TECHNOLOGY OF THE ANCIENT NEAR EAST

In this conversationally engaging volume, Baker has deftly collected the many materials, machines, and technological applications that defined and enriched the lives of those dwelling in the Ancient Near East into the Roman Era. Based firmly on a wide array of literary, artistic, and archaeological sources, *Technology of the Ancient Near East* provides an essential piece of the puzzle of the society, culture, and history of the region, and it fills a longstanding gap on the bookshelves of all who are interested in the history of technology, ideas, and the human quest to manipulate the natural world.

— Georgia Irby, *The College of William and Mary, USA*

Peoples of the distant past lived comfortably in cities that boasted well-conceived urban planning, monumental architecture, running water, artistic expression, knowledge of mathematics and medicine, and more. Without the benefits of modern technology, they enjoyed all the accoutrements of modern civilization.

Technology of the Ancient Near East brings together in a single volume what is known about the technology behind these achievements, based on the archaeological, textual, historic, and scientific data drawn from a wide range of sources, focusing on subjects such as warfare, construction, metallurgy, ceramics and glass, water management, and time keeping. These technologies are discussed within the cultural, historic, and socio-economic contexts within which they were invented and the book emphasises these as the foundation upon which modern technology is based. In so doing, this study elucidates the ingenuity of ancient minds, offering an invaluable introduction for students of ancient technology and science.

Jill Baker is an Independent Researcher in Ancient Near Eastern Archaeology and a Faculty Fellow (adjunct) in the Honors College at Florida International University, USA. She is the author of *The Funeral Kit: Mortuary Practices in the Archaeological Record* and co-author of *The Greensboro Blockhouse Project: An Historical and Archaeological Investigation in Greensboro, Vermont*.

TECHNOLOGY OF THE ANCIENT NEAR EAST

From the Neolithic to the Early Roman Period

Jill Baker

LONDON AND NEW YORK

First published 2019
by Routledge
2 Park Square, Milton Park, Abingdon, Oxon OX14 4RN

and by Routledge
711 Third Avenue, New York, NY 10017

Routledge is an imprint of the Taylor & Francis Group, an informa business

British Library Cataloguing-in-Publication Data
A catalogue record for this book is available from the British Library

Library of Congress Cataloging-in-Publication Data
Names: Baker, Jill L., 1964- author.
Title: Technology of the ancient Near East: from the neolithic
to the early Roman period / Jill Baker.
Description: Milton Park, Abingdon, Oxon: Routledge, 2018. |
Includes bibliographical references and index.
Identifiers: LCCN 2018008047 (print) | LCCN 2018012061
(ebook) | ISBN 9781351188111 (ebook) | ISBN 9781351188104
(web pdf) | ISBN 9781351188098 (epub) | ISBN 9781351188081
(mobi/kindle) | ISBN 9780815393689 |
ISBN 9780815393689q (hardback:qalk. paper) |
ISBN 9780815393696q (pbk.: qalk. paper) |
ISBN 9781351188111q (ebook)
Subjects: LCSH: Technology–Middle East–History. |
Middle East–Antiquities.
Classification: LCC T16 (ebook) | LCC T16.B35 2018
(print) | DDC 609.394–dc23
LC record available at https://lccn.loc.gov/2018008047

ISBN: 978-0-8153-9368-9 (hbk)
ISBN: 978-0-8153-9369-6 (pbk)
ISBN: 978-1-351-18811-1 (ebk)

Typeset in Bembo
by Sunrise Setting Ltd, Brixham, UK

Printed in the United Kingdom
by Henry Ling Limited

CONTENTS

FIGURES

ACKNOWLEDGEMENTS

This book has been a work-in-progress for a long time. The inspiration for this volume comes from my fascination with modern technology and by moments of invention and innovation among ancient peoples. Eventually, my fascination grew into a large body of research, then a class, and now, finally, a book. I hope those who read this book will be inspired by ancient peoples' knowledge and application of science and technology. I have been.

Numerous people have accompanied me along the way, offering their support and useful and creative thoughts. I am grateful for their involvement in this work. To the Routledge referees, I am grateful for and appreciate your constructive comments and useful suggestions. You have made this work stronger. To C. Chapman, S. Cohen, and S. Gitin, who read early drafts of the manuscript, I am grateful for and appreciate your support, ideas, and constructive comments. You have helped to shape this work, making it stronger and well rounded. To Janet Angelo of IndieGo Publishing, I am deeply thankful for your detailed, diligent, and creative editing. Your thoughts and suggestions have contributed much to this work. To the W. F. Albright Institute of Archaeological Research, to the Directors (Emeritus and current), to the Library Staff, and to the Staff, I am grateful for use of the library and for accommodation and meals; you provided a productive and collegiate base camp from which to conduct research. To Archaeological Horizons, Inc. thank you for providing a travel grant, making research for this book possible. To L. Northup, Honors College, Florida International University, thank you for the opportunity to share the ingenuity of ancient peoples with modern students. To the FIU Honors College students who have taken my class, I am grateful for your enthusiasm, curiosity, and insightful questions. You have been inspiring and thought provoking. I am also grateful to friends and colleagues, especially S. Cohen and S. Gitin, for friendly but useful banter and professional advice regarding the mechanics of the manuscript. Any inaccuracies in this work are my own.

Finally, but not least, I am deeply grateful to my family for their unconditional support, especially to my husband, J. Tidy, who has been supportive and patient while I have been 'in the zone'. This book is dedicated to you all.

MAPS

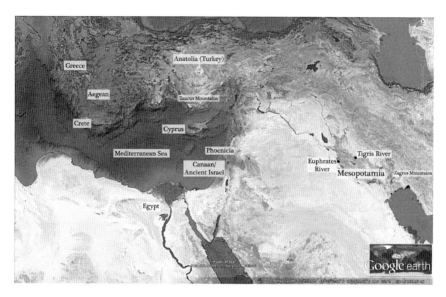

MAP 1   Depicting the major regions of the ancient Near East and eastern Mediterranean

Adapted from GoogleMaps.

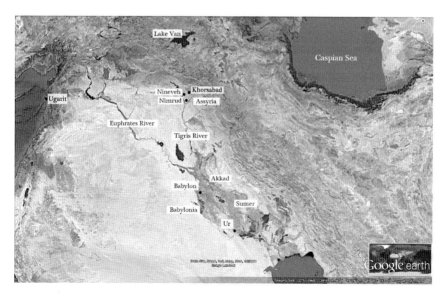

MAP 2   Select sites and kingdoms in Mesopotamia

Adapted from GoogleMaps.

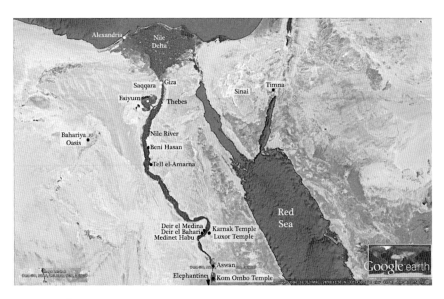

MAP 3   Select sites in ancient Egypt

Adapted from GoogleMaps.

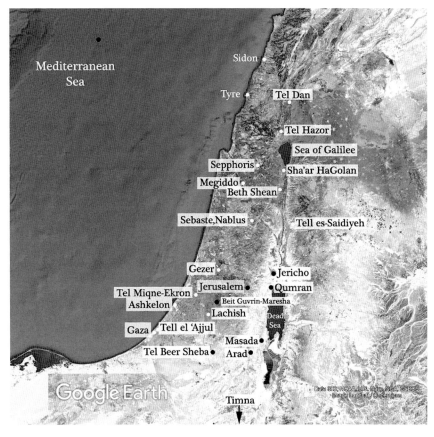

MAP 4   Select sites in Canaan/ancient Israel

Adapted from GoogleMaps.

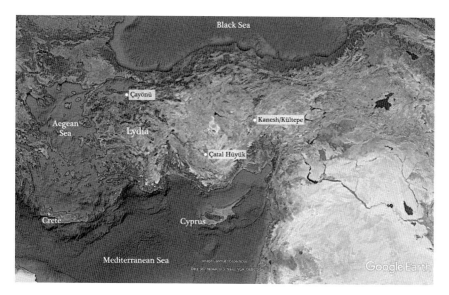

MAP 5 Select sites in Anatolia (modern Turkey)

Adapted from GoogleMaps.

Chronology of Mesopotamia, Egypt, Canaan, and Greece

The assignment of dates to chronological periods is complex and remains the subject of much discussion. The dates listed below are approximate and represent a middle-of-the-road approach to ancient Near Eastern chronology. These are meant to provide general dates for the periods discussed in this work and do not advocate for or against any specific chronological scenario.

(Dates based on *The New Encyclopaedia of Archaeological Excavations in the Holy Land*; University of Chicago, Oriental Institute Museum Timeline; Hamblin 2006.)

Unless otherwise noted, dates are BCE.

Mesopotamia	
Neolithic	10,000–6200
Hasuna, Samarra,	6200–5000
Halaf Periods	
Ubaid	5000–4000
Late Uruk	4000–3100
Jamdat Nasr	3100–2900
Early Dynastic I	2900–2650
Early Dynastic II	2650–2550
Early Dynastic IIIA	2550–2400
Early Dynastic IIIB	2400–2350
Akkadian	2350–2150
Neo-Sumerian	2150–2000
Old Assyrian/	2000–1600
Isin–Larsa–	2000–1600
Old Babylonian	
Middle Assyrian	1430–934
Neo-Assyrian	934–612
Neo-Babylonian	625–539
Achaemenid	538–331
Persian	547–334
Macedonian/Seleucid	330–64
Parthian	250 BCE–224 CE

Egypt	
Neolithic	7000–4500
Pre-Dynastic	4500–3000
Archaic	3000–2686
Old Kingdom	2689–2125
1st Intermediate	2166–2055
Middle Kingdom	2055–1650
2nd Intermediate	1650–1550
New Kingdom	1550–1069
3rd Intermediate	1069–664
Late Period	664–332
Ptolemaic Period	332–30
Roman Period	30 BCE–395 CE

Canaan	
Neolithic	10,000–5500
Pre-Pottery	8500–6000
Pottery	6000–5500
Chalcolithic	5500–3300
Early Bronze I	3300–3050
Early Bronze II	3050–2700
Early Bronze III	2700–2300
Middle Bronze I	2300–2000
(EB IV/Intermediate)	
Middle Bronze IIA	2000–1750
Middle Bronze IIB-C	1750–1550
Late Bronze I	1550–1400
Late Bronze II	1400–1200
Iron Age I	1200–1000
Iron Age II	1000–586
Babylonian and	586–332
Persian Periods	
Hellenistic	332–37
Roman	37 BC–324 CE
Byzantine	324–638 CE
(late Roman)	

1
INTRODUCTION

When considering the concept of technology, what comes to mind? Most people living in the twenty-first century immediately think of computers, mobile phones, tablets, smart watches, voice-interaction apps, global positioning system (GPS) devices, 3D printers, and other types of high-tech equipment. Some might also include machines such as power tools, kitchen appliances, automobiles, airplanes, and bulldozers under the umbrella of technology. Equating the notion of technology with electronic gadgets and machines has become commonplace because they have become so permanently integrated into the fabric of our lives and our very being. Today, some people have never known life without computer technology, and many people have never known what it's like to live without basic electronic machines such as electric stoves, dishwashers, washing machines, clothes dryers, and fans.

For many, it seems impossible to imagine a productive or comfortable life without these conveniences, yet in the distant past, people lived comfortably in cities that boasted monumental architecture, running water, access to doctors and medicine, knowledge of mathematics and astronomical events, and artistic expression in the form of sculpture, music, and theater. They enjoyed all the accoutrements of modern civilization without the aid of modern technology.

The purpose of this work is to explore some of the technologies employed by the peoples of the ancient Near East. In doing so, we will consider the unique function and contribution of these technologies to the construction of civilization, as well as their evolution and continued use in modern civilization. To achieve this goal, this study will specifically offer a survey of technologies utilized in Mesopotamia, Egypt, Canaan, and Anatolia from the Neolithic to the early Roman period (ca. 8500 BCE–132 CE). This is not meant to be an exhaustive survey, but rather an examination of selected technologies that contributed to the creation, development, and perpetuation of these ancient civilizations. Narrowing the chronological and geographic range for the purpose of this study is deliberate.

The primary foci of this work will be on earlier pre-Hellenistic and Roman periods; however, important technologies that migrated to the Near East from Greece and Rome will be discussed, such as aqueducts and Roman cement. An exhaustive study of the technologies of the Hellenistic and Roman periods in the Near East is best left to a dedicated volume. To be sure, the technologies brought to the Near East by the Greeks and Romans were impactful; however, the use and complexities of Graeco-Roman technology in the Near East deserve to be addressed in a separate volume. Additionally, numerous Classical scholars have expertly and meticulously discussed Greek and Roman technology (Humphrey et al. 2006; Oleson 2008; Landels 2000). To do so here would be redundant, and would significantly add to the length of this volume.

This study is intended to be a kind of first resource for those who wish to learn about the technologies of the ancient Near East but who will go beyond this work. It is meant to begin a discussion and inspire students of all fields and generations—professional and proletarian—to dive deeper into the topics presented here. It will present a broad picture of technologies used over a wide region by summarizing in one volume the ancient resources, excavation reports, focused studies, research, and recent discoveries that have formed an important foundation for our understanding of ancient technology. While these works provide important data, they are so specific that they are rarely integrated into broader studies. Here, these foundational works will be illuminated in an attempt to underscore the breadth and interconnection of ancient technological knowledge.

Finally, it is my hope that the reader will be inspired by the ingenuity, research, problem-solving ability, tenacity, and curiosity of these ancient peoples to achieve organized and sophisticated civilizations without the aid of electricity, combustion engines, electronic gadgets or computers. There is room in our knowledge bank to learn from the technologies designed, built, and used by these ancient peoples, and to consider how those technologies can be applied in our world today. Ancient systems were not necessarily simplistic or irrelevant when compared to modern ones. With an open mind, one can apply ancient technologies in new and innovative ways or be inspired to create entirely new approaches or systems that may prove useful in resolving present and future problems.

While teaching a course entitled Ancient Technology, it became clear that numerous academic resources discuss technology beginning in the eighth/seventh century BCE onward and focus mainly on the achievements of the Greeks and Romans. Certainly, this was a vibrant period of scientific advancement and engineering marvels, and many of the philosophic, scientific, and engineering concepts that we use today were developed or advanced during that time. Philosophers such as Thales of Miletus (ca. 624–546 BCE), Anaximander of Miletus (ca. 610–546 BCE), and Pythagoras of Samos (ca. 570–495 BCE) advanced the basic tenets of mathematics, physics, science, and medicine. There were notable inventors, such as Archimedes of Syracuse (ca. 287–212 BCE), who invented (among other things) a screw consisting of an evenly measured spiral that wound around a central cylindrical shaft, and Heron of Alexandria (ca. 10–70 CE), who developed a wind-powered organ, a force pump, a steam engine called an aeolipile, and temple doors that opened and closed automatically. These machines are antecedents to many of our own devices, and deserve recognition as such. However, many achievements of the Greeks and Romans were made possible by an extensive and solid foundation of scientific and mechanical knowledge already theorized and applied in Mesopotamia, Egypt, and Canaan long before the Greek or Roman periods. The experience, knowledge, and research of Near Eastern peoples, together with that gained from China and India, provided the foundation upon which the early Greek philosophers and scientists made their discoveries and developed their innovative technology that propelled humankind toward automation and mechanization.

Some modern academic resources acknowledge the technological and scientific achievements of the peoples of the ancient Near East; however, few of these achievements have been explored in detail or synthesized into one volume. While it is recognized that a thorough discussion of Bronze and Iron Age technology is necessary and worthwhile, it is understood that such a discussion would require a separate study (Oleson 2008:3). After cobbling together outdated references and recent archaeological reports and articles for my class, it became clear that enough material exists to compile a handbook dedicated to an integrated study of the technology of the ancient Near East. This work will focus mainly on the Mesopotamians, Egyptians, Canaanites, and Israelites and some of the technologies they employed to create their magnificent urban centers and cultures.

One might pose the question, why study ancient technology? After all, humankind and technology have progressed significantly since the period from 8500 BCE to 132 CE in the ancient Near East. What can possibly be learned from scientists, engineers, architects, and doctors who lived millennia ago? A stock response from an archaeologist's point of view is that understanding our past can help us make informed decisions regarding the present and future. However, humankind rarely learns from the past, and if it does, that knowledge is rarely incorporated into the decision-making process to solve present-day problems. Instead, humankind often repeats the same mistakes and poor decisions without analyzing the consequences that can be gleaned from history. Nevertheless, much can be learned from the successes and failures of the past and applied to the present and future.

Archaeology, anthropology, history, and culture elucidate the resumé of humanity. When going to a job interview, one presents a potential employer with a resumé or CV summarizing the experiences and abilities that make one suitable for the position. Similarly, humankind's technological resumé establishes the foundation and skill set upon which to move forward. It shows how people adapted to their natural surroundings, including micro and macroclimate changes, and developed new technologies and strategies to cope with and manage those changes. It is important to recognize the contributions and diligent work of the scientists, physicists, medical practitioners, mariners, engineers, metallurgists, and artists who lived before us; to understand how new technologies interacted with and advanced society; and to ask whether ancient principles can be applied to our present and future world.

Additionally, significant technological, scientific, and industrial advancement stagnated and much knowledge was lost in the Near East and Europe during the Middle Ages due to the fall of the Roman Empire, movement of peoples, socio-political reorganization, scholasticism, and the controlling grip of the Christian Church in influencing every aspect of society and culture. Studying ancient technology helps to regain lost knowledge and incorporate some of it into the present. As we move forward locally, nationally, and globally, ancient lessons learned can inform present and future decisions to provide a better standard of living and quality of life for people the world over.

Methodological approach

This work will approach technology from the practical standpoint of an ancient person with a task to perform, a problem to solve, a structure to build, or a goal to achieve. We will attempt to observe what the ancient people knew, when they knew it, how they knew it, and the ways in which they applied or did not apply their knowledge.

Let's revisit the opening question: what is technology? The word technology is comprised of two Greek words: *tekhnologia/tekhne*, τέχνη, meaning art, skill, or craft, and *logia*, λογία, meaning subject of study or interest. Technology can be defined as "the practical application of knowledge especially in a particular area" (see www.merriam-webster.com/dictionary/technology) and as "the application of scientific knowledge for practical purposes, especially in industry" (see https://en.oxforddictionaries.com/definition/technology). Humphrey et al. (2006:xiv) describe technology as an "attempt by humans to control and master the natural environment, changing it into a more hospitable, if artificial one," and as a "process by which humans accomplish change." For the purpose of this work and the overall discussion, technology will be defined as the practical application of knowledge, scientific or otherwise, to resolve a problem, achieve a goal, satisfy curiosity, make life easier, or to facilitate change. With this working definition in mind, technology can encompass a wide range of strategies and systems, some of which may be less obvious and more passive than others, such as architectural design, artwork, military organization and tactics, judicial systems, and even religion, all of which were utilized by ancient peoples to realize their goals and to accomplish change. Though we may not be aware of it, we use these non-mechanical technologies for the same purposes today.

To facilitate this survey, previously published research will be synthesized and integrated to establish a foundation for these technologies. This work will be based on known studies as a way to assemble a wide variety and scope of resources into one volume. This work is not meant to be an exhaustive review of all technologies or previously published works on ancient technology in the Near East. Instead, the most ubiquitous, instrumental, and informative will be integrated into our discourse. For example, in his book *Ancient Mesopotamian Materials and Industries*, Moorey (1999) discussed stone working, agriculture, metalworking, ceramic and glass crafts, and building methods and materials in Mesopotamia. In *Ancient Egyptian Materials and Technology*, Nicholson and Shaw (2009) discussed topics such as materials used for building, tool making, textiles, leatherwork, and food technology in ancient Egypt. Scholars have discussed ancient warfare, including Yadin in *The Art of Warfare in Biblical Lands in Light of Archaeological Discovery* (Yadin 1963) and Hackett, *Warfare in the Ancient World* (Hackett 1989), both of which highlight the technologies used in warfare. And some scholars discuss textiles, such as Nosch, Koefoed, and Strand in *Textile Production and Consumption in the Ancient Near East* (Nosch et al. 2013) and Friend in *Tell Taannek 1963–1968 III: The Artifacts, 2: The Loom Weights* (Friend 1998). Each of these references provides valuable information; however, each focuses on specific aspects of the ancient world and related technologies, and does not necessarily integrate those technologies with the wider Near East. Henry Hodges integrates technologies from the Neolithic to the early Roman period in Mesopotamia, Egypt, and Canaan in *Technology in the Ancient World* (Hodges 1992) a valuable work, but one that needs updating. Equally important are the manuals, handbooks, histories, and observations written by ancient engineers, physicists, scientists, mathematicians, astronomers, historians, and doctors. These essential works record the research and development of theories and knowledge established by the world's earliest researchers. The work of people such as Mesopotamian astronomers, Imhotep, Thales of Miletus, Hesiod, Herodotus, Ctesibius, and Pliny the Elder, established the foundation upon which our principles of science, engineering, physics, mathematics, astronomy, etc. are built. Throughout this work, reference will be made to the ancient authors. The accompanying citations will provide the name of the ancient author, the title of their work, and the chapter and verse of the relevant text, followed by one or two modern references that provide easily accessible English translations of the cited passage. This is to encourage the reader to chase-down the ancient reference to get a sense of the ancient people's knowledge, sense of humor, and understanding of the world around them.

This volume is meant to emphasize and build upon disparate works that discussed ancient technologies; to summarize the various technologies in use from the Neolithic to the early Roman period in Mesopotamia, Canaan, and Egypt; and to illustrate how, when combined, each study contributes to our understanding of the technology that supported the social, cultural, and economic complexities of the ancient world.

For the purpose of this work, it is necessary to establish some regional definitions. This work will focus on the ancient Near East. The broader terms ancient Near East or Levant will be used to refer to ancient Egypt, Mesopotamia (modern Iraq, southwestern Iran, northeastern Syria), Anatolia (modern Turkey), Canaan (modern Israel, Jordan, Syria), and Phoenicia (modern Lebanon). Modern Israel will be referred to as such or in ancient terms such as Canaan, ancient Israel, or Palestine, as it was known in the Graeco-Roman periods. Use of these geographical terms is in no way meant to support or refute any current political or religious ideologies or associations.

Although the focus will be on the Near East and the Mediterranean basin, technological invention and innovation were not particular to this area and timeframe. Concurrently, there were remarkable achievements in technology, engineering, and medicine in India, China, Europe, and South America. Because humankind inhabited the whole of the earth, it is important to recognize concurrent uses of similar technologies and advances in other regions of the ancient world because the human experience is similar no matter the culture or location. So, throughout this work, reference will be made to other cultures in other regions of the globe that were developing and utilizing similar technologies contemporaneous to these developments in the ancient Near East.

Theoretical approach

What sparks technological discovery, invention, and innovation? What causes people to create a tool, device, or weapon? Before proceeding, these terms should first be defined.

Discovery is the act or process of finding, encountering, or gaining knowledge about something that already exists. For example, electricity exists in nature in the form of lightning, static electricity, and in creatures such as eels and fireflies (Lampyridae). Humans did not discover electricity; rather, we figured out how to harness, manipulate, and produce electricity based on its natural properties.

To invent is to originate, create, fabricate, or produce something as the result of one's own ingenuity, research, experimentation, or imagination. For example, Hero of Alexandria (first century BCE) invented the aeolipile based on his knowledge of hydraulics and physics.

Innovation applies changes to something that already exists or has been established to develop it further or to adapt it to a different set of parameters. For example, the Greeks invented the gastraphetes, a crossbow, as a weapon to hurl projectiles. Based on the crossbow, the Romans later developed variations of catapults, which also hurled projectiles, but in different forms and for different purposes.

Scholars have long debated the impetus behind these actions. Were the driving forces for discovery, invention, and innovation based on need, competition, revolution, conflict, original thought, curiosity, or a combination of these? Humans are complex beings, and the technologies we have invented throughout the centuries have primarily been purposeful. Therefore, the development of technologies must be understood within the historic, cultural, social, economic, and religious contexts within which they were created and utilized. Some technologies were created during times of war to outsmart and/or respond to the enemy, such as the catapult. Others were meant to dazzle and mesmerize, such as Heron's temple doors that opened and closed mechanically, without human intervention, to entice worshippers to devote their loyalty to one deity over others. Still other technologies were created at the behest of rulers and their monumental egos, usually in times of war.

The theoretical and practical development of technologies and their application will be discussed throughout the text. Where relevant, contemporaneous historic events and economic, cultural, and religious contexts within which certain technologies were created will be mentioned. This will provide a framework that may help to explain the reason certain technologies were deemed necessary.

Technology and society

Technology and society are inextricably interwoven. Without one, the other would perish. From the moment one individual created a stone tool, that individual gained an advantage in daily survival. The person/people who made tools for others and traded or sold those for goods and services they needed gained an even greater advantage economically, and thus began social complexity, trade, marketplace supply and demand, accumulation of surplus, and power and control. The creation of technologies irreversibly altered society forever—a pattern that repeats to this day.

A modern example is the smart phone, specifically the Apple iPhone, the technology of which greatly impacted society and economy. The introduction of the iPhone led to advances in voice-recognition technology, fingerprint identification, social and industrial competition, and broader forms of communication written and spoken. So too ancient technologies, such as agriculture, mills, and metallurgy led to complex societies, accumulation of surplus, and power for those who controlled the technology and surplus. Technology allowed for leisure time and the emergence of social classes and altered the way people interacted with each other. It led to a stronger economy, competition in the marketplace, domestic and international trade, and the exchange of ideas.

It can be argued that new, innovative technologies can have a positive and a negative impact on society. Technology can positively impact society by resolving problems, increasing production, improving health and food production, and making daily survival easier. However, technology widens the gap between socioeconomic classes, allowing the rich to become very wealthy and the poor to remain poor. Technology can also be harmful to the environment: air and water pollution due to smelting and the depositing of waste in rivers; deforestation from felling trees for construction and fuel; the irreparable scarring of the earth due to mining.

Some technologies were welcomed with great relief and enthusiasm. For example, water mills literally released people from the "daily grind" of having to pulverize grain into flour every day, which was celebrated by Antipater of Thessalonica (*Greek Anthology* 9.418):

> Cease from grinding, ye women who toil at the mill; sleep late, even if the crowing cocks announce the dawn. For Demeter has ordered the Nymphs to perform the work of your hands, and they, leaping down on the top of the wheel, turn its axle which, with its revolving spokes, turns the heavy concave Nisyrian mill-stones. We taste again the joys of the primitive life, learning to feast on the products of Demeter without labour.
>
> *(Paton 1917:232–233. See also Humphrey et al. 2006:31)*

Others cursed technology, such as in Plautus' *The Woman from Boeotia*, wherein the speaker was not pleased with the increased reckoning of time:

> The gods confound the man who first found out
> How to distinguish hours! Confound him, too,
> Who in this place set up a sun-dial
> To cut and hack my days so wretchedly
> Into small portions! When I was a boy,
> My belly was my only sun-dial, one more sure,
> Truer, and more exact than any of them.
> This dial told me when 'twas proper time
> To go to dinner, when I had aught to eat;
> But nowadays, why even when I have,
> I can't fall to unless the sun gives leave.
> The town's so full of these confounded dials
> The greatest part of the inhabitants,
> Shrunk up with hunger, crawl along the streets.
> My master Favorinus too, when I was reading the Nervularia of Plautus,
> and he had heard this line of the comedy.
> Old, wheezing, physicky, mere foundered hags
> With dry, parched, painted hides, shrivell'd and
> shrunk, delighted with the wit of the archaic words that describe the ugly
> defects of harlots, cried: "By heaven! just this one verse is enough to con-
> vince one that the play is Plautine"
>
> *(Fragments, Boeotia, 1, De Melo 2013:432–433.*
> *See also Humphrey et al. 2006:517)*

Today, technology continues to have positive and negative effects on society. For example, the introduction of the iPhone created marketplace competition, friendly social rivalry (iPhone versus Android), questions regarding workplace ethics and conditions in factories that manufacture iPhones (Mielach 2012; Bilton 2014), and medical ethical dilemmas created by stem cell technology, cloning, and artificial intelligence. This reliance on these technologies has also created what some are calling digital dementia (Greenfield 2015), the condition in which people no longer remember phone numbers, cannot do math without the aid of a calculator, cannot spell words correctly or write well-constructed sentences, and do not remember information because they can simply look it up on the internet. These are a few examples of how technology can change daily life and society for the better and for the worse. As humankind continues to create and integrate new technology, its effects on humanity and society must be considered.

The earliest technologies were based on naturally occurring, observable phenomena. Early peoples were acutely aware of nature's recurring cycles—spring, summer, autumn, winter—and adapted to each of them accordingly. The cyclical nature of the seasons was observable in the phases of the moon throughout the month and the sun's path throughout the day, in the movement of celestial bodies in the night sky, in weather cycles, and by the migration of animals and the growth cycle of vegetation. Humankind was also acutely aware of biological cycles—birth, life, death, and illness. Humankind's ability to understand nature's technology eventually led to the ability to harness and manipulate various aspects of it. Even as hunter-gatherers, people recorded the movement of celestial bodies in the night sky, enabling a better understanding of the passage of seasons and the reckoning of time, which was helpful for predicting the availability of food resources.

Because of their keen observation, and to meet their nutritional needs, people gradually domesticated the flora and fauna that were amenable to human intervention. The progression from hunter-gatherer to sedentary agriculturalist and the work of animal husbandry should not be underestimated. It required persistent attention to detail as well as observation, research, trial and error, and ingenuity on the part of early peoples who developed techniques and technologies, many of which remain in use today. As humankind progressed, technology and society became inextricably interwoven. As technology advanced, society became more complex, creating the division of labor and craft specialization. With the advancement of technology, leisure time and demand for luxury items increased, as did the accumulation of wealth, leading to greed, exploitation, and poverty. Although society advanced in food production, tool making, and weapons production, the divide between rich and poor grew exponentially.

How do we learn about ancient technology? The resources

Multiple resources will be utilized to piece together knowledge of technology in the ancient Near East. These include artifacts recovered from archaeological investigation, artwork such as reliefs and wall paintings, painted decoration on ceramics and figurines, and written texts. Much of what is known about ancient engineering and technology is revealed in the monuments and artifacts left behind by peoples who did not always record their achievements in the form of handwritten instructional manuals or journals.

Prior to the written word, knowledge was passed orally from one person to another, from generation to generation, through narratives, legends, songs, and poems. Dissemination of knowledge was also achieved through apprenticeship. Highly skilled master craftsmen passed their knowledge to the next generation in trades such as masonry, carpentry, metallurgy, textile production, and agriculture through hands-on training and guidance. For example, this type of information sharing is reflected in architecture, monumental and mundane. Eventually, information was written down, and there was a shift from a memory-based, oral tradition to a more permanent method of record keeping that employed writing. Pre-literate societies, however, did not lack technological knowledge, as evidenced in their architecture, ceramics, and material culture.

From the Bronze Age onward in Egypt, Mesopotamia, and Canaan, textual evidence contributes greatly to our knowledge of ancient technology directly and indirectly. Egyptian medical papyri provide detailed descriptions of disease, treatment, and pharmaceuticals, and cuneiform tablets from the library of Ashurbanipal discuss astronomical events, mythologies, and mathematics. Early forms of writing appear as glyphs, pictures used to represent a concept, phrase, or word, which eventually evolved into an alphabet comprised of symbols and/or letters. Early forms of these include hieroglyphics (later hieratic), Cuneiform, and Hebrew.

Writing was used by the state to record royal heredity, rations, labor, accounts of war, and legends; by temples to record religious rites, mythologies, offerings, rations; by merchants to record orders, income, expenditures; and by early doctors who created early medical handbooks (Egypt). Libraries and archives of tablets and scrolls kept at Ugarit (ca. 1200 BCE), Ashurbanipal (ca. 668–627 BCE), and the library at Alexandria, Egypt (ca. third century BCE) preserved literary works, census reports, astrological observations, calculations, and much more. As more people became literate, poetry and narratives were available for popular consumption as exemplified by multiple copies of the Egyptian Tale of Sinuhe (Lichtheim 1975:222–235).

The reliefs and paintings found in monumental temples, palaces, on stelae and on obelisks found in Egypt and Mesopotamia provide a wealth of information regarding war tactics, weaponry, architecture, law, historic events, religious beliefs, burial practices, and afterlife scenarios. State-sponsored information sharing, or rather propaganda, was disseminated via large-scale reliefs on the walls of massive temples and palaces, which functioned as the news media of the ancient world. These reliefs announced to all who set eyes on them the deeds and accomplishments of kings and pharaohs. For example, the exterior reliefs at Medinet Habu and Karnak Temple announced to the Egyptian public and to visitors the achievements of the pharaoh(s) and helped to legitimize his reign. Similarly, the reliefs from Sennacherib's palace at Nineveh (ca. 701 BCE) depict the siege of Lachish (Canaan), illustrating battle tactics, weaponry, and architecture.

The combination of pictorial representation and writing ensured that the literate and illiterate could understand who was in charge and the deeds that had been accomplished. A glimpse into daily life, occupations, and family life were also depicted in tomb paintings and reliefs, figurines, seals, and artifacts. Although paintings and reliefs in tombs, temples, and palaces may seem mundane and insignificant, they represent the daily realities of royal and non-royal peoples who comprised the nation-state and contributed to the vitality of the economy and complexity of society. These depictions describe relatively normal aspects of daily life that would otherwise go unnoticed or did not survive into the archaeological record.

The data gathered from archaeological excavation also contribute greatly to our understanding of ancient technology. The investigation of architecture allows us to understand construction technique and materials. Daily activities and foodstuffs are illuminated through installations such as beehives, altars, and olive and wine presses. Industry is revealed through the discovery of looms and loom weights, coins, and storage jars and warehouses. Personal hygiene and adornment are evidenced by jewelry, wigs, and combs made from bone and ivory. Pottery vessels, such as bowls, juglets, and jars, provide information regarding manufacturing techniques. Some ceramic forms were task-specific, and ceramic typologies can be arranged into chronological sequence, which is useful when determining dates for specific strata within an archaeological context. Thus, the architecture, pottery, and material culture found in the archaeological record contribute greatly to our understanding of technology in the ancient world.

The modern resources utilized in this work will include excavation reports, secondary studies, journals, and electronic sources, as well as scholarly websites. Given that this is a textbook about ancient technology, it is fitting that modern technology should be integrated. Many scholars remain reluctant to utilize electronic resources, especially websites found on the internet. As with any resource, however, including printed matter such as books and journals, the information contained within must be judged for its scholarly integrity and quality. That said, there are numerous organizations and independent scholars producing quality work and publishing it on the internet. Organizations such as the British Museum and the Metropolitan Museum of Art; online journals such as *Plos One* and *LiveScience*; and research institutes, such as the South Tyrol Museum of Archaeology and The Antikythera Mechanism Research Project, offer scholarly research and data. It is important to integrate the internet into academic discipline and discern between the websites that offer accurate data and interpretations and those that do not. Therefore, websites with high academic integrity will be referenced and their data woven throughout the fabric of this work.

2

EARLY TECHNOLOGIES

It might be surprising to learn that human technological invention and innovation began at least as early as the Palaeolithic and Mesolithic periods. When considering these seemingly primitive peoples, it is easy to imagine them living in caves, dressed in furry animal skins, carrying spears or clubs, and grunting to communicate with one another. Yet archaeological evidence and research continues to produce data that suggest these early peoples led a sophisticated existence, relatively speaking. For example, the decorated caves of the Upper Palaeolithic period in France (Figure 2.1) and Spain reveal that early humans engaged in abstract thought and artistic representation and appreciation, and deliberately acquired the materials and tools necessary to recreate aspects of their lives in artistic imagery. Dating to ca. 15,000 BCE, the painted walls of the Lascaux cave in France depict numerous animals, including horses, bison, mammoth, ibex, deer, bear, and wolves (Lascaux, http://archeologie.culture.fr/lascaux/en; Lascaux-Dordogne Vallée Vézère, www. lascaux-dordogne.com/en/lascaux-cave). These images illustrate the vitality of the natural world these early humans encountered. They also illustrate a variety of artistic skills, as some animal figures were rendered in a "twisted perspective," meaning their heads were in profile but their horns or antlers were front-facing (Metropolitan Museum 2000–2015b).

In another example, sandals made from sagebrush bark have been found in Oregon (USA) at Fort Rock Cave. These sandals date to ca. 10,000 to 9000 BP (Before Present) (University of Oregon) and consisted of a woven foot bed with straps to secure the sandal to one's foot. To appreciate the achievements of the peoples of the ancient Near East, it is important to consider some earlier technologies that made later accomplishments and advancements possible. This chapter will briefly describe some of the technologies of the stone ages, which established a basis of knowledge and skills upon which the Bronze Age peoples of the Near East developed.

FIGURE 2.1   Lascaux Cave

Adapted from Wikipedia.org, by Prof saxx – Own work, Public Domain, https://commons.wikimedia.org/w/index.php?curid=2846254.

Palaeolithic and Mesolithic

Technology from the Palaeolithic period is evidenced by the Oldowan culture, from the Lower Palaeolithic, ca. 2.6 million years ago, and by the Acheulean and Mousterian cultures from the Middle Palaeolithic, ca. 120,000–45,000 BCE (Klein 2009; Clark and Coinman 2005). At this stage, these peoples were mostly encountering their environment, but they were also manipulating it to survive and make their daily routine and existence more efficient. As hunter-gatherers, people were mobile, followed their food sources, and migrated according to seasons and weather patterns. Because of this nomadic way of life, they needed basic tools for hunting, cutting, cleaning, gathering, and preparing objects for use. Tool making may be considered one of the first indications that humankind began manipulating their environment rather than simply encountering it and being shaped by it. The tool-making process reflects inventiveness, innovation, problem solving, and creation of task-specific tools. It reveals knowledge of raw materials and their properties, first by gathering and later by mining. It reveals use of purpose-specific materials as well as knowledge of processing materials, that is, converting materials from one form to another.

It is likely that one of the world's first industries was the production of stone tools, which suggests organized leadership, laborers, and the acquisition of raw materials, as well as processing and distribution. Each of these activities contributed to social complexity and established a kind of protocol for invention, innovation, industry, and marketplace. The need for stone tools was not limited to the Near East, though, as evidenced by discoveries of stone tool hoards and deposits from numerous and varied locations around the globe. In fact, the stone tool industry was thriving! Hoards such as those found in Buttermilk Creek, Texas (Palaeolithic, ca. 13,000–12,000 BCE), the Meadowcroft Rock Shelter, Jefferson County, Pennsylvania (Palaeolithic, ca. 14,000 to 16,000 years ago), the Mahaffy Cache, Boulder, Colorado (ca. 10,900 BCE), and the discoveries at Le Moustier in Europe, as well as the caches in South America and Africa, provide vivid evidence of a thriving stone tool industry.

Deposits like these are important for a number of reasons. The size, shape, technique, and style of stone tools exhibit a very high quality of craftsmanship that can be linked to specific people groups from various regions of the world. These can suggest possible migrations of people groups from region to region. The type of stone used suggests that people were obtaining raw materials from great distances. The range in size and shape suggests task-specific tools, including those that were likely reserved for ceremonial purposes. Finally, the location of discovery and the residue found on these tools are indicative of the ancient environment.

For example, from the Mahaffy Cache, which was discovered in Colorado in 2008, the Clovis period blades suggest that they were of very high-quality craftsmanship and probably made by the same person. The raw materials came from a great distance and from at least four different regions. The cache was likely buried next to an ancient stream in sandy sediment covered by dark, clay-like soil and deliberately buried for later retrieval. The bloodstains found on some of the blades belonged to North American camels, wooly rhinos, giant ground sloths, saber-toothed cats, wooly mammoths, and others that were extinct by the end of the Pleistocene period, possibly due to over hunting or climate change at the end of that ice age (University of Colorado, Boulder 2009, 2015; Shea 2013).

To make stone tools, a technique known as flint knapping was utilized throughout the ancient world and is still in use today. This technique was used to make hand axes, hammers, knives, scrapers, chisels, awls, smoothers, spear heads, arrowheads, adzes, harpoons, and numerous other items. At first, just the stone tool was utilized. Later, wood, bone, antler, and ivory were added as handles and shafts. To prepare a stone tool, a suitable type of stone must first be chosen, usually one made of chert, obsidian, jasper, agate, gaspeite, basalt, porcellanite, or any conchoidal fracturing stone. Percussion flaking and hammer flaking—forming a tool by striking the core or flakes—was accomplished by using bone, ivory, antler, wood, or a hammer stone made of harder stones. The core was held in one hand and the hammer stone in the other. When the core was struck, bits of it flaked off. The flakes were then shaped into the desired tool. Finishing of the blade edge was done with smaller pieces of wood, antler, or even a fingernail (Shea 2013:17–47; paleomanjim, Flintknapping-Beginners Part 1, www.youtube.com/watch?v=wyzNIa-U5Nc).

In the Upper Palaeolithic and Mesolithic periods (ca. 50,000 to 10,200 BCE—worldwide average; Levant—ca. 45,000–8,500 BCE), humankind's main focus was food collection—hunting and gathering. During this time, humans generally traveled to their food source by hunting the animals (fauna) they knew to be obtainable and edible, and gathering plants, berries, roots, fruits, vegetables, and grains (flora) they knew to be easily obtained and edible. They were mobile, migratory, and nomadic, moving with the seasons and according to the movement of their prey and to the growth of wild crops. To accomplish these tasks, stone tools were designed for collecting and processing these wild food sources (McClellan and Dorn 2006:9ff). There was little surplus of foodstuffs or belongings. Social structure was relatively simple with little or no ranking or dominance. Social groups were egalitarian or maintained some sort of clan-based leadership with perhaps elders functioning as decision-makers. Males and females contributed to the well-being and continued survival of the clan or group. However, stone tools were not the only factor in these ancient people's lives (McClellan and Dorn 2006:9–11; Clark and Coinman 2005).

Archaeological data and cave paintings evidence the use of tools made of wood or antler for activities such as food preparation and lunar observation. Figurines further suggest some sort of cultic activities, perhaps to induce fertility. Basketry, textiles such as leather for clothing, reeds for matting, flax for cloth, and stone for grinding grains comprised the ancients' use of early technologies. Intentional burials of the dead and care for elderly and disabled family members illustrate care and compassion among family/clan members. In the Mesolithic period, tools exhibit a greater diversity of type. The repertoire included knives, scrapers, awls, grinders, hooks, and a variety of projectile points. Wooden handles were added to stone blades for greater force of energy.

During the Palaeolithic period, people mostly reacted to their environment: eating what they encountered, following their food sources, living in caves or rock-shelters. However, toward the end of the Mesolithic period, there is evidence for a shift, whereby people planned several stages ahead by making task-specific tools and by combining one or more components, such as a knife blade with a wooden handle. Humankind was no longer passive, simply reacting to their environment, using only that which they encountered. Instead, they had become proactive, manipulating their environment to fit their needs. They were purposefully looking for the best materials, and fashioning them into the tools that best fit the task. In so doing, as living conditions improved, humans could focus less on daily survival and more on refining various aspects of settled life, such as agriculture and science.

It is at this turning point in human development that our discussion will begin.

Neolithic

The term Neolithic is comprised of two Greek words: νέος, (neos), meaning new, and λίθος, (lithos), meaning stone. Thus, the New Stone Age emerged ca. 12,000 to 10,200 BCE (McClellan and Dorn 2006:17–23; Rollefson 2005a). Significant changes took place in the Neolithic period, most notably the development of sedentary living and the domestication of flora and fauna. Humankind embraced a radically different lifestyle. Instead of chasing their food, people grew and raised their own food sources and constructed their own dwellings rather than searching for natural shelters such as caves and rocky outcrops.

The shift from hunter-gatherer to sedentary agriculturalist was probably much more gradual than the archaeological record indicates. It is likely that after millennia of observing and applying skills taught from generation to generation, people had learned to reseed the wild flora they gathered to ensure abundance for the next crop. Thus, domesticating and relocating wild crops to a fixed location was probably a next logical step. The reason for this shift has long been debated; however, recent research and data suggest that climate change may have prompted the shift. Based on core samplings and other data, it is clear that a major shift in climate occurred at about the same time that humankind became sedentary and domesticated flora and fauna.

The change in climate may have resulted in the migration or scarcity of food sources thus prompting people to grow and raise their own in a controlled environment. The Late Natufian culture, ca. 10,500–8500/8000 (ca. 10,800–9500 BC) in the northern Levant during the Younger Dryas period, experienced cold climatic conditions and drought. This change probably caused some wild food sources to diminish and eventually disappear. People learned the skills of agriculture to grow a reliable food source that would feed them in seedtime and harvest. They began with the domestication of wild grains (barley, einkorn, and emmer wheat) and animals such as sheep, goat, cattle, and pig, and eventually, they built permanent dwellings and storehouses (Bar-Yosef 1998; Rollefson 2005a; Issar and Zohar 2007; Yeakel et al. 2014).

People of the Pre-Pottery Neolithic period (ca. 8500–5500 BCE) continued to grow crops and raise animals; practiced selective breeding; established settlements including enclosure walls, animal pens, round houses of stone and mudbrick, and towers; and maintained regular contact with other people groups through trade. Examples can be found at Jericho, Byblos, and Göbekli Tepe. By the Neolithic period, settlements consisted of organized streets, blocks of houses, complex societies with designated leaders and a centralized community, a non-agrarian workforce, and technological advancement (Rollefson 2005a, 2005b).

The new demands of a sedentary agriculturally-based lifestyle created a need for specialized tools and crafts. New stone tools such as plough blades and sickle blades were developed. The production of foodstuffs resulted in a readily available food supply, surplus, and the accumulation of wealth. With the accumulation of wealth came power for those who controlled the surplus, all of which contributed to the ever-increasing socio-economic complexity of Neolithic society.

Sedentary living revealed the need for non-agrarian professionals: civil engineers, merchants, cultic functionaries, and crafts-peoples such as potters. These non-agrarian roles led to more formalized leadership—chieftains, kings, and administrative officials who managed public works such as maintaining streets, city gates, and walls. Well-organized infrastructure made it possible for villages and cities to thrive, ushering in rapid technological advancement, population growth, class stratification, leisure time, and an expanded and specialized non-agrarian workforce. Some of the best examples include Jericho, Sha'ar HaGolan, and Çatal Hüyük.

Additional ancillary industries resulted from the domestication of flora and fauna and a sedentary lifestyle. These included the textile industry (wool, linen, cotton), dairy (milk, cheese, yogurt), ceramics, and metalworking. Merchants near and far delivered goods to consumers, which created a need for transportation, accountants, and scribes, thus creating a local and long-distance market economy. Now that daily survival was not so tenuous, humans could also focus on religion and the development of cults and rituals.

With the advent and achievements of the Neolithic period, people shifted from encountering and reacting to their environment to manipulating and exploiting it, and even to enjoying it. They established the building blocks of complex society, industry, and artistic and religious expression.

The concepts, inventions, and discoveries made in the Neolithic period provided the foundation upon which the Bronze Age peoples of the Near East based their achievements. From the Bronze Age onward, the quest for knowledge, better technology, and sophisticated living propelled humankind forward and established the building blocks of civilized society that remain recognizable today.

3
STONE

Choosing the appropriate materials for buildings, furniture, fasteners, tools, weapons, and household items was critical. The type, quality, and combination of materials could determine the overall effectiveness and durability of the finished product. For example, today, we would not choose to build a commercial airliner or fighter jet using wood. Wood could not withstand the pressures and stresses placed on it, especially during takeoff and landing. Similarly, the ancient craftsperson carefully chose task-specific materials.

Ancient peoples used three main types of materials: organic, inorganic, and manufactured. Organic materials included wood, bone, sinew, and hide; inorganic included stone, metal, and ivory; manufactured included brick, baked clay, mortar, and glass (Nicholson and Shaw 2009). The latter are described as manufactured because their chemical composition changes to create the final product. It was (and remains) important to know the overall characteristics and behavior of the material: whether it is strong or weak, as well as flexible, resilient, malleable, or flammable, and how much it will degrade over time. One also has to determine whether the material will be compatible with other materials, such as fasteners, when the two are joined. Today, these issues may be referred to as "materials technology" (White 1984:73; Oleson 2008:256), a field of study that examines the characteristics and uses of materials and the design of new materials.

Additional factors were the availability, transportation, and cost of raw materials, and all that would be involved in the processing of raw materials for use. Choosing the proper material for the job was essential, and each craftsperson had to be keenly aware of its properties and how it would perform.

As an abundant resource, stone was utilized very early in human history. As an inorganic material, it served as raw material for tools, weapons, vessels, figurines, and in construction. Its abundance, strength, variety, and workability made stone an optimal material for early humans to exploit. Its endurance in composition and attractiveness made stone a much relied upon material, which remains true today. Before discussing the use of stone in the ancient Near East, a brief review of region-specific stone types that were exploited by the ancients is appropriate.

In general, the Levant is situated in the eastern regions of the Mediterranean basin, nestled within the wider geography of the Black Sea, Caspian Sea, and mountain ranges, including those in Turkey, Lebanon, Israel, and Iraq. This region is also situated along a fissure known as the Afro-Arabian Rift Valley, a fault line that extends from southeastern Turkey in the Amanus, Zagros, and Taurus Mountains southwestward through western Syria and Lebanon, along the border between Jordan and Israel, over to the Gulf of Aqaba, through the Red Sea to Ethiopia. This rift separates the Arabian Peninsula from Africa (Beitzel 2005:4). The geographical configuration of this region was influential not only for the location of settlements and cities, as well as for trade and transportation, but also for the availability and type of raw materials that could be utilized to the greatest extent, including stone.

In Canaan (modern Israel, Jordan, Lebanon, and Syria), the geological formations "consist of a thick packet of sediments lying in parallel order on a fairly flat, planed-off igneous basement" (Perath 1984:6). Four intersecting peneplains, dating from the Late Protezic pre-Permian, separate the basement from the sediments. Metamorphic mountain roots truncate the basement at various locations including the central and south Sinai, out-croppings in the Dead Sea Rift Valley near Eilat and Timna, and in the Transjordan (Perath 1984:6). Egypt's geology consists of a layer of limestone overtop sandstone, which forms the surface rock in Nubia and Upper Egypt, northward to approximately Edfu and Luxor.

The stone found in Egypt can be divided into three main groups: igneous, sedimentary, and metamorphic (University College, London 2003). These translate into volcanic, plutonic, and veinstones; clay, lime, and quartz; and sandstone, granite, and marble, respectively. In northern Mesopotamia (modern Syria and Turkey), the geological formations were complex and prone to earthquake and volcanic activity, producing extensive deposits of basalt and obsidian (Moorey 1999:21). Although stone resources were limited, Southern Mesopotamia (modern Iraq and Iran) was rich in alluvial silt transported by rivers in the highland regions and deposited in the plain of southern Mesopotamia. The south was also rich in the softer stones such as gypsum, limestone, and sandstone along the Euphrates west of Uruk, and extending into the desert region. From the Arabian Desert, granite was available. Other stones such as breccia, bituminous stone, calcite, marble, quartz, schist, and serpentine were also readily available and utilized. (Moorey 1999:21).

When choosing stone for construction, tools, or artwork, the craftsperson had to consider the stone's properties, making certain its characteristics were commensurate to the project. For example, rocks chosen for tools and weapons had to be workable and produce a strong finished product. In construction, stones had to correspond with the building's location, size, and function. The mason had to consider the stone's bulk volume and density, as well as its bearing capacity and strength; water absorption and evaporation; resistance to erosion from wind, rain, temperature, and weathering; and corrosion, especially near the sea (Perath 1984:14). In other words, the craftsperson had to know how the chosen stone would survive harsh weather conditions, bear weight, hold up under repetitive daily use, and consider whether it would be aesthetically pleasing. Knowledge of a stone's properties was probably acquired through experience: experimentation, and trial and error. Additional considerations included availability, quantity, location of the source, and transportation time between quarry and building site.

It is not known exactly when humans began using stone tools; however, archaeological and anthropological studies have revealed that humans began using stone tools ca. 3.4 million years ago (australopithecine) to ca. 2.6 million years ago during the Lower Paleolithic period in Gona Ethiopia. Recognizable stone tools appear in Oldowan Industry found in the Olduvai Gorge, Tanzania. These tools consisted mostly of cores made into spherical hammer stones with a sharpened tip. This phase was followed by the Acheulean Industry from Saint-Acheul, France, and tools consisted of a core with a bifacial cutting forming a hand axe. The Mousterian Industry followed, which exhibited refinement into smaller sharper knives and scrapers produced by Neanderthals. That phase was followed by the Aurignacian Industry of the Upper Palaeolithic, the Microlithic Industry, and the Neolithic Industries, the latter of which have already been discussed.

With each new phase, stone tools became more sophisticated, precise, and task-specific; furthermore, their use was planned in advance. By the Neolithic Period in the Near East, tools included knives, scrapers, sickles, microliths, arrow and spear heads, mace heads, chisels, and loom weights.

The stone tool industry became one of the most important industries of early human history. Based on blade types and materials, this industry clearly enjoyed a wide market. For example, obsidian blades reflect long-distance acquisition and trade of raw materials for a specific purpose. In the Near East, obsidian can be found in Turkey, Italy, Greece, and Armenia, though much of the obsidian found at Near Eastern sites probably originated from Turkey (Moorey 1999:21). Early examples of chipped-stone tools come from the Acheulian Industry, which produced hand axes, choppers, cleavers, and flake tools that became increasingly functional and sophisticated. These tools were made using the percussion technique and retouching to achieve a serrated edge. Examples from the early Acheulian stone industry have been found at the southern edge of the Sea of Galilee at 'Ubeidiya (Rollefson 2005b:254).

The widespread distribution of obsidian blades suggests intentional mining, refinement, and transportation of raw materials for fashioning into tools and weapons. Obsidian continues to be used for surgical blades because it is "infinitely sharper than a honed steel edge," which allows for super-precise incisions that heal without complications, "and these blades can be produced in a wide variety of shapes and sizes" (Buck 1982:265).

Flint-knapping, the technique of forming tools and weapons from stone through lithic reduction, was widely practiced. The most frequently used stones were flint, chert, quartz, obsidian, and other conchoidal fracturing stones that were easily dug or removed from the ground without the need for quarrying. The rocks selected were those that left a smooth surface when fractured. To create a blade, the flint-knapper held a core (stone) with one hand and held a stone hammer in the other. Striking the core at the correct angle produced thin chips, called flakes, with smooth surfaces and razor-sharp edges. The flakes were then fashioned into the desired tool with other smaller stones or pieces of wood. The knife could have a smooth or a serrated blade (Hodges 1992:22–27).

Stone was fashioned into numerous other utensils used in daily life, such as fishing hooks, needles, awls, grinding stones, and mortises and pestles. Basalt was regularly fashioned into pillar figures, bowls (flower-pot shaped, rounded, footed, and fenestrated footed), querns, grinding stones and pestles, hoses and agricultural tools, hammers, weights, and basins (Epstein 1977). In the central Golan where Dalwe Basalt was abundant, it was used for fashioning household items, whereas olivine basalt was used for milling equipment, agricultural tools, and pillar figures. Basalt can be worked, dressed, and smoothed using a flint blade such as an adze (Epstein 1998:229).

Basalt as a raw material or a finished product was not transported or traded over long distances. The evidence thus far suggests that those who used basalt in the Chalcolithic Golan, Negev, and Transjordan, for example, availed themselves of local deposits because it was abundant and easily obtained (Epstein 1998:229).

Quarrying stone

The acquisition of stone gradually shifted from collection to quarrying. Keen knowledge of the properties of various stones was developed, and techniques were devised for controlled extraction by breaking, cutting, and pulverizing using chisel, axe, adze, and hammer (Wright 2005:34). There were two basic quarrying techniques: extracting from the surface downward, also referred to as open cut quarrying, and horizontal extraction by digging galleries into a rock slope (Wright 2005:34).

Ancient quarrying activities remain evident throughout the Near East, especially in Egypt from the Old Kingdom (ca. 2689–2125 BCE) onward. Examples can still be seen in Aswan with the Unfinished Obelisk (Figure 3.1), thought to be from the

FIGURE 3.1 Unfinished obelisk and quarry at Aswan, Egypt. Left and middle: Unfinished obelisk, Aswan, Egypt. Example of open-pit *in situ* quarrying. Right: trenching and chisel marks left in the stone from quarrying

Photographs by Jill L. Baker.

time of Hatshepsut (reign ca. 1479–1458 BCE). In this case, a full-size obelisk remains unfinished, *in situ*, probably abandoned due to a stress crack that formed during extraction. Megaliths such as these were carved *in situ*, removed, and transported in one piece. Quarrying is a human activity that has caused irreparable damage to the earth's surface, as is so blatantly evident at the Aswan quarry in Egypt.

Recent research at Tell el-Amarna, by the Amarna Project of the McDonald Institute for Archaeological Research, University of Cambridge, has revealed much regarding ancient Egyptian quarrying techniques (www.amarnaproject.com/index.shtml), which took place in the hills north of the ancient city. Known as Queen Tiy's quarry, hundreds of limestone blocks were removed using several techniques simultaneously: vertical quarry facing, open quarrying, and cutting into the cliff facing. Blocks of all sizes, shapes, and finish were extracted. Some blocks were abandoned and left *in situ*, providing valuable insight into the quarrying techniques.

The blocks extracted from quarries were finished to near perfection, and many of them bear masons' marks, which suggests an orderly administrative connection between the quarry and the building site (Aston et al. 2000:15). Once extracted, the prepared blocks were transported to a workshop or a construction site.

At the quarry, building blocks were likely fashioned into reasonable sizes and shapes that could be realistically transported. The size would have been commensurate with the needs of the project and distance of the quarry to the site (Aston et al. 2000:17). However, depictions of Egyptians transporting mammoth obelisks or statues (Figure 3.2, top) suggest they were capable of moving massive blocks as well (as with the above-mentioned Obelisks of Queen Hatshepsut, with each obelisk 29.6 meters long and weighing ca. 323 tons; Transporting a Colossus, Tomb of Djehutihotep at Deir el Bersha, ca. 1900 BCE). Scenes such as Transporting a Colossus and the Unfinished Obelisk in Aswan further underscore that some megalithic pieces were quarried and carved *in situ*, extracted in a finished or semi-finished state, and transported to their final destination (Aston et al. 2000:15). In Mesopotamia, moving giant statues and stone blocks was accomplished in a similar manner. Reliefs from Sennacherib's palace at Nineveh depict workers pulling a bull statue on a sledge using rollers and a lever to propel it forward (Figure 3.2, bottom).

Another form of *in situ* quarrying involved cutting and removing stone from the area that was used as the building site. This method not only cleared the area for construction, but it reduced travel time between quarry and building site. This technique was practiced, for example, in Egypt at the Giza Plateau to facilitate the construction of the pyramids (see AERA website: www.aeraweb.org/gpmp-project/great-pyramid-quarry/).

Throughout the ancient Near East, quarry tool kits were relatively standard, consisting of stone or metal (bronze or iron) chisels, wooden wedges, levers, hammer (hand-held stone or wooden mallet), and drills. For example, quarrying tools were found at a recently discovered first-century quarry site in Jerusalem, which included wedges and chisels (Bryner 2013b). Extraction methods were also relatively standard. To extract stone from rock outcroppings, masons determined the desired shape and size of the block they needed, drilled holes, inserted wooden wedges, and soaked

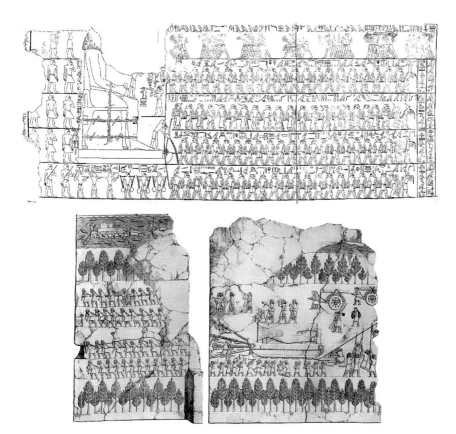

FIGURE 3.2 Transporting colossal statues. Top: Tomb of Djehutihotep, Nomarch, Twelfth Dynasty. Moving a colossal statue on a sledge. Bottom: Relief from the Palace of Sennacherib at Nineveh

Adapted from Newberry 1895, Pl. XV (Public Domain, PD-1923) (top); adapted from Layard 1853, Pl. 13 (Public Domain, PD-1923) (bottom).

the wedges with water. Drills consisted of a drill bit of a hard stone, harder than the one being cut, and a shaft around which a stringed bow was wrapped. With one hand the mason held a capping stone over the shaft, and with the other hand, or operated in concert with another mason, the bow was moved back and forth to produce a drilling motion (Arnold 1991:50–51). Wooden wedges were inserted into the holes and soaked with water to cause the wood to expand. As the wedges expanded, fractures were created, thus allowing quarry workers to chisel/pick a trench from which blocks could be extracted (Figure 3.1, right). This is referred to as the trenching method, which remained in use well into the Classical Period (Fant 2008:122–124). The trench created an isolated area wherein blocks could be fashioned and extracted. In addition to drilling and wedges, metal picks were also used, especially once iron became strong enough to chip away at rock. Once the block was isolated, wedges were inserted to remove the block from its base, and chisels could finish the process (Aston et al. 2000:7). Another way to split stone was along a natural vein, fracture, or a plane of weakness.

Once stone blocks were set into place, the masons added decorative elements and finishes (see Figure 8.1), such as borders or polishes, or they fashioned the blocks into sculptures using axes, hammers, chisels, plumb bobs, right angles, calipers, and bevels, which flattened and shaped the exposed face of the block (Wright 2005:44–58). Numerous blocks still contain the chisel marks of the ancient masons (Arnold 1991:32–34).

The bow drill was used to make holes of various sizes, which fashioned stone into blocks, vessels, door sockets, and the like. The bit consisted of a round wooden shaft attached to a hollow copper tube. The top of the shaft was held with a cap-stone, and the copper tube sat atop sand, the abrasive that cut the rock. Around the wooden shaft was strung the bowstring. With one person holding the capstone over the wooden shaft and one or two people moving the bow back and forth, the friction and pressure of the copper drill tube and sand created the desired cut in the stone (Figure 3.3, left). Alternatively, stones were attached to the top of the shaft providing weight and energy when turned (Figure 3.3, right).

Once extracted, the transportation of the mammoth blocks was an engineering marvel. To move the large blocks, several techniques were employed. A block or finished statue could be tied to a sledge and dragged, as depicted in the Tomb of Djehutihotep and at Sennacherib's palace in Nineveh (Figure 3.2). The sledge would have been pulled by hundreds of workers while one or several workers lubricated the construction road ahead of it. In addition to or in concert with sledges, wooden rollers were also used to move stone blocks. This method may seem simplistic or even impossible, but today, rollers are regularly utilized to move substantial objects, as in the loading of cargo onto an aircraft, which the author observed at Fort Lauderdale Airport (Figure 3.4).

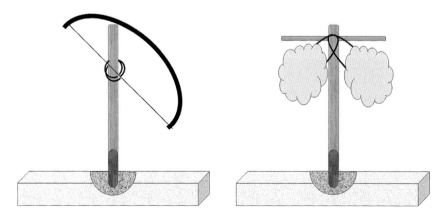

FIGURE 3.3 Stone drill. Wooden shaft with copper bit powered by a bow with string wrapped around the shaft (left) or stones attached atop the shaft (right)

Graphics by Jill L. Baker.

FIGURE 3.4 Cargo loaded onto an aircraft using rollers

Photographs by Jill L. Baker.

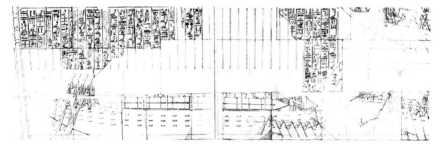

FIGURE 3.5 Depiction of an obelisk loaded onto a barge from the Mortuary Temple of Queen Hatshepsut

After E. Naville 1908 Pl. CLIV (Public Domain, PD-1923).

At some ancient sites, roads and ramps were created specifically for the purpose of moving materials to a construction site. For example, in the Middle Kingdom, the Egyptians constructed an 80-kilometer road that connected the diorite-gabbro and anorthosite gneiss quarries near Gebel el-Asr with the Nile at modern Tushka (Aston et al. 2000:18). To move large, heavy stone over a greater distance, the stone was set onto barges and floated to its destination along the Nile River. Queen Hatshepsut's temple at Deir el Bahri depicts the loading and transportation of an obelisk onto a barge (Figure 3.5). Similar scenes have been found in the temples of Unas at Saqqara (Fifth Dynasty) and Senedjemib Inty at Giza (Fifth Dynasty, tomb G2370). The barges themselves are equally impressive. Ship builders had to engineer a vessel that could accommodate the size, shape, and weight of the cargo without capsizing or sinking. Finally, once the stone arrived at the destination site, it would have been positioned into place using rollers, wedges, ropes, levers, and planks.

The Egyptians quarried several types of stone including granite, limestone, sandstone, diorite, basalt, and porphyry. Many of these were used for construction; however, minerals such as azurite were used for pigments and malachite for eye paint. So, in addition to mining stone for construction, it was also procured for use as pigments in paint, cosmetics, artwork (sculpture and inlay), scarabs, and jewelry (Aston et al. 2000:20).

In Canaan/ancient Israel, organized quarrying enterprise and techniques did not develop until the Iron Age when limestone was fashioned into building blocks. In ancient Israel there were three types of limestone: mizzi yahudi, which is very hard, not easily procured or dressed, but was used for thresholds and door sockets due to its durability; and mizzi hilu and meleke, which were more easily obtained and manipulated and used mostly for column capitals and bases. Meleke was the most used limestone, an example of which is the enclosure walls of the Temple Mount constructed during the Herodian period (Reich 1992:1).

Another type of stone, nari, a chalky, friable rock, was used extensively for architectural features, ashlar blocks, and the proto-Aeolic capitals adorning monumental buildings. While workable, the final product was not as smooth as the mizzi hilu and meleke stones; however, its durability made it desirable. Finally, basalt, found mostly in northern parts of ancient Israel in the Galilee, Golan, and Bashan regions, was very hard and durable. Basalt could withstand heat, water, and weathering in a way that limestone could not. It was used for building elements that bore a lot of weight, such as foundations, and that received the brunt of weathering and endured the most wear and tear, such as door sockets. It was also used for grinding stones and architectural elements such as city gates and roads (Reich 1992:2).

Limestone blocks were locally sourced from open-air quarries or areas close to the building site. Horizontal quarrying, which created artificial caves, was rare. For example, the quarrying site dating to the Second Temple Period (ca. 530 BCE to 70 CE), recently discovered in East Jerusalem in the Ramat Shlomo Quarter, was an open-air quarry (Bryner 2013b). There, in the process of removing the rock, the workers created columns, steps, and craters. Excavators estimate some of the blocks removed ranged in size from ca. 2 to 8 meters in length (ca. 6.5 to 26 feet). The rock found there is meleke rock, soft and easily hewn, and shaped at the time of quarrying because it hardens immediately after removal. Next to the quarry was a road that may have served to transport the blocks out of the quarry. Some tools were also discovered at the site including pick axes, metal wedges, and a key (Bryner 2013b).

While limestone functioned as the most used building material, higher quality stone such as marble was imported and generally reserved for palaces and temples. It is interesting to note that Levantine masons formed guilds; the Hebrew Bible refers to "Phoenician masons" (1 Kings 5:18), and tool sets remained the same for generations. Perhaps tools were passed from master to apprentice.

During the Iron Age, stone building blocks took on a distinctive style, referred to as an ashlar block. These consisted of six dressed sides with well-defined right-angled edges. They were laid in multiple horizontal courses in header-stretcher pattern, with the exposed faces receiving a smooth finish (Isserlin 2001:122–123). The quarrying techniques practiced in Canaan/ancient Israel paralleled those from Egypt, as evidenced by negative impressions left at abandoned quarry sites in Jerusalem from the Iron Age and the Roman period (Figure 3.6). In Mesopotamia, stones such as breccia, calcite, dolomite, gypsum, limestone, sandstone, basalt, granite, marble, quartzite, agate, amethyst hematite, cornelian, lapis lazuli, and turquoise

FIGURE 3.6 Locations from Jerusalem's ancient quarries. Left: Quarry stone in the Western Wall Tunnel, Jerusalem. Right: Quarry under the Church of the Holy Sepulcher, Jerusalem

Photographs by Jill L. Baker.

were used for jewelry, seals, sculpture, vessels, as stelae, and in the construction of buildings (Moorey 1999).

Once the stone was extracted, fashioned into the desired shape, and transported to the building site, it was incorporated into the construction, where stone was combined with other materials such as wood and mortar to complete the project.

4

WOOD

The variety of woods used in the Near East as well as the entire Mediterranean basin were numerous, task specific, and essential to domestic and international economies. Like stone, wood was an indispensable and much used material, just as it is today. Wood is an organic material that is subject to decay and is flammable and combustible. Nevertheless, it was valued and utilized in numerous aspects of ancient life. Its use began very early throughout Egypt, Mesopotamia, Canaan, and the entire Mediterranean basin. Every part of a tree was utilized, and little was left to waste. Evidence for the use of wood comes from physical remains such as decayed wood in postholes, negative impressions in mudbrick and cement, wattle and daub walls, pictorial representations and literary references, and artifacts. Timber was utilized in construction as structural elements, such as posts and lintels, and as decoration, such as paneling. It was used to make furniture, bowls, boxes and chests, handles for tools and weapons, and utensils. Wood was also used to fuel fires including domestic hearths, ovens, kilns, and for smelting and refining metals. Tree bark was used for fuel, roofing material, interior paneling, flooring, the soles of shoes (Pliny *Natural History* 16.34–42, Henderson and Jones 1963; Humphrey et al. 2006:338–340), basketry, mats, containers, and rope. The bark of the cork tree was used on ships for anchor ropes and fishermen's nets. The bark of beech, lime, fir, and pitch pine were used for containers and baskets to harvest grain and grapes. Tree leaves were given to livestock as food. Finally, charcoal was used as fuel for fires for smelting ores, in pottery and glass kilns, and in domestic fireplaces. As with masons, textile workers, and artisans, carpenters were prolific in the ancient Near East and probably formed guilds. This chapter will discuss the importance of wood in the ancient world and the archaeological record, as well as timber resources, felling and curing, and some tree species and their uses.

In drier climates like Egypt, wooden artifacts have been recovered having survived millennia due to lack of moisture. Textual references and depictions in friezes and murals describe the numerous ways that wood was utilized. The Palermo Stone, from the Royal Annals of the Old Kingdom, records the kings of Egypt from the First to the Fifth Dynasties, who sailed ships to Lebanon where trees were felled and then rafted down the Mediterranean coast and stored in timber yards in the Delta. In fact, the ancients' insatiable appetite for wood led to deforestation, contributing to the artificial creation of arid microclimates and soil erosion in some places. Their use of wood was so prolific that according to Plato, by the end of the Bronze Age, Greece had been largely deforested (Plato, *Critias* 111b-c. Humphrey et al. 2006:337–338). Wood artifacts recovered from the archaeological record are useful not only because they provide insight into the employment of wood as a building material or luxury item, but also because it may help to provide dating and sourcing data. The wood itself provides insight into trade routes, economy, the ancient climate, and the natural environment.

Dendrochronology, that is, tree ring dating, establishes the age of the tree at the time it was felled, which can contribute to wider chronological discussions. Dendrochronology can also establish climatological conditions during the tree's lifetime. Each ring represents one year's growth and records climate conditions for that period. Dendrochronology can help establish past ecologies and climate variations. Timber can be aged using radio carbon dating, C14, which can provide an estimated felling date, and the tree's age can be found by counting the rings. In the cross-section of a tree, growth rings, or annual rings, are visible (Figure 4.1). The rings are the result of new growth in the vascular cambium layer of cells close to the bark. The variation of each annual ring can reveal the amount of growth throughout that year. Wide growth rings mean a good growth year; thin rings mean a poor growth year. It can also aid in understanding the timber trade and interspecies analyses. Dendrochronology, and the additional data it can provide, has become useful in the analysis of wooden artifacts found in Egypt—in particular, coffins, boxes, and boats, such as the Dashur boat (Kuniholm et al. 2014). In another example, the year 1816 in North America was known as the year without a summer due to the volcanic eruption of Mount Tambora in the Dutch East Indies (Klingman and Klingman 2013). Tree rings from that year

FIGURE 4.1   Dendrochronology, or tree ring dating, relies on annual growth rings of trees to establish chronology and atmospheric conditions during the life of the tree

Photographs by Jill L. Baker.

show little or no growth because it was so cold. The abnormally low global tempera-tures ranged from 0.7 to 1.3° F below normal.

The horizontal cross-section also reveals the sapwood and heartwood. Sapwood is the new growth, and heartwood is the older growth. Heartwood is very dense, can be as strong as iron, and is resistant to pests. It is from this wood that many timber structures of Europe and colonial New England were constructed, many of which remain standing today, such as the House of Seven Gables in Salem, Massachusetts (1668), the Thomas Lee House in East Lyme, Connecticut (1660), and the Feake-Ferris House in Old Greenwich, Connecticut (1645, Greenwich Point Conservancy). No doubt, the craftsmen of the ancient Near East utilized heartwood for their projects as well.

The most abundant woodlands were sometimes found at great distances from the urban centers that coveted the wood. Coniferous woods, such as cedar, were found in northern regions such as Lebanon, which exported cedar wood to Egypt (Palermo Stone) and Canaan/ancient Israel (2 Samuel 5:11, 7:2,7; 1 Kings 4:33, 5:8–10, 6:9–20, 6:36, 7:2–12). Timber was also obtained from the Taurus and Zagros mountains, and tree species from there can be divided into three broad categories (Moorey 1999:348; Meiggs 1982:53–54). The lower slopes of the mountains, up to ca. 500 m, supported cypress, coastal pine, and green oak. The middle slopes, ca. 500 to 1200 m, supported cypress, coastal pine and evergreen, as well as deciduous oak, ash, elm, juniper, and maple. The upper slopes, over ca. 1200 m, supported conifers, cedars, firs, and junipers (Moorey 1999:348; Meiggs 1982:53–54). The Mesopotamians also made use of trees and plants that grew near the Tigris and Euphrates rivers, according to Ur III texts, which included poplar and willow (Moorey 1999:349). Other wood types included cultivated trees, box-tree, and Kanis oak (Nicholson and Shaw 2009:353). Finally, some woods were imported from farther east, such as from Pakistan (Moorey 1999:352). In Greece, Theophrastus (*Enquiry into Plants*, 5.2.1, Henderson and Hort 1916) also discussed some of the regions where the best woods were found and imported into Greece. These included Macedonia, the Black Sea, Rhyndacus, and Aenianes (Humphrey et al. 2006:338).

In Egypt, where forests are scarce, wood was imported, sometimes from distant lands. The Temple of Hatshepsut at Deir el-Bahari recounts an expedition to the land of Punt, where workers are depicted cutting branches and carrying logs of timber and live trees in pots onto the ship. It has been suggested the potted plant depicted is an ebony tree. Archaeological investigation and scientific analysis have identified numerous woods used by the ancient Egyptians. These include acacia, maple, cork, silver birch, common box, carob, African black or ironwood (Egyptian ebony), sycamore fig, common ash, storax balsam, olive, plum, almond, willow, tamarisk, lime, elm, palm, Cilician fir, cedar, cypress, juniper, Aleppo pine, and yew. Because tree types and their uses have been researched and described in Nicholson's and Shaw's work for Egypt (Gale et al. 2009:335–352) and in Moorey's for Mesopotamia (1999:347–361 (esp. 360–361)), it is not necessary to repeat all of that information here; nevertheless, some types of wood shall be mentioned.

As with stone, the type of wood chosen for a project had to correspond with the function it performed. The carpenter had to be aware of the characteristics and properties of each species of wood, as well as its strengths and weaknesses, durability, and aesthetic qualities. One of the best known and much sought-after wood types was cedar, Cedrus libani, which was found in present-day Lebanon. It could grow to 30 to 40 meters in height with trunks spanning 1 to 2.3 meters in diameter. They were conical to flat in shape, and boasted numerous branches, needles, and cones. The wood was pinkish-brown in color, had a straight grain, was aromatic, highly durable, and easy to work with (Gale et al. 2009:349). Cedar was used for doors, as in the Nuzi II Palace; temple facades, as at Khorsabad; planking, paneling, roofing, and ceilings as in Solomon's Temple (1 Kings 6); and as boxes, boats, coffins, and chests, as well as architecturally in Egypt (Gale et al. 2009:349–350). Pine was used for structural and architectural elements, furniture, roof timbers, boxes, and chests. Acacia was a hard and durable wood used for construction, furniture, coffins, bows, and arrows. Pine was also useful for fuel, and its charcoal fueled fires for activities such as smelting.

Field maple was a small tree, ca. 15 meters high and shrubby. It grew at an altitude of 200 meters above sea level and was native to Europe and the Balkans, northern Turkey, the Caucasus, and the southern coast of the Caspian Sea. It was a strong hardwood with an even grain. Its heartwood and sapwood were pale or yellowish-brown in color. It was used for boxes, culinary utensils, furniture, domestic items such as knife handles, musical instruments, boats and wagons, bows and arrows, and fuel. African Black, also called ironwood or Egyptian ebony, was found in the dry woodland of tropical Africa and western India. It was black or dark brown in color and very hard, which made it an excellent wood to use in furniture construction, inlay, veneer, and sculpture (Gale et al. 2009:338–339; Moorey 1999).

The process of felling trees and preparing them can be found in Egyptian tomb paintings and reliefs (Figure 4.2). In the Tomb of Sekhemkara, a vizier from the Fourth Dynasty depicts a tree being felled using a single-notch technique and the wood then being prepared for use (LG89; Hassan 1943:115, Figs. 15–17). The overseeing of felling trees and the preparation of them have also been depicted in the tombs of Khnumhotep II at Beni Hasan, Ipuy at Thebes, and Nefer and Kaha at Saqqara, where the double-notch technique is depicted (Nicholson and Shaw 2009:353).

This technique allows for more control as the tree falls, and it reduces the likelihood of "thunder shakes" upon impact with the ground, which could affect the grain, as depicted in a scene in the Hypostyle Hall in the Temple of Amun at Karnak, dating to the time of Seti I (Gale et al. 2009:353).

After felling, trees were transported from forest to destination by land and water, with water being the preferred method (Figure 4.3, left three). For example, cedar logs were rafted from Lebanon, along the Mediterranean coast, to the Nile Delta for use in Egypt (Gale et al. 2009:353). Reliefs from the Sargon II (reign ca. 722–705 BCE) palace at Khorsabad depict the transportation of timber by boat. The reliefs depict workmen lugging logs down a mountain and piling them next to the water's

FIGURE 4.2   Egyptian woodcutters felling a tree

Adapted from P. Newberry (1893a), *Beni Hasan,* Tomb No. 3. Pl. XXIX. (Public Domain, PD-1923).

FIGURE 4.3   Scenes of maritime transportation and preparation of timber. Left three: Maritime transportation of timber from source to destination from the palace of Sargon II (ca. 721–705 BCE), Dur-Sharrukin, present-day Khorsabad. Right: Cleaving a tree in Egypt. Tomb of Iteti, Deshasha, Sixth Dynasty

Adapted from Botta and Flandin 1849 Pls. 32, 34, 35 (Public Domain, PD-1923) (left three); adapted from Petrie 1898 Pl. XXI (Public Domain, PD-1923) (right).

edge for removal. The logs were then loaded onto boats or floated behind them. Once at their destination, workmen transfer the logs onto land for further transportation to workshops.

Very tall trees were felled by several people using ropes tied to upper branches to control the fall, as depicted on the northern wall of the Great Hypostyle Hall in the Temple of Amun, Karnak, dated to the time of Seti I. Great care was taken to prevent branches from being damaged because they could be used for table, chair, and bed legs without too much modification. Once felled, the tree was prepared for use. Green timber had to be reduced through seasoning. The timber was cut into planks by a process known as cleaving (Figure 4.3, right), using an axe to cut green wood into long boards, and splitting the log along the grain. The planks then had to be seasoned, or dried, to prevent warping, splitting, cupping, and shrinkage. To accomplish this, the planks were stacked with spacers to allow air ventilation between them. In Egypt, boards were stacked at the carpenter's workshop and sometimes covered with reed mats to control the rate of drying. The Egyptians were such experts at this process that the moisture content of their timber was between 8 and 12 percent (Gale et al. 2009:355).

Woodworkers used an array of tools to procure timber and prepare it. Axes made from copper and/or bronze and later iron were used to fell the trees. As depicted in Figure 4.2, axes were used to notch the tree for felling and to remove branches and bark. Planking was achieved with saws, poles, and chisel supporting the lob/board vertically while a man split it with a saw, which was the most common depiction, or by laying the board horizontally with one person wedging it with a pole-wedge and another prying off the plank (Figure 4.3, right).

Saws made of copper were used for planking along the grain-line and for cutting across it. Several have been discovered in various sizes and shapes, such as those found at Saqqara in tomb S3471, an Early Dynastic tomb. Some of these saws had a curved cutting edge with closely spaced teeth alternately set to the left and right. The handles were made of wood to fit the craftsman's hand perfectly. The adze was used to shape the wood, with one edge being the metal blade and the other end weighted more heavily for even cutting, but it could also have a cutting edge. Leather sinew was saturated in water then used to attach the metal head to a wooden handle. The leather shrank when drying, which secured the blade to the handle (Gale et al. 2009:355).

Adze blades came in a variety of shapes and sizes depending on the type of finishing work being done. Copper chisels and wooden hammers from the Predynastic period have been found, attesting to their use for boring holes and forming grooves. Chisels generally had a flat head and round body, while other chisels boasted different shaped heads for cutting, prying, and finishing. Awls were used to bore holes and as engraving tools for decoration. Planes helped to sand and smooth the planks. Bow drills were also used for boring holes. Examples from Egypt can be found in the tombs of Rekhmira at Thebes (TT100), Ipuy at Thebes (TT217), and Ty at Saqqara, a tomb from Kahun that contained two bow drills now at the Petrie Museum in London (UC7085 bow and UC7084 drill) (Nicholson and Shaw 2009:356). Examples from Mesopotamia can be found on the Stela of Ur-Nammu of Ur (ca. 2112–2095 BCE), and copper and bronze saws from Farah, Kish, Ur, and Susa to name a few (Moorey 1999:353–354).

5
METALS

Metals are considered inorganic, though some can corrode, such as iron, and their properties can change due to smelting and carburization. Metals have been in use since at least the Neolithic and Chalcolithic periods and continue to be one of the most important materials in industry and daily use. The use and value of metals differed from one culture to another and from one chronological period to another; however, metals remained one of the most prominent commodities in the ancient world and helped drive the economy. As society evolved, so too did their need for and use of metals. For example, the introduction of coinage increased the demand for silver and gold, which in turn resulted in improved purification techniques. With knowledge of metals and metallurgy, humankind shifted from using stone-based tools, weapons, and objects to metal ones. This resulted in stronger, more durable implements, which led to scientific development, increased production, technological advantage in battles, new professions, and economic growth. Metals, especially iron, became integral to the growth and development of civilizations, and the role of the metalsmith became increasingly important. This chapter will discuss mines and mining, smelting and refining, and some of the most commonly used metals in the ancient Near East.

The main metals employed in Mesopotamia, Egypt, Canaan, and throughout the Mediterranean basin included copper, bronze (tin and copper alloy), iron, lead, gold, silver, electrum (silver and gold alloy), mercury, tin, antimony, and zinc. Metals could be combined to make stronger materials. For example, copper and tin were alloyed to make bronze, a stronger more durable metal. Purification techniques could be chemical based. For example, mercury was used to refine gold. Softer metals such as gold, silver, copper, and lead were used for jewelry, ceremonial items, and decoration or overlay on figurines, cups, bowls, plates, and vases.

In the Bronze Age, metals, specifically copper and bronze, replaced stone as the material of choice for tools, weapons, ceremonial objects, and utensils. Since metals

FIGURE 5.1   Native copper, gold, silver. Left to right: Native copper, gold, and silver

Adapted from Wikipedia.org By Native_Copper_Macro_Digon3.jpg: "Jonathan Zander (Digon3)" derivative work: Materialscientist (talk) – Native_Copper_Macro_Digon3.jpg, CC BY-SA 3.0, https://commons.wikimedia.org/w/index.php?curid=60483070 (left, copper). Adapted from Wikipedia.org By Alchemist-hp (talk) www.pse-mendelejew.de (Own work) (FAL or CC BY-SA 3.0 de (http://creativecommons.org/licenses/by-sa/3.0/de/deed.en), via Wikimedia Commons (middle gold). By Alchemist-hp (talk) (www.psemendelejew.de) – Own work (additional processed by Waugsberg), CC BY-SA 3.0 de, https://commons.wikimedia.org/w/index.php?curid=7394995 (right silver). All images Public Domain.

were deeply integrated into society, it is important to note how the metal was obtained, processed, and fashioned into useful items, but also its place in the economy. As with stone and wood, metals have been discussed at length by Ogden (2009:148–176) for Egypt and by Moorey (1999:216–301) for Mesopotamia; therefore, the treatment of metals here is meant to be a summary and to initiate a wider discussion regarding metals' sourcing, extraction, preparation, and use.

One of the earliest metals used by peoples in the Near East was copper; however, Pliny suggests that gold may have been the first metal that humankind used (*Natural History* 33.58–63, Henderson and Rackham 1952:46–51; Humphrey et al. 2006:207). Lucretius (*On the Nature of Things* 5.1241–1265, Henderson and Rouse 1992:474–476; Humphrey et al. 2006:206–207) suggests that gold, copper, and iron were discovered at the same time, as was silver and lead (Figure 5.1). Copper, like gold and iron, is a native metal; that is, a metal found on the Earth's surface as a pure metal or an alloy, without having to extract it from an ore or smelt it. Other native metals include silver, nickel, cobalt, titanium, mercury, manganese, arsenic, and tin. These can also be found as an ore, but they must undergo the smelting process to remove the surrounding impurities.

Archaeological evidence suggests that humankind was using copper as early as the Chalcolithic period. At first copper was used in its pure form, that is pure copper not alloyed with another metal. Pure copper is very soft and does not necessarily make for useful tools or weapons. It is often assumed that in its pure form, copper was used to make objects that evoked prestige, such as jewelry, ceremonial, and ritualistic objects such as crowns and maces, and for votive objects (Muhly 2003:174). A well-known votive hoard from the Chalcolithic period comes from the Nahal Mishmar cave near the Dead Sea, wherein some 432 copper, bronze, ivory, and stone objects were discovered (Bar-Adon 1980). Other supplicatory deposits were found at the Obelisk Temple in Byblos (Muhly 2003:174), and in burial deposits such as those from Ashkelon, Megiddo, and Jericho.

Mines and mining

The process by which the ancients identified mineral deposits is not yet known (Ogden 2009:148; Oleson 2008:96–99). Since no real knowledge of scientific geology had been formulated, it was likely that observation of the natural environment, trial and error, and experiential knowledge about native metals, ores, and deposits formed the basis for knowledge and subsequent methods of detection and extraction (Ogden 2009:148; Oleson 2008:96–99). Keen observation of the flora associated with certain deposits and rock formations also may have provided reliable clues. For example, acacia, *Lychnis alpine, Haumaniastrum Katangense*, and pine trees have been associated with the presence of copper and lead ores (Ogden 2009:148; Hand 2015). In another recent example, geologists have noticed that a newly discovered species of tree, Pandanus Candelabrum, a type of palm tree in Liberia, grows only on top of kimberlite pipes formed by volcanic activity. These natural formations deliver diamonds from deep in the Earth to its surface (Haggerty 2015). In the Greek and Roman periods, significant progress was made in identifying geological features and surface indicators of buried deposits (Oleson 2008:96–99). It is also probable that quarrying activities provided valuable practical information regarding not only stone but also geological formations and the type of metal deposits they held.

Miners extracted vast quantities of ore and created huge galleries or open pits without the use of explosives, a remarkable feat. Numerous ancient mines remain visible today. Some early mines include a Neanderthal chert mine in Bulgaria, and the Ngwenya Mountain Lion Cave in Swaziland (ca. 43,000 years old), where people extracted hematite and red ochre. In the Near East, Timna (Figure 5.2) and Feinan provide some of the earliest examples of mining, from ca. 4000 BCE onward. Miners collected copper from the surface but also dug extensive mines to extract the copper ore, and their shafts and galleries remain visible today. Early mining tools and methods were similar to those used by quarry workers. Picks, chisels, hammers, and harder rocks were used to extract the desired ore. Methods such as coring, separating rock by inserting wood into fissures or hollowed-out cores and then soaking it so the wood expanded, thus loosening the rock, were also employed.

In the late first millennium BCE, substantial developments were made in mining techniques, from Greece to Spain to China. Ventilation and drainage were improved, as was the strengthening of tunnels and galleries. Much of the credit for these improvements was due to advancements made in mathematics, physics, and pneumatics, which provided new technology to the mining industry. Such technology included the adit, screw (Archimedes invention; Diodorus *History* 5.36–38), pumps (Ctesibius), water wheels, and an understanding of airflow. Tools such as picks, hammers, wedges, chisels, hoes, and rakes were made of iron and steel, and thus were much stronger and more durable than earlier tools made of stone, antler, and bronze.

In most ancient nations, the ruling authority staked claim and held sole rights to valuable mine deposits. The state worked the mine with royally appointed officials organizing and administering the day-to-day logistics. In a letter from

FIGURE 5.2 Timna mines in southern Israel. Remnants of a shaft mine. Footholds visible in the rock face were once used to provide access to a mining shaft, mostly removed by ancient miners, along with the copper ore. Some of the original shaft remains at the bottom of the left photo

Photograph by Jill L. Baker.

Hemiunu (ca. 2570 BCE), an Egyptian Vizier, prince, architect, and priest, to Iahbty-Semyt, Administrator of the Eastern Desert and to Biah-Ahky, Overseer of the Expedition to Sinai (Sesen 2010), some of the tools, equipment, operations, quality, and skills of workers are described, and quotas of copper production are detailed. Fifty highly-skilled workers were to be chosen for this expedition. They could not be slaves or prisoners, and a company of soldiers was provided for protection during the journey and while extracting the copper ore. Although the work would be hard, Hemiunu assures that there would be heavenly rewards. Judging from this letter, mine working was a noble profession performed by highly skilled and valued laborers. This is in contrast to later Greek and Roman periods when mine-work was scorned and regarded as unsafe, and those employed to work the mines were of low status, usually slaves and prisoners (Diodorus III.12–14, Henderson and Oldfather 1935:114–123; Humphrey et al. 2006:173–192).

One site that provides a wealth of information regarding ancient mining is Timna, in the Wadi Arabah, located in modern-day Israel. The copper from Timna has been exploited since very early periods. In the Chalcolithic period, copper was taken from the Timna and Feinan areas as early as the second half of the fifth millennium BCE. Copper objects were found at Tuleilat Ghassul dating to this period, and the copper originated from the Feinan region. In the Chalcolithic period, the ore appears to have been transported to Jordan for smelting at sites such as Tell Abu Matar and Shiqmim. In the Early Bronze Age II–IV (ca. 2900–2000 BCE), the copper mines of Timna and Feinan were exploited, and the smelting was done at the extraction sites. Some fifteen smelting sites have been identified in Timna and Feinan (Muhly 2003:177).

The Egyptians systematically mined and marketed copper from Timna from as early as the Old and Middle Kingdoms (Figure 5.3). In the letter from Hemiunu, some of the tools needed to extract the copper were chisels, picks, saws, and drills, and to avoid the transportation of unnecessary waste materials, all of the smelting took place near the mines. Workers were provided with mudbrick to build the kilns, granite pounders for crushing the ore, and molds for pouring copper into 50-deben ingots. A deben is an Egyptian weight unit, ca. 13.6 grams in the Old and Middle Kingdoms. A supply train made regular deliveries of wood for the kilns, and donkeys were loaded with supplies and equipment needed for the process of refining the copper and making ingots but also for the workers' daily needs (Ogden 2009:149–161).

Recent excavations at Timna have revealed mining techniques and aspects of daily life in a mining settlement (Sapir-Hen and Ben-Yosef 2014:775–790). Mining techniques include pit mining from the fifth to fourth millennia BCE, shaft mining during the fourth millennium BCE, and shaft mining with chisels in the Late Bronze Age. Geomagnetic dating reveals that the site was active during the Bronze and Iron Ages and that a substantial community lived at and worked in the Timna mines. An area known as Slaves' Hill testifies to the amount of copper processed during the Iron Age.

Nearby was a workers' camp, the presence of which reflects a complex community of highly regarded and highly skilled workers. The village consisted of structures used mostly as dwellings and for storage. The workforce consisted of people who operated the mines, smelted, and provided support to those working in the mines and processing areas. Thus, there were industrial and domestic workers. Judging from the faunal remains, the diet of the Timna workers consisted of sheep–goat (98 percent), donkey (6 percent), fish (catfish, mullet, etc.), and pig (not in the Iron Age). It is clear that these workers were skilled, elite, and well provisioned and supported, and not necessarily slaves (Gannon 2014). Based on the human remains, industrial area workers had diets higher in meat content; those in the domestic areas ate meat but not in the same quantity. Presumably, it was important for workers engaged in physical labor to eat a meat-rich diet.

The fuel source for the smelting of ore and purifying of copper came from wood: acacia (87 percent), retama (10 percent), and tamarix (3 percent) in the earlier phases. In the later phases, timber used for fuel included acacia (54 percent), retama (31 percent), haloxylon, and juniper; however, having depleted the local timber reserves, they had to use what they could find. To support this massive endeavor, a complex system was established whereby resources were brought in from distant places to provide the Timna workers with what they needed (The Central Timna Valley Project, http://archaeology.tau.ac.il/ben-yosef/CTV/, Accessed 30 August 2017; ASOR Annual Meeting, 20 November 2014, The Central Timna Valley (CTV) Project: Revolutionizing a Fifty-Year Consensus, M. Cavanaugh and D. Langgut, "Fuel Use at Iron Age Timna Site 34: The Anthracological Perspective"). It should be noted that the supply trains also transported copper ingots and finished goods to their export destinations.

The miners engaged in extremely difficult physical labor, evidenced by the skeletal remains found at Timna. Hemiunu's letter also attests to the Egyptian miners' difficult work, but he assured them their hard labor would be rewarded in the afterlife, which would "hold every luxury" (Sesen 2010). According to Hemiunu, laborers were to be chosen from the best of the miners; there were to be no slaves and no prisoners. Presumably, this means that those chosen possessed great experience and skill. Additionally, the mining community was provided with all the necessary supplies to mine the copper and process it, and to protect the workers as they traveled to the mine. Defensive forces were provided throughout the mining operation. Data from the Slaves' Hill excavation suggest that this later mining community was well provisioned, their work was deemed important, and the laborers highly skilled. It was not until the Greek and Roman periods that mining was consigned to slaves and prisoners because the work was deemed dangerous and degrading (Humphrey et al. 2006:183–184).

Copper smelting

Although labor and resource intensive, copper smelting is a relatively simple process. To smelt copper ore, a pit was dug into the ground with a channel on one side to allow airflow from a bellows. Using a hammer stone, copper ore was crushed into a fine powder on an anvil stone. In the pit, a fire was started using charcoal. The crushed copper ore was placed on top of the initial layer of hot charcoal, and more charcoal was placed on top of that. A final layer of soil capped the pit fire. Extending from one side of the pit near the bottom was a tube attached to a bellows made from animal skins. When pumped, the air from the bellows increased the fire temperature and the oxygen level. The carbon monoxide produced by the fire bonded with the carbon in the ore and produced carbon dioxide and copper metal. This chemical reaction changes the ore into metal, not necessarily the temperature of the fire. The color of the flame indicates when the change has taken place (see Ancient Arts: Prehistoric Copper Smelting in a Pit! www.youtube. com/watch?v=8uHc4Hirexc).

When complete, the soil cap was removed and the contents of the pit, including the charcoal, soil, and metal, were placed into a large vessel of water. This process separated the metal from the rest, which appeared as pinkish-yellow blobby fragments (Ancient Arts: Prehistoric Copper Smelting in a Pit!). Fragments like these were transferred to a crucible for further refining (Figure 5.3), and large ingots of nearly pure copper were produced for transportation. The copper ingots, referred to as oxhide ingots, looked like the stretched out hide of an animal, but sometimes they were fashioned into a bun shape. Numerous examples were discovered in the Cape Gelidonya and Ulu Burun shipwrecks (Institute of Nautical Archaeology). The Ulu Burun shipwreck, for example, sank ca. 1300 BCE off the coast of Turkey and contained 354 oxhide ingots and 121 bun-shaped ingots, totaling ca. 10 tons of copper.

The shipwreck also contained 120 ingots of tin, approximately 1 ton, which corresponds to the ratio of tin to copper that produces bronze (Hauptmann et al. 2002). Copper and tin were alloyed to create bronze, generally 90 percent copper to 10 percent tin, though there were variations. The refining process removed sulfur, iron, and other impurities to purify the copper as much as possible. This process involved achieving a reaction of iron sulfides with oxygen to produce sulfur dioxide and iron oxides, which produces slag. By adding silica, the melting point of the slag reduces, so smelting can take place at a lower temperature. At Timna, evidence for

FIGURE 5.3 Timna copper smelting site and copper smelting in the tomb of Rekhmira. Left: Timna copper smelting site. Right: Copper smelting depicted in the tomb of Rekhmira (TT100), who was an Egyptian noble of the Eighteenth Dynasty, Governor of Thebes and Vizier during Thutmosis III and Amenhotep II

Photograph by Jill L. Baker (left); adapted from Newberry 1900 Pl. XVIII (Public Domain, PD-1923) (right).

smelting can be found in the giant slag mound created there referred to today as Slaves' Hill (The Central Timna Valley Project). This method was employed throughout the ancient world from the Near East to Britain.

In Egypt, scenes of copper smelting and processing have been found in the Eighteenth Dynasty Theban tomb of Rekhmira (TT100), a vizier (Figure 5.3). People are depicted as operating bellows, tending the fire, holding crucibles over the fire, and processing the baked ore in bowls. The finished products appear as doors and ingots. As mentioned earlier, the metal ore was processed on site, and if it was not turned into something specific, such as doors, it was fashioned into ingots that resembled the hide of a cow or sheep. These ingots were a standard size, weight, and shape, making them easy to transport and creating a marketable standard. Such practice illustrates the standardization of the economy, which would have been useful not only for domestic trade but international as well.

Gold

Gold is a native metal and considered to be one of the first used by humankind because it could be found as nuggets at the Earth's surface or as an ore (Pliny *Natural History* 33.62, Henderson and Rackham 1952; Humphrey et al. 2006:207). In addition to being collected as nuggets from the surface, gold was mined, especially in Egypt. Gold can be found in quartz rock veins, known as reef gold, in alluvial sands, or in gravel, known as placer gold (Moorey 1999:217). Gold is naturally alloyed with silver to varying quantities. Additionally, it can be naturally alloyed with copper and iron. Gold was found in Egypt, but not in Mesopotamia or Canaan.

Gold mines in Egypt were located in the south, in the Eastern Desert from approximately Qena-Quseir to the Sudanese border. Gold also was located in the Eastern Desert in the Hammamat to Abbad region, and was referred to as "gold of Koptos," Koptos being an important center of trade on the Nile River (Ogden 2009:161). Further south was the "gold of Wawat" along the Allaqi and Gabgaba Wadis, and gold was obtained from Ethiopia, called the "gold of Kush" (Ogden 2009:161). One of the oldest known maps, the Papyrus Turin, dates to the Twentieth Dynasty, ca. 1189–1077 BCE (Figure 5.4). This map measures ca. 2.8 meters long and 0.41 meters wide and depicts 15 kilometers of the Wadi Hammamat. It was discovered at Deir el-Medina in Thebes, drawn by Amennakhte, scribe of the Tomb and son of Ipuy. It was prepared for Ramesses IV and his quarrying expedition to the Wadi Hammamat in the Eastern Desert. It depicts the confluence with Wadis Atalla and El-Sid, the surrounding hills, the bekhen-stone quarry, and the gold mine and settlement at Bir Umm Fawakhir. It is also annotated. The top of the map is oriented southward, and distances, sizes, and gold deposits are all marked. The map is topographical and geographical (Harrell and Brown 1992).

Gold is highly malleable and can be alloyed with silver to form electrum or with mercury to form an amalgam. It resists corrosion and most chemical reactions but can be dissolved by nitro-hydrochloric acid. Due to its malleable and non-corrosive

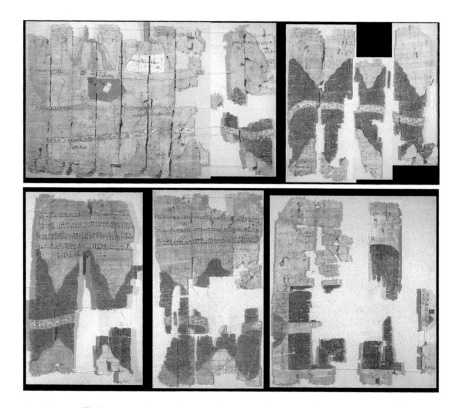

FIGURE 5.4 Turin papyrus map. An Egyptian map depicting directions to a gold quarry

Adapted from Wikipedia.org. By Zyzzy – Photograph at the Turin Museum courtesy of J. Harrell, Public Domain, https://commons.wikimedia.org/w/index.php?curid=359165. Public Domain (top); By Zyzzy – Photograph courtesy of J. Harrell, Public Domain, https://commons.wikimedia.org/w/index.php?curid=359172. Public Domain (bottom).

properties, it was used for jewelry, coinage, and figurines. Gold's non-corrosive quality was especially advantageous for coinage when introduced by the Lydians in the seventh century BCE, where the first coins were made from gold and later from silver as well. Gold also conducts electricity, which was exploited in later centuries. For example, today gold cables are used for televisions, computer monitors, and battery chargers because they transfer data faster. Gold usually contains between 5 to 30 percent silver. Gold containing less than 75 percent gold and more than 25 percent silver is considered electrum. Gold containing more than 75 percent gold and less than 25 percent silver is considered gold (Ogden 2009:162). Gold can also contain copper. The ratio between gold, silver, and copper determines the color of the gold. Upon discovery, gold can be used without alteration, or it can be refined and purified or alloyed with other metals, such as lead or copper (Ogden 2009:162–164; Moorey 1999:218–219).

In Egypt, some tomb paintings depict gold refining. The Old Kingdom tomb of Baqt III at Beni Hasan (BH15), ca. 1900 BCE, depicts gold being sorted (washed) and ground, and a washing table. The tomb of Kha'y, at Saqqara (ca. 1279–1213 BCE) depicts gold washing, grinding, a sloping table for washing, and smelting (Ogden 2009:162). A written description of Egyptian gold mining and processing was provided by Diodorus of Sicily in The Library of History (Diodorus III.12–14, Henderson and Oldfather 1935:114–123). A gold refinery was discovered at Sardis in central Turkey dating to the second century BCE, where gold and silver were highly purified.

To purify gold, granules and dust were mixed with salt and sometimes alum in an earthenware vessel. The vessel was placed into a furnace and heated to a temperature of 600 to 800° C for hours and sometimes days. The hot salt vapors penetrated the gold, removing the silver and silver chloride, leaving pure gold. Silver was also collected from the clay parting vessels and furnace walls by cupellation. Because gold and silver were used for coinage in the second century BCE, their purity became increasingly important, and standards of purity were established.

Mercury, which was known to the Egyptians as early as 1500 BCE and even earlier to the Chinese, was useful in purifying gold. Mercury attracts gold but repels everything else. When gold is placed into mercury, it floats; everything else is repelled. Once the gold has been extracted, it and the mercury are placed into a leather bag through which the mercury passes, leaving only the gold. Pliny explains this process in his *Natural History* (33.99–100, Henderson and Rackham 1952:75–77; Humphrey et al. 2006:210).

Silver

Silver also occurs in a native form or as an alloy with gold, known as aurian silver, which may have come from Egyptian and Nubian gold mines. Silver with less than 1 percent gold has been found in Predynastic contexts. This is important because it was not until later that gold and silver could be extracted from each other, suggesting that early silver was extracted from ore, known as argentite (silver sulphide). However, due to the lead content, it is also likely the silver came from lead ore. When lead is heated, it is converted to lead monoxide, leaving shiny silver globules (Ogden 2009:170–171).

Lead was being smelted as early as the seventh and sixth millennium BCE in other parts of the world and at least as early as 3000 BCE in Egypt (Ogden 2009:170). Native silver was a rare occurrence, generally not found in abundant quantities, but it was found deep in the ground (Moorey 1999:232). It is generally accepted that in much of the ancient Near East, silver was probably extracted from argentiferous lead ores (Moorey 1999:232). It has been suggested that most of Egypt's silver came from naturally alloyed silver and gold, known as aurian silver, which came from the Egyptian and Nubian gold mines; however, silver containing 1 percent or less gold probably came from ores (Ogden 2009:170).

Silver was worked in much the same way copper was. Silver is soft and malleable, but slightly harder and heavier than gold. It is highly conductive and possesses the highest conductivity of any element and the highest thermal conductivity of any metal. It was used for coins, jewelry, bullion, cups, bowls, figurines, eating utensils, mirrors, boxes, and lids. Refined, pure silver quickly became the standard metal used for coinage throughout the Greek and Roman worlds. Even before coinage, several hordes of silver ingots and rings were found, presumably used as an early form of monetary exchange (Gitin and Golani 2001).

Iron

Iron came into use in the first millennium BCE, almost completely replacing bronze tools and weapons. Iron has been used as wrought iron, phosphoric iron, cast iron, steel, and crucible steel. It was used extensively in Canaan/ancient Israel, Egypt, Mesopotamia, Anatolia (Turkey), among the Sea Peoples, the Aegean, and Greece. A long-standing explanation for the end of the Bronze Age and beginning of the Iron Age was the introduction of iron into the Levant by the arrival of the Sea Peoples into Canaan. It has long been thought that the superiority of iron weapons gave the "invading" Sea Peoples military advantage, leading to their dominance over the Israelites. However, very little evidence or data have been produced to support this theory, and it no longer remains a convincing argument. It is more likely that since iron was more easily obtained and prevalent in more regions than copper, its availability in raw form may have been a factor in its frequent use (Muhly 2003).

On the other hand, iron was labor intensive and difficult to work with (Muhly 2003:180). Smelting iron was achieved by a bloomer process, named for the type of furnace used for smelting iron from its oxides. The iron-smelting furnace produced a bloom, a spongy mass of iron and slag. The slag was called sponge iron, which was hammered to consolidate the mass into wrought iron. The hammering was done when the mass was quite hot to squeeze out the slag and consolidate the iron particles (Muhly 2003:180). Small quantities of phosphorus in iron ore had the same effect as carbon in iron but could cause brittleness. Nevertheless, phosphorous iron was selected because it remained sharp. Iron could be found in Egypt and the Sinai Peninsula at sites such as Wadi el-Dabba in the Eastern Desert, the Bahariya Oasis in the Western Desert, Naukratis, and Tell Defena (Odgen 2009:166). Iron was obtained from native iron; telluric iron, whose use was minimal; iron ore; and chance findings of meteoric iron. Some early examples of iron use in Egypt date to Predynastic periods, with more frequent use occurring in the late second millennium BCE (Ogden 2009:166–167).

In a furnace, at a temperature of 1200° C, iron turns to liquid, and when removed from the furnace, it contains 3.5 to 4.5 percent carbon. This process produced cast iron, which was utilized in later periods. Carbon caught in wrought iron was steel, which is much stronger than iron. Ideal iron consisted of ca. 0.1 percent uniformly distributed carbon and no slag. This was achieved by reacting wrought iron with charcoal and wood in small sealed crucibles at very high temperatures of ca. 1500° C.

High-quality wrought iron was shaped by hammering when red hot, and joins were made by hammering red-hot pieces together.

Wrought iron could be turned into steel by a process known as carburization, which adds carbon to the iron, thus making it harder and producing steel, which can be quench-hardened then tempered to obtain substantial hardness (Ogden 2009:168). Examples of carburized tools have been found in Canaan, such as a carburized-iron pick head dating to the twelfth century BCE (Ogden 2009:168). One can gain some idea of the tools and furnace used to process iron by examining decorated Greek vessels dated to ca. 525 BCE (Figure 5.5).

Although iron was abundant in Egypt and the Sinai Peninsula, Egyptians did not use iron much during the Dynastic periods. Iron ore can be found at Wadi el-Dabba in the Eastern Desert, at Bahariya Oasis in the Western Desert, and at Aswan (Ogden 2009:166). Ironworking sites have been identified at Wadi Abu Gerida in the northern part of the Eastern Desert and may date to the Roman period, and Naukratis and Tell Defena (Daphnae) in the Delta area, sixth century BCE, based on slag by Petrie (Ogden 2009:166, with reference to Petrie 1886:39, 1888:79). An additional source for iron was found in meteorites, called meteoric iron, which contains high amounts of nickel (Ogden 2009:166–167). By the second half of the second millennium BCE in Egypt, the use of iron was increasing. The Amarna letters describe high quality iron objects given to the Egyptian court by foreign rulers (Ogden 2009:167–168). By the mid-first millennium BCE, iron had become commonplace among the materials used for tools and weapons across the Near

FIGURE 5.5   The Berlin Foundry Cup. Fifth century BCE depicting a bronze foundry with furnace on left

East, including Egypt. Although copper/bronze remained in use, iron came to nearly replace copper and bronze, and in Mesopotamia by the Neo-Babylonian period ca. sixth century BCE, iron became cheaper than copper and bronze (Moorey 1999:263).

Casting

Casting is the process by which objects, including tools, weapons, figurines, and sculpture, are created by pouring molten metal into a mold made of stone, clay, sand, or wax/resin. Casting is known to have been in use as early as the Chalcolithic period in Canaan, ca. 4500–3500 BCE, as evidenced by the 429 copper objects discovered in a cave in the Judean Desert, known as the Nahal Mishmar cave, near the Dead Sea. In Egypt, casting started in the early Predynastic period at Matmar (Ogden 2009:156; Bar-Adon 1980). In Mesopotamia, casting is known to have been in use in the fourth millennium. Stone molds for jewelry were discovered at Assur, Uruk, and Sinjirli (Moorey 1999:269).

Molds were made of one or two pieces, also called bivalve molds, or even three pieces. A craftsperson first created a mold of stone, clay, or wax. In Egypt, it has been discovered that molds were probably a mixture of wax and resin; otherwise, the molten metal would melt the mold too quickly. More commonly, the mold was made from wax, and an investment material, such as clay, was applied around the mold. When the clay was baked in the kiln, the wax melted, leaving only the clay mold. Once the clay mold had been fired, molten metal was poured in and, when cooled, the clay mold was broken, leaving the metal object. The surface protrusions and rough spots were cut off and the object polished and/or decorated. Hollow core casting was also in use. This was when wax was molded around a central core. This type of casting was in use in Egypt during the Early and Middle Kingdoms (Ogden 2009:157–158; Moorey 1999:269–270).

Lead

Although native lead occurs, it is relatively rare. However, lead is easily obtained from ore, specifically galena, lead sulfite, or cerrusite, lead carbonate. Lead is easily identified due to its shiny, metallic appearance, and is easily extracted from its ore by smelting over a low heated charcoal or wood fire. Lead was also found in abundance in Egypt near the Red Sea coast and the Eastern Desert, and from southern Anatolia (Turkey), and possibly in the Tiyari mountains near Nineveh (Ogden 2009:168; Moorey 1999:292–293).

Evidence suggests that lead was used as early as the sixth and seventh millennia BCE. An artifact discovered in Grave 1257 from Naqada, ca. fourth millennium BCE, was in the form of a hawk of hollow-casted lead. Later, in New Kingdom Egypt and in Mesopotamia, lead was used for eye paint (kohl in Egypt), vessels, pipes, as covering in thin sheets, door sockets, weights, and as jewelry (Ogden 2009:168–169;

Moorey 1999:292–293). Its malleability made it easy to use and configure into desired shapes.

Recent research has determined that lead can be sourced. Using lead isotope analysis, the isotopic characteristics of lead can be observed, and based on the ratios of them, a diagnostic pattern can be devised. This pattern can be matched to known sources, and the origin of the lead can be traced. This is useful to the understanding of commodities trading in the ancient economy.

6

BONDING AGENTS

Glue, plaster, mortar, cement, bitumen

The ability to bind one item to another is something we take for granted each day. Shoes, books, and furniture are just a few of the many items held together with the aid of adhesives. When repairing a torn sail or backpack, duct tape comes to the rescue! Adhesive technology has become an integral part of modern life, yet we tend to overlook its importance. Binding materials are a significant part of our economy and a multibillion-dollar industry. Enormous and varied resources go into the development of this technology, allowing us to bind items together more efficiently, safely, and cost-effectively. Binders in the ancient world were equally important and much utilized. This chapter will review select adhesives and binders exploited in the ancient world, many of which formed the foundation for products in use today.

The subjects discussed in this chapter may seem inconsequential; however, they represent a significant factor in the development of humankind. The use of binders, plasters, and bitumen, and the making of mudbrick, mortar, and cement, reflect humankind's knowledge and ability to change the chemical and physical properties of raw materials for intended purposes. No longer were people simply encountering their environment, making use of that which they found by happenstance. Rather, they were actively manipulating their environment to suit their needs, and by doing so, were exhibiting complex cognition (Wadley 2010). They were gathering raw materials, adapting them for use, and integrating them to make tools and daily items such as furniture. Similarly, instead of living in natural shelters such as caves, they were constructing dwellings using man-made materials such as mudbrick and mortar. As with the stone tool industry, adhesives demonstrate the gradual accumulation of knowledge, growing social complexity, an enlarged centralized authority, organized labor, standardization of manufacturing, and international and domestic trading, all of which contributed to a stable economy. When combined, these seemingly small factors represent impressive advancement.

Glue, or adhesive, is defined as a substance that is used "for sticking objects or materials together" (*Oxford Dictionary*, https://en.oxforddictionaries.com/definition/us/glue). The practice of binding objects together is ancient. For example, when making tools from more than one component and material, such as arrowhead and shaft, bonding agents were required to hold them in place. An early example of adhesive comes from the Middle Pleistocene period in central Italy, where three stone tools were found, two of which were partially covered with "birch-bark tar" (Mazza et al. 2006). Ötzi's arrowheads (ca. 3359–3105 BCE; Bonani et al. 1994), for example, were held together with thread and birch tar (sap), and the three-part radial fletching was attached using thin nettle thread and birch tar (South Tyrol Museum of Archaeology, www.iceman.it/en/node/282). Similarly, Ötzi's axe consisted of a copper blade set into a forked shaft of smoothed yew attached with birch tar and leather straps tightly wound around the wood and blade (South Tyrol Museum of Archaeology, www.iceman.it/en/node/277).

In Babylon, ca. 5000 BCE, in addition to tools and daily items, bonding agents were also used in building construction. These included animal blood and protein, plant resins, and asphalt (bitumen). Tar-like glue was used as early as 4000 BCE by the Babylonians to affix ivory-carved eyes into the sockets of statues. This glue held materials in place for millennia. For the Egyptians, professionals called *Kellopsos*, or adhesive-maker, created glues by boiling ingredients. In Egypt, glues and resins were utilized as bonding agents to assemble furniture, to affix decorative inlay, to coat paintings, or to mix with paint as a preservative that also served as a bonding agent. Tutankhamun's wooden coffin, for example, was bound together using glue, and wood laminate was glued to boxes and furniture as decoration. In the tomb of Rekhmira at Thebes (TT100), part of the woodworking scene depicts glue being spread onto a box in preparation for gilding.

Adhesives also occur naturally in numerous organic sources, including albumen in egg white, beeswax, gums, tree and bush resins and saps, bees' honey, animal fats, bitumen, and some oils. Inorganic adhesives come from clay, gypsum, natron salt, and solder; however, these have to be processed and mixed together with other substances. Adhesives were also made from animal fats from which the protein collagen acted as the binder (Newman and Serpico 2009; Mazar and Panitz-Cohen 2007).

Adhesive/Glue from protein collagen

Protein collagen formed the basis for most glues. This is a primary structural protein found in animal connective tissue such as cartilage, tendons, skins, and bones (Nicholson and Shaw 2009:475; Lucas and Harris 2011:3–4). The chief animal sources may have included horses, cattle, sheep, and goat, and collagen may have been collected during the butchering process. Glue could also be made from fish, particularly the skin of non-oily fish. One ton of fish produces about fifty gallons of clear, high-quality glue (Newman and Serpico 2009:475). To prepare adhesives from animal collagen, the relevant animal parts were cleaned, boiled in water, and strained. Next, the mixture was cooled until it congealed into a jelly, and then it was dried, resulting in brittle chunks. To produce the adhesive, the chunks were crushed into a fine powder and warm water was added. The glue mixture had to be used while warm, above ca. 30° C; otherwise it would congeal. Similarly, fish-glue had to be used while liquid (Newman and Serpico 2009:475). This type of glue was used in woodworking for binding furniture joints or affixing inlay, as well as for binding fabric to wood, or as a binder in pigments or on plaster surfaces (Lucas and Harris 2011:3–4).

Eggs

Glue made from birds' eggs, came mostly from waterfowl such as duck and geese and from chickens in later periods (Newman and Serpico 2009:475, 485; Lucas and Harris 2011:1–2). The egg white, the egg yolk, or the two of them combined could serve as binders. Each component of the egg contains proteins, albumen, and ovalbumin, all of which can function as adhesives. The white and yolk were used together or separately, depending on the type of binding desired. Egg white could be dried and mixed into a solution or whipped and used unaided. The yolk was also whipped, but it had to be used immediately because dried yolk could not be reconstituted. The presence of egg as a bonding agent can be determined by amino acid analysis; however, this type of analysis cannot distinguish between white and yolk since the same lipids and triglycerides are present (Newman and Serpico 2009:475, 485; Lucas and Harris 2011:1–2). Egg was frequently mixed with paint or applied to paintings as a stabilizer. This method has been detected in the Twelfth Dynasty tomb of Kahun, the Eighteenth Dynasty paintings at Tell el Amarna (Lucas and Harris 2011:1), on the paintings in the tomb of Nefertari (QV66), and as a coating or varnish, especially over red and yellow paint (Newman and Serpico 2009:485).

Gum—From plants

In Egypt, the most frequently used gum was made from acacia, specifically acacia *spp.* and astragalus *spp.* Other commonly used gums were tamarind and cherry. These grew naturally in Egypt, probably near Sudan and Africa. To collect the gum, the bark of the tree or bush was scored and tapped allowing the sap to run out. Collected sap appeared as small teardrops and could be easily transported. In Turkey, Syria, Palestine, Iraq, and Iran, tragacanth gum (Astragalus *spp.*) was more commonly available and tapped for its gum (Newman and Serpico 2009:476–477).

Gum was used to bind linen bandages, especially those used to wrap mummies after the embalming process. Gum-saturated bandages have been discovered on mummy remains (Lucas and Harris 2011:6). Herodotus (*Histories* 2.86.6, Strassler and Purvis 2007:152–153) referred to this practice, and noted that embalmers preferred to use gum rather than glue. Paint may have been mixed with gum, such as acacia, or covered with a gum mixture then applied as a varnish (Lucas and Harris 2011:6). Gum may also have been used as a thickening agent in perfume, and some gums have medicinal qualities, such as myrrh and frankincense. The sticky properties, however, make gum a natural and effective adhesive (Newman and Serpico 2009:476).

Beeswax

Beeswax is produced from the eight abdominal glands of worker bees. Initially, the wax is clear, but it becomes more yellowish or brownish in color with the addition of pollens from the worker bees. The temperature in the hive must be 33° to 36° C (91° to 97° F) for the bees to secrete wax (Sanford and Dietz 1976; Ahnert 2015). Through a labor-intensive process, the bees produce the honeycomb, which is harvested to obtain the wax (Ahnert 2015). Beeswax had many uses and was frequently used as a bonding agent, varnish, and as a binder in paint during the early Eighteenth Dynasty in Egypt. It was used as a varnish to preserve tomb paintings only between the reigns of Amenhotep I and Amenhotep II in Egypt; however, beeswax has been detected on some mummy portraits (first to fourth centuries CE) in the Fayum region. Because of its adhesive qualities, beeswax was also used in mummification, shipbuilding, bronze casting, the sculpting of figurines, and as a surface coating on writing tablets. Wax was also used to seal lids. For example, the lids of five alabaster vases in the tomb of Tutankhamun were sealed with wax, as were two uraei, and some alabaster vases were affixed to pedestals. Beeswax was also used to hold the plaits of wigs in place (Lucas and Harris 2011:2–3; Newman and Serpico 2009: 489–491).

Resin

Resins were utilized at least as early as the Neolithic period, evidenced by flint blades affixed into the shaft of a sickle using resin as a bonding agent (Lucas and Harris 2011:7). Resin is naturally secreted from plants and trees, particularly coniferous trees, and comes in the form of sap, latex, or mucilage, which can be used as adhesives, varnishes, and glazing. As with gums, resins can be obtained by scoring the bark of a tree or shrub and collecting the exuded substance in the form of a liquid or a dried clump. Resins were used as incense, especially in religious ceremonies and funerals; to scent oils and perfumes; and to anoint a corpse during the process of mummification. Well-known resins include amber, frankincense, and myrrh. The value and ritual significance attributed to frankincense and myrrh is attested to in the New Testament narrative when these, along with gold, were presented to the newborn Jesus by the three kings (Matthew 2:11). Resins were used in Greece and Rome as attested by Theophrastus of Greece (*Enquiry into Plants Book IX*, Henderson and Hort 1926) and Pliny the Elder (*Natural History Book XIV*, Henderson and Rackham 1945:266–273). The most used and best-known resins from the Mediterranean region come from pine, fir, spruce, cedar, and cupressaceae, specifically juniper and cypress (Serpico 2009:431). Resins from softwood pines when heated make excellent pitch and tar.

Discovered in the First Dynasty tomb of Hemaka in Egypt was a narrow-neck jar that had been sealed using a mixture of resin and quartz sand. At Saqqara, tesserae from the Third Dynasty were held in place by a cement mixture of resin and powdered limestone, and a sarcophagus was held together with a resin-based cement.

This cement typically was a mixture of resin with powdered limestone or quartz sand. Resin was also used to affix inlay pieces and to hold mummy bandages in place (Lucas and Harris 2011:7). The Egyptians acquired resins from Punt, as depicted in the relief in Hatshepsut's tomb of resins being delivered from an expedition to that region. No doubt resins were obtained and distributed from numerous points throughout the Levant and Mediterranean regions.

Amber is an organic material that comes from resin-bearing trees that fell millions of years ago in the Middle Cretaceous to Tertiary periods. The fallen trees were eventually covered by sediment as they settled into the ground, thus producing fossilized resin, known as amber (Serpico 2009:451). Amber occurs as a pale yellow or brown color that can turn to brownish-red over time. Deposits have been found around the Baltic Sea, across the European continent from Russia to England, and in Sicily, Austria, Israel, Jordan, Lebanon, Romania, and Poland (Serpico 2009:451).

In Mesopotamia, amber was considered to possess magical qualities because it has some magnetic properties, it polishes to a brilliant sheen, and it has a certain amount of static electricity. It was also thought to have medicinal properties. For these reasons, amber was worn as an amulet on occasion and as beads (Moorey 1999:79–81). It was also worn as an amulet in Middle Bronze Age Crete and Greece. In Egypt, amber was used for amulets, beads, and jewelry. Amber beads were found in Tutankhamun's (KV62) tomb (Serpico 2009:451).

Gypsum and lime plaster

Plaster was made from gypsum and lime, and because these can seem similar, differentiating between the two is more accurately achieved by scientific analysis. In Mesopotamia, gypsum and lime plaster were utilized but for different purposes, and it appears that gypsum was more frequently utilized than lime. To make plaster from gypsum, calcium sulfate dihydrate, it was heated to 100–200° C to remove the water, resulting in hemihydrate (Moorey 1999:330). The hemihydrate was crushed and rehydrated producing a plaster paste, which could be used alone or as mortar mixed with sand or another temper. In general, gypsum plaster could be used as a whitewash on floors, interior walls, or roofs. However, it was not practical for exterior use in damp climates because it absorbed water and could disintegrate, but it was excellent for dry climates (Moorey 1999:330). In Egypt, gypsum was used as an adhesive; for example, it was used to repair a large Predynastic ceramic vessel from Ma'adi and a sarcophagus at the pyramid of Sekhemkhet at Saqqara from the Third Dynasty, and in Tutankhamun's tomb, a ceramic lid was affixed to a jar by gypsum plaster (Lucas and Harris 2011:6). Gypsum was also used as a mortar and floor plaster in Egypt (Lucas and Harris 2011:6–7).

The production of lime plaster was more complex. First, limestone was heated to ca. 800–900° C for three to four days, reducing it to calcium carbonate and calcium oxide. The powder was then rehydrated with water, producing a paste. The newly formed paste was mixed with sand, ground limestone, and other temper.

Once mixed, it could be applied. As the plaster dried and water evaporated, it lost plasticity, hardened quickly, and continued to harden over time. Lime plaster was used as a wall plaster, white wash floor plaster, and in mortar. In Mesopotamia, lime plaster was commonly used in domestic and public buildings. Plaster was used at Yarim Tepe I and Choga Mami in open passageways between houses (Moorey 1999:330–331) and at Nuzi on streets (Moorey 1999:331). In Canaan, plaster was also very commonly used, and remnants were found in the Middle Bronze Age Gate at Ashkelon.

An additional use for lime plaster has been rediscovered in a sixth-century bridge abutment in France. Merovingian bridges used a hemp mortar known as hempcrete, which construction industries in Europe, Australia, and the United States have been producing and using since this discovery in the 1980s. Hempcrete is a bio-composite material made from the inner woody core of the hemp plant, called the shiv, which is high in silica and binds well with lime and pozzolana (volcanic ash). When combined with lime, hempcrete forms a lightweight cement (it weighs one-seventh or one-eighth that of concrete) with excellent insulating properties. It is also fire resistant. Hempcrete can only be used as fill between supportive and structural components. Nevertheless, those who have built modern homes using this material have seen a significant reduction in heating/cooling bills. Hemp is very easy to grow, is a renewable resource, and does not need fertilizer, weed killer, pesticide, or fungicide. This is a case where the rediscovery of an ancient technology may prove to be useful for our own present and future. Certainly, these natural materials can be grown and found in less industrialized countries and could help provide inexpensive housing and buildings (Chaban 2015; see also American Limetechnology, www.americanlimetechnology.com/ and Hemp Technologies Global, https://hemptechglobal.com. Accessed 3 May 2018).

Bitumen

Bitumen (pitch), or natural asphalt, called *esir* by the Sumerians and *iddu* by the Akkadians (Bilkadi 1984), comes from deposits of organic matter comprised from the accumulation of land and marine plant sediment, which result from anaerobic conditions and elevated temperatures causing a change in the chemical composition resulting in the formation of petroleum (Figure 6.1). Bitumen occurred in various forms ranging from liquid to semi-viscous to solid blocks (Conan 1999; Nicholson and Shaw 2000:454–455). Bitumen could be found in several areas in antiquity: at the Dead Sea; in small deposits in Egypt on the Red Sea coast; in Helwan, Iraq, and Iran; and in Ethiopia (Forbes 1964:26–27; Conan 1999; Moorey 1999:333; Serpico 2009:454–455). It would seem that the Mesopotamians, Canaanites, and Egyptians exploited the bitumen resources located nearest to them.

Evidence for the use of bitumen has been found as early as the Palaeolithic period, by the Musterian peoples at Umm El Tlel, Syria, where flint implements coated with bitumen were found. Neanderthals from this period used bitumen as

FIGURE 6.1   Bitumen. Left: Exposed pool of liquid bitumen, Puy de la Poix, Clermont-Ferrand, France. Right: Solid, natural bitumen from the Dead Sea

Adapted from Wikipedia.org (By Vales – Own work, Public Domain, https://commons.wikimedia.org/w/index.php?curid=9551544) (left); adapted from Wikipedia.org (By Daniel Tzvi – Own work, Public Domain, https://commons.wikimedia.org/w/index.php?curid=1960710) (right).

an adhesive to affix handles to flint tools (Conan 1999:33–35). During the Neolithic period at Tell Atij in Syria, around 4500 BCE, Ubaid dwellings were made with bundled reeds and bulrush fiber as the structural elements, reed matting for roofing materials, and mud plaster that contained bitumen. The bitumen-filled mud plaster was an efficient insulator because it was waterproof and required no maintenance. As a mortar, bitumen was mixed with straw, clay, and sand (Conan 1999:34). By 4000 BCE, the Ubaids used bitumen to waterproof and strengthen their coricles, round basket-like boats made from reeds (Bilkadi 1984).

Bitumen was used as an adhesive in Canaan from the Chalcolithic period through the Bronze Age and onward. Examples of bitumen as an adhesive were found at Ras Shamra dating to ca. 1600–1200 BCE. In Mesopotamia, bitumen was used as an adhesive, mortar, waterproofing, and possibly as fuel, evidenced by a container of baked brick placed above a firebox at the Early Dynastic II installation in the North Temple at Nippur (Moorey 1999:332–333; also Serpico 2009:456; Conan 1999:33–35). Bitumen was also used to make sculpture and jewelry.

At Ur, in the Ubaid period, baskets were used to transport prepared bitumen cakes. Evidence for bitumen cakes was also found at Tell el-Oueili and at an early third millennium BCE Villate at Sakheri Sughir, which is also in the region of Ur (Moorey 1999:334). The bitumen was heated and formed into cakes, which could then be transported, reheated, and used for its intended purpose. Throughout Mesopotamia, by at least 3000 BCE (Bilkadi 1984), bitumen was used in mortar and to make bricks. It has also been found in the mortar used to build temples, palaces, ziggurats, and roads.

Further evidence of bitumen has been found at Susa in the Darius Palace at Babylon, in temples and ziggurats, roadway surfaces, and in terraces such as those in the Hanging Gardens of Babylon (Serpico 2009; Conan 1999). Herodotus (*Histories* 1.179, Strassler and Purvis 2007:97) mentions the use of hot bitumen as mortar in Babylon. At Mari and Haradum, bitumen was used to waterproof baskets, ceramic jars, and storage pits, as well as wooden posts, roofs, bathrooms, sarcophagi, coffins, and mats, and to seal containers. As an adhesive, it was used to repair broken statues and to affix eyes into statues, as well as to attach decorations to various objects. Bitumen was used for similar purposes in Egypt and Canaan (Conan 1999:33–35; Bilkadi 1984; Serpico 2009:454–456). In later periods, in Egypt, bitumen was used during the mummification process. This was mentioned by Diodorus and Strabo; however, it is a practice dating to the Hellenistic period and onward (Lucas and Harris 2011:303–305; Serpico 2009:464–468).

Mortar, cement, concrete

The subtle difference between mortar, cement, and concrete should be noted. Mortar binds materials together, such as bricks or stones in building a wall. Mortar is comprised of sand and cement, and when mixed with water this material can be spread as a binding agent. Cement is a binding component for concrete and mortar, and is generally made from limestone, clay, shells, and silica. These ingredients are combined, crushed, heated, and turned into a fine powder, which when rehydrated with water forms the basis of cement. Cement can also be used as a bonding agent. Concrete is strong enough to be used to build a foundation, wall, or structure. It is comprised of cement, sand, gravel, and/or any type of aggregate. When water is added to this mixture it forms a solid object.

Ancient Near Eastern construction techniques used mortar and cement from very early periods. However, the Romans developed a much-improved concrete recipe, which significantly impacted building technique. Their mixture consisted of slaked lime, quartz sand, and water, plus volcanic ash, called pozzolana. When crushed ceramics were added to this mixture, it produced a hydraulic concrete. The addition of pozzolana produced a chemical reaction that altered the concrete and made it extremely hard (Oleson 2008:260–261). Knowledge of pozzolana and the basic cement recipe comes from Vitruvius (*On Architecture* Book II.VI, Morgan 1960:46–49). However, the exact recipe is lost. The innovative nature of concrete made it useful as more than just a bonding agent; it could be fashioned into solid structural features such as arches and domes, walls, steps, and floors.

Hydraulic concrete could be used to waterproof cisterns or build harbors. Several ancient authors discuss the methods used for constructing a harbor including Vitruvius, *On Architecture* 5.12.1–7, Pliny the Younger, *Letters*, 6.31.15–17, and Procopius, *On Buildings* 1.11.18–20. The most impactful example of the use of Roman hydraulic concrete in the Near East is the Sebastos Harbor at Caesarea, built by Herod the Great ca. 25–15 BCE. Measuring 100,000 square meters and including two jetties, the Sebastos Harbor was the largest artificial harbor in the Near East. The south breakwater was some 500 meters long, and the north, 275 meters long. They were constructed using ca. 35,000 cubic meters of concrete including 24,000 cubic meters of pozzolana, 12,000 cubic meters of kurkar, and 12,000 cubic meters of slaked lime (Hohfelder et al. 2007). The pozzolana from the Bay of Naples was transported by ship to Caesarea and mixed with local ingredients. Although pozzolana was used to build the Sebastos Harbor, mixing it with local ingredients resulted in a weaker concrete than that which was mixed in Italy, but it was still of high quality, strength and durability (Hohfelder et al. 2007).

Three systems of construction were used to build the harbor. The first technique involved pounding vertical wooden boards into the sea floor, strengthened by posts and cross beams, to form boxes that served as wooden molds into which concrete was poured. A second approach involved constructing a "double-walled hollow box" (Hohfelder et al. 2007) on shore, then towing it by water to the desired location and filling it with concrete before sinking it into place. Finally, barges were partially filled with concrete then towed to the desired location where they were filled completely with concrete and sunk into place (Brandon 1996; Blackman 1996; Hohfelder et al. 2007).

Mudbrick

One of the most used building materials in the ancient (and modern) world was mudbrick. The ancient Egyptian word for mudbrick was *djebet*, in later Coptic it was *tobe*, and in Arabic, *tub(a)*. The Spanish word is adobe, probably derived from how the Spanish heard the Egyptian and Arabic words pronounced. Mudbrick was in use from very early periods as a plaster or to form bricks. In Pre-Roman Egypt, Canaan, and Mesopotamia, mudbrick was one of the primary building materials. Just as today, mudbrick was bound by mortar made from mud (clay) or from a mud and lime/gypsum mixture. Some of the buildings of Babylon exhibit mortar made from a lime and bitumen mixture (Moorey 1999:331). In Egypt, mortar was made from alluvial mud, and some mortar was mixed with gypsum, especially when mortar was used with stonework (Kemp 2009:92). In Canaan, it was common practice to dig a trench and build a foundation of fieldstone or worked stone into it. The superstructure was made of mudbrick, which was set on top of the stone foundation. In Egypt, however, bricks were set directly onto the leveled sand or bedrock. Courses were generally set in a header-stretcher manner for stability, and multiple patterns could result. Generally, after a layer of brick had been set, a layer of mortar was spread over the top. The mortar would fill any gaps and create a level surface for the next layer of brick. Sometimes a wooden beam or pole was inserted to strengthen and align the wall and to allow for airflow and flexibility. Once finished, the entire structure was covered with a lime/gypsum plaster for waterproofing and protection from the elements.

Mudbricks were simple and inexpensive to make because there was an abundance of suitable soil. Four basic ingredients are needed to make mudbrick: course sand or aggregate, fine sand, silt, and clay (Figures 6.2 and 6.3). The course sand (aggregate) provides the strength, and the fine sand is the filler that locks together the grains of the aggregate. The silt and clay bind the other ingredients together. Changing the quantities and ratios of these ingredients determines the strength of the brick and its resistance to water and weather. Temper, such as grass, straw, reeds, or hay, can be added to the mix to provide more strength.

At first bricks were molded by hand, and later the brick batter was pressed into wooden molds and then set out to dry in the hot sun (Figure 6.3). It has been estimated that two brickmakers could produce 2000 to 6000 bricks per day. Eventually, standard sizes were established. The average size of a brick during the Predynastic period was ca. 24 x 12 centimeters; in the Old Kingdom ca. 42 x 21 centimeters; in the New Kingdom and onward, ca. 30 x 15 centimeters. The length-to-width ratio was always 2:1 no matter the chronological period or geographic region (Kemp 2009:83).

Mudbricks were manufactured with equal precision in Canaan and Mesopotamia, and were used for constructing houses, gates, city walls, and temples. To waterproof the bricks, they were plastered with lime and gypsum. When laying the bricks, masons set them in header-stretcher fashion, overlapping the seams below, and inserting wood or reed separators to allow airflow and to mitigate condensation that might compromise the integrity of the brick from within. Pharaohs also left an imprint of their seal on bricks, in part to determine the age of the brick and for maintenance purposes, but also to claim responsibility for building magnificent

FIGURE 6.2 Middle Bronze Age mudbrick gate complex, Ashkelon, Israel

Photograph by Jill L. Baker.

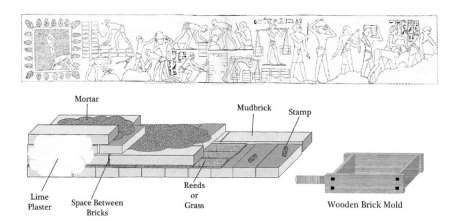

FIGURE 6.3   Egyptian mudbrick manufacturing and laying. Top center: Brickmaking scene from the Tomb of Rekhmire in Thebes. Depicts collection and processing of materials, molding and drying bricks, transporting to building site, and laying a brick wall. A right-angle frame helps keep the wall straight. Bottom left: Bricks laid in header-stretcher fashion, overlapping first course seams, separated by reed mat and a gap for air flow and the Pharaoh's brick stamp. Not to scale. Bottom right: Wooden brick mold. Not to scale

Adapted from Newberry 1900 Fig. XXI (Public Domain, PD-1923) (top); graphics by Jill L. Baker (bottom).

structures. Some knowledge of the brickmaking and construction process comes from the Tomb of Rekhmire in Thebes (Figure 6.3, top). Rekhmire was a noble officer of the Eighteenth Dynasty, a vizier, or governor, of Thebes (modern Luxor). He served under the reigns of Thutmosis III (ca. 1479–1425 BCE) and Amenhotep II (ca. 1427–1401 BCE). Apparently, overseeing brickmaking was one of his responsibilities (Kemp 2009; Hodges 1992; Reich 1992; Netzer 1992).

While sun-dried mudbrick was most frequently used because it facilitated monumental building projects throughout the Near East, fired bricks were more durable. Dating to ca. 3500 BCE, Mesopotamians fired smaller bricks, which made it easier to fit them into a furnace and to transport them later, and provided greater flexibility for architectural features such as the arches at Ur. Intricate patterns could be achieved with the careful layering of bricks of various sizes, colors, and materials, such as alternating bands and herringbone patterns. Fired brick could also be made into various shapes such as curves and cones. For example, fired cones were used in a wall mosaic at Ur (Hodges 1992:77–79). Furnace-fired bricks were also better able to survive wind and rain than mudbricks, and were used to strengthen vulnerable areas. The furnace the Mesopotamians used for firing bricks was much like the kilns used by potters. More will be said about kilns later.

In his book *On Architecture*, Vitruvius described the brickmaking process in the first century BCE (Figure 6.4). The best clay was white and chalky or red, or coarse grained and gravelly. The best time of year to make bricks was in spring or autumn

FIGURE 6.4   Examples of Roman fired brick. Left: Bathhouse at Beth She'an National
Park, Israel. Right: Pompeii

Photographs by Jill L. Baker.

so that the bricks dried evenly and without cracking. They were cured for two years
prior to use. Vitruvius describes three types of bricks: the Lydian, which is 1.5 feet
long and one foot wide; the πεντάδωρον (*pentadoron*); and the τετράδωρον
(*tetradoron*).

In Greek, *doron* means palm, and "a brick five palms square" is a *pentadoron*.
A four-palm square brick is called a *tetradoron*. Private structures were constructed
with tetradora, and public buildings of pentadora. Half-size bricks were also used
(Morgan 1960:42–43). As with concrete, the Romans used bricks in their building
campaigns throughout the empire. Public and private construction demanded vast
quantities of brick, which helped create a specialized industry. The standard sizes
of bricks made them easy to produce and transport, and a reliable resource for
engineers in any region. Bricks were stamped with the names of emperors, estate
owners, workshops and even managers, possibly to verify the standard of manufacture (Oleson 2008:400–401). As the Romans conquered the Near East, their brickmaking traditions and industry became standard in that region as well. Buildings in
which Roman-style bricks were used include the bathhouses at Beth Shean and
at Masada in Israel (Figure 6.4).

7

ENGINEERING, MACHINES, POWER, AND ENERGY

The Mesopotamians, Egyptians, and Canaanites constructed monumental buildings and elaborate cities using tools that we might consider rudimentary. To construct on such a grand scale required inventiveness, ingenuity, resourcefulness, and knowledge of mathematics, geometry, and physics. For example, based on the Rhind Papyrus (ca. 1650/1550 BCE), the Moscow Mathematical Papyrus, and the Lahun Mathematical Papyri, which date to approximately the Twelfth Dynasty (ca. 1991–1778 BCE), the Egyptians had this knowledge. They knew how to find the volume of a granary and the area of a triangle, rectangle, circle, and a hemisphere, knowledge that was useful when building pyramids and temples, and establishing lotting plans. Another example is Plimpton 322, a Babylonian clay tablet in the G. A. Plimpton Collection at Columbia University. This tablet dates to ca. 1800 BCE and includes four columns and fifteen rows of numbers and text, part of which contains what is now known as the Pythagorean triples, that is $a^2 + b^2 = c^2$ (Mansfield and Wildberger 2017). Scholars from the University of New South Wales refer to it as "one of the oldest and possibly most accurate trigonometric tables of the ancient world" (Gibbens 2017). The true purpose for the complex tables is not presently understood; however, they reflect the ancients' sophisticated mathematic and scientific knowledge.

Building on a grand scale also required human incentive, such as the ego of a ruler, because these monumental structures conveyed statements of power, established a permanent legacy, paid tribute to a person or event, or reflected afterlife scenarios. Large-scale building also required organization, obedience, and a centralized authority. According to the Merriam-Webster website, engineering is "the work of designing and creating large structures (such as roads and bridges) or new products or systems by using scientific methods." Further, it is "the application of science and mathematics by which the properties of matter and the sources of energy in nature are made useful to people" (www.merriam-webster.com/dictionary/engineering), characteristics found in ancient and modern engineering. Engineering and construction methods today use modern adaptations of ancient techniques as well as machines. Much of the technique, physics, mathematics, and engineering behind the machines in use since the nineteenth century were initially worked out in antiquity and adapted for modern use. This chapter will discuss the antecedents to some of those machines and to some of the mechanical methods and techniques the ancients used to build their cities.

Pulley/block and tackle

The pulley (Figure 7.1) was one of the five simple machines described by Philo in the third century BCE (referenced by Pappus of Alexandria in *Mathematical Collection* 8.52), Hero of Alexandria (*Mechanica* 3.1–5; Humphrey et al. 2006:48–49; Oleson 2008:342), and Vitruvius in the first century CE (*On Architecture* 10. II, Morgan 1960:285–290). In actuality, the pulley was probably in use much earlier; however, it did not resemble the ones we know today. Antecedents to modern-day pulleys could

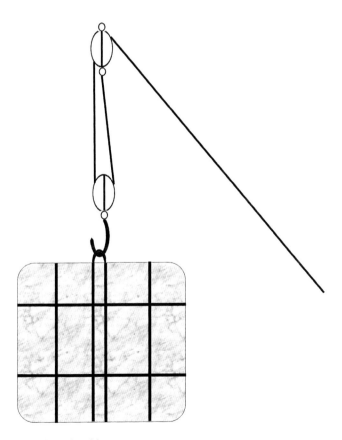

FIGURE 7.1   Block and tackle

Graphic by Jill L. Baker.

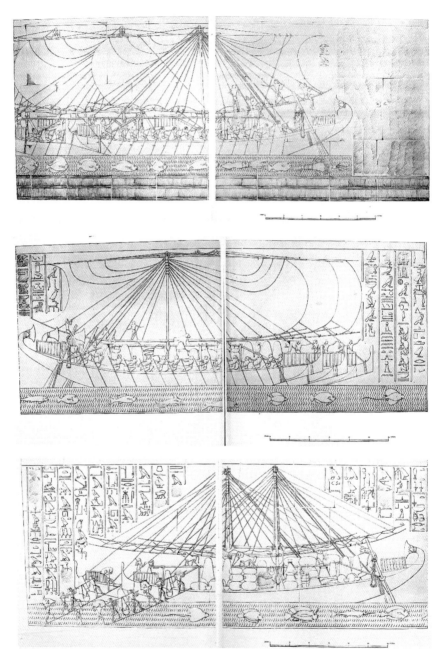

FIGURE 7.2 Deir el-Bahari, Hatshepsut's Temple, the Voyage to Punt

Adapted from Naville 1989 Plates LXXIII–LXXV (Public Domain, PD-1923).

be found in Mesopotamia and Egypt. For example, at Tell Halaf, ca. 6100–5100 BCE, wells were in use, and water was likely obtained with a bucket and pulley (Moorey 1999:4). This, of course, would have been a crude pulley that resembled what might be described as a block and tackle.

These ancient pulleys probably had stationary wooden rollers consisting of wooden block(s) through which a rope was threaded. The immovable wooden rollers may have been lubricated with olive oil or some other lubricant to help the rope slide more easily. Like today's pulleys, the wooden blocks bore the weight of the load being hoisted and allowed the person to lift heavier loads. Block and tackle pulleys were used to transfer power over a distance via ropes, and could lighten the hoisting load or change its direction (Landels 2000:10). The mechanical advantage corresponds to the number of blocks through which the rope (tackle) travels. The block and tackle reduce the input force by the lifter, thus allowing the lifter to move heavy objects with relative ease.

The Egyptians used block and tackle pulleys to raise and lower ship sails, as depicted on the ships painted on the walls of Hatshepsut's tomb (Figure 7.2). Simple pulleys made of wood would have contributed greatly to reducing the weight of the sail and boom, or any load that had to be moved from one place to another.

Even without a separate rotating wheel, wooden blocks would have become worn and smooth from the friction of the ropes. If plated with copper/bronze or with oil, the friction would have reduced even more. Once the wheel was introduced into the pulley, the load-bearing weight was reduced even more, and people could manipulate slightly heavier loads.

Another type of pulley is the stone or rope roller, which some speculate was used to lower the large doors, portcullis, that sealed the Grand Gallery of Khufu's Pyramid (Figure 7.3). A stone or rope roller consisted of stone or wooden rollers

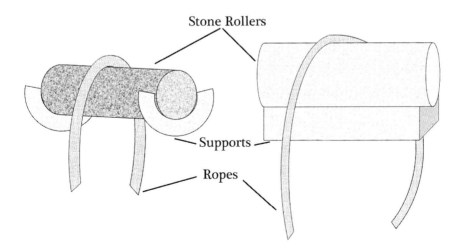

FIGURE 7.3 Recreation of a rope roller

Graphic by Jill L. Baker.

around which ropes were threaded and attached to large stone blocks. The blocks were suspended by a kind of pulley system known as Löhner's rope roll. The ropes moved over the beams, acting as pulleys, allowing the doors to be closed or opened as desired.

Recently, a mechanical engineer, Stephen Blakely, has suggested that the Egyptians may have constructed this type of pulley he terms the "Egyptian pulley" (Figure 7.3). This device consisted of a cradle that was carved to look like a half-pipe and polished to provide a smooth surface that would accept a solid stone cylinder. The cylinder was also polished and may (or may not) have been carved with a roughed groove to accept and guide a rope. As the rope pulled the load, the cylinder rotated within the cradle, thus reducing the stress and weight of the load. In his experiment, Blakely was able to elevate a 5000-pound load, which was thought to be the average weight of Egyptian building blocks. The Egyptian pulley would have been portable, easily transportable from one part of a building site to another, and would have left no archaeological trace (Blakely 2015; Blakely and Blakely 2014).

In Egypt, the pulley may have been in use as early as the Old Kingdom (ca. 2649–2150 BCE), although it was probably limited in the weight it could lift. The Book of Ecclesiastes (12.6) in the Hebrew Bible refers to a wheel over the well, or cistern. Although late, ca. 450–180 BCE, this passage seems to refer to the wheel or pulley that was commonly found over wells during that period, which helped deliver water from the depths of the well to the user.

Crane

The *shaduf*, also *shadoof*, may have been the earliest working crane. The *shaduf* was a manually operated counterbalanced crane used for transporting water from a lower elevation to a higher one (Hodges 1992:117–119). It was used mainly for irrigation to deliver water from a primary source, such as a river, to irrigation channels. Made from timber, it was formed into a long pole and attached to a fulcrum, which was secured to a horizontal beam, also made of timber. Vertical supports at each end, or mudbricks, secured the machine. The end of the pole extended over the water and was outfitted with a bucket, while the opposite end was weighted with clay or stone as a counter balance when the bucket was full.

It is not known exactly when these machines were first used. The earliest depiction of a *shaduf* appears on a cylinder seal from the late third millennium BCE in Mesopotamia. Another depiction comes from reliefs at Sennacherib's palace, ca. seventh century BCE (Moorey 1999:4). Although few, if any, of these ancient devices survived, they remain in use today along the Nile, Tigris, and Euphrates Rivers (Figure 7.4).

The Hellenistic Greeks are generally credited with inventing the crane and combining it with the pulley. The stone blocks that were used to construct temples and administrative buildings in Greece were carved with fittings to receive metal lifting tongs and Lewis bolts. A Lewis bolt was a metal fitting inserted into a

FIGURE 7.4 *Shaduf* in use in modern-day Egypt

Photograph by Jill L. Baker.

quarried and dressed stone, which was then attached to a hook or lifting tongs, thus allowing the block to be lifted into place (Landels 2000:91). It is likely that knowledge and use of the crane/pulley combination was present in Canaan/ancient Israel, Egypt, and Mesopotamia prior to the Hellenistic period. It is speculated that ongoing construction of the Temple Mount in Jerusalem utilized this machine (Figure 7.5).

Early cranes were made of timber consisting of two vertical poles, referred to as the jib by Vitruvius (*On Architecture* 10.2, Morgan 1960:385–288). These were joined together at the top by a metal bracket and iron, and separated at the base by some distance, creating a V-shape, with the wider part set on the ground. Ropes called rear stay-ropes were attached to the metal bracket at the jib and pulled behind the legs at ground level. These were staked into the ground to hold the crane firmly in place. Also attached to the jib was a rope, called a trispaston, to hold the pulley block. There could be one or several pulleys depending on the load. The load could be hoisted using a rope and pulley attached to the jib or by a crank known as a capstan, a type of winch, which was added later and became more elaborate as time progressed. The capstan was attached to the vertical legs and could be turned to reel in the rope and lift or lower the load (Landels 2000:84–98; Hodges 1992:220–224; Oleson 2008:342–345).

FIGURE 7.5 Life-size crane replica and graphic recreation of a crane. Left: Life-size recreation of a crane likely used to build Hellenistic and Roman period walls and buildings of and around the Temple Mount, Jerusalem Archaeological Park. Right: recreation of a crane

Photograph and graphic by Jill L. Baker.

FIGURE 7.6 Jerusalem, Western Wall Tunnel. The massive stone blocks supporting the Temple Mount

Photograph by Jill L. Baker.

Gigantic stone blocks, such as those that support the Roman Period Temple Mount in Jerusalem (Figure 7.6) and the Temple of Jupiter at Baalbek, weigh between 60 to 1000 tons, and some blocks measure 68 x 14 x 14 feet. Upon close examination, one can see that the masons carved notches into these massive stones, which likely received pegs or Lewis bolts that were then connected to multiple cranes for positioning into place.

Sledges and rollers

Moving massive, heavy stone blocks from one place to another was challenging; however, ancient engineers cleverly employed their knowledge of mathematics and physics to accomplish this task, particularly in Egypt and Mesopotamia (Davison 1961). Sledges and rollers have been discussed previously but are worth revisiting here (Figures 3.2 and 3.4). Some of the methods employed to move massive stone sculptures, obelisks, and blocks are known from Egyptian tomb paintings, reliefs, and archaeological evidence. These scenes depict massive objects being transported by vast numbers of workmen, with some pouring oil or water across the path to lubricate it. A painting from the tomb of Djehuti-hotep at Deir el Bersha, often entitled Transporting a Colossus, dating to ca. 1800 BCE, illustrates how a colossal statue was transported in ancient Egypt (see Figure 3.2, top). The Assyrians also moved colossal structures using this method, as depicted at the Palace of Sennacherib at Nineveh (Figure 3.2, bottom).

Sledges transported statues, obelisks, stone blocks, and other large objects. The sledge and its cargo were placed onto a well-built road or rollers. Roads were built to transport blocks from quarry sites to construction sites. Some of these roads remain *in situ* today, and several can be seen around the Giza Plateau. The roads were constructed of mud, sand, limestone chips and gravel, and wood. When moistened with water and/or oil, the combination provided enough lubrication for a team of workmen or oxen to pull a sledge along the road to its destination (Aston et al. 2000:18–19). Once at the construction site, levers and cranes situated the blocks into place.

Wheels and carts

Carts and wheels were also used to move blocks from place to place. It is not known exactly when humankind began using wheels; however, based on archaeological evidence, the wheel was known as early as the Neolithic period, ca. 9500–4500 BCE. The Halafian culture utilized wheels made of wooden disks with an opening for an axle. The potter's wheel (ca. 4500 BCE) was a round wooden or stone slab on which ceramic vessels were thrown. Used as a mode of transportation, large solid wooden wheels were made from the center of a tree (Figure 7.7). The outer sapwood was removed leaving the heartwood, the inner hardwood. The wheels were made in sections consisting of three planks: one large center plank with rounded ends and two smaller flanking ones joined together by cross struts. A large round hole was carved to receive an axle and hub, and from there, the upper portions of the wagon were constructed (Hodges 1992:84–87). Wagons took on numerous different shapes commensurate with the task they were meant to perform. Wheeled vehicles such as these appear in Mesopotamia as well as in

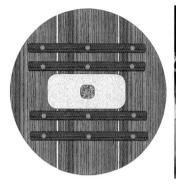 

FIGURE 7.7   Early wheels. Left: Recreation of a wooden wheel. Right: Egyptian chariot
with spoke wheels, Egypt, Cairo Museum

Graphic and photograph by Jill L. Baker.

the northern Caucasus and in Central Europe around the fourth millennium.
Recently, a Bronze Age wheel made from wood planks was found at the Must
Farm in England (www.mustfarm.com/).

In Mesopotamia, ca. 2600, the Battle Standard of Ur (British Museum, Museum
number 121201), a wooden box triangular in shape and adorned with war and
peace scenes made of inlaid mosaics using lapis lazuli, limestone, and shell, and
bound together with bitumen, measuring 21.59 centimeters (8.50 inches) wide
by 49.53 centimeters (19.50 inches) long, depicted four-wheeled vehicles,
generally interpreted as chariots (see Figure 9.1). The wheels appear to be solid
wooden wheels, and there are four wheels per vehicle. The upper portion of the
vehicle appears to be made from wood, and the vehicles are drawn by at least two
onagers. The wheel and cart/wagon developed rapidly, shifting to spoke wheels
and lighter baskets, especially for chariots used in battle and sport (Figure 7.7,
right).

Carts to move cargo, however, were generally made from wood; they were heavy
and usually pulled by oxen or onager. This basic design remained in use for a long
time. Examples can be seen in the reliefs at Medinet Habu (ca. 1186–1185 BCE).
These reliefs depict the "invading" Sea Peoples, some of whom were arriving in
carts being drawn by a team of two oxen, carrying women, children, and their
belongings. These carts appear to be made of wood with large solid wooden wheels,
and were probably heavy and slow moving.

Wooden wheels were also used to move stone blocks. In this instance, the stone
block served as an axle between two wheels with a frame attached to a team of
oxen. Replicas can be seen at the Archaeological Park in Jerusalem as well as at the
site of Beth Shean, Israel (Figure 7.8).

These carts would have been used to transport blocks from quarry to construction site. In this case, the cart is comprised of two large wooden wheels, and the
stone block itself functions as the axle.

FIGURE 7.8 Stone block functioning as axle between wheels for easy transport from quarry to site. Left: Beth Shean. Right: Jerusalem Archaeological Park

Photographs by Jill L. Baker.

Scaffolding

A scene found in the Eighteenth Dynasty tomb of Rekhmira at Thebes (TT100) depicts artists working on colossal statues, some standing on scaffolding that had been erected around the unfinished statues. At Amarna, postholes have been discovered next to large walls suggesting that scaffolding was erected to construct large, high, brick and stone walls. To build these walls, scaffolding would have been erected next to and/or over the wall during construction of it. In his description of the building of the Pyramids, Herodotus (Histories 2.125, Strassler and Purvis 2007:174) described what many interpret as cranes and scaffolding used to lift stone from a lower elevation to a higher one. The Berlin Foundry Cup, ca. fifth century BCE, depicts an oversized warrior statue on Side A surrounded by wooden scaffolding. In the fourth century CE, the Tomb of Trebius Justus depicts Roman masons building a brick wall using scaffolding and ladders (Sear 1982:72).

The Egyptians, however, were not the first to use scaffolding to reach great heights for artistic purposes. The artists who adorned the walls of the Lascaux Caves in France with magnificent paintings depicting animals may have also used scaffolding to reach the upper portions of the walls they painted. Holes in the walls, presumably made by humans, may have held the scaffolding to support the artists (Howley 2010). Early scaffolding such as this would have been made from wood.

Lever

The word lever comes from the Latin word *levare* and from *levis*, which means light (Figure 7.9). Listed as one of the five simple machines by Hero, Philo, and Pappus (Humphrey et al. 2006:46–50), the lever can help move extremely heavy objects. This simple machine consists of a lever, which can be made of very strong wood, or of a metal beam or rod and a fulcrum. The fulcrum is placed near the object being

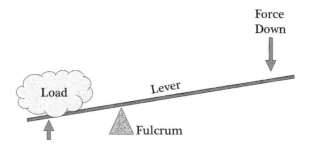

FIGURE 7.9 Lever and fulcrum lifting a heavy load

Graphic by Jill L. Baker.

moved, and one end of the lever is wedged under the object and over the fulcrum. When force is applied to the opposite end of the lever, the end under the object is lifted up, thus moving the large heavy object. The longer the lever extending between the fulcrum and the mover, the greater the force exerted on the object. Thus, "the weight of the load and the force needed to lift it are inversely proportional to their distances from the fulcrum" (Landels 2000:195).

This simple machine, in concert with pulleys, sledges, and rollers, was used to maneuver very large blocks of stone into place during construction. In the relief from Nineveh (Figure 3.2, bottom), a lever is used to move the colossal bull statue.

Construction ramp

Together with scaffolding, engineers likely used ramps to aid with the vertical challenges presented in building massive structures, especially pyramids and temples (Figure 7.10). Recent hypotheses suggest that ramps were used to transport the large, multi-ton blocks up to the higher elevations as the pyramid was built. Three types of ramps have been suggested: straight, zigzag, and spiral.

The straight ramps were built at a right angle to the pyramid on one or several sides. The length, width, height, and angle of a straight ramp would have been commensurate with the height of the pyramid under construction. The ramp's angle was important because it had to be relatively gentle not to create more work for those pulling up the blocks.

Additionally, as the pyramid increased in height incrementally, the right-angle ramp had to increase in length and the angle recalculated, which posed another problem. To achieve a practical incline, a ramp has to be extremely long once a structure reaches a certain height, which makes a right-angle ramp impractical at a certain point (Arnold 1991; Lehner 1992, 1997). Perhaps the straight right-angle ramp was more useful for lower levels of a structure or shorter structures.

The zigzag ramp would have started at the bottom of the pyramid, presumably in a corner, and ascended up one side of the pyramid in a zigzag fashion, much like

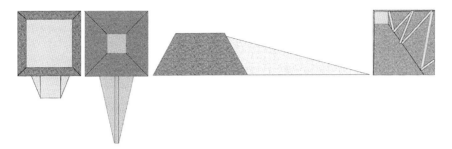

FIGURE 7.10 Possible ramp scenarios used by ancient Egyptians to construct the pyramids

Graphic by Jill L. Baker.

a snake path on a very steep mountain. As the pyramid increased in height, so too did the zigzag ramp, providing access to each new construction level of the pyramid. The spiraling ramp would have started when the pyramid was one or two courses high, extending up and around each side of the pyramid at an angle commensurate with the ever-increasing height of the structure. The spiraling ramp provided consistent access to each level and each side of the pyramid during construction. The spiraling ramp itself was under constant construction as the height of the pyramid increased. Both the zigzag and spiraling ramps are thought to have begun from within the quarry, providing direct access from where the block was quarried to the construction site. Once the blocks were hauled up to the desired level, they were maneuvered into place, presumably by using levers and possibly rollers. Several construction ramps have been discovered (Arnold 1991; Lehner 1997).

Once the pyramid or temple was built and decorated, the earthen ramps were removed, leaving no trace of their existence. Just as today, once a building or dwelling is completed, the scaffolding and cranes used to construct them are removed, leaving no evidence of their use. However, some ramps were not completely removed, which lends support to the earthen construction ramp theories. The remains of ramps have been discovered at several sites, including Dashur, Meidum, Abu Gurab, and Abusir; at the pyramids of Sahura, Nyuserra, and Neferirkara; at Saqqqara at Pepi II's pyramid; at the Giza Pyramids such as at Kafre's pyramid; and behind the first pylon at Karnak Temple.

Surveying and measuring

The first step to any building project involved surveying, which in Egypt was also used to establish property boundaries for agricultural fields as well as residential dwellings in villages and cities (Figure 7.11). Surveying involved mathematics and geometry, and a keen awareness of special dimension. One of the best and earliest examples of the important role of surveyors comes from Egypt. Egyptian surveyors were responsible for establishing boundaries between neighboring farms; for the

FIGURE 7.11   Depictions of Egyptian surveying scenes. Left: Tomb of Djeserkereseneb (TT38). Right: Tomb of Menna (TT69)

Adapted from Salmon 2003 and Livet 2001 (left); adapted from Salmon 2003 and Schultz 1998 (right).

layout of cities, such as Kahun (el-Lahun, ca. 2025–1700 BCE), which used a gridiron plan and major and minor streets; and for establishing the size, shape, and orientation of construction projects.

Determining boundaries, especially for individually-owned farmland, was important for calculating tax rates and reestablishing field boundaries after the annual inundation of the Nile, which altered the landscape. Tax rates were also established by a nilometer, which will be discussed in Chapter 12 (Figure 12.1). At first, in the Old Kingdom, the pharaoh owned the land and granted it to others as and when he deemed fit. However, from the Third Dynasty onward, land was initially given to officials and later to temples and individual citizens, although the latter were required to pay taxes to the state. Hence, the tax collectors were an integral part of the pharaoh's administration, and re-surveying the land was an annual task (Salmon 2003; Lyons 1927; Brock 2005).

Surveyors, known as rope stretchers and scribes of the field, were members of the scribal class, meaning they were well-educated members of Egypt's upper class. Four surveyors are known from their rock-cut tombs in Thebes (Luxor), northeast of the Valley of the Queens and southeast of the Valley of the Kings, in the Eighteenth Dynasty cemetery called Shaykh Abd al-Qurna.

Amenhotep-Sise (TT75), also called the "Second Prophet of Amun," worked during the time of Thutmose IV, ca. 1400–1390 BCE. The tomb painting on the left wall depicts temple craftsmen and field surveyors at work. Some carry a coiled measuring rope (Lyons 1927).

Khaemhet (TT57), also known as Mahu, was a royal scribe during the reign of Amenhotep III, ca. 1390–1352 BCE. His title was Overseer of the Granaries of Upper and Lower Egypt, and his tomb contained a rope-surveying scene. Menna (TT69) was known as the Scribe of the Fields of the Lord of the Two Lands of Upper and Lower Egypt (Figure 7.11). A surveyor and archivist responsible for keeping land ownership records, he was also known as a cadaster scribe. Menna had two sons, Kha, who was a Uab, or libation priest, and Sa, who was scribe of the fields,

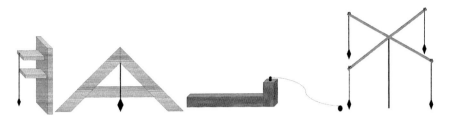

FIGURE 7.12   Surveying instruments. Left to right: F-level, A-frame level, *merkhet*, *groma*

Graphics by Jill L. Baker.

or scribe of grain reckoning. Djerserkereseneb, a.k.a. Zerkereseneb, ca. 1400 BCE (Figure 7.11), was surveyor of crops under Thutmose IV (ca. 1400–1390 BCE). His tomb contained the typical measuring scene depicting Zerkereseneb with a scribal palette in one hand and a long staff in the other, and wearing a long transparent kilt and white sandals (Salmon 2003; Lyons 1927; Brock 2005).

Surveyors' tools included the *groma* (a Roman term) (Sloley 1926), *merkhet*, a *gnomon*, which is a measuring rod or cubit stick, rope, an A-frame level with plumb bob, writing materials, and a bag or bucket that contained the cord or writing materials (Figure 7.12). Initially, surveying in Egypt was conducted by stretching out rope that was knotted at cubit intervals. Ropes could be 100 cubits in length. The gnomon was used to create a shadow to mark the path of the sun to establish orientation. Their measuring system included the typical length of a man's thumb and palm, a cubit, a royal cubit (ca. 52.4 centimeters), *khet* (100 royal cubits), *iteru* (ca. 20,000 cubits, ca. 10.5 kilometers), and area, or *khet, aroura*, and *setjat* (ca. 0.25 hectares) (Salmon 2003; Lehner 1997).

Distance and orientation also may have been established by using a merkhet ("instrument of knowing"), which was actually a timekeeping instrument. It consisted of a handle with horizontal bar and plumb line. The horizontal bar could be made from wood or ivory and was usually incised with marks that corresponded to the night sky. Two merkhets had to be used together to determine north, south, east, and west. It is possible that the groma was based on the merkhet.

The groma is well known from Greek and Roman periods (Figure 7.12). It consisted of a vertical pole with a pointed metal end, which was stuck into the ground. At the top were two horizontal cross pieces joined at right angles to a bracket. From each of the four tips hung plumb bobs. This instrument was used to create straight lines, right angles, squares, and rectangles. These instruments and surveying methods were also used in Mesopotamia, where surveyors were called Boundary Stores or Draggers of the Rope. The groma was widely used in Greece and Rome and helped to build the Roman road system and empire. It is likely that the groma was originally used in Egypt and Mesopotamia and imported to Greece when Greek engineers traveled to the East (Lyons 1927; Salmon 2003). A groma dating to the first/second century BCE was found in Egypt's Fayum region.

Once boundaries were established, boundary stones were put into place. These delineated the plots of land for which people were responsible and upon which taxes were based. Moving boundary stones was forbidden, as stated in Amenhotep's *The Instruction of Amen-em-opet*, Chapter VI, dated to ca. 1400 BCE: "Do not carry off the landmark at the boundaries of the arable land, nor disturb the position of the measuring-cord; be not greedy after a cubit of land, nor encroach upon the boundaries of a widow" (Wilson 1992b:422). Psalms 22:28 and 23:10 also warn against moving boundary markers. Surveying and boundary marking were also used to establish the boundaries of nations and city-states.

To level an area, the Egyptians used an A-frame level with a plumb bob (Figure 7.12). The horizontal part of the A-frame was marked at specific intervals, and when the legs of the frame were placed on a surface, the pendulum of the plumb indicated whether the surface was flat. Leveling using the A-frame appears to have been nearly exact, for the pavement upon which the Great Pyramid at Giza sits is almost completely flat, with a slope of only 6 millimeters east to west and 14 millimeters north to south, which covers a distance of 230 meters in each direction (Lyons 1927:136). The A-frame was also used to level the stone courses of the pyramids and other buildings such as temples, palaces, and homes, as well as walls. Water also may have been used to level a surface. This could be achieved by filling a chiseled trench with water, marking the waterline, which would have been level, emptying the trench, then measuring down to see if the bottom was level. Additionally, a container with level horizontal markings also could have been used.

The office of Surveyor in Egypt was highly organized and involved the Treasury, Land Registration, and Survey departments; the latter was part of the capital works program in the Old Kingdom, the period when the great pyramids were built. Surveyors, also considered to be scribes, came from the upper class and were highly educated. Rigorous training began at the age of twelve, and they learned over 700 hieroglyphic signs and worked from dawn to dusk. Surveying was multidisciplinary, and involved not only surveying skills but also calculation, agronomy, engineering, mathematics, geometry, and astronomy (Lyons 1927).

Although the best evidence for survey technique comes from Egypt, these methods were likely used throughout the ancient Near East well into the Roman period and beyond. Modern survey techniques are based on the aforementioned ancient technique; however, the instruments have changed by incorporating lasers and computers.

Presses

The pressing process was used to extract essential oils and juices from fruits such as olives and grapes. The olive oil and wine industries of the ancient Near East were two of the main economic drivers. Olive oil and wine were also two of the main staples of daily life. However, exactly when humankind began manufacturing oil and wine remains the subject of discussion. Nevertheless, it is not surprising that olive and wine presses were ubiquitous throughout the region. Numerous installations and types of presses have been discovered throughout Canaan/ancient Israel and the Mediterranean basin. Most of the examples in this work, however, will focus on those from Canaan/ancient Israel and Egypt.

Pressing installations range from simple rock-cut treading floors, basins, channels, and vats to weighted lever presses and the screw press (Frankel 1999). As technology improved and the industry grew, the production process included more efficient presses, vats, and the buildings to house them. The process for pressing olives was nearly identical to that used for grapes. To make olive oil, the olive had to be crushed to a mash. The mash was then pressed to extract the expressed fluid. Approximately 20 to 30 percent of this was oil and the rest was the darker, heavy, watery lees (Frankel 1999:41). To make wine, the grapes had to be trod upon to obtain the must. The remaining skins and stalks were pressed to obtain the rest of the must, which was then fermented (Frankel 1999:41).

Olive pressing

Use of olive wood and olives is evident as early as the Palaeolithic period; however, use was greater in the Chalcolithic period, with the cultivation of the olive tree and its fruit. By the Early Bronze Age, especially in Canaan, at Teleilat Ghassul north of the Dead Sea, and in the upper Jordan Valley region, olive wood and fruit was commonplace (Serpico and White 2009:399). Similarly, in Egypt the olive and grape were in use from Predynastic times. Widespread knowledge of the cultivation, processing, and production of olive oil was probably disseminated by the Phoenicians and/or the Greeks throughout the North African region (Wolff 1996:129).

The main method of extracting the oil and juice was by pressing, and various methods and press types were used. Some presses were above ground, while others were subterranean. Some were rock-cut; others a series of stone presses and basins. This section is not meant to provide an exhaustive summary of press types and techniques; rather, it will highlight those presses that reflect the basic principle of pressing.

At Tel Miqne-Ekron, simple lever-and-weight presses were employed (Figure 7.13). These generally consisted of a central basin with two flanking presses conjoined by channels allowing the oil to flow from the presses into the basin. Levers were inserted into specially prepared niches in the wall behind the presses, which rested on reed mats piled high on the press and filled with olives for crushing. Stone weights were attached to the lever, which applied weight to the olive-filled mats, crushing them and releasing their oil (Frankel 1999:62–63). At Tel Miqne-Ekron in the Iron Age, 184 installations were discovered; of those, 164 were used to manufacture olive oil, comprising 115 oil-press complexes (Eitam 1996:169).

These included one rectangular basin flanked on each side by crushing presses carved out of local Na'ari stone. With these were found crushing stones and rolling stones. The crushing presses were square with channels directing the flow of oil into the collection vat. The pressing stones also contained a collection basin. This is known as the Ekron-type press (Gitin 1990).

FIGURE 7.13 Olive presses at Tel Miqne-Ekron. Left: Archaeological remains including weights, press, and collection vats. Right: Recreation of pressing procedure

Used with permission and courtesy of Seymour Gitin.

To crush the olives, workers placed them onto round reed mats, which were stacked and placed on top of the press. A wooden lever was inserted into a niche built into the wall of the building that housed the crushing apparatus. The lever rested on top of the olive-filled reed mats and was weighted down by stones hanging from the end of the lever (Figure 7.13). The weight of the stones pressed down on the lever and reed mats, thus crushing the olives and extracting the oil (Eitam 1996:172). By using the reed mats, the meat of the olive was pressed and the oil was extracted without crushing the skin or olive stone, which could make the oil bitter tasting. Simple weight-and-lever presses were also discovered at Gezer, Bet Mirsham, Megiddo, and Qurnat el-Harmiya (Frankel 1999:63). Freestanding presses such as these date to the seventh century BCE onward.

Rollers and pounders (mortar and pestle) were also used in conjunction with freestanding or rock-cut basins that were round or rectangular. Rectangular basins were generally used with a roller rather than a pounder. Some regional diversity within Canaan/ancient Israel has been detected. At many northern sites, mortars were used for crushing, as well as at sites such as Balata, Rosh-Zayit, Shiqmona, Maresha (Figure 7.14), and Qiri. In the southern coastal plain and eastern foothills, rectangular basins and rollers were used for crushing (Frankel 1999:68).

In the first millennium, the mechanical principle of the potter's wheel was adapted and applied to the crushing of olives (and grapes) with a rotary crusher, which included a round basin into which a round stone (or stones) was set. The crushing stone contained a hole, circular or square, which received a horizontal shaft that rotated in a socket. The horizontal shaft and stone were pushed, allowing it to roll in a circular motion around the basin, thus crushing the olives. The oil drained from the basin into collection vessels for further processing. Exactly when this device came into use is not known; however, this machine was used throughout the Iron Age, and is still in use to the present day in some places (Frankel 1999:68–71). Rotary crushing machines have been found at sites such as Sur Natan, Tabgha, Zabadi, and Marisha.

FIGURE 7.14   Olive presses at Maresha. Left: Weight-and-lever press. Right: Rotary grinder

Photographs by Jill L. Baker.

FIGURE 7.15   Processing grapes to make wine. Top: Tomb of Nakht and Tawy, Thebes, dating to the New Kingdom. Scenes depict harvesting grapes and the treading and pressing process. Bottom: Tomb-chapel of Bakt III at Beni Hasan (BH 15). Scene of straining and pressing grapes to extract juice

Adapted from de Garis Davies 1917 Plate 26 (Public Domain, PD-1923) (top); adapted from Newberry 1893b Plate VI (Public Domain, PD-1923) (bottom).

Wine pressing

Wine presses have been found extending from the Chalcolithic period onward at sites such as Megiddo (Frankel 1999:51). Early wine presses tended to be relatively simple rock-cut installations consisting of a treading floor, channels, and collection basins. These were carved directly into the bedrock and remain visible today. Simple installations such as these remained in use throughout history, especially in rural areas. Treading floors tended to be ca. 2.5 to 3.1 square-meters. The collection vats ranged from 1.00 to 1.24 square-meters. There also were freestanding and built treading installations with associated collection basins.

In Egypt, the treading method was employed, though it is estimated that treading accounted for only two-thirds of extracted juice. The remains of the grapes, crushed skins, stalks, and seeds were pressed using a cloth or sack press. After treading, the remnants were placed into cloth or sack and twisted until all the juice had been extracted (Figure 7.15).

Screw

The "endless screw" was one of the five machines discussed by Hero and Philo, and was used for its mechanical advantage. Best known as Archimedes' screw, it has been suggested that the screw was in use by the Egyptians and Babylonians long before Archimedes made it famous (Landels 2000:58). Based on a cuneiform inscription, Stephanie Dalley suggests that Sennacherib (reign, ca. 704–681 BCE) devised a water-lifting screw to hydrate the Hanging Gardens of Babylon. Accounts from ancient authors such as Diodorus Siculus describe large amounts of water being raised by great machines hidden from view (Dalley 2013, Diodorus Siculus, *The Library of History*, II.10.6, Henderson and Oldfather 1933:386–387). Several hundred years later, Archimedes rediscovered this machine and integrated it into the classical world. This simple machine, constructed of a round beam around which horizontal threads snaked from bottom to top, carried water or grain from a lower level to a higher one. This machine could also be used to move large objects with ease, as Archimedes demonstrated to King Hieron by moving a ship (Plutarch, *Marcellus* 14.7–9, Henderson and Perrin 1917:472–473). Adaptations of the screw allowed it to be used in presses, in a pulling-down motion as in a lever press, and as a screw press (Oleson 2008:341). The screw mechanism delivered the force needed to squeeze the grapes or olives, and reduced the amount of force required of the operator.

Electricity

If asked when electricity was discovered, most would probably answer in the 1600s with the research of William Gilbert, in 1791 with Luigi Galvani's research into bioelectricity, or in the 1800s with Alessandro Volta's research into batteries. However, electricity was known to the Mesopotamians and Egyptians, and probably also to much earlier peoples, based on their experience of electrical phenomena found in nature. As early as 2750 BCE, the Egyptians were aware of electrical fish such as eels, catfish, and rays, as were Greek, Roman, and Arabic natural scientists and physicians in later periods. Another natural occurrence of electricity was static electricity, which was observed by rubbing amber against fur or wool or from rubbing wool clothing or blankets together in cold dry climates (James and Thorpe 1995:145–147). Electrical storms producing lightning were another natural occurrence of electricity. These natural occurrences of electricity can be observed today.

In medicine, early physicians were aware of the numbing effect of an electrical shock received from touching electric fish, such as the torpedo fish. Patients suffering from headaches or gout were instructed to touch an electric fish with the hope of shocking the system into a cure (Tsoucalas et al. 2014). Even though the ancients knew about the existence of electricity, it remains unclear whether they understood it or knew how to harness it for useful purposes.

One artifact suggests that someone in antiquity may have been experimenting with electricity, though the true nature of this artifact remains the subject of debate (Figure 7.16). Known as the Baghdad battery, several jars containing metal objects suggest that deliberate chemical reactions were used to produce an electrical current (Paszthory 1989; Keyser 1993).

In 1930 in Baghdad, Wilhelm Konig of the University of Michigan excavated four small, unglazed earthenware jars sealed with bitumen from the Seleucid trading post of Opis on the Tigris River (Paszthory 1989). These date to the Sassanian period, ca. 225–640 CE (some sources date these to the Parthian period, ca. 250 BCE–224 CE). The jars were ca. 15–20 centimeters high and of various shapes, some with two handles, each surrounded by at least four metal rods, most of which were bronze but at least one per set was iron, and the rods measured 20–25 centimeters long. Within each jar was a bronze cylinder, ca. 3 centimeters in diameter and 7.5 centimeters long, sealed at both ends, and compressed rolls of papyrus (Paszthory 1989).

FIGURE 7.16   Baghdad battery. Left: Artifacts from Khuyu Rabbou'a, Baghdad, including the ceramic vessel (ca. 14 centimeters high), copper cylinder (ca. 9.8 centimeters long), and iron spike (ca. 7.5 centimeters long). Right: Drawing of the Khyuyt Rabbou'a objects

Adapted from Paszthory 1989:31, Figure 1 (left); adapted from Wikipedia.org, By Ironie – Own work, CC BY-SA 2.5, https://en.wikipedia.org/wiki/File:Ironie_pile_Bagdad.jpg (right).

In 1931, a German team of archaeologists excavating on the east bank of the Tigris River at Ctesiphon found six unglazed, earthenware jugs. Each was sealed with bitumen, save for two holes, and contained copper and/or tin rolls or iron nails and small lead plates. At a third site, Khuyut Rabbou'a, Baghdad, in 1936, Late Parthian, unglazed ware jars were discovered. Each was sealed at both ends with bitumen and contained a copper cylinder, a copper plate at one end, and an iron spike inserted into the copper cylinder, held in place by bitumen. Traces of lead were found in the negative impression found at one end of the cylinder stopper. All of these have been interpreted as components for Galvanic cells or batteries (Paszthory 1989).

A Galvanic cell converts chemical energy into electric energy. The jars containing the metal objects would have been filled with a liquid containing electrolytes, which have conducting properties, such as citrus fruits (oranges, lemons, and pomegranates) or vinegar. The liquid would react with the metals and produce an electrical current (Paszthory 1989). Basically, a galvanic cell, named after Luigi Galvani, who discovered bioelectricity, is comprised of two different metals, copper and zinc, which are connected. When they come into contact with an electrolyte solution, an electrical current is produced.

Archaeologists continue to debate whether this was an actual battery used to produce an electric current. However, any first-year electrical engineering student will say that these artifacts comprise the ingredients necessary for the construction of a rudimentary electrical device. In 2013 *National Geographic* magazine (see Charland 2013) demonstrated how an orange, galvanized nails, and copper wire could power a 3.5-volt light for 14 hours. In my class, for their final projects, two students made batteries based on the Baghdad batteries and demonstrated how a rudimentary electrical device such as this could power an LED bulb and LCD clock (Figure 7.17).

Assuming the Baghdad battery was in fact constructed to produce an electrical current, what function could it have performed? It has been speculated that the

FIGURE 7.17   Baghdad battery experiment in the classroom. Left: Electricity produced from two oranges powering an LCD clock. Right: Replica of a Baghdad battery producing electricity measuring almost 4 volts. My thanks to two of my students

Photographs by Jill L. Baker.

device may have been used for electroplating, as "a local electrical analgesic" (Keyser 1993:98), or in temples to perform magical acts. For example, it could have been attached to an idol made of a conducting metal to deliver a small shock when touched. Or perhaps it was used for medicinal purposes, in much the same way fish were but without having to actually catch the animal. Unfortunately, the true purpose for this device remains unknown. Whatever the purpose of this "battery," its presence suggests electrical experiments were being conducted. This is not unreasonable to surmise since the artifacts date to an age of discovery and experimentation, and the ability to combine and convert the chemical properties of materials had long been known. If in fact these artifacts represent electrical energy, they also represent knowledge gained and lost, only to be rediscovered centuries later.

8

CONSTRUCTION

Chapters 3–6 presented some of the materials used to build ancient Near Eastern cities. Chapter 7 discussed some of the tools and engineering techniques applied during construction. Drawing on these data, this chapter will discuss the manner in which those materials were incorporated into building projects. Just as it is important to recognize the unique characteristics of materials, it is equally important to appreciate how they worked together to achieve a single purpose.

Beyond the practicalities of construction, the architect had to consider the purpose of a structure. Would it be for public or private use? Would it be for government, business, or industrial use? Would it be a palace or a temple, a house or a bakery? The function or purpose of a structure determines the form or architectural style it will take and the features it will include. For example, the architectural style and features of a railway station differ from those of a bank. A railway station is generally a tall, slender, timber structure with an open, sparsely decorated interior, made to efficiently accommodate the movement of people from entrance to ticket booth to train. A bank is generally a solidly built structure of stone, brick or concrete, also sparsely appointed, and meant to serve a smaller number of people with greater privacy and security. So, the architectural style (form) is a reflection of the activities (function) that take place within the space.

Furthermore, structures, whether public, industrial, or domestic, convey information. The architectural style, materials, size, layout, and decoration convey significance within the structure's community and can be used to communicate information, such as political propaganda, laws, or cultic tradition. Temples reflect religious beliefs, and palaces reflect centralized power and government structure. In ancient Egypt, temples conveyed important information to the public. The exterior walls boasted the Pharaoh's achievements while interior walls provided mythical narrative and ritual instruction. Three examples include Medinet Habu, Luxor Temple, and Karnak Temple. In Greece, monumental buildings such as bouleuteria, treasuries, and temples reflected their system of democracy. These structures included large, open spaces so that people of all classes could gather and participate. Meeting halls included seating that allowed participants to see and face each other during assemblies. In the United States, buildings such as the White House, Supreme Court, and treasury building mimic ancient Greek structures in architectural style and layout to demonstrate our democratic system of government.

Equally important was the organization of structures within urban centers. City planning determined the location of government, religious, industrial, business, and residential zones to ensure an organized, well-run city. By establishing activity-specific zones, the movement of residents, workers, and visitors could be controlled. Aided by a network of well-planned streets, the flow of foot and wheeled traffic provided efficient movement throughout the city while maintaining control. This organization ensured that residential areas would remain private and public areas could accommodate visitors and professionals.

To some, the form and function of architecture, architectural layout, and city planning may not seem like technology. However, in keeping with our working definition of technology, these may be considered technologies because they help to resolve problems, achieve goals, and improve quality of life, aspects which will be worked into the discussion below.

Masonry methods

It has already been mentioned that urban construction began in the Neolithic period and stone was the primary construction material. Building types included domestic dwellings, community and government structures, silos, storage facilities, and temples/shrines. Additionally, pit graves, wells, and storage pits could be carved into bedrock or dug into the ground and lined with stone.

By way of reminder, harder, igneous rocks were usually used for foundations and walls, and softer stones were used for decorative facing. Softer limestone such as Iskander and yabis were mostly ornamental, while Nari limestone was used for building, exterior facing stone, piers, and capitals. Mizzi Yahudi, a dolomite lime-stone, was also used for building. Marble was dense and compact, and several varieties could be found in Canaan/ancient Israel. Because marble could be highly polished, it was used as an interior decorative finishing, and its strength made it suitable for use in construction (Bar-Yosef 1992).

Some of the earliest Near Eastern dwellings that have been found thus far were in Epipalaeolithic Natufian villages dating to about the fifteenth to tenth millennia BP. Natufian sites include 'Ein Mallaha in the Huleh Valley, at the entrance to the Hayonim Cave near Nazareth, Oren Valley, Mt. Carmel, and at Mt. Tsin in the Negev. Villages of the contemporary Kebarian culture include' Ein Gev Creek near Lake Kinneret. These were generally round enclosures, up to 8 meters in diameter, with cobbled floors and mud-plastered walls, and were constructed with unworked fieldstone. One pillar in the center provided support for roofing. Houses of the Neolithic Period (ca. ninth to sixth millennia BP) were also round and partially sunken, had one room as a living space, and were made of fieldstone with mud-plastered walls. Buildings consisted of shrines, graves, and storehouses. At sites such as Sha'ar HaGolan, Jericho, and Çatal Hüyük, buildings were rectangular, contained one or several rooms, and were built in clusters that formed villages with streets (Bar-Yosef 1992).

Perhaps the best example of Neolithic construction can be found at Sha'ar HaGolan (Garfinkel and Ben-Shlomo 2009). Making use of stone, clay, wood, and reeds, the people built an extensive urban center. Abundant river pebbles comprised the basic building material, used in foundations and lower walls, surfaces/pavements for streets, courtyards, thresholds and rooms, postholes, hearths, and grinding installations. Stone foundations and lower walls provided stability for the mudbrick superstructure, which formed the main part of the building. Mud plaster generally covered stone walls (Garfinkel and Ben-Shlomo 2009).

Fieldstones collected from the surrounding landscape were chosen for their size, shape, and durability. Masons fit the stones together to produce a solid wall or structure, and, if done properly, mortar was not necessary to hold the stones in place. Since these stones were collected and not reshaped, the walls took on a relatively random course or pattern. Eventually, masons learned to shape, or dress, the stones to produce a more uniform course and pattern.

In the Bronze and Iron Ages, dressed stone and ashlar blocks became the norm, especially for monumental public buildings. Ashlar blocks were quarried from stone and hewn to a specific size and shape, usually rectangular. Dressing was achieved with a chisel and hammer and exterior faces of the stone blocks were usually smooth, straight, and at right angles. If prepared properly, these blocks fit together perfectly without need for mortar or a bonding agent. Decorative elements were added to ashlar blocks to mimic molding and paneling. Monumental examples of dressed blocks may be found on the remaining exterior block facing of the pyramids on the Giza Plateau and on the ashlar blocks of the Herodian period portions of the Temple Mount in Jerusalem (Figure 8.1).

FIGURE 8.1 Stone detail on Temple Mount, Jerusalem. Left Two: Southern wall of the Temple Mount. Right Two: Southern wall of the Temple Mount, the Kotel

Photographs by Jill L. Baker.

These blocks were cut to specific dimensions and finished with flat surfaces, especially the exterior, and with decorated faces. Dressing tools consisted of wooden mallets, copper chisels, stone hammers, scrapers, adzes, and files, all of which were used to chip and smooth the facing (Wright 2005:48–51). Once positioned, the blocks fused together leaving few if any gaps.

Stone walls

The construction method and materials used to build stone walls of structures varied and were dependent upon available resources and terrain. Also, the size and shape of the structure's walls was commensurate with the function of the structure, whether a house, palace, or city gate. If the structure was a two-story house, the walls had to be thick enough to support the weight of a second floor and roof without bowing and collapsing. To achieve the construction of a solid structure, various methods were employed.

The first task was to lay a solid foundation. Most foundations were partially subterranean to establish a solid and stable footing for the superstructure. A trench was dug into the ground, usually 0.5 to 1.0 meter in depth, depending on the thickness of the wall and the load it was expected to carry. The bed of the trench was leveled and lined with rubble or solid bedding stones. The initial course of stones may not have touched the trench walls, thus forming a gap that was packed with rubble and/or mortar (Figure 8.1). This created a firm foundation upon which to construct the walls of the structure.

Construction methods of walls

Several types of wall construction have been observed, including simple walls without a core, walls with a core, walls made of fieldstone and dressed stone, and walls constructed with or without mortar. In general, a combination of stone and mudbrick with a lime plaster comprised buildings. In regions where mudbrick was scarce, structures were predominantly made of rock, and in other regions where stone was scarce, structures were mostly made with mudbrick. Very early structures could be round, square, or rectangular, though the latter two became standard design.

The most basic walls did not have a core. They were made of rough fieldstone, or fieldstone with one or two finished (dressed) sides, or dressed blocks (Figure 8.2). In general, walls were set into a trench and the foundation was strengthened using fill and/or mortar. Simple walls were usually one to three stones wide and the height varied. To keep the length, width, and height straight, or plumb, masons established a straight edge by stringing rope between stakes and constructing the wall within the confines of the rope. As they built the wall higher, the strings were reset to guide the next course. Right angles and plumb bobs were also used to keep vertical lines straight. To build high walls, scaffolding and ladders were erected. Building supplies could also be hoisted onto the scaffolding (Netzer 1992:21–22).

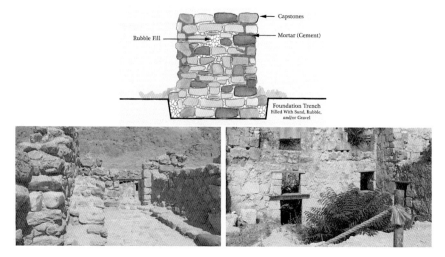

FIGURE 8.2 Examples of stone masonry construction, depiction of wall construction and two examples from Qumran and the Jerusalem Archaeological Park. Top: Example of stone masonry construction. Below left: Qumran building with steps (left) next to wall that once provided access to a second floor. Below right: A building at the Jerusalem Archaeological Park showing timber beams, lintels, above the doorway and windows

Graphic and photographs by Jill L. Baker.

Most structures, including domestic dwellings, storehouses, and administrative buildings, were constructed with a stone foundation and lower wall with a mud-brick superstructure. Generally, the foundation wall measured 1 to 3 meters in height, and the mudbrick superstructure was covered with a lime plaster. Steps leading to the second floor were usually made from stone covered with mudbrick and/or lime plaster (Figure 8.2, bottom left). This was the most cost-effective method of construction and comprised the majority of buildings in Canaan, Egypt, and Mesopotamia. Structures of greater importance, such as palaces, administrative buildings, city gates, and temples, were often constructed of mostly stone with less use of mudbrick and lime plaster (Netzer 1992; Mazar 1992; Moorey 1999). Core walls were wider and stronger, and could bear the weight of multiple stories. These generally consisted of two rows of fieldstones, often with the exterior sides dressed, at a distance from each other, with the inner space filled with rubble and/or mortar. Once settled, core walls could be very thick and strong. For even more strength, double core walls were constructed, consisting of two outer facing columns with one column midway between the two. Rubble and/or mortar were deposited between the two outer columns and the center columns, which made the wall strong and sturdy (Netzer 1992).

To accommodate doorframes, windows, ceilings, second floors, and roofs, wooden beams spanned the walls (Figure 8.2, bottom right). Timber beams were

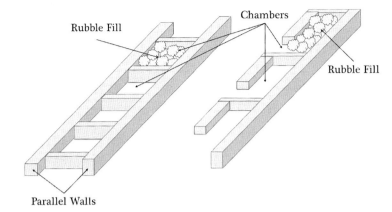

FIGURE 8.3 Casemate walls. Left: Closed casemate wall with rubble-filled chambers. Right: Usable chambers that could be filled as needed

Graphic by Jill L. Baker.

worked into the construction of the wall. Timbers had to be strong enough to support upper floors, and crossbeams were generally covered in mudbrick packing and plaster. Roof beams were covered with mudbrick or clay tiles (Netzer 1992).

Casemate walls were generally made from fieldstone, dressed stone, and rubble, and were mainly used in defensive structures, such as fortification and city walls (Figure 8.3). This type was utilized mainly in Iron Age Israel from about the tenth century to the eighth century BCE. There were two types of casemate walls: free-standing and integrated. A casemate wall looks much like a ladder, consisting of two parallel walls joined at regular intervals by partition walls extending perpendicularly between the two parallel walls. The partition walls created smaller chambers that could be used as homes or shops, but when necessary, were filled with rubble to create a very thick and stable defensive structure, as the one found at Hazor Str. X, tenth century BCE. Freestanding casemate walls were those that stood alone and whose chambers were used as homes or shops during peaceful times, as at Masada (see Figure 9.7). Integrated casemate walls were incorporated with dwellings inside the city, for example at Beersheba, Str. III (ninth century BCE). Casemate walls could also be permanently filled, never allowing the chambers to be utilized for anything other than defensive purposes (Herzog 1992).

Architectural layout of buildings

The architectural layout of buildings demonstrates a relatively steady progression from simple to multifaceted, reflecting society's increasing complexity, engineering skills, and use of materials. Architectural engineers also exploited natural resources such as wind and rain to create comfortable and productive living and working spaces. These aspects are best observed in the architectural configuration of domestic structures, courtyard palaces, temples, and fortifications. Some of these ancient building techniques remain in use today, such as architectural layout and use of materials such as concrete, whereas other techniques could be incorporated into modern and future construction practices, such as exploiting natural resources, thus making modern constructions more energy efficient.

The use of private and public space within structures became more prevalent in the Bronze Age. Specific portions of houses, palaces, and temples remained accessible to some and off limits to others. In Egyptian, Canaanite, and Israelite temples, for example, inner chambers and holy of holies were accessible only to priests and high priests while outer spaces were available to the masses. In domestic dwellings, front rooms closest to the street were used as shops or to conduct business while second floors and back rooms were private, with the courtyard functioning as a divide. Thus, the layout of rooms within a building conveyed information to its inhabitants and to visitors.

The configuration of rooms and the overall orientation of a building also determined interior temperature control. If situated properly, a building could take advantage of cool breezes in the summer and the sun's warmth in the winter. Tall ceilings and open windows allowed the hot air to rise and cool air to sink, resulting in a cooling circulation of air. The winter and summer palaces at Masada offer excellent examples of such planning. Well-configured courtyards and roofs offered shade from the sun and collected rainwater into pools and subterranean cisterns.

The engineering and ingenuity that went into the construction of buildings was complex, extending beyond mere protection from the elements. The form of a building reflected its function, and its form and function reflected a host of technologies. The division of public and private space continues to be used today and is reflected in modern architectural layout. For example, when walking into a doctor's office, one first enters into a reception area, which is public and separated from the examination rooms, which are more private. In many homes, the living room and dining room, tend to be toward the front of the house while family rooms and bedrooms are toward the back of the house or on upper floors. The needs of social interaction, conducting business, religious ritual, daily routine, and comfort of living influenced the architectural layout of buildings. In keeping with our working definition of technology, architectural layout represents an overlooked technology because it achieves specific goals and facilitates functional living and working spaces.

Domestic structures

In Canaan, early domestic dwellings were round, square, or rectangular (Figure 8.4). Round and ovoid dwellings were commonly used during the Neolithic and Chalcolithic periods and among nomadic and migratory groups. From an engineering standpoint, round structures were easier to construct.[1] Round/ovoid dwellings were utilized from the Neolithic throughout the Early and Intermediate Bronze Ages. Circular or oval dwellings generally had peaked, timber-framed roofs, and walls made of fieldstone. Circular and ovoid dwellings occurred in clusters,

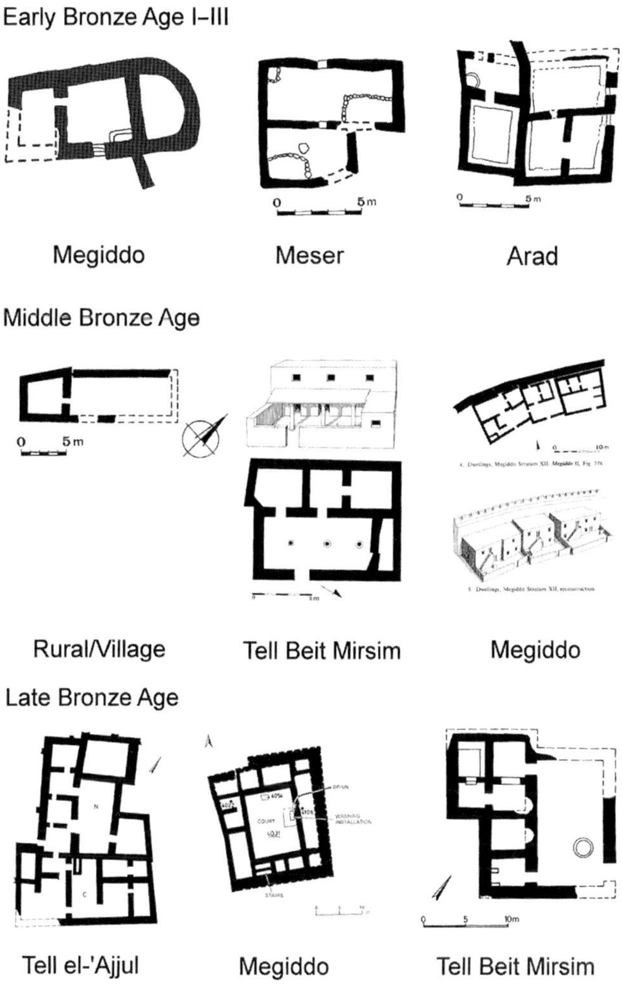

Early Bronze Age I–III

Megiddo   Meser   Arad

Middle Bronze Age

Rural/Village   Tell Beit Mirsim   Megiddo

Late Bronze Age

Tell el-'Ajjul   Megiddo   Tell Beit Mirsim

FIGURE 8.4   Select examples of domestic dwellings of the Bronze Age. Early Bronze Age I–III, left to right: Megiddo Meser; Arad. Middle Bronze Age, left to right: Rural/village from the Jordan Valley, Tell Beit Mirsim village/urban dwelling; Megiddo urban dwelling. Late Bronze Age, left to right: Patricians' houses Tell el-'Ajjul; Megiddo; Tell Beit Mirsim

Adapted from Ben-Tor 1992:61 (Megiddo); adapted from Ben-Tor 1992:65 (*IEJ* 9 (1959:16, Figure 3) (Meser); adapted from Ben-Tor 1992:55 (Arad, Pl. 183, No. 2318a) (Arad); adapted from Ben-Dov 1992:100 (*Qadmoniot* 10 (37) 1997) (Rural/Village); adapted from Ben-Dov 1992:102 (Tell Beit Mirsim II, Pl. 56:6) (Tell Beit Mirsim); adapted from Ben-Dov 1992:101 (Megiddo II, Figure 397) (Megiddo); adapted from Oren 1992:116 (Ancient Gaza II, Pl. LIV) (Tell el-'Ajjul); adapted from Kempinski 1992c:195 (Megiddo); adapted from Tell Beit Mirsim II, Pl. 55 (Tell Beit Mirsim).

possibly representing familial relationships. Some circular structures were likely used as storage for food, and others as animal pens (Bar-Yosef 1992; Porath 1992).

Square and rectangular dwellings usually consisted of a courtyard with roofed living spaces on one side. The courtyard consisted of a main entryway in the wall, providing access to/from the compound. The living space was partitioned from the main courtyard by a large wall containing a doorway, usually on the short wall if the compound was rectangular. The living space could be further subdivided if necessary. Presumably, this was where the inhabitants sought shelter from the elements, stored food, clothing, and belongings, and slept. The walls of the living spaces also contained benches, generally 0.5 meters high, which were covered with mudbrick and lime plaster. Courtyards served as the daily activity center, housing animals, the hearth, food storage, preparation, and cooking, and water collection. From this point forward, the courtyard became one of the most used and important features of homes throughout the Near East and Mediterranean basin and remained so throughout the Roman and Byzantine periods. The courtyard became technologically integral to the overall function of a dwelling or building. Although somewhat vestigial, courtyards remain in use today.

Dwellings of this configuration, and variants of it, were utilized from the Neolithic through the Early and Intermediate Bronze Ages (Kempinski 1992c; Ben-Tor 1992; Cohen 1992). Canaanite domestic dwellings of the Middle Bronze Age (Figure 8.4) onward became more complex, boasting multiple rooms, multiple stories, and architectural styles that can be distinguished as rural and urban.

Rural village dwellings resembled those from earlier periods, consisting of a large forecourt with one or two sides enclosed, and possibly a second story. In this configuration, ground floor rooms were used for storage and to house animals, and the second floor functioned as living space. The courtyard remained the focal point for daily activities, including food preparation, cooking, and storage. Housing animals in ground floor rooms allowed their body heat to rise, thus heating the upper rooms during winter months.

In Egypt, examples of domestic dwellings have been found at Tell el-Dab'a, Lahun, Elephantine, Deir el-Medina, Wah-Sut (Abydos-South), and Tell el-Amarna. Clay models of ancient Egyptian houses have been found in tombs, such as those found at the Metropolitan Museum (Accession Numbers 07.231.10, www.metmuseum. org/art/collection/search/544249; 99.3.4, www.metmuseum.org/art/collection/search/558274) and at the British Museum (Museum number EA2462, www. britishmuseum.org/research/collection_online/collection_object_details. aspx?objectId=119429&partId=1&searchText=Egypt+model+house&page=1). Most Egyptian houses generally consisted of one to three stories, a front entrance, a courtyard, a front room, living room(s), sleeping room(s), steps or a ladder to the upper floor(s), and a shrine, with cooking and toilet areas generally toward the back or detached from the main dwelling (Peck 2013). Dwellings of the upper class were generally larger and contained more rooms for storage, servants' quarters, toilets and bathrooms, workshops, stables, and halls for receiving and entertaining guests.

Canaanite urban dwellings developed new features while retaining some rural ones. The architectural layout of the urban house included a courtyard with attached rooms on the long side rather than the short, and a second story. Entrance into the house was through a courtyard gate in the long wall opposite the enclosed rooms and allowed access to the street. These urban dwellings are often referred to as courtyard houses. At Megiddo in Area B-B (Figure 8.4), a row of courtyard houses was found. These houses consisted of two to four ground-floor rooms with corresponding second-floor rooms. Access to the second floor appears to have been from the house's exterior in the courtyard. Similar houses were also discovered at Beth Shemesh and Tell Beit Mirsim (Ben-Dov 1992).

Throughout the ancient Near East, as people accumulated wealth, architectural design reflected socio-economic stature in the so-called patrician-style house. From the Middle and Late Bronze Ages onward, the size and architectural layout of one's dwelling was commensurate with and emphasized one's socio-economic position. Although this was true in earlier periods, it became more pronounced at this time. The basic courtyard-house style, with unroofed or partially roofed courtyard, surrounded on one or several sides by roofed enclosed living space, endured and came to characterize domestic dwellings (and nearly all building types) in the Mediterranean basin for centuries to come. However, based on function, need, and socio-economic status, slight variations on this basic style occurred. As the function of the domestic structure changed, so too did its architectural components.

These changes can be seen in patricians' houses at sites such as Tell el-'Ajjul, Tell Beit Mirsim, Ashdod, Tell Ta'anakh, Beth Shean, and Aphek. The needs of patricians, who were merchants, landowners, craftspeople, or administrative officials, and those who comprised the wealthy upper class, dictated the function and layout of their dwellings. While the courtyard remained an integral part of the home, it was not necessarily the center of activity in the same way it was for contemporaneous rural and village dwellings. The courtyard functioned more like a garden and a passageway to the rooms that surrounded it. However, the household well, roof drainage, water collection, and wastewater to the street were usually located in the courtyard.

As the needs of the upper class changed, so did their dwellings. The courtyard side rooms became service rooms, bathrooms and toilets, sleeping quarters for domestic workers, storerooms, kitchen and food processing areas, and an office or meeting space. Second stories functioned as living and sleeping quarters for the patrician and the family. In a single-story house, the owner's living rooms and bedrooms were on the ground floor as well.

Patricians' houses did not follow any particular architectural layout. These were built to accommodate the needs of the owner. However, there were some common elements. The houses were usually located near areas of administration, the marketplace, or the city gate. The layout of these dwellings typically progressed from public to private, with the public areas of the house, such as meeting rooms or offices, near the front, and the more private rooms, such as bedrooms, toward the innermost or back of the dwelling. In light of Vitruvius' later discussion regarding positioning buildings to benefit from the warmth of the sun and cool breezes, it may be that the architects of patrician homes took these environmental factors into consideration.

Courtyard palaces

In the Middle and Late Bronze Ages, courtyard palaces developed in Palestine and Syria (Figure 8.4). These were well planned and usually located near the city gate and temples, occupying a considerable amount of public space. The ratio of space between courtyard and rooms tended to be 1:1 or 2:3. In general, high quality materials were used to construct these palaces. Courtyard palaces have been discovered at Megiddo, Kabri, Aphek, Tell el-'Ajjul, Tel Sera', Shechem, and Ugarit (Oren 1992).

The primary feature of a courtyard palace is, of course, the courtyard. As with the patrician-style house, the architectural layout of palaces met the needs of the occupants, making the layout unique to each structure. Activities traditionally performed in the courtyard, such as food preparation, moved to side rooms next to the courtyard. These rooms became the kitchen, the bathroom and toilet, storage rooms, and workers' quarters. The royal family's living and sleeping quarters were located on the second story, or if there was no second floor, in rear rooms on the first floor. In some courtyards, such as at Aphek, pillar bases were discovered, suggesting use of pillars to support a partial roof. Courtyard palaces also contained a throne room, as was found at Megiddo, Stratum VII, and Area D-D. Courtyard palace walls were 2 to 4 meters thick made of dressed stone foundations with mudbrick superstructures. Some of the walls were constructed of dressed stone to a height above the foundation. Walls were thick to support a second floor and for defensive purposes (Oren 1992).

Palace layout also distinguished between public and private. Public rooms were usually located toward the front of the building with a throne room acting as a receiving room. Other public spaces possibly included storage, administrative offices, and dining rooms. Visitors to the palace and administrative officials were likely restricted to the public spaces with no access to the private portions of the palace. The layout of the palace and division of public and private spaces would have been obvious to visitors and to the inhabitants.

In Egypt, palaces were large complexes generally located within or near temple complexes. These palaces provided housing for the pharaoh and his/her family. The location of the palace within temple complexes underscored the divine nature of the pharaoh. Palace complexes included a courtyard(s), pool, chapel, garden, reception room, magazines, servants' quarters, living rooms, and bedrooms. Examples include palaces at Tell el-Amarna, Medinet Habu, and Malkata.

Temples

Temples were constructed using high quality materials (Figure 8.5) since they were considered the dwelling places of deities. Early temple structures were unassuming

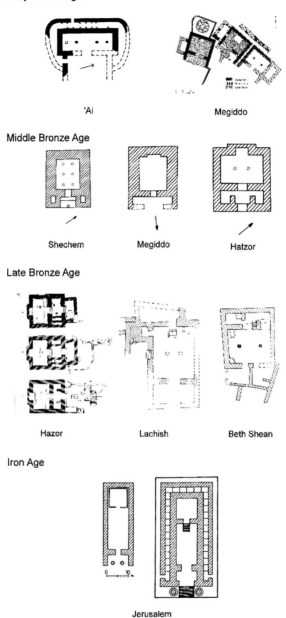

FIGURE 8.5 Select examples of temples. Early Bronze Age: 'Ai. Megiddo, Area BB, Str. XV. Middle Bronze Age: Shechem, Megiddo, and Hazor Area H. Late Bronze Age: Hazor. Lachish Stratum VI and Beth Shean Stratum VII

Adapted from Kempinski 1992d:55 ('Ai); adapted from Aharoni 1993:1007 (Megiddo); adapted from Mazar 1992:211 (Middle Bronze Age); adapted from Gonen 1992:225 (Hazor); adapted from Mazar 1992:252 (Lachish and Beth Shean).

and built as open-air structures, as at Megiddo and Gezer, or as single-room structures in the EBIV/MB I periods. In the MB II B-C periods, temple architecture developed rapidly, presumably the result of evolving cultic mythologies and practices. Thus, the form of a temple often reflected its mythology and practices, or its function.

Early single-room temples gave way to those with partitioned rooms, and eventually a tripartite layout became the dominant type. This layout generally included a porch with two pillars, an entryway, and the cella, which was the main room, presumably where cultic activities took place. As mythologies and rituals evolved, the tripartite division allowed for a porch (or porches), an entryway, an outer room, and an inner holy of holies (cella). The progression from the doorway through the outer room to the holy of holies restricted visitors' movement, with the holy of holies accessible to only the high priest and possibly select attendants.

The general public was likely restricted to the outer courtyard and the porch with the wealthy, elite classes allowed into the hall preceding the cella. By the Late Bronze Age, this tripartite division was commonplace; however, irregular temples consisting of one room with benches and raised platforms continued to be used. Anomalous, irregular type temples had an indirect access into the main hall and cella. These include Arad's Israelite Temple, Lachish Fosse Temple, and Beth Shean Str. VI.

Temples were solid structures. Their sizeable walls were very thick, some more than 2 meters wide, with solid pillars to support timber beams that may have supported a second floor. In addition to those mentioned, additional rooms surrounded the main halls and cella. These auxiliary rooms were probably used for storage of cultic objects such as statuettes and icons, as well as food and drink, and may have functioned as living quarters for temple personnel. An enclosure wall surrounded the wider compound and may have included outbuildings functioning as storage of cult objects, food, drink, and other items brought as offerings to the temple precinct.

In Egypt, there were two types of temples: cultic temples dedicated to the worship of a deity and mortuary temples dedicated to the worship of a dead king (Murray 2009a:2). The temple complexes of Egypt, such as Luxor Temple, Karnak Temple, and Medinet Habu, contained numerous buildings for processing and storing foodstuffs, and for housing priests and temple staff; the complexes also contained halls where ceremonies, festivals and rituals were conducted, and where the deity or pharaoh could be worshipped. Temple complexes also functioned as schools, dispensed rations, owned and farmed surrounding land, and contained nilometers to monitor the annual Nile flood.

Architecturally, Egyptian temples were always rectangular, subdivided into sections with the public portions at one end and private (sacred) at the opposite end. Upon entering the first pylon, one entered a large peristyle courtyard, a public space for the masses. The hypostyle hall was entered through a second pylon, a dark and mysterious room sparsely lit by high clerestory windows, giving the feeling of being in a dense forest, represented by massive columns and a high ceiling. This room was available to most worshippers. From then on, the spaces became smaller, restricted, and sacred, available only to priests and pharaohs where the sacred rituals were performed (Murray 2009a; Shafer 2005).

In Canaan, temples were considered the dwelling places of deities. They were built using the same engineering techniques and construction methods as houses and administrative buildings; however, high-quality materials were used, including large-hewn stones, core-built walls, mudbrick superstructure, and paved or lime plastered floors (Mazar 1992). With these large, extensive structures, the relationship between form and function can be observed. Cultic activities dictated the architectural layout and interior features such as walls, columns and capitals, and paved or plastered floors (Iron Age).

Fortifications

Fortification systems were one of the most important urban structures because they provided protection for the city and its inhabitants. Fortification systems have been found at Megiddo, Ashkelon, Tel Dan, Jericho, Gezer, Alalakh (Turkey), and Lachish. These defensive systems consisted of several components: city walls, towers, gate(s), and ramparts, all utilized to achieve the safety of the city and its inhabitants. Each component will be discussed individually.

Walls

Fortification walls were solid structures made of a stone foundation with mudbrick superstructure or entirely of stone. Defensive walls were usually set into a deep and stable foundation trench and were solid stone, rubble core, or casemate (Figures 8.2, top, 8.3). The hewn stone blocks were set in a header-stretcher manner for maximum stability and to support the mudbrick superstructure. In general, the stone walls were constructed using the dry masonry method. In most cases, city walls included bastions or towers, which functioned as lookouts and provided firing advantage since they protruded from the wall. Towers were well planned and occurred at regular intervals. At Gezer, for example, towers were ca. 20 to 30 meters apart. Bastions usually contained one or two rooms and steps leading to the open rooftop. For added tactics, walls were sometimes constructed in a zigzag or offsets-in-sets fashion. The upper portions of city walls and towers were usually constructed of mudbrick with a lime plaster. By using mudbrick for the uppermost portions of the city wall, architects could achieve specific defensive features and impressive architectural features for city gates. Defensive walls have survived either in part or whole at Megiddo, Lachish, Dan, and Ashkelon. Remains suggest they may have originally measured as much as 15 meters high and 2 to 5 meters thick (Kempinski 1992b).

Ramparts

Two of the most important components of the urban defensive system were the rampart or glacis (Figure 8.6). These originated in Mesopotamia and Syria and were commonly used in Canaan in the Middle and Late Bronze Ages. Ramparts and

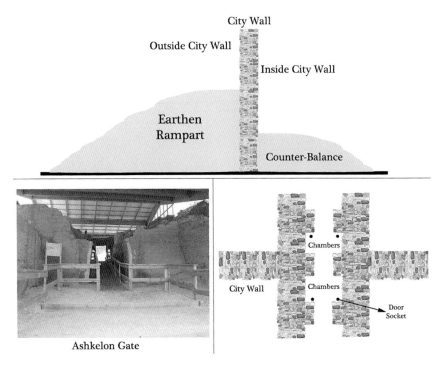

FIGURE 8.6   Illustration of a rampart and city gate. Upper: Depiction of a fictitious city wall and earthen ramparts. Lower left: The Middle Bronze Age gate at Ashkelon. Lower right: Depiction of a chamber gate with three piers and two chambers. Depictions do not represent any specific gate

Graphics and photograph by Jill L. Baker.

glacis were earthen works used in combination with city walls for added defense, creating an artificially raised city wall and extremely wide and dense base, making penetration difficult. Ramparts and glacis have been discovered at Hazor, Dan, and Ashkelon (Kempinski 1992b).

Ramparts were man-made earthen works that could stretch from 25 to 40 meters wide and 10 to 15 meters high with an angle of ca. 40°. The earthen berm abutted the exterior side of the city wall, burying the lower portions of it and creating a very steep slope leading up to the wall. In some cases, a dry mote, or fosse, was located at the foot of the rampart, adding to the immensity of the entire fortification. The earthen rampart was constructed with multiple layers of soil with strategically placed stone and/or mudbrick retaining walls to prevent the soil from shifting due to the weight and angle. The rampart surface was coated with loose stone or rubble making it difficult for invaders to climb. To keep the city wall from collapsing due to the pressure of the rampart, a counter balance had to be constructed against the interior side of the wall. A glacis was similar to a rampart; however, it made use of natural slopes as a base upon which to build the human-engineered earthen berm (Kempinski 1992b). In addition to raising the height of the city wall, these super-wide ramparts made it difficult for invaders called sappers to dig tunnels into the city. Sappers were specialized units that dug tunnels under city walls to gain access into the city (Bentley 1999:17, 51–57, 104, 114; Ancient Discoveries 2008a; Oleson 2008:685).

City gates

City gates were an essential component in the urban defense system. Most cities had one large main gate (Figure 8.6); however, depending on the size of the city, there were also smaller, secondary gates. Impressive Middle and Late Bronze Age gate complexes have been discovered at Dan and Ashkelon from the Middle Bronze II period, Lachish, Yavneh-Yam, Shechem, Hazor, and Alalakh (Turkey).

Early Bronze Age gates were relatively simple, some consisting of just two piers and doors. It was in the Middle and Late Bronze Ages that gates developed into strategic passageways. There were two types of entrances: direct and indirect. Gates with direct entrances could be barrel-shaped with an arched roof, like those from Dan and Ashkelon (Figure 8.6, lower left). The purpose of the arches was to direct the weight of a superstructure downward, away from the opening. These were used extensively in Egypt and later in Roman construction. Most gates, however, were rectangular and flanked by piers on either side of the entrance. Some piers contained rooms and some housed steps that provided access to the rooftop and walkway. The space between piers formed chambers, either four chambers or six (Figure 8.6, lower right). The piers were outfitted with doors, adding further control of who entered the city. The gate at Yavne-Yam, Tell el-Far'ah (South), Hazor, and the North Gate at Shechem were constructed in this manner. Indirect entry gates obscured one's approach to the gate. These are known as bent-access gates, which put the person entering the gate at a defensive disadvantage, leaving their vulnerable, unshielded side facing the city wall and gate upon approach. Like with city walls, gates were constructed with hewn stone, solid foundations, and thick walls. The upper portions of the city gate were constructed of mudbrick with a lime plaster. On the interior wall of the Ashkelon gate, some plaster still remains.

Woodwork in construction

Wood was used in building construction, for decoration, to make furniture, and to carve household items and tools. By the Third Dynasty, Egyptians used thin sheets of timber for laminate. Woodworkers also turned wood on a lathe and bent it into desired shapes for furniture, inlay, decorative architectural elements, and bows. Wood inlay was held together with small pegs or mitered joints. Examples of these techniques are depicted in wall paintings in the tomb of Amenemhat at Beni Hasan (BH2) from the Middle Kingdom and in laminate from the sarcophagus of Djoser at Saqqara from the Third Dynasty. Wooden furniture has been discovered at Mesopotamian sites such as Hasanlu, Period IVB (ca. ninth century BCE). These include turned stool legs, decorative furniture legs, and an iron saw blade with incised decorative features (de Schauensee 2011; Moorey 1999:347–354).

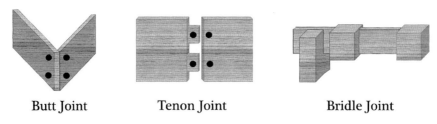

Butt Joint   Tenon Joint   Bridle Joint

FIGURE 8.7   Selected wood construction techniques

Graphic by Jill L. Baker.

Methods for crafting furniture were sophisticated and well established by the Predynastic period in Egypt. The Egyptians were particularly adept at exploiting wood's physical properties; specifically, they recognized that timber's strength is along the grain, and they cut timber accordingly, accounting for shrinkage during seasoning. Without the existence of nails as we know them in the twenty-first century, various methods were devised to hold a wooden piece together. Nails were used only for boxes and decorative objects and were made from gold or silver. They were not used for furniture or larger wooden items. Instead the Egyptians fashioned butt joints, edge joints, mortise and tenon joints, and half-lap joints, and they used dowels, dove tails, mitre, joints and scarf joints to assemble tables, chairs, beds, boxes, and beams (Figure 8.7). Veneering, inlay, varnishing, painting, and gilding were employed to make various wooden objects decorative and ornate (Gale et al. 2009:358–367). When waterproofing was needed, as in boat building, bitumen and tar were used. Joints could also be strengthened with glue.

Throughout the ancient Near East, wood was incorporated into the construction of buildings (Figure 8.8). Structurally, wood was used as beams to support upper floors, and as roofing beams and pillars. The large support beams were covered with smaller beams covered with mudbrick packing when constructing a second floor, and with tiles for roofing. The tree species most commonly used for roofing included palm, acacia, cedar, sycamore fig, oak, elm, juniper, pine, and cypress (Moorey 1999:355; Gale et al. 2009:335–352). Wooden roof beams were used in Canaan/ancient Israel (2 Samuel 5:11, 7:2,7; 1 Kings 4:33, 5:8–10, 6:9–20, 6:36, 7:2–12) and Mesopotamian kings such as Shalmaneser III, Adad-Nirari I, Assurnasipal II, Shalmaneser III, TiglathPileser III, and Sennacherib, as well as Neo-Babylonian kings listed several of the above-mentioned woods, such as pine and oak, as imports for use as roofing beams (Moorey 1999:355–356). Archaeological evidence for timber roofing beams has been found at Nimrud from Shalmaneser's Fort and has been identified by the Forest Products Research Laboratory, Princes Risborough, as *pinus halepensis var brutti*, also known as Aleppo or Calabrian pine (Moorey 1999:355).

Columns were used to support stretcher beams, and these were fashioned from various types of timber (Reich 1992:7–8). Timber was also used as reinforcement in the lower portions of buildings and walls, especially those made of mudbrick. Although most wood samples did not survive, their negative impression in the

FIGURE 8.8 Jerusalem Archaeological Park near the southern end of the Temple Mount. Note the wood used to span the door and window frames

Photograph by Jill L. Baker.

plaster and mudbrick did, as well as niches in bricks and walls that once accommodated wooden beams. Furthermore, doors, lintels, shutters, and moldings were also made of wood (Figure 8.8). Structural remnants have been discovered in Mesopotamia at the Temenos at Ur (second millennium BCE), the palace at Mari, the palace of Nabopolassar, and the doorframe at Ninmakh Temple at Babylon, where wood reinforcements were coated in bitumen. Doors, doorframes, and lintels could also be reinforced with copper or bronze sheeting (Moorey 1999:356).

Timber was also used to fuel fires. As humankind became more industrial, nearly constant fuel sources were needed. Aside from the domestic hearth, fires were used for smelting metal ore, and in baking ovens, pottery kilns, and limekilns, as well as in the glass and faience industry. The firing temperature needed to smelt copper, for example, is 1000° C; to produce glass, 1000–1700° C; to fire ceramics, between 500–1000° C; and to produce quicklime, between 850–2400° C. At the site of Timna, at Slaves' Hill, slag mounds and the workers' village have been recently excavated and studied. Research based on charcoal indicates that woods such as acacia, retama, and tamarix were used in the Bronze Age as a fuel source for smelting copper ore. In the Iron Age, acacia and retama were replaced with Haloxylon and Juniper Tree, probably due to over use of the preferred timber sources (Sapir-Hen and Ben-Yosef 2014).

Technological invention and innovation in construction

Technological invention and innovation has also been motivated by rulers' ambition and ego. The monumental building campaigns of Egyptian pharaohs, for example, specifically in the form of pyramids and temples, contributed to advancement in engineering, architectural design, and quarrying techniques. The machines and engineering techniques used by ancient peoples allowed them to build magnificent cities and structures. Their ability to think theoretically, to develop mathematics, physics, and geometry, and then apply theoretical knowledge to practical engineering resulted, in part, in the above-mentioned machines that powered their construction goals. The process behind ancient research and development was much the same as it is for us today. If a person can dream it, one can also build it. These massive structures and cities reflect the highly organized nature of the ancient Egyptian, Mesopotamian, and Canaanite societies and governments.

The process of developing mathematics, physics, and engineering principles and construction techniques and then putting them into practice can be seen in the building campaigns of the ancient Near East. An excellent example resides in the construction of Egyptian pyramids. When considering pyramids, those of the Giza Plateau generally come to mind, specifically those of Kufu (Cheops) ca. 2598–2566 BCE, Khafre (Chefren) ca. 2558–2532, and Menkaure ca. 2532–2503 BCE.

The construction of giant pyramids required much planning and development of tools and building technique. Planning included determining where to build, choosing a proper surface on which to build (sand or bedrock), surveying, clearing and leveling the land or bedrock, orientation, and determining the size and shape of the structure. Engineering included geometry, physics, and choosing building materials; determining the weight of materials and weight distribution of the overall structure; maintaining the proper angle and dimensions, and planning for interior passageways and chambers. Construction technique involved quarrying the stone blocks, building construction ramps and roads, transporting the blocks to the building site, and positioning them into place, as well as perfecting a dry masonry technique. Additionally, architects and engineers had to incorporate aesthetic as well as practical features—form and function. The form of the structure had to be commensurate with its function. For example, a residential dwelling would not have the same architectural features or requirements as a temple.

Refocusing on the pyramids, the actual construction of them involved a learning process (Figure 8.9). Examples of this can be seen in several pyramids that

FIGURE 8.9   Egyptian pyramids. Left to right: 1) Step Pyramid. 2) Meidum Pyramid. 3) Bent Pyramid. 4) Red Pyramid

predate those of the Giza Plateau. The Step Pyramid at the Saqqara necropolis is considered one of the earliest attempts at pyramid building. The architect was Imhotep (ca. 2650–2600 BCE), an architect, physician, and engineer who received divine status, which was unusual for a nobleman. The Step Pyramid was to be the burial place for Pharaoh Djoser (ca. 2679–2651 BCE) of the Third Dynasty and was constructed from ca. 2667–2648/2630–2611 BCE. It consists of six mastabas (a type of burial structure that was in use from the Predynastic to New Kingdom Eighteenth Dynasty), one set on top of the other, resembling steps. Using the steps as a base, the gaps between the steps were filled in to create the smooth sides of a four-sided pyramid. The base measures 109 x 125 meters (358 x 410 feet) and is some 62 meters (203 feet) high. Below the massive superstructure are shafts and chambers where the pharaoh would have been buried. However, the angle of the steps was too steep, and the materials used to create the smooth outer pyramidal shape collapsed, leaving heaps of rubble at the base and exposing the mastaba steps.

A second attempt at pyramid building is the Meidum Pyramid begun by Pharaoh Huni (Uni), ca. 2837–2814 BCE, in the Third Dynasty and continued by his son, Sneferu ca. 2613–2589 BCE. It is located ca. 100 kilometers south of Cairo. The architect of this structure did not follow Imhotep's schematics. It was made of two steps. The first was made of multiple mastabas, and the second was more of a true pyramid. However, here too the slope was too steep, and the outer casing stones that formed the true pyramid shape collapsed. It measures ca. 65 meters (213 feet) high today and was probably originally 93.5 meters (307 feet) in height. The base measures ca. 144 meters (472 feet) wide. The slope is ca. 51°, 50', 35".

The third attempt was more successful and established the formula for those to follow. The Bent Pyramid at the Dashur necropolis remains the third largest after those of Khufu and Khafra at Giza. Built by Sneferu in ca. 2600 BCE, it represents a transitional phase between the step pyramids and a true straight-sided, smoothed pyramid. There are stages: the base measures ca. 188 meters on each side and rises to a height of ca. 49 meters with a slope of 54°, 27'; the upper portion is ca 56 meters and has a slope of 43°, 22'. The slope of the upper portion became the standard for pyramid-building thereafter.

The first successful pyramid, a true pyramid, was built by Sneferu, ca. 2600–2576 BCE, and is known as the Red Pyramid at Dashur. This is the third pyramid built by Sneferu and was the most successful of all. It is a four-sided pyramid measuring ca. 104 meters (341 feet) in height and 220 meters (722 feet) at the base with an angle of 43°, 22'. Additionally, the burial chambers for the Meidum, Bent, and Red Pyramids are located in the superstructure and not below the pyramid.

The construction of these structures illustrates the practical application of theoretical knowledge, the process of trial and error, learning from mistakes and making adjustments based on knowledge gained, and the determination to persist until the desired goal was achieved.

Another intriguing aspect of pyramid building was the labor force, which probably consisted of noblemen, paid professional tradespeople, peasant farmers performing annual state-required labor, and possibly prisoners of war. Based on our working definition of technology, administrative organization can be considered a form of technology, and the highly organized labor force that built structures such as the pyramids, temples, and palaces was outstanding. Recent excavation of the workers' village at the Giza Plateau has provided valuable data regarding those who built the pyramids (see the AERA website at www.aeraweb.org/projects/lost-city/). This village boasted barracks that could accommodate up to 20,000 people, bakeries and cooking facilities, copper working, and other structures that housed masons, quarry-men, artisans, doctors, officials, and overseers (Handwerk 2002).

Not only was the labor force (those building the structure) impressive, but so, too, was the elaborate supportive network of those sustaining the labor force in the village. Similar workers' villages have been found at Deir el-Medina, which housed those who helped construct and decorate the tombs in the Valley of the Kings, and at Tell el-Amarna, Akhenaten's (1349–1332 BCE) capital city. Organizing the popula-tion into a workforce achieves unity, loyalty, diligent work, and a relatively peaceful existence among not only the workers but also the population. Involving the entire citizenry in state-sponsored projects creates a sense of involvement, investment, pride, and ownership. Although subtle, this too is a powerful form of technology.

Finally, the structures themselves were a form of information technology. Monumental buildings, walls, and gates boast an organized society led by a powerful entity, the king or pharaoh. In Egypt and Mesopotamia, massive reliefs and painted walls depict historical events such as battles, religious rituals, and daily lives of the upper class. In Egypt, for example, temples functioned as the news media of the ancient world. The exterior walls depicted events and achievements of a pharaoh(s), while the interior was a kind of instructional for ritual and ceremony.

There were two types of temples: cult and mortuary. Cult temples, such as Luxor and Karnak Temples, were the houses of the deities, and the deities' statues lived in the temple. A temple could be dedicated to one or several deities for the purpose of conducting festivals and ceremonies, collecting offerings, distributing rations, and the schooling of children. The temple employed much of the population and warded off chaos, providing an interconnection between the pharaoh and high priest. It also served as a medium for state propaganda.

Mortuary temples, such as Medinet Habu, were usually dedicated to one king for the purpose of conducting ceremonies during the king's lifetime, and after his death, they were used for propaganda. Just as in a domestic dwelling, there were public spaces where the masses could gather to worship the deity, participate in ritual, and perform obligations, and private spaces where only the priest, clergy, and king gathered to perform ceremonies and daily rituals. The temple interior con-tained information and instruction regarding cultic ritual, mythology, festivals, and some direction for participants. The temple's exterior walls boasted the pharaoh's achievements, victorious battles, peoples who had been conquered, captives taken, and boundaries extended. Finally, the architecture and layout of temples set the mood by making use of the size of interior and exterior space and lighting. Similarly, Mesopotamian reliefs, such as those from Sennacherib's palace at Nineveh depict-ing the siege of Lachish, function as information technology.

Architecture and artwork informed local populations and visitors about the power and success of the ruling entity; internal organization; engineering and technological advancement; evolving afterlife scenarios (tomb architecture); and evolving religious beliefs (temple architecture). These same structures and scenes continue to inform us today about the might and success of the ruling class and help us to reconstruct ancient events and interactions. Without the aid of electricity or combustion/diesel machines, television, radio, or the internet, ancient peoples engineered and constructed elaborate monumental structures that were practical, meaningful, and symbolic.

Today, monumental architecture reflects our understanding of ancient knowledge, techniques, materials, and ideals as well as the theoretical and technological development of these. For example, the White House and other structures in the Greek Revival style reflect the use of ancient construction techniques, materials, and a democratic style of governing. Modern skyscrapers such as the Empire State Building in New York, the Willis Tower in Chicago, and the Burj Khalifa in Dubai represent advanced knowledge of mathematics, physics, engineering, and building materials.

Note

1   Personal communication with R. Padilla Pulido, certified engineer and architect. I am grateful to R. Padilla Pulido for our many conversations about modern and ancient engineering and architecture.

9

WARFARE

Urbanization, social complexity, and communal living are often considered progressive accomplishments that benefit the people, but these also present greater opportunity for conflict. One of the most powerful driving forces behind technological advancement has been warfare. Other than making tools for hunting and agriculture, human invention, ingenuity, and innovation have focused on designing weapons and military-specific tools.

Throughout the Epipaleolithic period in the Near East there was little organized warfare (Hamblin 2006:16). People probably lived in relatively nomadic, kinship-based groups that established camps wherever reliable food sources were available according to the seasons. With low population density, it is likely that conflict was limited to tribal clashes over resources (Hamblin 2006:15–16). As people became more established and formed organized settlements with a surplus of food and other resources, conflict became more frequent, but it was not until the dynastic periods in Mesopotamia and Egypt, and the Neolithic period in Canaan, that rulers established armies and specialized military units.

Early signs of conflict and the evolution of organized defense and warfare can be found in the archaeological record at sites such as Jericho, Tell es-Sultan. At Neolithic period Jericho (ca. 8000 BCE), for example, a tower and city wall have been interpreted as one of the earliest defensive structures discovered thus far (Watkins 1989:16–18). The tower and city walls were ca. 13 feet thick, 10 feet high, and enclosed ca. 10 acres. They were made from stone and included a deep exterior ditch. The tower contained steps leading to the top. To some, this is a clear indication of conflict (Kenyon 1981).

The progressive rise of warfare has been discussed by others and will not be discussed here (Hamblin 2006; Watkins 1989). This chapter will focus on some of the technology employed in early warfare by reviewing the weapons, defensive gear, siege craft, fortifications, and tactics employed by ancient militaries. The evidence for these will be gathered from excavated materials, texts, and artwork such as friezes, paintings, and a battle standard.

In general, as humankind transitioned from hunting and gathering to growing their own food, their lives became more settled and sedentary. This gave rise to urban centers and organized government, including a ruler/king, government officials, regular religious practices with places of worship, and armies that engaged in military campaigns. A ruler and his administrators controlled centralized governments known as city-states. A ruler could annex multiple villages into his kingdom to possess vast territories and resources, thereby establishing a powerful city-state. Although high-ranking military officials and mercenaries comprised professional military personnel, most early armies consisted of ordinary citizens— agriculturalists, craftspeople, and merchants—who served in the military for a portion of the year. Eventually, city-states in Egypt, Mesopotamia, and Canaan were absorbed into larger nation-states, which resulted in greater organization of resources, including militaristic ones. Use of a predominantly citizen-based army lasted well into the fourth century when Philip II of Macedon and Alexander the Great shifted from a citizen-based army to a professional one that included specialized military training and standardized equipment.

The Sumerians of southern Mesopotamia formed one of the earliest armies. The Battle Standard of Ur, also known as the Royal Standard of Ur, ca. 2600 BCE, provides visual evidence for the clothing and weaponry of the Sumerian army (Figure 9.1). It was found in one of Ur's richest royal graves, Tomb PG 779, belonging to Ur-Pabilsag, who died ca. 2550 BCE. The Battle Standard is a hollow wooden box with scenes of war on one side and peace on the other. It measures ca. 21.59 centimeters wide x 49.53 centimeters long (8.50 x 19.50 inches) and is inlaid with

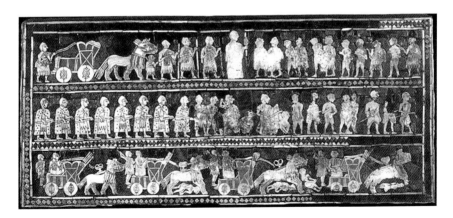

FIGURE 9.1   Royal Battle Standard of Ur. The war side depicting a defeated enemy, including warriors and horse drawn chariots

Adapted from Wikipedia.org (https://commons.wikimedia.org/wiki/File:Standard_of_Ur_-_War.jpg). By Unknown – "Royal Standard of Ur" – Mosaic With Sumer Images, Awesome Stories, Public Domain, https://commons.wikimedia.org/w/index.php?curid=458495, accessed 21 September 2017.

FIGURE 9.2   Stele of the Vultures. Victory stele of King Ennatum of Lagash, who was victorious over Umma. Depicts Sumerian phalanx

Adapted from Wikipedia.org by Unknown – Eric Gaba (User:Sting), July 2005, CC BY-SA 3.0, https://commons.wikimedia.org/w/index.php?curid=37082486, accessed 21 September 2017.

a mosaic of shell, red limestone, and lapis lazuli. The sides of the box were glued together using bitumen (Watkins 1989:18–21; Hamblin 2006; Yamauchi and Wilson 2016 vol. III:340–342).

Another example can be found on the Vulture Stele from Lagash in southern Mesopotamia (Figure 9.2). It commemorates a military victory won by King Eannatum, ca. 2500 BCE. The scenes depict a phalanx—weapons, shields, helmets, and even the unique hairstyle of the soldiers—and the king riding in his battlewagon. A further resource is the Epic of Gilgamesh, ca. 2150–2000 BCE, a text from the Third Dynasty of Ur that describes military organization (Watkins 1989:21). The Sumerian army utilized a phalanx of troops standing shoulder to shoulder protecting the line with their shields, helmets, and metal-studded capes. Weapons consisted of spears and axes with bronze heads and handles made of wood bone and ivory. Opposing phalanxes met on the battlefield, each trying to break through the other, pushing, shoving, and slashing with axe and spear. Special forces used bows and arrows, slings, and smaller spears, and operated separately but in concert with the phalanxes. This method of engagement did not change until the Hellenistic period.

Chariots

Sumerian armies may have been among the first to employ wheeled vehicles in battle, specifically chariots, sometime around 3000 BCE. These were pulled by four horses or by a team of onager-donkey hybrids (Hamblin 2006:129). They were yoked to a draft-pole and controlled with reins that ran through a rein-ring mounted on the draft-pole. The chariot was an advance from the war-cart and consisted of a platform with breastwork of basket weave, which appears to have been mounted directly over two axles at first and one axle later on. The wheels (see Figure 7.7) appear to have been made of three wooden pieces forming solid discs covered with skins (Hamblin 2006:129–153).

Each chariot was equipped with a shield, a driver, and a warrior armed with spears, the purpose of which appears to have been to break the opposing phalanx by simply running over opposing fighters. Each wagon carried two men and a large quiver filled with various types of lances, and one fighter carried a battle-axe. Judging from the depiction, the turning radius was probably quite wide, if it even turned at all. These vehicles were large, heavy, and cumbersome; hardly vehicles fit for battle. It is speculated that perhaps these were meant to carry high-ranking officers or the king to and from the battle zone (Watkins 1989; Hamblin 2006).

There is evidence for a smaller two-wheeled chariot in clay models. This chariot consisted of a "straddle-car" with one axle and two wheels and a saddle on a vertical post with a draft-pole directly over the axle. This may have been more maneuverable and better suited for battle (Watkins 1989:21). The smaller chariot was drawn by two horses, wheels were spoked rather than solid, and the carriage was smaller, which made it a much lighter and more maneuverable vehicle. Later, ca. eighth century BCE, Mesopotamian (Assyrian) war chariots were lighter, with the basket situated over the axle, a larger, eight-spoke wheel, and drawn by two horses carrying a driver, bow-man, and shield-man, as depicted in the Battle Relief in Sennacherib's Palace, Nineveh (Watkins 1989:21).

In Anatolia (modern Turkey), Hittite chariots were much lighter than Mesopotamian chariots but more fragile, sacrificing strength and weight for speed. Consequently, they tipped over when making tight turns, were splintered by arrows, and broke easily on rough terrain. The Hittite chariot consisted of a wooden axle ca. 4 feet by 4 inches, and wheels 3 feet in diameter with four spokes, or six or eight for added strength. The pole was 7 feet 10 inches long. The chariot basket was a wooden frame enclosed with leather. The axle was fastened to the basket with leather straps. The wooden wheels were secured to the axle by wood or metal lynch pins. The outer rims of the wheels were covered with metal for added strength and durability. A vertical pole was attached to the yoke with leather straps, and the yoke went over the backs of the horses, attached around their necks (Hodges 1992; Watkins 1989).

Hittite chariots could accommodate more people because the axle/wheel was in the middle of the basket, which added stability. Generally, three people rode in a chariot: the driver, who had to be from the upper class, and two warriors. Warriors stood on the left side and were outfitted in helmet, armor, breastplate, and arm protector. Weapons included bow and arrow, spear, sword, dagger, and mace. Originally, these chariots were drawn by two horses and later by four, which could be clad in armor made of chain mail or leather robes or wooden breastplates. Horses were kept lean and strong and had to accept commands. Drivers and their horses developed a close relationship. Drivers gave their horses names, and if a horse was killed, the driver wept and withdrew from battle, as exemplified in the Horses of Achilles (Hodges 1992; Watkins 1989).

It has been traditionally believed that chariots were introduced to the Egyptians by the Hyksos in the sixteenth century BCE (Booth 2005:36–37). Egyptian chariots were lightweight and made of wood, and two horses were used to pull them. There were two wooden wheels with six spokes for strength. The basket, which was open at the back and sometimes at the sides, held one warrior who drove the chariot with reins connected to the horses and strapped around his waist. Chariot scenes depict warriors or pharaohs wielding a battle-axe, shooting bows, and launching spears. Examples can be found in reliefs at the Ramesseum on the second pylon and at Medinet Habu depicting the battle with the Sea Peoples (Watkins 1989:35).

Although lightweight, the Egyptians used strong, rigid wood that did not splinter or crack, such as elm, oak, and ash. They also introduced a new yoke saddle around 1500 BCE, which more naturally fit the contours of the horses' bodies. The revised shape probably made it much more pleasant for the horses, which in turn probably made them more productive and willing to cooperate. In some scenes, such as those depicting the Medinet Habu battle with the Sea Peoples in the Nile Delta, ca. 1178 BCE, a chariot is shown with two quivers: one presumably filled with spears and the other with arrows. Numerous intact chariots were discovered in the tomb of Tutankhamun and remain on display at the Cairo Museum. (Hodges 1992:163). Although ceremonial, these provide examples of battle chariots, their construction and functionality (see Figure 7.7). The back edge of the platform and basket were perched directly over the axle and there were two wheels. Thus, the weight of the load in the chariot was positioned in front of the wheel, and supported by the pole and yoke over the shoulders of the horses, which prevented the horses from being choked. A pad was also inserted between the yoke and the backs of the horses (Hodges 1992:163). This configuration, plus the independently moving wheels, made this a highly maneuverable vehicle in battle. Warriors were probably able to make lightning-quick strikes.

The dynamic that chariots introduced into the battlefield was chaos. Charioteers drove around and through the battlefield to disrupt the phalanx and immobilize as many soldiers as possible. They probably had the effect of being an annoying but effective gnat, buzzing around the scrum. It was not until the conquest of Alexander the Great that chariots were fully integrated into the Greek arsenal. Alexander's successors incorporated the Near Eastern chariots into their armies and preferred the scythed chariot, which was used by the fourth century BCE Achaemenid Persians (Oleson 2008:681). A scythed chariot was outfitted with blades protruding horizontally from the axles and the bottom of the chariot basket (Xenophon *Cyropaedia* VI.2.17, Henderson and Miller 1914:158–159; Joshua 17.16, 18; Judges 1:19). Pulled by four or six horses and driven by one man accompanied by two warriors, the scythed chariot was driven through infantry lines, running over and through enemy soldiers in its path.

Weapons

In addition to artifactual evidence, the Battle Standard of Ur, the Vulture Stele (Figure 9.2), and reliefs and paintings depict some of the weapons used in the ancient Near East, all of which provide data essential to understanding the type of weapons utilized and the ways in which they were employed.

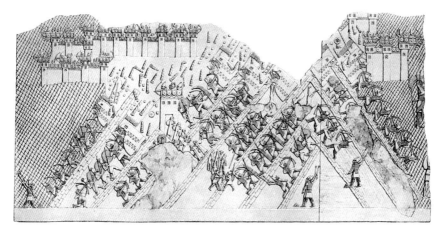

FIGURE 9.3   Siege of Lachish, by Sennacherib, King of Assyria, ca. 701 BCE. Biblical References include 2 Kings 18:14–17; 2 Chronicles 32:9; Jeremiah 34:7; Joshua 10

Illustration from Layard 1853, Plate 21 (Public Domain, PD-1923).

Nearly all soldiers seemed to carry a standard array of weapons: heavy spear, battle-axe, and dagger. The spears had heads with a long tang attached to the shaft. A hook at the end of the tang ensured it would fit snugly in the shaft. Battle-axes were produced in Mesopotamia as early as the third millennium BCE and reached a high level of manufacturing quality. The head was cast with a cylindrical hole for the wooden shaft. It was meant to pierce helmets and skulls and to inflict large slash wounds. Levantine battle-axes had a curved edge and three flanges that aided attachment to the shaft. The dagger was a small, simple but effective weapon. It was made with a bivalve mold, which allowed the metalworker to carve elaborate, intricate details on the blade. A sheath covered the blade, and was often beautifully decorated as well (Watkins 1989:23–25). Numerous of these weapons were depicted in the reliefs at Sennacherib's palace in Nineveh (Figure 9.3). However, these more formal weapons were those of the upper class: wealthy noblemen, landowners, or businessmen who could afford an array of weapons and armor. The soldiers who comprised the rank and file brought to battle whatever was available, whether farming tools or rudimentary weapons.

Bow and arrow

Some of the oldest known bows come from Denmark and date to ca. 6500 BCE (Sachers 2009). Together, the bow and arrow were probably one of the earliest human-made weapons, utilized worldwide. The bow consisted of two flexible limbs, usually made from wood joined by a riser, with the limbs connected by a string. Placing an arrow against the string and pulling backward on the string creates

FIGURE 9.4 Reliefs from Sennacherib's palace in Nineveh depicting the Siege of Lachish dating to ca. 701 BCE. Scenes depicting bowmen, slingers, and spearmen

Adapted from Layard 1853, Plate 21 (Public Domain, PD-1923).

compressive force on the belly (middle) of the limbs and places the back section under tension. When this stored energy is released, the arrow is propelled forward. The bow could be made from wood such as ash, oak, and yew.

In the Near East, the composite bow has been traditionally attributed to the "Asiatics" or Hyksos, who introduced it to the Egyptians probably in the early second millennium BCE (Booth 2005:37). The composite bow was made from a combination of wood and horns; although the exact materials varied by region based on the availability of resources. Composite bows were difficult to make, and the craftsperson had to be skilled to make an effective one. When made properly, a composite bow could deliver an arrow at a much higher velocity than a bow made from only one type of material.

Due to its strength, the composite bow could be shorter, which made it easier to store, carry, and use in battle, and could remain strung for longer periods. The shorter composite bow was perfect for shooting arrows from horseback or while riding in a chariot (Hodges 1992; Watkins 1989:28).

Bowmen comprised a significant portion of the infantry, functioning as individuals or groups (Figure 9.4, left) and were most effective at a distance of 250 to 650 meters (Wiseman 1989:45). Arrowheads were made of stone, bronze, or iron. Arrow shafts were made from wood or reed, and the tails were generally made from bird feathers. Although extremely effective on the offensive, bowmen were also vulnerable to attack since they did not carry a shield, but they may have been accompanied by a shield-bearer. Bowmen usually wore light armor and a helmet (Wiseman 1989:45). Arrows were held in a quiver that could hold up to fifty arrows at a time. The quiver was usually worn slung over the arrowman's shoulder (Yadin 1963).

Sling and shot

A simple and surprisingly effective weapon was the sling and shot (Figure 9.4, middle). This weapon consisted of two cords made of rope and/or sinew with a flexible pocket or pouch and a smoothed rock or projectile. The rock was placed into the pouch, and the loose ends of the cords were held in one hand and swung. At just the right position, the thrower released one cord, which released the projectile. The length of the sling was commensurate with distance and speed. Projectiles could be slung 1500 feet (450 meters) at a speed of approximately 250 mph (400 kph).

To a skilled thrower, this could be a remarkably accurate and deadly weapon. When the rock was released, it became kinetic energy. As it rose into the air, the kinetic energy transformed into potential energy, and as the rock descended, hitting its target, the energy transformed into kinetic energy.

The importance of slingmen in the Assyrian army has been commemorated in the reliefs from Nineveh recounting the Siege of Lachish. Sling-bullets from that battle have been recovered via archaeological excavation. Some Greek sling-bullets have been recovered dating to the fourth century BCE, inscribed with messages to the enemy such as "DEXAI," or "take that!" (thuleanperspective.com) (Yadin 1963). In the Biblical story of David and Goliath (1 Samuel 17), David is described as killing Goliath with a single well-aimed stone using a slingshot. Because Goliath, a Philistine, was a tall, muscular, well-trained soldier outfitted with scale armor of bronze, a large bronze javelin, and shield, he was the presumed victor in a duel against David. David is described as small in stature and without armor or shield, his only weapon a slingshot. The astonishing aspect of this tale is that David kills Goliath with a single shot. However, although a simple shepherd, David also served in Saul's army (1 Samuel 17:12–15) and was probably a well-trained, highly skilled slinger. So what seems an edifying tale of a victorious underdog may actually be one of intellect and skill versus brawn. Slingers continued to serve through the Roman period. Oval shaped lead shot inscribed with propaganda messages has been recovered from the site of a siege in Perugia (ca. 41–40 BCE) and at Numantia (Oleson 2008:698; Cantarella 2002:159; Bishop and Coulston 2016:58–59).

Spear or lance

Spears consisted of a long wooden pole with a large pointed head at one end made of bronze, iron, steel, flint, or obsidian (Figure 9.4, right). Spearheads were shaped like a lozenge or a leaf and were utilized very early in human history. Initially used in hunting, fishing, and combat, they were designed for thrusting or throwing. In the archaeological record, the wooden shaft generally disintegrates while the metal or stone head remains. Some of the earliest copper weapons found in Canaan come from the Nahal Mishmar hoard, which dates to the Chalcolithic period (Bar-Adon 1980). Bronze spearheads found in archaeological context date from the Early Bronze Age onward and consist of large and small tanged and socketed spearheads, some of which were hammered from a cast billet or cast from molds (Philip 2003:184–186). Spearheads from the Middle Bronze Age IIA included socketed spearheads secured to the shaft with twine (Garfinkel and Cohen 2007:105–106). Spears are depicted in reliefs and paintings, and texts describe the length and use of these weapons. A relief at Beni Hasan depicts "Asiatics" carrying a spear. One text,

1 Samuel 17:7, describes the spear of Goliath, a Philistine, as having a "shaft … like a weaver's rod, and its iron point weighted six hundred shekels." To some this describes an Aegean spear and to others a modified Canaanite weapon (Gabriel 2003:26). This does, however, reflect the variety of length and style of spear available to Canaanite and Israelite armies. The Assyrian army, for example, utilized the spear in concert with shields to form a single mobile offensive unit (see the Vulture Stele in Figure 9.2).

In the fourth century BCE, Philip II of Macedon and Alexander the Great modified the spear, developing the *sarissa* (ca. 4–5 meters long), which when used in a phalanx presented a formidable fighting unit. The infantry and cavalry used the sarissa, which "consisted of a long shaft made from cornel wood" with an iron head attached to one end with a socket (Hackett 1989:105–107). The butt end consisted of another iron head or a "conical butt-spike" (Hackett 1989:105–107).

The Romans developed the *pilum*, which measured approximately 2 meters long and included an iron shank about 55 to 60 centimeters long, making it a heavy weapon. The head was pyramidal in shape, and sometimes was barbed. When thrown it could penetrate a shield or helmet without hesitation. If it did not kill the intended target upon impact, it certainly caused significant damage to equipment and body (Bishop and Coulston 2016:52–53). With the conquest of Alexander, the Great and the later Romans, the sarissa and pilum were introduced into the ancient Near Eastern military repertoire.

Sword and daggers

Initially, swords were made from flint and obsidian and were somewhat fragile. Lithic blades were replaced by copper, bronze, and iron, which were stronger and more effective in battle; however, swords made of copper were mostly ceremonial. Hilts were made from wood, bone ivory, or bronze. This weapon was used for thrusting and striking and could measure 45 to 60 centimeters, but could be as long as 100 centimeters. Sizes varied depending on the type of battle and one's role as a soldier.

The earliest known sword comes from Turkey at Arslantepe and dates to ca. 3300 BCE. Canaanites probably initially used a sickle sword, which was replaced by a straight sword (Gabriel 2003:22). In Egypt, the *khepesh*, or sickle sword, was in use from the third millennium to ca. 1300 BCE, as well as in Mesopotamia. It was depicted on the Vulture Stele (Howard 2011:34–35; Loades 2010:1–21), and one was discovered in Tutankhamun's tomb. The *khepesh* was derived from an agriculture tool, the sickle, a curved blade used to harvest grain or cut brush or foliage, a tool that had been in use since at least the Neolithic period. Examples of straight swords have been found at Tell es-Sa'idiyeh, Jordan Tomb 102 ca. 1273–1194 (Pritchard 1980:43, Figure 5:13) and at Ugarit, where a sword inscribed with pharaoh Merneptah's name was discovered (Gabriel 2003:25).

The Romans developed the *gladius Hispaniensis*, which they adopted and adapted from Spain. This weapon could thrust and cut, which allowed a soldier to slash and stab his opponent. In general, the *gladius* was long and had double-sided blades that tapered to a point. It could be 55 to 65 centimeters in length. Another type of sword, the *spatha*, was longer and narrower than the *gladius* and used mostly by the cavalry for slashing while on horseback. This blade could measure from 62 to 91 centimeters (Oleson 2008:697; Bishop and Coulston 2016:82; Connolly 1989:153).

Smaller handheld weapons such as daggers were much like swords but shorter. These were important because they could be concealed and were easily maneuvered. These worked in concert with swords on the battlefield.

Gastraphetes, petrobolos, catapults

At the turn of the century, 399 BCE, a new arsenal of weapons was developed—the catapult. The invasion of Alexander the Great brought these mechanized weapons to the Near East. Originally designed by craftsmen hired by Dionysius of Syracuse in preparation for war with Carthage (Diodorus; Ancient Discoveries 2008b; Henderson and Oldfather 1954:128–133, 152–153), the first of these was likely the *gastraphetes*, or belly shooter, similar to a modern-day crossbow (Landels 2000:99–132; Oleson 2008:346; Humphrey et al. 2006:566). The gastraphetes was a glorified bow attached at a right angle to a stock that contained a slot for the bolt (modified arrow) propelled by the bowstring. To load it, one end of the stock rested on the ground and the other against the shooter's belly. The string, attached to the ends of the bow, was drawn up and secured by a locked notch on the stock. The bolt was placed in the slot and against the string. A trigger released the lock, which released the string, propelling the bolt forward (Oleson 2008:346–347). The advantage of this weapon, as opposed to a traditional bow and arrow, was the amount of energy stored in the bow. It shot a bolt at greater velocity over a longer distance, allowing the shooter to maintain a greater distance from the target and deliver a deadlier blow.

Based on this design, a myriad of ballistic machines were devised, including the petrobolos (stone thrower), onager catapult, and lithobolos, which were first used by Alexander the Great in the Siege of Halicarnassus in 334 BCE. Some of these also fit inside siege engines. Stone throwers, also called catapults, employed similar mechanics to the gastraphetes by ratcheting down an arm that would contain the ballistae to create tension against the torsion spring, which when released would launch the object toward its target (Landels 2000:106–107). Springs were crafted from tightly wound rope made from flax, hemp, horse, or human hair. The stone throwers could hurl rounded stones up to 180 pounds, which would shatter into smaller pieces of shrapnel upon impact. The Ptolemies of Egypt developed a research program that identified the exact formulae needed to produce task-specific uses for the machines. Not only was the throwing power of these machines impressive but the mechanics of them and the numerous working parts were as well, such as the cogs and triggers.

Ballistic machines were adopted and adapted by the Roman military. A wide array of mission-specific catapults was developed and integrated into their strategies. Most machines were made of wood; however, working parts that broke or wore out quickly were replaced with metal ones. In addition to hurling stones, catapults were used to throw fire, buckets of snakes, urine, rotting corpses, and anything else that would surprise and disperse the enemy.

Catapults remained useful in the battlefield as recently as World War I when they were used to propel grenades from trenches. In 1904, Samuel Langley and the Wright Brothers used catapults to help planes take off where space was limited. Today, aircraft carriers continue to use catapults to launch aircraft. Although the task has changed, use of this ancient technique remains the same.

Crossing water and using underwater apparatus

As the Assyrian army advanced, it encountered bodies of water such as rivers or moats that had to be crossed. Crossing water had to be done quickly and stealthily. To meet that requirement, the Assyrians made flotation and breathing devices using pigskins sewn closed and inflated (Figure 9.5, middle and right). An inflated skin could be used as a flotation device for a soldier, or multiple inflated skins could provide buoyancy for a watercraft, such as a raft. Partially sewn skins, with all sides sewn except for the end of one leg, for example, were utilized as an underwater breathing apparatus. The skin functioned as a flotation device that also provided air to an underwater swimmer. Swimmers depicted in Assyrian reliefs are often referred to as special forces soldiers who performed specific offensive tasks (Figure 9.5).

Armor

Early Sumerian armor was depicted on the Royal Battle Standard of Ur (Figure 9.1) and the Vulture Stele. Soldiers appear to wear an armored cloak, possibly made from thin leather with metal disks with raised centers or spines sewn into the cloak and leather caps or metal helmets fastened below the chin. Some have interpreted the cloaks as being leopard skins or colorful designs rather than actual armament (Hamblin 2006:49). Although it may not seem like effective protection from projectiles, this cape may have functioned like a samurai Horo, which was made of silk and prevented arrows from reaching the wearer (*History* 2008). An engraved shell plaque from Mari, ca. 2500 BCE, depicts a warrior wearing a metal helmet and holding a battle-axe and a sickle sword. From the Royal Cemetery of Ur in the Tomb of Meskalam-dug (PG 755) dating to ca. 2500 BCE, an engraved helmet was discovered. It was made from gold and depicted the wearer's hair, complete with knotted bun at the back of the head and woven band around the head. Holes at the bottom held a cloth chin strap and the interior lining. There were holes in the helmet for each ear so the wearer could hear. Scaled armor has been found at Nuzi from the house of Shilwi-Theshub dating to the fifteenth century BCE and from Egypt. Both were depicted in a tomb painting from the tomb of Kenamon during the reign of

FIGURE 9.5 Assyrian soldiers using inflated pigskins to cross bodies of water, as an underwater breathing apparatus, or to float rafts

Images adapted from Layard 1849 Plate 33, Layard 1867 Plate 43:1, Layard 1853 Plate 41 (Public Domain, PD-1923).

Amenhotep II (ca. 1436–1411 BCE) and from the palace of Amenhotep III in Thebes, ca. fourteenth century BCE (Yadin 1963:196–197).

Later Assyrian armor was made from metal and remained the same from the fourteenth century to the first millennium BCE based on reliefs from Nuzi and Nimrud (Wiseman 1989:45). Pointed helmets worn until the seventh century BCE were replaced by crested helmets. Conical helmets can be seen in Sennacherib's reliefs depicting the Siege of Lachish in 701 BCE. Cavalry and foot soldiers wore body armor that covered the torso to the waist allowing flexibility for legs and arms. The reliefs depicting the Siege of Lachish illustrate Assyrian soldiers' armor and helmets (Figures 9.3–9.4). These were commensurate to the soldier's role and rank, and indicated from where in the empire he originated. The Assyrian helmet was made of bronze or iron hammered out of a single sheet. It covered the head and was conical in shape, and some included flaps to protect the ears. The pointed shape of the helmet deflected downward the force of a spear or arrow. When battle-axes became the weapon of choice, the helmet shape changed to deflect its force.

Archers and spearmen usually wore full-scale armor, depicted in reliefs as knee-length tunics. These were made from wool or linen with the scales sewn into the fabric. Scale armor was easier to wear than solid metal armor because it allowed for full range of motion during battle. Soldiers wore a shoe with minimal leather; however, at the Siege of Lachish soldiers wore thick leather boots with shin guards. These appear to have been plates of bronze or iron sewn into the fabric above the boot lacing.

In Old and Middle Kingdom Egypt (ca. 2686–1650 BCE), soldiers rarely wore armor based on the few depictions of soldiers wearing armor. Soldiers most often were depicted as wearing a belt and triangular loincloth (Hamblin 2006:324). During the Middle Kingdom soldiers and workmen were depicted wearing the same kilt, suggesting these were civilian soldiers performing annual duty. Beginning in the New Kingdom, soldiers wore various types of body armor, probably related to their rank. The most frequently worn type was a cuirass, which protected their torso. The Egyptian cuirass was made of very thick linen that could stop the force and impact of projectiles. Full-scale armor also was worn; however, from depictions it seems that pharaohs primarily wore this type, possibly for ceremonial purposes. For example, Ramesses II was depicted as wearing full-scale armor that covered his arms and torso. He is riding in a chariot, which protected his legs. Full-scale armor was made from linen with copper or bronze scales sewn into it (Robinson 2002:1–2). A wall painting in the tomb of Qenamun (ca. 1427–1400 BCE, Theban tomb TT93) also depicts scaled armor, with a collar, that covered the entire body (Robinson 2002:1–2; Metropolitan Museum of Art, Accession number 30.4.75).

The friezes at Medinet Habu show the Sea Peoples wearing body armor. Based on these, Aegean armor covers the torso, and it appears to have been constructed of an unknown material forming a sort of horizontal or chevron pattern. Some speculate this armor may have been made from bone or ivory or may have been a smooth, one-piece breastplate (Dothan and Dothan 1992:14–18). Bronze figurines from Sardinia (ca. 800 BCE), often interpreted as depicting the "Sherdan," which were also depicted in the Medinet Habu reliefs, illustrate Aegean armor and weaponry. The body armor appears to be made of metal, and was possibly segmented for ease of movement. It may have had a linen base with metal overtop. The helmets were made from metal and included horns.

Hoplite armor of the eighth to the fourth centuries BCE consisted of a bronze cuirass made of two pieces covering the torso, a bronze helmet, some with cheek plates, and bronze greaves to protect the lower legs. As battle tactics and weaponry changed, so did armor and helmets. For example, the cheek plates of early helmets became a fixed part of the Corinthian helmet, and from the seventh/sixth century onward, the linothorax, which means "wearing a breastplate of linen," replaced the bronze cuirass (Lazenby 1989:57–59; Oleson 2008:674–678). Macedonian and Hellenistic soldiers use linothorax armor, as did Alexander the Great, according to Herodotus (*Histories* 2.182, 3.47, 7.63, Strassler and Purvis 2007; Livy, *History of Rome* 4.19.2–20.7). It was a cheaper, lighter, cooler and a more flexible choice than metal armor.

Linothorax was made from laminating multiple layers of linen together, possibly reinforced by a sheet of metal or metal mail. Seams and edges were reinforced with leather trim, and sections were held together with metal fastenings. The University of Wisconsin–Green Bay Linothorax Project has been researching the viability of this body armor. It is their belief that a linothorax 1 centimeter thick, that is eleven to eighteen layers of linen, could protect the wearer from an arrow or slashing sword (www.uwgb.edu/aldreteg/Linothorax.html).

Roman armor was probably influenced by the Celtic and Gallic invaders to northern Italy. For example, the Montefortino helmet used during the Republican period was likely derived from the Gauls. This helmet resembled a deep bowl with cheek plates hinged or riveted to the edge and a flanged neck guard at the back. Later, the Coolus helmet was introduced during the Late Republican period. This was more streamlined, resembling a shallower bowl with longer cheek pieces and ribbed neck guard. The Imperial helmet provided the best protection with longer and wider cheek pieces, a neck guard, and a fixed brow over the front of the helmet. In later periods, helmets made of solid metal became the norm rather than those made of individual pieces. Body armor included the Greek-style cuirass or a scaled linothorax, lorica squamata, lorica segmantata, or chainmail. These could cover some or all of the body, and variations were as numerous as the wearers (Oleson 2008:700–702).

Shields

A shield was an important part of a soldier's protective gear. Assyrian shields were made from wood, wicker, hides, and bronze. They came in numerous shapes and sizes depending on the soldier's battle position (Figures 9.2–9.4). Large shields covered the entire body and provided protection from archers and spear throwers. Smaller round shields were carried by spear throwers and those who wielded daggers and battle-axes. Egyptian shields were large and semi-rectangular, that is three sides were rectangular with the top side rounded, presumably for ease of vision and for throwing spears. The Sea Peoples' shields were round and probably more easily maneuverable than the Egyptians' shields. Most shields were outfitted with a handle and arm brace on the inside, the defender's side, and the exterior could have spikes or solid metal plates so that the shield could be used as an offensive weapon.

The Sea Peoples' shields resembled those of hoplites, which leads some to believe this reflects their Aegean origin. Hoplite shields were round, convex, and made of wood encased in bronze plating. There were interior arm and hand grips, and a strap to go around the soldier's neck. These could measure 0.91 meters in diameter, be 25 to 38 centimeters thick, and weigh ca. 7 kilograms. Shields were decorated with city-state, family, or clan emblems. Shields were used to protect the body and as a weapon in combat.

The Romans used shields of various sizes and shapes; however, the *scutum* was the most used and recognized. The *scutum* was large, rectangular, and curved. An example found at Dura-Europus in Syria dating to the fourth century BCE measured 1.06 meters high, curved width of 0.86 meters, and 0.5–0.6 millimeters thick. Another example comes from Kasr al-Harit in the Fayyum in Egypt, which measured 1.28 meters long and 0.635 meters wide. These shields were made from multiple layers of laminated strips of wood laid crisscross, horizontally and vertically, with the center being thicker, tapering to the edges (Bishop and Coulston 2016:61; Oleson 2008:700). This construction allowed the shield to be flexible, not rigid, and less susceptible to fracture. The wooden core was covered by leather or felt, which was stitched together with bronze or rawhide in later periods. The exterior of the shield contained a metal boss attached with iron nails. Inside the shield was a handle at the boss, and straps could be attached to rings on the internal framing (Bishop and Coulston 2016:61; Oleson 2008:700). The shield was used as individual protection and in turtle formation, *testudo*, in which soldiers formed an armored unit with their shields, as depicted on Trajan's column.

Siege craft

From the ninth century BCE onward, the siege engine, or tower, was utilized in battle (Hodges 1992:169–171, 275–277). Initially these consisted of a wagon covered in wickerwork and a domed turret for protection, mounted on four or six wheels, with a battering ram that was flat-ended with a metal tip for shattering masonry or a pair of large lances for gouging chunks from walls after being driven into cracks created by the flat ram (Figure 9.6). The upper portions of the engine allowed fighters to shoot arrows at the enemy. Meanwhile, defenders shot arrows, threw spears, and hurled buckets and arrows of fire. However, attackers were prepared and carried buckets of water. One relief in Sennacherib's Palace depicts a soldier pouring water with a ladle over the vehicle (Hackett 1989:46–49).

The siege engine with battering ram was so effective that it became a regular part of ancient warfare. There were also mobile assault towers from which archers

FIGURE 9.6   Reliefs depicting siege engines from Sennacherib's Siege of Lachish from the Palace of Nimrud. Wheeled battering ram with archers in adjacent siege tower attempting to break down the city wall

Adapted from Layard 1853 Plate 21 and Layard 1849 Plate 17 (Public Domain, PD-1923).

could engage defenders on city walls on the same level. Reliefs from several sources depict various types of battering rams and mobile towers, including Ashurnasirpal II, Nimrud Palace, ca. 883–859 BCE; Shalmaneser III ca. 858–824 BCE, relief depicting assault of the city of Dabigu, capital of Bit-Adini; Tiglath-pileser III (ca. 744–727 BCE) Nimrud Palace; Sargon (ca. 721–705 BCE) from Khorsaad; and Sennacherib's Siege of Lachish (ca. 704–681 BCE) (Yadin 1963:16–18, 313–316, 390–408, 422–425; Wiseman 1989). Based on these reliefs, siege engines appear to have been large, cumbersome, and heavy, but very effective.

Exactly how these vehicles were powered in battle remains unclear. Perhaps they were pulled by draft animals, propelled in some way by people from within, or transported in pieces and assembled near the battlefield. A cylinder seal from Nabada suggests people may have pulled the wheeled engines by ropes (Hamblin 2006:216, Figure 5:g). Additionally, ramps and pathways had to be constructed on site to get the siege engine close to city walls and gates. Ramps were built of earth and paved with brick and stone. The newly assembled ramps were wide enough to accommodate several siege engines at one time. Building siege engines and ramps likely comprised another unit of special forces whose skills and labor were devoted to these tasks (Hamblin 2006:216–221, 228–229).

Eventually siege engines became more mobile, fireproof, and elaborate. Polyidus of Thessaly, ca. 340 BCE, invented what came to be known as the *Helepolis*, or the "city-taker" (Sekunda 1989:133–134). Epimachus of Athens built such a machine. Based on Assyrian siege towers, the helepolis measured ca. 25 square meters at the bottom and tapered upward. The frame was made from squared timber held in place with iron spikes. The tower was nine stories tall with room for soldiers to stand on each floor. The first floor of this tower measured ca. 430 square meters, and the top floor ca. 90 (Sekunda 1989:133–134). To move

FIGURE 9.7 Masada. Left: Roman encampment. Right: A "room" in the casemate wall
Photographs by Jill L. Baker.

the tower, it was set onto eight wheels covered with iron plates, each wheel a meter in width. The tower was equipped with iron plates on three sides held in place by iron spikes. On the attacking side, square portholes with doors allowed artillerymen to shoot using catapults and bows and arrows. Approximately 3400 men moved the tower forward, most pushing from the rear. Shuttered windows adorned the front face of the tower, the size and shape of which was commensurate with the type of catapult and projectile that would be hurled from them. The shutters were made of hides covered with wool to absorb impact from stones. Internally, steps provided access to each floor. Some siege engines had gangplanks with grappling hooks for providing access from the tower over the wall of the besieged city (Sekunda 1989:133–134).

The armored siege engine was adapted into Roman warfare as part of their circumvallation tactics. Earthen ramps were constructed to provide vertical access to city walls for individual soldiers and for the mobile tower. Not only did towers provide vertical assault but also a bridge from tower to city wall providing easy entrance for soldiers. At Masada, the Roman army built a ramp that reached just below the casemate wall (Figure 9.7). They built an armored siege tower at the top of the ramp, which also contained a battering ram. Eventually the battering ram broke through the wall, only to find an earthen berm behind it. Nevertheless, the Romans were able to breach the wall and enter the city.

Fortifications

Canaanite city walls, towers, and gates were discussed in Chapter 8; however, it is appropriate to briefly revisit them here because their intended purpose was to provide protection for inhabitants during times of attack. During the Bronze Age, Canaanite city-states developed fortification gates, walls, ramparts, and towers, making them the main line of defense against invaders. Later, during the Iron Age, the Israelites advanced fortification systems, making them better and stronger (see Figures 8.3 and 8.6). In general, Early Bronze Age fortification systems

FIGURE 9.8   Ashkelon Middle Bronze Age gate. Left: Ashkelon ramparts rising above the sandy beach. Right: Remnant of the rampart

Photograph by E. Christensen (left); photograph by Jill L. Baker (right).

consisted of a relatively simple gate with two piers, an entryway, and a thick wall surrounding the city, some with towers. During the Middle Bronze Age, fortification technology improved. Walls continued to be constructed with a fieldstone foundation and mudbrick superstructure; however, walls could take on different shapes. Some were in the form of offset-inset style, which added strength as well as defensibility. Gate technology improved as well. In addition to continuing direct access from the Early Bronze Age, some gates incorporated a bent access and/or additional chambers. Megiddo employed offset-inset style city walls during this period. In addition to the walls and gates, the Canaanites also employed ramparts (see Figures 8.6 and 9.8).

In the Iron Age, fortification walls were strengthened by casemate walls and multi-chambered gates (see Figure 8.3). Casemate walls were large stone walls that looked much like a ladder. The empty spaces of the casemate wall were used as shops, storage rooms, or living quarters during peaceful times; however, during times of conflict these spaces were filled with rock and rubble, creating a very thick and solid wall. Some were as thick as 7 meters. Casemate walls have been found at Hazor, Khirbet Qeiyafa, and Masada. Gates continued to be direct or bent access with two to six chambers.

Battle tactics

Although battle tactics are not a machine or device, they can be considered a technology because they are a practical application of knowledge to solve a problem, achieve a goal, and to facilitate change. A tactic can be defined as "a device for accomplishing an end" or "a method of employing forces in combat" (see www. merriam-webster.com/dictionary/tactic). Battle tactics organize personnel, weapons, and specialized units to creatively and successfully engage an enemy in battle, taking into account geography and terrain, and consider how to use all of these factors advantageously (Clausewitz 1832). The strategic and organizational nature of tactics functions as a type of technology that achieves goals in an attempt to accomplish progress.

Initially, battle tactics were crude and simple. Troops fought in a phalanx (Figure 9.2), whereby fighters stood together in a tight formation, each armed with spears, daggers, battle-axes, and shields. This formation was rectangular in shape, and the soldiers moved as one body, each soldier standing shoulder to shoulder, protecting the line with their shields, bodies, helmets, and armor. Members of the phalanx used spears and axes. The phalanx consisted of several rows of soldiers each extending spears forward. This formed a massive wall of shields and spears with which to strike the opponent. When opposing phalanxes met, they broke through the enemy's formation by pushing, shoving, and slashing with spear and axe. The phalanx advanced first at a walking pace, probably increasing to a run as they approached the opposing side. The main objectives of the phalanx were to break apart the enemy phalanx and to eradicate its troops. Using this tactic, the Sumerians dominated Mesopotamia, and soon these tactics were adopted by neighboring peoples, making the phalanx a standard battle formation until the invasion of Alexander the Great in the fourth century BCE. Although the phalanx formed a tight unified formation, the special forces units moved in smaller groups and strategically orbited the phalanx. While the focus was on the main attacking unit, the phalanx, slingers and bowmen, and eventually cavalry and charioteers provided cleverly placed auxiliary firepower and protection. These smaller units stealthily orbited the embattled phalanxes, eliminating fighters one by one.

Orchestrating a battle plan, successfully controlling multiple moving parts, and outwitting the enemy was an impressive feat. Geography and terrain were additional factors to consider. Mountainous regions, deserts, and bodies of water influenced and challenged the movement of troops and equipment as well as battle tactics. The rocky, sandy terrain of the Near East was not conducive to wheeled vehicles such as carts and chariots to carry supplies and engage in battle. The route taken by an invading army was crucial to retain an element of surprise and control. In the campaign of Pepi I (ca. 2350 BCE), in an effort to control northern Canaan, troops were sent by land along the Via Maris and by sea to Acco and the Mt. Carmel region. This provided a sort of pincer attack from north and south resulting in a successful campaign (Aharoni and Avi-Yonah 1977:25). In Thutmose III's Battle of Megiddo, strategic decisions led to the Canaanites' defeat. Approaching from the south, the Egyptians could take three possible routes: northern, middle, and southern. At Yaham, on the Sharon Plain, Thutmose and his officers considered the alternatives. Meanwhile, the Canaanites divided their troops and abandoned Megiddo's vertical advantage by placing troops at strategic points along the northern and southern routes, dismissing the middle route because the pass was too narrow and vulnerable. By choosing the middle passage, Thutmose gained strategic advantage and defeated the Canaanites (Aharoni and Avi-Yonah 1977:32–33; Watkins 1989:29–32).

Early Greek armies, comprised of hoplite soldiers, utilized the tight formation of a phalanx of eight, twelve, or sixteen rows of troops or more. Hoplite soldiers were citizen-soldiers from the Greek city-states. Hoplite means heavily armed soldier and refers to the equipment they carried: spear, shield, and armor, also referred to as the hoplite panoply (Oleson 2008:674–675; Humphrey et al. 2006:543–545). Primarily the landed gentry could afford the equipment and customized shield decorations of designated city-state, family, or clan emblems. Opposing phalanxes met with spears down, ready to impale, engaging collectively and individually in hand-to-hand combat (Lazenby 1989:58). The *othismos*, "the shoving," was the initial clash of spears and shields and ongoing pushing and shoving until one side was overcome and defeated (Lazenby 1989:58). During the Persian Wars, the phalanx remained in use; however, troops were divided into smaller units. This provided strategic advantage as the Persian phalanx attempted to break up the Greeks, which provided a path for the smaller units to circle around and envelop Persian troops, as exemplified with the battle at Marathon in 490 BCE.

Philip II of Macedon (ca. 382–336 BCE) revolutionized the Greek military, which influenced military organization and tactics for centuries to come. One of his most important innovations was creating a professional standing military. Until that time, most soldiers, other than officers, were citizens conscripted into service as needed. When not performing military duty, the rank and file soldiers were agriculturalists, craftspeople, and merchants. Only the noble class and officers could afford to purchase equipment, weapons, shields, and armor. Philip II made military service a paid profession, which meant that because soldiers were paid a regular salary throughout the year, they did not need to engage in another profession to make a living. Now, any citizen could become a soldier with the only prerequisite being citizenship, not necessarily social class. Philip also outfitted each soldier with standardized equipment. Each received a *sarissa*, a long spear ca. 4–5 meters long, a shield, and armor. By providing standardized equipment, each soldier contributed equally to the unit, which created unity. By creating a standing professional army, each could devote attention to training and tactics full time. The ability to achieve this was due in part to the invention of coinage to compensate soldiers rather than paying them with foodstuffs.

Philip modified the phalanx formation into multiple units with ten or more rows of soldiers placed close together. The first three or four rows held sarissas down and the rear rows held spears up, ready to lower once the first rows had engaged. Auxiliary units, foot companions, peltists, slingers, and archers provided support to the phalanx, as did the companion cavalry, an elite fighting unit. Philip's phalanx units had freedom of movement to maneuver around their opponent's inflexible mass. This flexibility resulted in great success for Philip and for his son, Alexander the Great, who adopted and adapted these tactics, allowing him to conquer much of the Near East. Alexander's units were small, flexible, and highly mobile, and included infantry, cavalry, and special forces. Their tactics and lightning-fast assaults were unequaled.

10
TEXTILES

Among the basic needs of humankind is clothing. Textiles and the textile industry are often overlooked aspects of ancient technology, yet the textile industry held a prominent role in the economy and daily life of all peoples. Textiles were marketed as raw materials and finished goods. The procurement, refinement, and production of textiles required specialized skill and labor. Textiles were utilitarian, artistic, and symbolic. They could be fashioned into prized possessions, and were given as gifts. Textiles were used for clothing, blankets, bedding, shelter, flooring, bags, nets, and as decoration. They have facilitated human activity, stimulated the economy, and communicated cultural traditions and values. The form and function of textiles addressed basic human needs and festooned the immediate environment by being functional and pleasing to the eye and soul. Early evidence for the manipulation of wild flax, twisted and dyed, appears in the Dzudzuana cave, Georgia, dated to ca. 36,000 BCE. References to skins versus clothing throughout The Epic of Gilgamesh implies that wearing woven cloth was the mark of a civilized nature, whereas the wearing of skins reflected one's wilder nature (Gilgamesh; Speiser 1969). The same need for textiles exists today as in antiquity, as clothing, furnishing, and ornamentation. Therefore, textiles remain an essential component of modern life and culture. This chapter will discuss the textile industry in the ancient Near East: its importance, the materials, weaving, market, and the role of women in the industry.

The materials from which textiles are made are perishable; however, fragments of textiles, and in some cases entire garments, have been recovered from the archaeological record. In addition to the textiles themselves, knowledge of materials, the textile industry, clothing styles, tapestries, and the like were recorded in texts, and artwork such as figurines, reliefs, sculpture, paintings, and coins. Clothing styles and fabric quality could also carry symbolic meaning. Clothing styles depicted in Mesopotamian artwork, for example, such as friezes and cylinder seals, illustrate garments worn by the elite members of society. These garments ranged from a simple short skirt to a full long skirt or toga. The range in style may be age-specific, representing the rites of passage from birth to old age, or it may reflect status within society, or both (Breniquet 2013:12–13). Egyptian clothing styles were also depicted in their artwork and represented status within society and the life cycle, and prized textiles were given as royal or state gifts, as wedding gifts, or could be used as currency. It is clear from these data that the textile industry was inextricably interwoven into the fabric of the ancient economy. That phrase alone illustrates the importance of the textile industry in daily society, culture, and economy.

In the ancient Near East, specifically Mesopotamia, the textile industry appears to have been managed predominantly by women. Women prepared the raw materials for weaving, conducted the actual weaving, and managed the weaving employees. Young girls and boys were taught to spin and weave, and women from within the village and neighboring villages worked in household-based weaving businesses. Clan-specific, culture-specific, and region-specific patterns were developed. Patterns, color, and quality of material also indicated socio-economic status. The men were responsible for providing the raw materials, wool, cotton, flax, and hemp, by shearing and cleaning the wool, and growing, harvesting, cutting, and drying the vegetable fibers, and picking the cotton. Men also transported and sold the finished goods. Some insight into this ancient industry can be gained through letters written by women at *kārum Kanesh,* modern Kültepe in east-central Anatolia (Turkey), regarding their textile businesses (Thomason 2013:93). As this was the commercial quarter of Kanesh, most households kept archives. Some 23,000 tablets have been recovered thus far, a portion of which have been translated. These tablets contain letters between traders and merchants, family members, and business owners, and discuss subjects such as legal statutes, treaties, and contracts. They also contain inventories, caravan details, official administrative decrees, and calendars (Thomason 2013).

These tablets provide a wealth of information and an intimate glimpse regarding ancient business practices and daily commercial activities. The tablets also reveal numerous people of Mesopotamian origin living in Anatolia and vice versa as goods were traded between the two regions. It is assumed that the practices discussed in these Anatolian tablets also reflect practices common in Mesopotamia. Based on the tablets, it is clear that finished goods were more valuable than raw materials and were produced in Mesopotamia and sold along a caravan route that spanned from Ashur to Kanesh and other trading posts along the route. Finished goods predominantly included wool and linen cloth (Thomason 2013).

It is also clear from these tablets that women were self-employed or employed under the umbrella of their family firms, and their goods were exported from Assyria to Anatolia by relatives, such as sons or husbands, or by business partners. The businesswomen acquired the raw wool usually in Ashur or Babylonia, spun and wove the wool into cloth, pieced together fragments to make larger items, employed other women from outside the clan, or used slaves to produce cloth. They completed the fulling process, dyed the fabric, contracted with caravans to transport the cloth, and contracted with buyers. All of this indicates that women could read, write, and send and receive letters; produce, buy, and sell their own products;

understood and managed taxes, tariffs, and judicial procedures; managed other traders and associates; hired and fired employees; managed currency, property, and merchandise; and were productive and active members in family households and firms as textile producers and as merchants (Thomason 2013). That the textile industry was under women's direction, and remained so into the Roman period is evidenced by Lucretius' description of the way in which textiles came under their direction, and why (*On the Nature of Things* 5.1350–1360; Humphrey et al. 2006:347). In the New Testament, Lydia of Thyatira, known as "the Seller of Purple," was a textile merchant, specifically a dealer of purple cloth (Acts 16:14–15). It is also probable that textile guilds regulated the industry and provided professional dialogue and advancement for its members.

It is not known exactly when people began making cloth and wearing clothing. Presumably, the reason for wearing clothing was for protection from cold and heat, the elements (rain, snow), and from the wild environment (forest, rocks, sand). Presumably leather, from animal skins, was one of the earliest materials used for clothing, footwear, containers, equipment, tents, saddles, and the like (Humphrey et al. 2006:367–371; Oleson 2008:483–495). Leather was versatile, durable, functional, and was usually stronger than textiles; basically, it was "antiquity's plastic" (Oleson 2008:483). Animal skin could be worn with or without hair/fur. It had to be dried, or cured, with smoke, fat, or by soaking it in a mineral bath or by tanning it with vegetable extracts or tannins. In Mesopotamia, sesame oil was the standard dressing and skins were treated with sesame oil and stretched to produce a soft light-colored leather.

The ancient tanning industry was massive, and leather-producing techniques have changed very little to this day. Large vats were used to bathe the leather in the liquor, water vats were used for rinsing, and drying rooms allowed the liquor to evaporate. A vivid example of the use of leather is Ötzi, ca. 3359–3105 BCE, from the European Chalcolithic period (www.iceman.it/en). Although numerous other materials were available, leather remained an integral part of humankind's wardrobe and was used for daily items such as clothing, bags, shoes, boots, and containers throughout the Roman period. Based on sewing needles found from Solutrean culture in France, people were wearing clothing at least as early as 19,000 to 15,000 BCE. Textiles were also found at other sites such as at Neolithic Çatal Hüyük in Anatolia (Turkey), flax from ca. 5000 BCE, and at Egypt and Nahal Hemar in the Judean Desert ca. seventh millennium BCE based on radiocarbon dating. Domestication of flax appears to have been around 5000 BCE in Egypt, Syria, Iraq, and Turkey. It also appears that flax was dyed during this early period as well (Barber 1991:10–18). The materials that were most used for textiles were wool, flax, hemp, cotton, and silk. A tannery was also discovered at Masada.

Basketry

Basketry is a broad term that can refer to baskets, matting, netting, rope, boxes, storage bins, coffins, pit liners, sandals, brushes, and furniture, and can be considered a textile. Innumerable paintings and reliefs depict baskets holding foodstuffs, commodities, or used for storage, or even as boats. Some of the earliest evidence for basketry comes from Çayönü and Çatal Hüyük in modern Turkey, Nahal Hemar Cave, and Egypt, dating to the Neolithic Period (Wendrich 2009; Potts 2012:337; Wendrich and Ryan 2012). Although labor-intensive and time-consuming, basketry did not require sophisticated technology in the same way ceramics or metallurgy did. The tools needed for basket making were blades (Peck 2013:148), needles or awls to make holes, and a loom, if the baskets were woven (Wendrich 2009:261). The weaving process may have included a horizontal loom; however, the main weaving was accomplished by hand.

The materials used to create basketry include, but are not limited to, reeds, palm fibers from numerous palm species, sedges, rushes, and grasses (Wendrich 2009: 254–255; Lucas and Harris 2011:128). In Egypt, the date palm and doum palm were the most commonly used material for baskets. Their large feather and fan-shaped fronds and side leaves were the useful parts of the tree. In later periods, the fibrous leaf-sheaths of the date palm tree were used to make rope and matting (Wendrich 2009:255). Grasses, such as halfa grass, were used for basketry as well as matting and ropes (Lucas and Harris: 2011:130; Wendrich and Ryan 2012).

One of the earliest and most common basketry techniques was coiling. Coiled baskets were common to nearly "all emerging societies" (Peck 2013:148) and remain one of the most common techniques today. This technique starts with a wad of material, such as palm frond or grass, which is twisted and bound by another frond, leaf, or grass. The coils could be fashioned into a deep basket by winding the coil upward and securing each layer with a cord or into an open form or even into sandals, which kept the coils flat (Peck 2013:148; Wendrich 2009:256). Other techniques include weaving, which usually involves a loom, in which several strands of grass, palm leaf, or fiber are interwoven between cords; twining, wherein multiple wads are fixed together with cord; plaiting, in which fronds or leaves are interwoven; looping, a kind of netting, wherein cord is looped around wads; piercing, in which sticks are pushed through pre-punched holes in stems, wads, or fronds; and binding, wherein a cord is passed through a hole to bind sticks or wads together (Wendrich 2009:256; Peck 2013:148–149). Matting was used in burials as bedding, such as in the Naqada Period burials, and to make boxes or containers. Furniture was also made from these materials, much like modern rush furniture.

Wool

Wool was a byproduct of sheep, though it was less important than their meat, milk, and milk byproducts. Sheep's wool is relatively waterproof, warm in the winter, and cool in the summer, a temperate and durable material for any time of the year and for multiple climate zones. Once domesticated, sheep were selectively bred not only for their meat but also for the color and quality of wool they produced. Fine woolen sheep were protected with a jacket of skin to protect their wool from dirt and damage (Varro *On Agriculture* 2.2.18, Henderson and Hooper 1935:342–343;

Humphrey et al. 2006:353). Selective breeding was employed by the Egyptians, Canaanites, Greeks, and most ancient cultures to produce the finest sheep. Fiber diameters suggest fleece types that included a hairy, medium-weight wool, a generalized medium, and medium-fine, semi-fine, and true-fine wool types. The dominant gene color for sheep is white; however, there were color variations that included yellows, reds, and grays, which were used for making patterns. Wool could also be dyed (Thomason 2013).

Originally, wool was plucked during molting; however, once iron shears were invented, these were used to acquire wool. Plucking the wool, however, extracted the finest wool and left the coarser behind. Recently, an Iron Age woolen tunic was discovered in Breheimen National Park on the Lendbreen glacier, along with shoes, tent pegs, hunting tools, and horse dung, all preserved by the glacier. The tunic was made of overhair and underwool. Old Norwegian sheep had two layers of hair: an outer layer, called overhair, which is long and stiff and virtually water repellent, and the inner layer, called underwool, which is soft and fine and similar to wool on modern sheep. Each type of wool was used for different purposes or combined. Garments and textiles made from overhair were more durable and water resistant. The Lendbreen tunic was constructed with inner-layer fine wool. To obtain each type of wool for yarn, the finer inner layer had to be separated from the coarser outer layer, a painstaking and time-consuming task (http://phys.org/news/2014-11-recreating-iron-age.html).

In Egypt, rock art depicting the wild Barbary sheep in Southern Egypt and lower Nubia suggest the use of this wool as early as the Neolithic or Predynastic period. Two types of domestic sheep have been depicted in Pharaonic tomb paintings: *Ovis longipes Palaeoaegyptiacus*, with a long, spiraling horn, which likely produced coarse wool, and the *Ovsplatyura aegyptiaca*, whose horns grew downward and curled forward close to the head, and whose wool was shorter and less coarse (Vogelsang-Eastwood 2000:268). Woolen textiles were utilized in Egypt from the Predynastic and Early Dynastic periods onward and fragments have been found at Naqada, Helwan, Kahun, and the Workmen's Village at Amarna (Vogelsang-Eastwood 2000:269).

Once shorn and before dyeing, the fleece was washed to remove any suint (dried perspiration), excess lanolin, and dirt. Soap was made from fats and oils from animals and plants mixed with alkali and used to wash the wool (Pliny the Elder *Historia Naturalis*; Ebers Papyrus; Levey 1958; Firth 2013:142–143). Once prepared the wool was ready for dying. At Dura-Europos (Syria) records of sold wool indicate that some had not been degreased, and other wool had been washed, sorted, and sold by weight. Washing the wool decreased the weight by ca. 30 percent. The wool was then combined to align fibers for spinning and to separate short from long fibers.

Combing was a low-status task, but a necessary one. Combs were flat, rectangular, and made of wood or iron, and had iron teeth that were cut or welded on the ends. They were hand-held or mounted on a wall. Once combed, the wool was spun into yarn, which was then ready for weaving. Goat hair was also collected and processed for weaving; however, it was of minor commercial value and was used mainly for sacks and tents because it was coarse and tough.

Flax

Vegetable fibers, such as flax, have been utilized as textiles since at least 12,000 BCE. Artifactual evidence has been found at Natufian period sites in present-day Israel and in Egypt as early as 5000 BCE (Janssen 1995:383). Flax, *linum usitatissium*, is a hardy annual herb that grows best in well-watered fertile soil, such as the soil found in Egypt and the Peloponnese. Although linum was grown in Egypt, it was not native and was probably brought to Egypt from the Levant (Vogelsang-Eastwood 2000:269). It is thought that two types of flax were grown in Predynastic Egypt: *Linum angustifolium* and *Linum usitatissimum*. Each grows to about 1 meter high and produces flowers (Vogelsang-Eastwood 2000:269–270). *Linum Usitatissimum* was used most commonly, and was depicted in Egyptian artwork and paintings. Linen is made from the bast fiber, or flax.

Growing, harvesting and preparing the linum plant for use as a textile was labor intensive. This activity generally involved entire families, usually of the lower classes. Proper timing of planting and harvesting was essential, especially harvesting because that determined the quality of the fibers. Once planted, usually mid-November, linum took about three months to be mature enough to harvest. To obtain fine fiber, plants had to be harvested when young and green. If harvested later, the older fiber was used for rope and coarse cloth (Vogelsang-Eastwood 2000:270). All of this was done so the bast fibers of the flax plant could be separated from the woody core and bark.

In Egypt, the entire linum plant was pulled from the ground, rather than cut, to obtain as much of the plant as possible. The stalks were dried, seeds collected for replanting, and the pericyclic fibers were bundled. After drying, the fiber bundle was prepared for spinning. This process included retting, cleaning or "scutching," and twisting the flax filaments into initial slivers or roves (Vogelsang-Eastwood 2000:271). Vogelsang-Eastwood (2000:270–274) discusses this laborious and complex process in detail, which will not be repeated here. This process is depicted in the tombs of Urana at Sheikh Said (Tomb 25, De Garis Davies 1901:19, 21–22, Pl. XVI) and Paheri at Elkab (EK3, Tylor and Griffith 1894 Pl. III) from the Middle and New Kingdoms, respectively. From these depictions, it appears that men and women participated in the harvesting and processing of flax.

The Egyptians employed two techniques for making flax into thread: spinning and splicing. Spinning produced long twisted thread that could measure from ca. 1 centimeter to more than 2 meters. Various techniques were developed that were not unique to the Egyptians and included the use of spindle and whorl, or an upright arm with weight (Vogelsang-Eastwood 2000:272–273).

Once dried, stalks were retted, which diminished bacterial activity stimulated by moisture to loosen the fibers. Retting was done in ponds or in tanks or by exposure in fields. Stalks were then dried and broken with a wooden mallet and scutched with a wooden blade to remove bark and core. Fiber bundles were combined to remove residual cellulosic matter called tow and to isolate individual fibers. From the tow were made cord, rope, and sacs.

In Egypt, linen was the most used material for textiles, so much so that ancient authors such as Herodotus (*Histories* II.81, Strassler and Purvis 2007:151) erroneously claimed that the Egyptians did not use wool or that it was a religious prohibition to use wool in favor of flax (Vogelsang-Eastwood 2000:269). Based on archaeological discoveries it is now known that this was a misunderstanding on the part of the ancient author; however, given the climate, it is not surprising that linen was favored over wool.

Hemp

Hemp, Latin *cannabis sativa*, also contains a bast fiber, but it is tougher and coarser than flax. Hemp was used for cordage, netting, and sailcloth. This plant was harvested and processed in a manner similar to flax (Hamilton and Milgram 2007).

Cotton

Pliny described cotton trees as "wool bearing trees" (*Natural History* 12.38–39, Henderson and Rackham 1968:26–29). Cotton was grown in India and the Persian Gulf. It was plucked from the pod, combed, and spun into yarn. It was often combined with flax and called "fustian," named after a suburb of Cairo known as Fostat (Humphrey et al. 2006:349–350).

Silk

According to legend, silk was developed in China by Lady Hsi-Ling-Shih, wife of the Yellow Emperor (mythical), who supposedly ruled China in ca. 3000 BCE. She is also referred to as the Goddess of Silk. Lady Hsi-Ling-Shih is said to have cultivated silkworms and invented the loom. In Qianshanyang in Zhejiang Province, China, woven fragments, threads, and ribbons were found that date to ca. 3000 BCE. In 1927, near the Yellow River in Sanzi Province in northern China, part of a silkworm cocoon was discovered that dates to ca. 2600–2300 BCE. The production of silk came from a single species, the Bombyx mori, which probably came from the Bombyx mandarina Moore, which lives on the white mulberry tree in China. Although there are other species that produce silk, the Bombyx mori was favored due to its exquisite filament, which is rounder, smoother, and finer than others (www.silk-road.com/artl/silkhistory.shtml). Silk production, or sericulture, was time consuming and required patience. Cultivating the worms included controlling their diet and not allowing the moth to hatch. Once hatched, baby worms feed twenty-four hours a day on prepared mulberry leaves until they attain the optimal size. The worms must be kept in specific conditions including a temperature between 65 to 77° F, and in an environment devoid of loud noises, drafts, or unpleasant odors. Once ready, the worms construct a cocoon from "a jelly-like substance in their silk glands, which hardens when it comes into contact with air" (www. silk-road.com/artl/silkhistory.shtml). It takes three or four days for the cocoon to be constructed, and after eight or nine days, when the cocoon dries, it can be unwound. To obtain the silk, the cocoon is steamed or baked to kill the worm, dipped into hot water to loosen the filaments then unwound from the cocoon onto a spool. Each cocoon can contain 600–900 meters of filament (www.silk-road.com/artl/silkhistory.shtml).

Silk became a valuable and desirable commodity in China and much of the ancient world. One of the earliest examples of silk trade outside of China comes from Egypt, at Deir el Medina, near Thebes and the Valley of the Kings, where a female mummy that dates to ca. 1070 BCE was adorned with silk (www.silk-road.com/artl/silkhistory.shtml). During the Achaemenid Empire (ca. 500–330 BCE), the Persian Royal Road extended from Susa in northern Persia to the Mediterranean Sea in Turkey, on which raw and finished goods were transported as well as messages and letters. After the invasion of Alexander the Great, the soldiers who stayed behind, and the Graeco-Bactrian king Euthydemus I (ca. 260–195 BCE) extended their control as far as the empire of Seres, as China was known to the Greeks and Romans. Seres means "the land from where silk comes" (www.ancient.eu/Silk_Road/). Silk quickly became increasingly popular and was considered exotic and associated with licentiousness by conservative Romans in the first century BCE through the early first century CE (www.ancient.eu/Silk_Road/).

According to Aristotle, silk was first produced in the Mediterranean by Pamphile of Cos, an island in the Aegean (*History of Animals* 5.19 (551b), Henderson and Peck 1970:176–177). Silk was made into cloth to create clothing for men and women, and to make rugs. Aristotle describes the process by which a carefully selected worm produced cocoons from which the silk was unraveled and turned into thread (McLaughlin 2016:6–8).

Spinning

Although already mentioned, yarn spinning was taught to young girls and prepubescent boys, and was an important social and economic task performed by women. The quantity of yarn spun and the way in which it was spun determined the quality of the fabric produced. Without this important task, nothing could be produced. Yarn spinning was done with a distaff, which held the bundled raw fibers from which a strand was drawn, and a spindle—a short rod, usually made of wood, with a hook where the strand from the distaff attached then threaded down to a tapered shaft below the whorl, which was located at one end of the spindle to serve as a weight (Figure 10.1). Spindle whorls have been found all over the ancient and modern world. Whorls were usually made from stone, ceramic, bone, or wood and could be elaborately decorated or simply left plain. Twisting and rotating the yarn into an exact pattern was clan-specific, region-specific, and culture-specific (Oleson 2008:469–470; Humphrey et al. 2006:363–364; Lassen 2013). Yarns could be spun very thin and fine or wide and coarse, depending on the type of cloth desired.

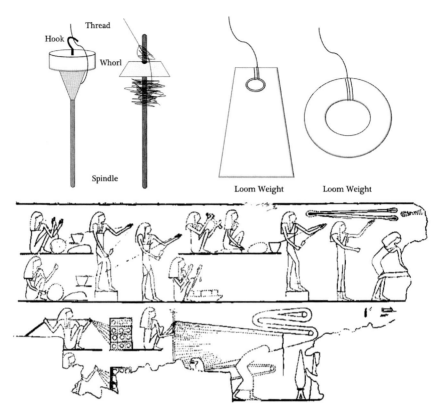

FIGURE 10.1 Recreation of spindles and whorls and loom weights and Egyptian spinning scene. Top: Spindles and whorls (left) and loom weights (right). Bottom: Spinning raw material into yarn from the tomb of Djeutihotep

Graphic by Jill L. Baker (top); adapted from Newberry 1895, Plate 26 (Public Domain, PD-1923) (bottom).

Looms and weaving

The use of looms for weaving textiles appears to have developed during the Neolithic period, ca. 8500–4300 BCE, beginning in Anatolia and spreading to the Levant, Egypt, and then westward, and was an evolution from the hand loom, which had been in use for some time prior (Friend 1998:1). The basic technology and technique for weaving has remained the same ever since. Basically, weaving relies on tension applied to one set of parallel fibers, known as the warp, into which another set of fibers, the weft, is interwoven (Friend 1998:1–2). Early depictions of looms come from Mesopotamia, ca. 3500 BCE, from a seal (Hodges 1992:112) and from paintings in the Middle Kingdom tomb of Khnumhotep II, Beni Hasan (BH3). In each scene, the loom and the operation of it look very similar. These were horizontal or ground looms with two pair of pegs/stakes pounded into the ground supporting two beams, between which the length of the warp was stretched (Figure 10.2, top).

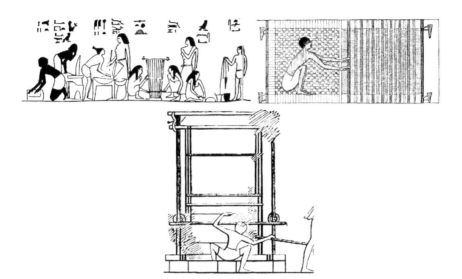

FIGURE 10.2   Depictions of horizontal and vertical looms from ancient Egypt. Top left: Horizontal loom from the tomb of Khnumhotep at Beni Hasan (BH3). Top right: Horizontal loom from Beni Hasan. Bottom: Vertical loom

Adapted from Newberry 1893a, Plate XXIX (top left); adapted from Wilkinson 1878:134, Figure 353 (top right); adapted from Wilkinson 1878:135, Figure 354. Images Public Domain (PD-1923) (bottom).

A shuttle carried the weft through the warp and rods, called a Laze rod or heddle rod, which separated the warp threads and tightened each row after the shuttle passed through. Sometimes two "jacks" were used to support the heddle rod. Other rods called "sword-beaters" and wooden combs were used to beat in the weft once the shuttle and thread had passed through (Vogelsang-Eastwood 2000:276–277; Friend 1998:2–4; Barber 1991:83–91).

Another type of loom, the vertical or fixed two-beam loom or warp-weighted loom, developed from the earlier one, and the two may have been used simultaneously (Figure 10.2, bottom). The vertical loom consisted of two fixed beams, one over the other, and the warp threads were strung between these for tension. This loom was fixed vertically into the ground or leaned against a wall. Weavers could stand or sit while working this loom. Depictions of such looms have been found in the New Kingdom tomb of Thutnefer at Thebes (TT 104). Between the warp threads was a warp beam, which turned the warp threads between shuttle passes (Vogelsang-Eastwood 2000:277–278; Friend 1998:2–4; Barber 1991:113–116). The shuttles that passed the weft threads were used to separate warp threads, and to bead down the weft weave could be made from wood, bone, ivory, or stone. Usually these were elongated with rounded ends. The warp threads were held taut by weights, hence the term warp-weighted loom, which could be made from fired clay or stone (Friend 1998).

Loom weights have been discovered in various sizes and shapes, each performing a specific task in the weaving process. They were generally cylindrical, triangular, or round with a center hole for attaching the warp yarn. In Mesopotamia, a crescent-shaped loom weight was also utilized. Numerous crescent-shaped loom weights that date to the second millennium BCE have been found in central Anatolia; however, crescent-shaped weights have also been found at Early and Middle Bronze Age sites in that region. A recent study suggests the crescent-shaped loom weight may have aided in separating specific warp threads thereby producing different patterns in the weave. Some suggest that stamped crescent-shaped weights may be indicative of a palace economy (Lassen 2013).

Dyeing

Ancient dyeing is perhaps best known from the Phoenicians' purple and the Canaanites'/Israelites' blue dyes, the colors of royalty and the sacred. Purple and blue pigments were extracted from the glandular fluid of a sea snail commonly known as the murex. The process of extraction and dyeing was described by Pliny the Elder in his work *Natural History*. Modern experiments have successfully duplicated the process (Koren 2005). The earliest purple dyeing may have occurred ca. 4000 years ago on Minoan Crete, based on large quantities of murex shells having been recovered from archaeological contexts. During the Iron Age, blues and purples were utilized for priestly garments in addition to royalty. However, overuse caused the murex to die out, and the blue and purple dyeing industry ceased to operate along the Phoenician (Lebanese) coast.

The purple murex dye was extracted from the snail by smashing the shell, which punctured the gland. The entire smashed creature was placed into a container so the fluid, which initially emerges as a clear substance, turns purple upon contact with air. The mixture was allowed to sit for several days to oxidize and turn purple. The best way to dye the raw material, such as fleece or linen, was in a large vat. In the dyeing vat sodium carbonate and the murex were mixed. This minimized the amount of oxidation and retained the purple color. After four days of fermentation with the alkaline solution, the concoction turned green. Wool was then bathed in the mixture, which upon extraction was initially green; however, after contact with the air, oxidation caused the wool to turn purple. To achieve the desired hue, the fleece could be submerged several times.

Several large basins that resemble modern bathtubs have been discovered at Philistine sites in present-day Israel, one each at Tel Miqne-Ekron and Ashkelon. The example from Ashkelon was discovered in the room of a large building that also contained numerous loom weights next to the basin, and fibers were extracted from the soil samples taken from the hard-packed floor. It is now believed that these basins were dyeing vats (Mazow 2013).

The Egyptians also made use of ochre and plant dyes. Ochre is a natural earthen pigment comprised of hydrated iron oxide and clay, and can be yellow, deep orange, or brown in color; however, yellow was the most commonly used color. Yellow ochre can be made red by heating dehydrated iron oxide and mixing the two. Red ochres come from anhydrous ferric oxide (Vogelsang-Eastwood 2000:278), or from ochre that contains a large quantity of hematite. The practice of dyeing linen with iron oxide dates to at least the Early Dynastic period and the Tarkhan textile. For example, textiles dyed with iron oxide have been found at the village of Amarna (Vogelsang-Eastwood 2000:278–279).

The Egyptians also made dye from plants; however, few produced robust dye. Plants used for dyes included the *Indigofera*, specifically *indigofera tinctoria* and *indigofera suffruticosa*, and Isatis, specifically woad. These produced blue color for dyeing. To produce reds, the most used plant was *Rubia tinctorum*, known as madder. The roots of this plant produce the chemicals known as anthraquinones, specifically alizarin. Use of this plant for dye dates to the Eighteenth Dynasty and was brought to Egypt from the Levant. Pliny the Elder references this plant and its color in his work *Natural History*. The safflower, *Carthamus tinctorius*, henna, *Lawsonia alba* or *L. inermis*, and alkanet, *Anchusa tinctoria*, also produced red dye (Vogelsang-Eastwood 2000:278–279).

As with purple dye from murex, the number of times the fabric was dipped into the dye mixture determined the depth of color attained. To obtain deep coloration, fabrics had to be dipped numerous times. Once dyed, the raw material could be spun into yarn and woven into cloth.

For the fabric to absorb the dye, the fibers had to be treated with mordants such as natural alum, urine, or soapwort (Humphrey et al. 2006:358). The easiest recipe for mordanting includes 3 oz. potassium aluminum sulfate for fine textured wool or 4 oz. for heavy texture, 1 oz. cream of tartar, 4 gallons of water, and 1 pound of wool. The alum was dissolved in warm water, which was then added to the larger vat of water and heated to ca. 160° F. To make colors brighter, cream of tartar dissolved in warm water could be added to the mix. Once the mixture heated to 160° F, the wool could be added and brought to a boil after thirty minutes, then left to boil for forty-five minutes for fine wool and one hour for heavy wool. (http://thelibrary.org/lochist/periodicals/bittersweet/su75h.htm). As with weaving, in some parts of the world, this process has experienced little change.

Sewing

Sewing was a practical matter, evidenced by the limited range of techniques and details in the textiles found thus far. Stitching included simple hems and seams, rolled and whipped, lap-over seams, over-cast seams, and run and fell seams, to name a few (Vogelsang-Eastwood 2000:282–284). Garments were not complicated and made use of draping instead of cutting and tailoring. Due to the resilience of the materials, garments and other textiles appear to have remained in good condition; however, there is evidence that mending was necessary on occasion. Repairing a ripped or worn garment or textile was accomplished with needle and thread and was mended, darned, or patched. All sewing was conducted by hand; sewing machines were not invented until the nineteenth century.

Prior to scissors (as we know them), cloth was cut using flint knives and tearing. Shears were used as early as 1500 BCE in Egypt and Mesopotamia. Shears were made of two bronze blades connected by a thin, flexible piece of curved bronze, which provided a spring-like action that aided in the cutting action. When the blades were squeezed together, they cut; when released, the blades sprung apart. Shears were used in Europe until the sixteenth century. The Romans invented scissors (as we known them) in the first century CE. Scissors consist of two blades attached at a pivot point between the handles and the blade tips. Manipulation of the handles causes the blades to close or open (Vogelsang-Eastwood 2000:282–284).

In addition to shears and scissors, sewing tools consisted of needles made from various materials including bone (animal, fish, bird), ivory, and metal (bronze, copper, silver). Needles looked much like those used today with a sharp tapered end for inserting into the cloth and an opposing end containing a fold-over, eye, or hole to take the thread. Needles have been found as early as the Palaeolithic period and were used to make fishing nets, to facilitate the weaving process, and to sew fabric.

Garments

Once the raw material was dyed and woven into fabric, it could be manipulated into clothing, which consisted of two basic styles: wrap-around or draped, and tailored or fitted. Wrap-around or draped garments include kilts, skirts, dresses, shawls, and cloaks, and tend to be little more than a large swath of cloth wrapped around the body and secured. Tailored or fitted clothing included triangular or rectangular cloths sewn on one or several edges with fastenings. These garments included tunics, loincloths, and sheath dresses. Although fitted, these were not form-fitting as modern clothing is today; there were no darts, tucks, or shaping to one's body. Most garments were loose fitting (Janssen 1995:384–385; Vogelsang-Eastwood 2000:286).

Loincloths (or undergarments) were worn by men and women. The cloth was placed between the legs then drawn up and secured around the waist with ties or a belt. Usually loincloths were made from cotton, gauze, or leather. Often a cotton loincloth was worn next to the body underneath a leather loincloth. This combination was worn mostly by men, usually soldiers, sailors, workmen, and servants. Two leather loincloths survived from New Kingdom Egypt, found in a box inscribed with the name Maiherpri (Janssen 1995:385; Vogelsang-Eastwood 2000:286–287).

The Egyptians, Canaanites, and Mesopotamians wore kilts, skirts, and dresses (Figure 10.3). In Egypt, there were three types of dresses worn by women: wrap-around, V-neck, and beaded (Vogelsang-Eastwood 2000:288). Examples can be found depicted in tomb paintings, for example the Eighteenth Dynasty tomb of Rekhmira at Thebes, and surviving garments such as a V-necked dress from Asyut Le Louvre (E12026), and one from Saqqara (Vogelsang-Eastwood 2000:288–289).

FIGURE 10.3   Depictions of some garments from Canaan and Egypt. Scene from the tomb of Khnumhotep II at Beni Hasan (BH3), a nobleman in the Twelfth Dynasty, ca. 1900 BCE, Egypt. Depicts male and female "Asiatics" in brightly colored garments and Egyptians in white kilts

Borrowed and adapted from Newberry 1893a, Plates XXVIII and XXX (Images Public Domain PD-1923).

Men and women in Mesopotamia wore dresses that initially consisted of one large piece of cloth wrapped around their body and secured with a clasp or pin. Women pinned theirs together on the left side while men secured theirs on the right (Stol 1995:490).

The Canaanites wore a wrap-around skirt that extended from the waist to mid-thigh, and women wore a wrap-around dress that extended from the shoulder to just above the ankle. These were held in place by a toggle pin, a pin inserted into the fabric and held in place by wrapping a cord around the ends of the pin. Canaanite garments also were quite colorful. Depictions from Egyptian tomb paintings illustrate the brilliant colors of their garments, especially those containing blue fringes. The painting in Khnumhotep's tomb (BH3) is often referenced regarding the brilliantly colored garments, as well as the tools and weapons of the "Asiatics" (Cohen 2015).

During the Median and Achaemenid periods, Persian clothing consisted of a short tunic and loose mantle; Indian style consisted of a kilt, with or without a mantle; and plains dwellers wore a long gown that reached to the knees or ankles, and a cloak. The main clothing style consisted of headgear, an over garment, a shirt or tunic, trousers, and footwear. Warriors wore red, priests wore white, and pastoralists wore blue (Collon 1995).

The style, length, and color of garments conveyed socio-economic status, cultural affiliation, religious position and affiliation, sex and gender, and age. Kings, queens, court officials, priests, soldiers, servants, and workmen could be identified by the costume they wore.

Miscellaneous

Textiles were not limited to clothing and were utilized daily for functional purposes in the household and workplace. Lamp wicks were made of cloth or fibers that were twisted and used as wicks in lamps providing light. Beds and cushions were most commonly used in Egypt. Frames were made from wood and mounted on four legs. Rope was strung from the frame to form a woven sling on which was set a mattress. The mattress was made from multiple layers of cloth bound by swaths of cloth. The mattress probably would have been covered with bedclothes and blankets. Mattresses have been discovered in the tomb of Kha (TT8) at Deir el-Medina, and a bed canopy was discovered in the tomb of Hetepheres (Vogelsang-Eastwood 2000:291). Cushions were more versatile and had numerous uses. They functioned as lounging cushions, chair cushions, footstool cushions, and possibly as pillows. Cushions were constructed from two pieces of linen stitched together and packed tightly with feathers. Cushions have been discovered in the tomb of Huya at Amarna (EAI), the tomb of User, Thebes (TT260), the tomb of Yuya and Tuyu (KV46), and the tomb of Ramose and Hatnefer at Thebes (Vogelsang-Eastwood 2000:291).

Rugs or carpets held essential and practical roles in the ancient Near East. The origin of rug manufacture and technique remains unknown; however, rugs adorned the floors of nomadic peoples' tents and the floors of temples, palaces, and churches. Rugs could be made from wool, cotton, silk, or a combination of these. They could be felted, woven, or knotted. Their designs could be geometric, abstract, or life-like. As with mosaics, rug design could be used to tell a story or to record history. In fact, rugs were closely connected with mosaic design, and often shared similar motifs. As with clothing, designs could communicate tribal affiliation or socio-economic status. In his book *Anabasis* (XII.3.18, 27), Xenophon (ca. 400 BCE) mentions Persian carpets as prized possessions and valuable diplomatic gifts (Dimand 1939; Eiland and Eiland 1998). Archaeologically, rugs rarely survive; however, a well-preserved rug was discovered in 1949 in the kurgan (burial mound) of a Scythian nobleman in the Pazyryk Valley in the Siberian Altai Mountains. This rug dates to the fifth century BCE and measures 183 x 200 centimeters (72 x 79 inches). It contains thirty-six symmetrical knots per centimeter squared (232 per inch squared) and was made of wool (see The State Hermitage Museum, www.hermitagemuseum. org/wps/portal/hermitage/digital-collection/25.+Archaeological+Artifacts/8798 70/?lng=vu, accessed 3 May 2018).

Various types of cloth were used as strainers for oils, juices, beer, and wine; as bags to transport spices, grain, and other commodities; and as padding or saddles on donkeys and other pack animals. In the military context, cloth was used as flooring for chariots, and as bandages, tents, flags, and sails. Finally, cloth was used in the funerary setting to dress the corpse, and in religious settings to dress the priest and other participants in festivals, rites, and ceremonies, as well as to dress the statues of deities.

Textile maintenance

Although cloth and textiles were durable, proper maintenance was important to extend the life of the item. It has already been mentioned that wherever possible, garments and other textiles were repaired when damaged or worn out and not thrown away and replaced by new ones. Equally important was the storage of cloth items. Garments and textiles were stored in baskets (some with lids), chests, sacks, and boxes.

An important aspect of textile maintenance was the washing of it. In Egypt there was a "chief washer of the palace," "washer to the pharaoh," and a "chief bleacher." Nobles and owners of large estates also employed washermen as part of their household. Washermen are known from textual reference, The Teaching of Dauf's Son, Khety, and from tomb paintings as in the tombs of Khnumhotep II at Beni Hasan (BH3, Newberry 1893a, Pl. XXIX) and Ipuy at Deir el-Medina (TT217). The Egyptians had washing down to a fine process. The cloth was moistened with water and rubbed with detergent made from natron (natural soda), potash, and soapwort (*Saponaria officinalis*). Then the cloth was beaten with sticks or wooden clubs on a stone or piece of wood. Finally, the cloth was washed in water, rinsed, rung out, and then set out to dry. Setting the cloth out to dry in the hot sun also bleached and, in effect, sanitized it. Pleating and creasing was performed by a dressmaker using pleating gauges or a pleating board, and was done when the fabric was still damp. Once dry, it was folded and stored (Vogelsang-Eastwood 2000:284–285). The washing was done in a large vat or tub or the running water of a canal, river, or stream. Undergarments were more numerous than outerwear and were washed more frequently. In most New Kingdom households, women performed laundry duties; however, wealthy households hired professional laundry services, which were run by and employed men. In Medinet Habu, for example, in the vicinity of the temple, 155 households shared the service of six washermen (Janssen 1995:390–392).

Footwear

Although not technically characterized as a textile, it seems appropriate to include footwear in this section. Like clothing, it is difficult to know exactly when people began wearing shoes, but foot coverings probably met a basic need to protect one's feet from rain, snow, stones, and thorns. This sub-section is not meant to elucidate the earliest use of footwear, but rather to discuss some of the examples that have been discovered and the construction of them.

The abovementioned versatility of leather was also applied to footwear. Two examples include a leather shoe discovered in a cave in Armenia (ca. 3500 BCE) and those found with Ötzi (ca. 3400–3100 BCE) in the Ötztal Alps, South Tyrol, Italy. The Armenian shoe was made of cowhide from one piece of leather. It was fashioned to the shape of the wearer's foot and contained grass, which possibly functioned as insulation or cushioning (Pinhasi et al. 2010; *National Geographic*, http://news.nationalgeographic.com/news/2010/06/100609-worlds-oldest-leather-shoe-armenia-science/, accessed 10 December 2014). The shoes worn by

Ötzi were more complex and included inner and outer components. The inner shoe consisted of grass netting that held in place hay, which functioned as insulation. The outer part was made from deerskin with the fur intact. The inner and outer upper were attached to an oval-shaped sole made from bearskin, which was held in place by leather straps. The collar extended around the ankle and was held in place by grass rope. A strip of leather was attached to the sole of the shoe to provide better gripping (see Südtiroler Archäologiemuseum, www.iceman.it/en/node/226, accessed 10 December 2014).

Reconstruction experiments suggest this shoe construction was effective and comfortable with the only down side being that it was not waterproof (Südtiroler Archäologiemuseum, www.iceman.it/en/node/226, accessed 10 December 2014). These shoes differ from other prehistoric European footwear in that they lacked a vamp and were made from soft leather. Shoes made of a single piece of cowhide with a vamp have been found throughout Europe in Denmark and Ireland from Bronze Age and Medieval contexts. This one-piece cowhide shoe technology was utilized for a long time and finds similarities with shoes in Southwest Asia. Ötzi's shoes find similarity with those of the Inuit and Native Americans (Pinhasi et al. 2010).

Leather footwear has also been found in Luxor Egypt dating to the Hellenistic period. In a temple, seven shoes were discovered inside a clay jar which, along with two other jars, had been deposited between two mudbrick walls. Two pairs were made for children and measured 18 centimeters/7 inches long. One shoe was made for an adult. Another pair of shoes, measuring 24 centimeters/ca. 9 inches, was also made for an adult who apparently had a limp based on wear patterns. The child-sized shoes were bound together with string made from palm fiber and stuffed inside the lone adult shoe. All of these shoes were placed inside one of the jars (Jarus 2005).

In Egypt, Canaan, and Mesopotamia, sandals were more common than leather shoes. The depiction of the "Asiatics" in the tomb painting of Khnumhotep II at Beni Hasan (BH3) illustrates the sandals worn by those considered to be Canaanites (above, Figure 10.3). Shalmaneser's Black Obelisk depicts Israelites wearing a Hittite high-top boot with a turned-up toe (Gruber 1995:642). Egyptian sandals (or evidence of sandals) have been found as early as Predynastic cemeteries at Badari, Naqada, and Mostagedda. Numerous examples have also been discovered in dynastic contexts including tombs such as Kha (TT8), an Eighteenth Dynasty workman's tomb at Deir al Medina, Tomb N at Gurob, an Eighteenth Dynasty tomb wherein a pair of red-stained sandals were covered with dirt and showed signs of wear, and in Tutankhamun's tomb, to name a few (Veldmeijer 2011; Van Driel-Murray 2000: 312–316). In the Nahal Mishmar cave, a Chalcolithic period (ca. 4000–3300 BCE) Ghassulian cave in modern-day Israel, sandals of similar construction have been found. The Nahal Mishmar sandals were made from several pieces of leather sewn together with straps extending from the footbed over the foot (Bar-Adon 1980: 186–187).

Egyptian sandals could be constructed from leather and/or plant materials. The soles could be manufactured from bundled halfa grass, palm fronds, papyrus, or vegetable fiber coiled into the shape of the wearer's foot, comprising the sole. The coil was held in place by sewing small strips of doum palm leaf, thus securing the coil. Similar to modern thong sandals, straps were sewn into the sole between the big toe and second toe and across the breadth of the foot, with a strap around the heel (Veldmeijer 2009).

Like today, ancient footwear came in a variety of styles, decoration, and of varying quality. Footwear could be open-toed, close-toed, or open with a turned-up toe; or it could utilize minimal strapping or multiple straps to secure the sole of the sandal to the foot. Footwear could be made from leather or plant-based materials. In Egypt, a scene from the tomb of Anta and Shedu at Deshasha, Fifth Dynasty, depicts sandal making (Van Driel-Murray 2000:313–314), and sandals were found in the Tomb of Anta (Petrie 1898).

Textiles are a kind of overlooked technology because they are such an integral part of everyday life; most of us do not give much attention to the manufacture or meaning of clothing and footwear. Yet it is a multi-million-dollar industry that stretches across the globe. In antiquity, those leading the garment industry learned to selectively breed sheep to produce a particular quality and color of wool. They learned how to clean and prepare the wool to take dye and how to spin the yarn to produce fabric of varying quality, thickness, and refinement. Knowledge of plant fibers and their characteristics translated into the use of cotton, flax, and hemp, which produced lighter clothing for warmer seasons and climates. An elaborate process for procuring and processing the raw materials for manufacture was developed. This knowledge was likely the result of trial and error, experimentation, and innovation.

It is upon this knowledge that today's textile industry is based. To a certain extent, little has changed. Fibers such as leather, cotton, wool, flax, hemp, and silk are still sought after and used today. The basic sourcing and manufacturing processes have changed little since antiquity, except that in many instances machines have taken the place of people. Modern technology has added synthetic fibers such as rayon, nylon, and polyester, and natural fibers such as lyocell, also known as Tencel, which is made from cellulose fiber from wood (www.lenzing-fibers.com/en/tencel/).

The ancient textile industry was an important component of the economy. It provided employment for men as well as women, especially in Mesopotamia. Many scholars view the ancient world as male-dominated; however, women possessed an integral, if not dominant, role in this industry, which likely also extended into culture and society as well. Women who ran their own businesses conducted business transactions and agreements, bought and sold raw materials and finished goods, hired employees, could read and write, knew arithmetic, and were entitled to profits. These and other industry-related activities suggest that women's roles in the ancient world were likely much more integrated than dominated than some modern scholars like to admit.

Although fashion has evolved, clothing continues to convey information. The uniforms worn by police officers, doctors, and military personnel convey their occupation, and the quality and style of clothing suggest socio-economic status and even gender. Fashion styles vary by region, cultural tradition, and ritual, and the evolution of clothing styles can be observed and reliably dated. The clothing a person chooses to wear or is compelled to wear can make a statement about an individual's character, hobby, cultural affiliation, or profession. Clothing served this function in antiquity and continues to do so today.

In that this may be a hidden technology, its importance in the ancient and modern worlds should not be taken for granted. The essentials of modern textiles are rooted in that which was developed long ago.

11

CERAMIC AND GLASS TECHNOLOGY

Perhaps the most ubiquitous artifact found at most archaeological sites is pottery. The ever-present nature of pottery has helped and hindered archaeologists' interpretation of the ancient record. Sir W. M. F. Petrie, in 1890 at Tel Hesi, and W. F. Albright, in the 1930s and 1940s at Tell Beit Mirsim, were among the first, if not the first, to recognize a correlation between pottery and the archaeo-chronological record. From thence forward pottery has been used to interpret aspects of the ancient past such as chronology, activity, ritual, economy, trade, social status, and artistic interpretation, developing an almost obsessive, unhealthy reliance on pottery. In recent years, however, a more balanced approach has been adopted, integrating ceramic analysis with data from architecture, flotation, material culture, and human remains, providing a more holistic interpretation of ancient peoples.

Pottery is considered among the earliest manufactured materials that humankind produced (Gheorghiu 2009:1; Quinn 2013:1). This is because the act of firing clay to produce hard, durable objects irreversibly changes the physiochemical properties of clay (Maniatis 2009:2). Some of the earliest ceramic sherds found thus far date to ca. 20,000 years ago based on ceramic fragments from the Xianrendong Cave in China (Wu et al. 2012; Bhanoo 2012; Patel 2012) and from ca. 16,500–14,920 BCE from Odai Yamamoto, Japan (James and Thorpe 1995:300–301); however, this chapter will focus on the development of ceramic technology from the ancient Near East.

Prior to the discovery of fired clay, people used skins, bark, reeds, wood, and stone to contain liquids, foods, and belongings. It is speculated that the discovery of firing clay was made by accident. People likely discovered the malleability and workability of clay by first making figurines and small vessels which when set close to or in fire transformed into a harder material which led to the development of fired clay vessels (Oleson 2008:496). Thus, by the Neolithic period (ca. 8000 BCE) in Mesopotamia, Canaan, and Egypt, ceramic production was well underway and quickly became a specialized industry.

Why study pottery?

As ceramic technology developed, the quality and type of vessels produced evolved as well. Certain sizes, shapes, and decorative elements became popular, with some style elements enduring through the centuries, and others just momentary fads. Vessel type was commodity specific, region specific, and task specific. Based on Petrie's realization, archaeologists' subsequent observations of specific characteristics within broader typologies led to the formulation of a typological chronology for ceramic vessels found in the archaeological record. In other words, by documenting the changes in size and shape of vessel types and observing smaller changes in the rim, handle, and base within each vessel type, such as bowls, jugs, and jars, specific characteristics and changes could be assigned to specific regions within specific chronological periods. Additionally, the surface treatment of pottery, such as decorative features, is also chronologically, culturally, and regionally specific. Thus, vessels with certain characteristics are assigned to specific periods, places of origin, and possibly also functions, which helps the excavators interpret the overall context of the room, building, or location being investigated.

Vessel type can be related to activity. For example, cooking pots suggest that the people living in a structure routinely prepared and cooked their food in certain spaces or rooms. Large bowls and platters suggest the serving of food. Smaller bowls and plates suggest eating portions of food. Pitchers and jugs indicate decanting liquids. Large jars suggest the storage of raw foods, such as grain, or liquid, such as wine. Some vessels were utilized only in ritualistic or religious contexts such as in temple rites and ceremonies, while others were purely for domestic use. When discovered, ceramic artifacts are carefully recorded so that when interpreted in relation to other artifacts found in the same space, one can suggest the type of activities that may have taken place there. In this way, rooms within buildings can be interpreted as dining rooms, kitchens, or storage rooms.

Finally, typological characteristics and manufacture techniques can also suggest the region from which the vessel and the commodity it contained originated. For example, certain vessels, such as Base Ring Ware that originated on Cyprus, indicate that Canaan was importing goods from Cyprus during the Late Bronze Age. In other cases, vessels appear to be local imitations of the foreign import, such as pyxis jars from the Iron Age. Imported ceramics reflect trade, which provides insight into international economic relationships.

To aid in understanding where a vessel may have originated, petrographic analysis proves useful. Based on its geochemical and mineralogical content, the composition of clay can be analyzed. Using geochemical techniques including instrumental neutron activation analysis (INAA), X-ray fluorescence (XRF), and inductively coupled plasma mass spectrometry (ICP-MS), the elemental signatures of ceramics can be obtained. Additionally, mineralogical techniques can be used to discover these elements within a given vessel, which can be observed under a microscope or by X-ray diffraction. The mineralogical components of a given sample can suggest specific clay sources found in specific geographical locations (Quinn 2013:1).

Thus, a thin section of a vessel or artifact when examined under a microscope can reveal the clay's place of origin, which in turn suggests trade of the raw clay material to distant workshops or local use of local resources and the subsequent distribution of the finished ceramic vessel to local and/or distant regions. Either way, petrographic analysis has become an important tool when trying to determine the movement of ceramic vessels throughout the wider ancient world.

Residue analysis

In recent years, the analysis of the organic residue trapped within the fabric of vessels has become an extremely useful and relatively accurate method to determine the contents of some vessels. The process is not without problems, such as contamination or lack of remains; however, when it is possible to obtain reliable data, this can support or surprise traditional interpretations. Ceramic vessels in particular tend to capture the various chemical components of the foods and drinks they contained, such as lipids and acids. Careful extraction and analysis of these can lead to remarkable discoveries.

Advances in residue analysis have been made by P. E. McGovern, a bimolecular archaeologist from the University of Pennsylvania Museum (www.penn.museum/ sites/biomoleculararchaeology/, accessed 24 January 2018). For example, while analyzing ceramic jars and a funnel from Godin Tepe in Iran (Mesopotamia), he discovered tartaric acid, a principle component of grapes. These vessels were discovered in a room associated with a citadel courtyard dating to Period V, ca. 3500–3000 BCE. It is thought that this room was a distribution center for commodities (Badler 1990:27; McGovern et al. 1996). Similarly, well-preserved residues from a drinking set found in the tomb of King Midas at Gordion from the Iron Age yielded a recipe for wine that included a mixture of grapes, barley, and honey, and beer and mead, which was served with a spiced lamb and lentil stew. This meal was recreated using chemical analysis and adapted to modern measurements using authentic ingredients as much as possible (McGovern et al. 1999; McGovern 2000). Residue analysis can be used not only for foodstuffs, but also to identify the purple dye produced by the Phoenicians (McGovern and Michel 1990).

The potter's workshop

Clay preparation

Clay occurs naturally and is a fine-grained substance that when mixed with water becomes flexible. So, the first step in procuring clay is to find a source with the finest grain and the least amount of inclusions. In Egypt, for example, clay was easily found, but collecting it would have required the permission of the landowner (Arnold and Bourriau 1993:11). Some clays were found at a distance and had to be transported to the potter's workshop, which was done by donkey according to records from Deir el-Medina (Arnold and Bourriau 1993:11).

Next, the clay was cleaned via a process called levigation, wherein the impurities were sifted out, but first the clay was dried to remove all water. This was so that when it was re-saturated with water, the clay would evenly absorb the moisture so that it could be properly levigated. Then it was placed into a pit dug into the earth or into a vat and soaked with water. Once soaked, the clay was manipulated by treading with one's feet or with one's hands or a paddle to work out the unwanted inclusions and air bubbles. The clay was then left to soak for several days, a process known as slaking (Rye 1981; Arnold and Bourriau 1993; Maniatis 2009).

Slaking allowed the lighter components of the clay to rise, producing the slip, which could be used for surface treatment. When a uniform suspension had been achieved, the slip could be sieved and settled, and the clay was ready for use (Rye 1981; Arnold and Bourriau 1993:12–13; Maniatis 2009:3). The amount of cleaning/levigation depended on the type of vessel being thrown and the desired quality. For example, cooking pots were generally made with clay that was not well levigated, whereas dining and drinking vessels were generally made with very well levigated fine clay.

Throwing a pot

At first, ceramic vessels were formed by shaping lumps of clay by hand or by the coiling method. Clay would be formed using hand and fingers to obtain the desired shape. Shaping was achieved by pinching and hollowing, and possibly by using a paddle or by pounding when making a large pot. Clay could also be shaped over a core made from stone or wood or from a mold. Once the basic shape was formed, the potter used scrapers— wood or stone— to smooth the surface and to form the base and rim. At this point in the process, external decoration such as applique, burnishing, or incising may be applied (Rye 1981; Arnold and Bourriau 1993; Moorey 1999; Maniatis 2009).

Coiling was another widely used method, especially when making large vessels. Clay is fashioned into a long round strand and coiled in an open stacked shape to form the body of the vessel. Then the coils are smoothed to create a solid wall. Even though smoothed, sometimes the coils remain visible (Arnold and Bourriau 1993:33–35).

The potter's wheel had humble beginnings. The first step toward developing the wheel seems to have been a reed mat. The clay was placed onto a mat that was turned by the potter or by an assistant. This method was extremely slow but allowed the potter to use both hands to form the vessel while benefiting from the rotation. To achieve a uniform shape, it is necessary to rotate the clay. The more continuous the rotation the more uniform the vessel.

Evidence for the use of a "wheel" or a turntable comes from depictions in reliefs and tomb paintings as well as literary references. Artifactually, evidence for a mat, wheel, or turntable can be found on the vessel itself in the lines created during the turning of the vessel. Pivoting wheels could have been made from ceramic, wood,

In Egypt, some of the earliest kilns have been discovered at Hierakonpolis and date to ca. 3650 BCE. This kiln measured ca. 6.1 x 5.0 meters. Another kiln from the same site dates to 3200–3100 BCE and was a shallow pit updraft type of kiln (Arnold and Bourriau 1993:108). Although the ceramics fired in this kiln were removed from the fire by blocks, the structure was not covered. Later in the Old Kingdom and First Intermediate Period, kilns depicted in the tomb of Ty at Saqqara show tall, biconical kilns made of brick with exterior ribbing for strength (Arnold and Bourriau 1993:108). At Buhen, three kilns (or furnaces for copper) were discovered. These were ca. 1.0 meter in diameter and 1.0 meter high. These were single-chamber kilns consisting of a pit dug into the earth with a brick superstructure. In the middle of the pit was a brick column rising above ground level with a "grid" radiating from the central pillar to the brick walls. There was also a rectangular stokehole that protruded from one side of the stack, part of which was covered (Arnold and Bourriau 1993:109).

In the New Kingdom, kilns were rather elaborate. One found at el-Amarna provides an excellent example. One from area G4, kiln 2984, was oval in shape and measured ca. 2.30 meters north-south and ca. 1.50 meters east-west and was preserved to a depth of 1.0 meters with 0.75 meters being dug into the ground. It had a brick stokehole on one side. Long bricks projected from the walls onto a central pillar to form a floor. Finally, kilns from the Late Period at Karnak, Phase D, and from Memphis, were elaborately constructed. These consisted of a pit, with ceiling/floor pierced with holes for ventilation, and a sophisticated brick-built superstructure that could be left open or capped (Arnold and Bourriau 1993:15–116).

In Canaan, several Middle Bronze Age II period kilns have been discovered at sites including Aphek, Nahal Soreq, Tel Jerish, Tel Mikhal, Tel Qasile, and Tel Ridan. Middle Bronze Age II period kilns were generally oval or elongated in shape, of the vertical updraft variety. They included a lower combustion chamber and upper baking chamber with earthen radial supports in the lower chamber to support the platform of the baking chamber, flues perforating the platform between the combustion, and baking chambers to allow airflow between the two. Clay stoppers for the flues have been discovered with some kilns at Aphek and Tel Mikhal. At Nahal Soreq, for example, one of the remaining kilns was of the two-story type and was round in shape (Singer-Avitz and Levi 1992:174). The subterranean fuel chamber sloped downward toward the front of the kiln and the collapsed remains of the pillars that once supported the platform of the upper chamber. The kilns from Tel Mikhal and Tel Qasile were similar. Both consisted of lower combustion chambers that were cut into the kurkar and boasted radial supports, flues that pierced the platform between the upper and lower chambers, and coloring on the walls indicating a firing temperature of ca. 700–1000° C.

Late Bronze Age kilns differ from those of the Middle Bronze Age in two ways: the combustion chamber is generally bilobate, possessing a central tongue that functions as a support for the platform, which serves as the roof of the firing chamber/floor of the baking chamber. Rather than utilizing radial platform supports extending from the walls of the combustion chamber, as did the Middle Bronze Age kilns, there was a single central supportive tongue or column. Examples may be found at Sarepta with Kilns E, F, and G (Pritchard 1975:71–77, Figures 13, 14) and at Haruba (Oren 1987:69–119, Figure 9, Pl. G).

At the Phoenician city of Sarepta, located in Lebanon, 50 kilometers south of Beirut, a series of nineteen U-shaped kilns and workshops was found (Pritchard 1975:71–84; Anderson 1987:41–51; Khalifeh 1988:24–35) in what has been described as "the potters' quarter" (Pritchard 1975:71). Only three kilns were well preserved, Kilns E, F, and G, and the adjacent workshop, Room 74. Of these, Kiln G was the best preserved. The kilns were built using a consistent construction technique and were of a similar architectural plan, including combustion chamber and a baking chamber. The lower combustion chamber was bilobate, partly divided into two sections by a tongue that protruded toward the center of the chamber from the wall opposite the stoking hole, providing support for the floor of the baking chamber. The baking chamber floor contained a series of vents or flues that controlled the updraft of heat from the combustion chamber around the pottery. The roofs were rounded, made of clay, and pierced by numerous flues allowing for additional controlled ventilation. The kilns were associated with rooms or structures that probably functioned as workshops and storage facilities. Other items found in these rooms, such as tools, wheels, and settling basins, would suggest that this was a pottery manufacturing site (Pritchard 1975:71–76; Anderson 1987:49).

Located in the northern Sinai, near the coast on the "Ways of Horus," Haruba's industrial quarter (Site A-345) contained a potter's workshop (Oren 1987:69–119; Figure 9, Pl. G). This Late Bronze Age II complex included installations for preparing and storing clay and fired vessels, in addition to the remains of a nearly complete kiln. This kiln was of the double chamber updraft type. In total, it measured approximately 1.50 meters in height. The dome of the baking chamber rose approximately 0.50 meters above the floor. The inner diameter was approximately 1.40 meters and the outer measured approximately 1.80 meters in circumference. The combustion chamber extended 1 meter beneath the floor of the baking chamber. The entrance of the combustion chamber was on the southern side of the kiln, probably to avoid the north wind. The floor of the baking chamber measured 0.20–0.25 meters thick and was perforated by a series of flues that allowed heat and air to flow freely between the combustion and baking chambers. The kiln wall also contained a clay pipe leading from the combustion chamber through the firing chamber to the outside, allowing the potter to control the temperature of the kiln (Oren 1987:99–102).

Although the size and shape of kilns may have altered slightly from kiln to kiln and from time to time, the basic technology and technique remained the same. For example, a kiln found at Qumran, second century BC to first century CE, continues the architectural traditions mentioned above.

Glass

In Egypt, glass and faience were considered precious stones, even if artificial. Glass was used as jewelry, was made into vessels, and was used as inlay for boxes and on statues, often for the eyes. Late in the Roman period, drinking vessels made of glass were preferred over ceramic because they were more hygienic. Detailed and comprehensive discussions regarding the manufacturing and working of glass have been undertaken by Moorey (1999), Nicholson and Henderson (2000), and Henderson (2013). These works should be explored for a more extensive investigation of glass and faience. For the purpose of this work, a brief summary of glass and faience will be offered, focusing mainly on Mesopotamia and Egypt.

Initially, humankind first encountered glass in the form of obsidian, a naturally occurring glass produced by volcanic activity. Raw obsidian was fashioned into tools such as blades; however, it could not be easily melted to make other objects, such as beads or vessels. As with ceramics and metals, glass production represents knowledge of converting the natural state and chemical composition of a material, yet glass was the last of these three materials to be produced (Henderson 2013:12). Knowledge gained from ceramics and metalworking was likely adapted and applied to the production and working of glass. Several manufacturing techniques shared by pottery and metal production include kilns/furnaces, creating a gaseous atmosphere and controlling heat, extracting impurities, slaking, and combining materials to achieve optimal fire temperature and melting point, annealing, coloration, and production of ingots (Henderson 2013:12–16; Rehren and Pusch 2005; Rehren 2000).

Glass was probably first made in Mesopotamia. The earliest known glass beads come from Nineveh, level 4 (ca. 3200–3000 BCE), from the Great Pit MM, in the form of two glass beads, although exact dating and quality is the subject of debate (Moorey 1999:190). Glass beads have been found at other sites with early dates as well: at Nippur in association with Akkadian period tablets; at Tell Brak also of the Akkadian period; and a raw lump of glass was discovered at Abu Shahrein (Eridu) in a rubbish heap associated with a house. Glass beads from Mesopotamia could be spherical or oblong in shape and could be clear, white, olive-green, blue, yellow, yellowish-green, blueish-green, blueish-white, or a complex of colors (Moorey 1999:190).

Glass was probably introduced to Egypt as a commodity. The seemingly abrupt emergence of glass in Egypt has led some to conclude that Mesopotamian craftspeople were relocated to Egypt by Thutmose III as a result of his campaigns to Mittani and Babylon. Soon thereafter, glassmaking thrived as an industry in Egypt with local craftspeople developing their own techniques and artistic styles (Nicholson and Henderson 2000:195; Peck 2013:159). This is further supported by words for glass used by the Egyptians, *ehlipakku* and *mekku*, which are Hurrian and Akkadian words. The vocabulary words, raw materials, and technique may have been transported to Egypt (Nicholson 2000:195). It is speculated that initially, Mesopotamian glassmakers were brought to Egypt to create a glass industry. From ca. 1500 BCE onward, Egyptians prized glass (and faience) as artificial precious stones. Letters from Tell el-Amarna mention glass as an imported commodity, but evidence of glass manufacturing has also been discovered at Tell el-Amarna. In Mesopotamia and in Egypt, glass manufacturing appears to have taken shape in the Late Bronze Age. Egyptian glassmakers would go on to produce some beautiful and intricate glass items (Moorey 1999; Nicholson and Henderson 2000:195). Recently, a glass production center dating to the Late Roman period was discovered in Israel in the Jezreel Valley while constructing parts of the Jezreel Railway Project.

The kilns that produced glass consisted of two chambers, a firebox, and a melting chamber where the raw materials (sand and flux, such as soda or alkali or pot ash) were melted together at ca. 1200° C, and a stokehole. Two kilns found at Tell el-Amarna were round, measured ca. 1.5 meters in diameter, and were made of brick. They consisted of a lower chamber and an upper one with vents allowing the heat to rise. Both kilns would have had a conical shape with a large opening for ventilation. Once the glass was produced, it was melted together into chunks or poured into crucibles to form ingots, which were transported to glass workshops. The ingots were melted again and fashioned into bottles, bowls, and other items. Kilns and workshops have also been found at Malkata in Egypt and a recently discovered Roman period kiln site in the Jezreel Valley, Israel (www.sci-news.com/archaeology/roman-period-glass-factory-israel-03779.html; Jackson et al. 1998; Shortland et al. 2017).

Raw materials for glass manufacture

Unfortunately, no recipes for making glass or working with it have been discovered. Knowledge of the raw materials has been obtained from analyses of discovered artifacts and gleaned from Mesopotamian texts. Today, glass is made from pure silica, which melts at over 1700° C, a temperature unattainable in ancient kilns. To lower the temperature at which silica melts, flux was added as 20 percent of the mixture. However, this made the glass unstable and susceptible to rapid decay. To stabilize the mixture, lime was added. Thus, ancient glass was a mixture of silicate, soda, and lime (Nicholson and Henderson 2000:195).

Silica can be found in desert sand, which was abundant in Egypt. Based on analyses of glass furnaces from Amarna, it is likely that only sand was being used to produce glass because neither the Assyrian texts (fourteenth to twelfth centuries BCE) nor Pliny mention adding lime to the mix. Desert sand naturally contains lime, an ingredient necessary to make pure silicate stable. Hence, scholars believe early glassmakers were not using pure silicate but the impure desert sand. Amarna sand is comprised of as much as 18.86 percent lime (Nicholson and Henderson 2000:195). As for alkali, it is possible the Egyptians were using sodium oxide (Na_2O), and/or sodium bicarbonate, also called natron ($NaHCO_3$). This hypothesis is based on the presence of 15–20 percent of soda (Na_2O) found in Egyptian glass (Nicholson and Henderson 2000:197). Another source was magnesia derived from potash, which was obtained by burning plants containing alkali. These include species Salsola herbavea, S. fruticose, and S. Lignosa. Using these raw materials, the glass would have been greenish or brownish due to the iron impurities within the sand (Nicholson and Henderson 2000:195).

To remove color from glass, manganese (Mn) may have been used. Manganese could also be used to give glass a purple color. Copper and manganese combined could be used to achieve black. Most coloration, however, was achieved by mixing minerals. The much-used blue was obtained from cobalt (Co), which could have come from central Europe or from Asia Minor or from the Kharga and Dakhla Oases in the Western Desert (Nicholson and Henderson 2000:196–198). Cobalt occurs naturally as a pinkish color and must be mixed with water, natron, potash, or ammonia and heated to 800–1000° C to bring out the blue. Copper was used to obtain a turquoise-blue color. Copper was mined in the Sinai and used for tools and weapons as well as pigment. To achieve a clear or white color, tin was used; with the addition of antimony (Sb), glass could be opaque as well as yellow, amber, brown, or, when iron was added, black. The color red was very difficult to obtain, but was probably achieved by mixing copper in a crucible heated with blowpipes (Nicholson and Henderson 2000:198–199).

Once the raw materials were sourced, they were ground into a fine powder and mixed together. The mixture was then heated, a process called fritting. Fritting was discussed by several ancient writers, including Pliny, Theophilus (tenth century CE), and Neri (1612 CE). The mixture would be heated to ca. 750–850° C. The mixture required regular stirring and could take five hours to one day.

Once fritting was complete, the frit was ground and large chunks were removed. Fritting was likely done in bowls ca. 25 centimeters (10 inches) in diameter and 7.5 centimeters (3 inches) deep. The glass was then melted into deeper, cylindrical vessels that produced a glass ingot, which was sized for transportation. Coloration could be added at this stage or perhaps during the initial mixing and heating (Nicholson and Henderson 2000:199–201). Some scholars argue the Egyptians never actually made glass but simply imported glass ingots, re-melted them, and produced glassware. The reason for this conclusion is the lack of glass kilns discovered thus far.

Techniques in glass manufacturing

Several techniques were used to make glass vessels: core-formed, mold, rod-formed, and cold cutting. Core-formed appears to be the earliest and most common way to create glass vessels. A form was made of clay, or a mixture of clay and dung, or another material, and was dipped into molten glass or, more likely, covered with glass coils. To flatten the coils, the form encased with glass coils was rolled on a flat surface, and to make patterns, the craftsperson used a stylus to slice through the coils to create a decorative ripple effect. Handles, bases, and rims were added separately or molded from the body (Moorey 1999:204; Peck 2013:159–160). Casting glass in molds was useful when making inlay pieces for jewelry, sculpture (such as the eyes in statues), and for furniture. Molds and castings were also useful for making bowls and other open vessels. Molds were made of clay, metal, or wood. Molten glass was poured into the cavity, which was probably coated with powdered glass (Moorey 1999:205; Peck 2013:160). Rod-formed glass produced beads. A clay or metal rod formed the base around which glass coils were wound. Finally, cold cutting started with a cold lump of glass that was formed into the desired shape by grinding, cutting, and polishing, much like in stone work (Moorey 1999:206).

Given the quantity of ceramic and glassware found at excavated sites, comparatively few pottery and glassmaking workshops have been thus far discovered, and little is known regarding the production and distribution of ceramic and glassware. The production of ceramic and glass goods was labor intensive and required varied and numerous resources. The natural resources had to be procured and transported to the workshop and then prepared for manufacture. Considerable amounts of fuel were burnt, most likely wood and dung, to achieve temperatures necessary for baking the clay and making the glass.

Craftsmen also maintained a keen knowledge of chemistry and how to manipulate various ores and minerals to achieve the desired color for paint and to color the glass. Those who produced ceramic and glass objects were likely independent craftspeople; however, some have suggested that the production of glass in Egypt may have been the monopoly, at least in part, of the pharaoh, as exemplified at Amarna (Shortland et al. 2001). Because glass was a new product, it was highly desired by the upper classes who could afford to buy it. It is likely that the pharaoh controlled glass production, at least initially.

Faience, an older well-known product, was readily available to the lower classes and therefore not the interest of a pharaoh's monopoly. Hence, in Egypt, glass production was established in Amarna at that time, while faience workshops were located in residential areas (Shortland et al. 2001).

Presumably, as with the textile industry, these goods were shipped via merchant caravans and ships, judging from shipwrecks and their cargo. For the most part, ceramic and glass vessels contained commodities such as wine, grain, perfume, and oil, so the vessels were merely packaging for the commodity. In some cases, it was not the vessel itself being traded but the product it contained. A vessel's size, shape, inscription, and perhaps also decoration probably revealed the product contained within, so that anybody looking at it would know what it held. Just as today when we see a Coca-Cola bottle, we know it contains a specific soda; or a specifically shaped bottle contains wine or gin; or a thin cardboard box contains cereal. The exterior decoration of these items communicates exactly what type of wine or cereal will be found within. So too it was with ceramic and glass vessels. Smaller glass vessels likely contained perfume; larger clay storage jars likely contained wine or olive oil. The decoration may have also conveyed information about the recipient and/or the manufacturer.

12

WATER MANAGEMENT AND TECHNOLOGY

Water is vital to life. Not only is it essential for humans and other animals to survive; it is critical for agriculture, manufacturing, hygiene, and the economy. One of the fundamental criteria for the founding of a settlement was its proximity to a perennial water source. At first people camped or established settlements near springs, rivers, lakes, or seasonal water sources while herding, hunting/gathering cyclical food sources, and even when forming permanent communities. For example, Jericho, one of the earliest known city/villages in Canaan, was established in the ninth millennium near a perennial spring that provided at least 4 cubic meters of water per minute (Wikander 2000:608). Water could be collected in jugs at the spring and transported into the home or workshop. The availability and quantity of water was directly commensurate to the size of the corresponding settlement it could support. Later, canals and aqueducts were constructed to bring water to cities. Given the importance of water, it is not surprising that engineers devised ways to gather water and transport it great distances to the settlement via canals and aqueducts. This allowed urban centers to exist in areas that lacked a nearby perennial water source but that may have been near other vital resources, such as a mineral deposit. This chapter will discuss water collection, management, and associated technology such as canals, wells, cisterns, irrigation, aqueducts, and drainage.

Wells

Wells were a Neolithic invention. Digging a well consists of first determining the location of a consistent subterranean water source and digging down to the water table from the surface. Most wells were ca. 0.5 to 2.0 meters in diameter and could be ca. 3 to 30 meters deep. The walls of the well, if dug through soil, had to be lined with stone, wood, and/or plaster to keep them from collapsing. Some wells were cut through soil until bedrock was encountered; then, the well diggers had to chisel away the bedrock. Once finished, the best way to retrieve water from a deep well was with a bucket or jug attached to a rope with or without the aid of a block and tackle, a *shaduf* (discussed earlier, see Figure 7.4), or a wooden crank. It was not until the eighth century BCE that the wooden pulleys (as we know them) were invented (Hodge 2000a:30–31). An excellent example of a Neolithic well was discovered at Sha'ar HaGolan (Garfinkel et al. 2006; Mithen 2010).

Some wells were very large and deep. Water systems such as those at Megiddo (MB/tenth century BCE), Gibeon, Lachish, and Gezer (Bronze Age) consist of a large pit-like opening at ground level with steps winding around the well walls or descending directly down to the water table. The steps were usually made of stone set into the earth or hewn from the bedrock below the soil level. These wells measured to a depth of 15 meters below soil-level, resulting in a lot of steps! Once at the bottom, the rock-cut entrance opened into one or several chambers, which may have included reservoirs or feeding channels, such as the well at Tel Beersheba (tenth century BCE) (Ohlig et al. 2004). Water was collected by descending the steps while carrying ceramic containers. Once filled, those steps had to be ascended while carrying those containers heavy with water. So not only did this type of well provide water but also strenuous exercise! Finally, water from subterranean wells would likely have been cool and relatively free from contaminants.

Irrigation canals

Irrigation is the intentional diversion of water from a perennial source, such as a stream or river, to another place such as to fields to water crops or into a collection reservoir. As early as the seventh millennium irrigation systems were employed in Khuzistan in southwestern Iran. Runoff from rivers in the Zagros Mountains was redirected for agricultural purposes. Irrigation in Egypt began soon after. Water from the Tigris and Euphrates in Mesopotamia and from the Nile River in Egypt was diverted into a series of canals and reservoirs from which water was guided into furrows in the fields. To move water from a lower to higher place a *shaduf* was used and continues to be utilized in Egypt today (see Figure 7.4) (Oleson 2000a, 2000b).

Evidence for elaborate irrigation systems comes from maps depicting the canal system at Nippur, Ur, and Babylon dating to the nineteenth century BCE. Canals were given names such as Canal of Burden, Side Canal, and Stream that Gives Drink, the name of a canal at Nippur. At Ur and Babylon, names were topographical, such as Sea-Canal, for example. Administrative documents describe the tasks involved in maintaining the canals, including excavation of new canals, cleaning canals, repair of dikes, and survey of boundaries. The eighteenth century BCE law code of Hammurabi describes the legal framework involving the irrigation network and individual rights and responsibilities. Later, Xenophon (ca. 430–354 BCE. Anabasis 1.7.14, 2.3.10, and 2.4.13) and Strabo (*Geography* 16.1.9–10, Henderson and Jones 1935:204–206) described canals from the Tigris and Euphrates that fed fields via irrigation canals (Oleson 2000a:192–195).

FIGURE 12.1   Nilometers in Egypt. Left: Elephantine Island. Middle: Kom Ombo
Temple. Right: Edfu Temple

Photographs by Jill L. Baker.

Egypt was fortunate to have the Nile River, which flooded annually. Thus, the
Nile provided not only water for irrigation, but the floodwaters brought new fertile
soil each year. As mentioned earlier, nilometers were used to record the height of
the floodwaters for determining annual tax rates (Figure 12.1). Nilometers were
situated at numerous points along the Nile to predict and determine the exact flood
level for each area along its path.

A nilometer consists of a shaft made of ashlar masonry with descending steps and
calibrated marks on the wall to measure the height of the water. Inside the well, or
freestanding in fields, there may also have been a marked, calibrated column situated
on a platform, another way to determine flood levels. Several nilometers have been
discovered at Philae, Aswan (ancient Elephantine), a temple at Kom Ombo, and at
Cairo on Rhoda Island (Figure 12.1). Recently, a third-century BCE nilometer
was discovered by workmen in the ancient city of Thmuis while installing a new
pumping station. Like the others, this appears to have been associated with a temple
complex (www.archaeology.org/news/4470-160518-egypt-thmuis-nilometer, accessed
9 June 2016). Nile-themed mosaics also depict nilometers such as those found at
Sepphoris and Tabghah in northern Israel. Nilometers were described by Herodotus
(Rawlinson 1875:297–300), Pliny the Elder (*Natural History* V 10.57–58, XVIII
47.167–70; Oleson 2000a), and Strabo (*Geography* 17.1.48). The nilometer determined
tax rates well into the Islamic period when the Abbasid caliph, al-Muttawakkil,
constructed a nilometer on Rhoda Island in Cairo in 861 CE.

The ancient Egyptian waterworks administration included an overseer of irrigation, as evidenced by various titles including Chief of Irrigation, Chief of the Water
Office, Chief of the Canal Workmen, Scribe of the Water Reservoir, Inspector of
the Inundation, and Watchers of the Nilometer (Oleson 2000b:201). While these

devices were not integral to the collection of water, they do emphasize the important role water held for the ancient Egyptian economy.

Elevating water

No matter the source of water, it is inevitable that water must be lifted from a lower place to a higher one, such as from a river or stream to a field, or from a well to a portable container. The simplest way to move water was by using a container and rope, as with wells. Containers could be made from skins, bark, wood, or reeds and usually had a handle to which the rope could be tied. Rope was made from hemp or flax. This method was used as early as the Mesolithic period and remained in continual use (Oleson 2000b:220). In Assyria at Nimrud, a nineteenth-century BCE relief depicts the use of a simple pulley to retrieve water. It is likely that the pulley was introduced around this period. Early pulleys were made from wood and consisted of a block or roller set into a frame over a well shaft. This was a much more efficient way of retrieving water from a well as the container did not hit or get stuck on the well walls. Using this method, larger containers could be utilized, allowing one or several people or even animals to pull up the container via the rope.

When lifting water from river/stream to field, a *shaduf* was employed. Already discussed earlier (Figure 7.4), but by way of reminder, this device consists of a wooden frame with a lifting mechanism or beam that extends out over the water source and to which the collection vessel or bucket is attached. The beam varies in length and thickness depending on the size of the container and thus the weight of the water being carried. The beam is loosely tied to the crossbeam so that it can be swung to the riverbank to deliver the water container to the irrigation ditch or collection basin. The limitations of this device include the range that the beam can swing and the size of the container, since the wooden beams are not usually very thick, and a too large and thus too heavy container can break the beam. Nevertheless, the *shaduf* remains in use in Egypt today. Use of the *shaduf* was at least as early as 2400–2200 BCE, evidenced by the depiction on a Mesopotamian seal of a *shaduf* in a later phase of development. This device was probably in use long before this depiction (Oleson 2000b:227).

It is possible that the water wheel was in use in Egypt during the Hellenistic period. The wheel was made of a wooden circle divided into equal compartments, which when turned captured and delivered water to a trough at a higher elevation. The wheel was turned by human or animal power. This wheel was called τύμπανον in Greek and *tympanum* in Latin, translated as drum (Oleson 2000b:229). The equally divided compartments generally numbered eight and were waterproofed with pitch and angled to catch and deliver the water. This device could lift a greater quantity of water than could the *shaduf*; however, it was limited by the diameter of the wheel in terms of the distance it could deliver the water. Nevertheless, it is upon this device that Archimedes is thought to have developed his water screw, which was used to move water from a lower to a higher place (Oleson 2000b:229).

It is said that Archimedes (ca. 287–212 BCE) invented the water screw (ca. 241–220 BCE) as a way to remedy irrigation problems in Egypt. One of its first non-agrarian uses was as a bilge pump for large grain ships. Scholars speculate that Hieron II King of Syracuse (308–210 BCE) loaned Archimedes' services to the Ptolemies of Egypt to help with the engineering problem. The water screw consisted of a large, solid, cylindrical axle around which a double or triple helix made of wood strips (sometimes bronze) were fixed. The axle and helix were inserted into a barrel casing to facilitate water flow. When the axle and helix were turned, the helix collected water in the spaces between the threads of the screw, thus moving the water up the cylinder. Vitruvius provides a description of a water screw in his work, *On Architecture* X, 6.1–7 (Morgan 1960:295–297; Oleson 2000b). Originally intended to move water, Archimedes' screw proved useful for moving grain, rubble, and dirt, and for olive and wine presses. Recent scholarship suggests that Sennacherib (ca. 704–681 BCE) may have used a bronze screw to deliver water to the Hanging Gardens of Babylon (Dalley 2013). If this interpretation is accurate, the screw would have been invented and utilized about 350 years before Archimedes developed his screw.

Bucket chain

To gain a higher lift, the bucket chain was developed. This contraption was a vertical lift that incorporated a tall frame, two axles, buckets or scoops, rope or chain, and a crank or perennial moving water source to turn the axles. When turning, the buckets rotated around the two axles, dipped into the water to collect it, and delivered water to a trough at the top. This device could be powered by humans, animals or automatically with a running water supply. This machine may have been invented by Ctesibius (ca. 285–222 BCE), an Hellenistic inventor from Alexandria, Egypt; however, it is described in detail by Philo of Byzantium in *Pneumatica* (65) and by Vitruvius (*On Architecture*, X.IV).

Pipes

To deliver water from its source to settlements, cities, and villages, pipes were the most efficient and direct method. Beginning from the tenth century BCE onward, Assyrian kings, such as Ashurnasirpal II (ca. 883–859 BCE) constructed a canal from Upper Zab that irrigated his garden and orchards at Nimrud. Similarly, Sennacherib (ca. 704–681 BCE) built a 55 kilometer-long canal, including a 300 kilometer dike over Wadi Jerwan, to deliver water to Nineveh. He also built several dams and canals to sustain his gardens and orchards. (Wikander 2000:618). To deliver the water to specific locations, clay pipes were utilized.

Clay piping delivered water to bathhouses and bathrooms within palaces and upper-class houses. For example, in Neo-Hittite cities in northern Syria, palaces and larger buildings were outfitted with bathrooms that included bronze tubs and toilets. The floors in these rooms were equipped with drainage pipes and sealed with bitumen. Clay pipes also removed wastewater from toilets, baths, and the roof (Wikander 2000:619).

Terracotta pipes were made by potters and measured ca. 20 to 25 centimeters in diameter and 40 to 60 centimeters long. The two ends were male and female to slip snugly into each other (Figure 12.2). Piping generally ran underground, especially

FIGURE 12.2   Sebastia, Nablus. Restored clay pipes in use

Photograph by Jill L. Baker.

FIGURE 12.3   Qumran canal system

Photographs by Jill L. Baker.

when carrying water across the countryside. The movement of water from one place to another was generally achieved through gravity. The force and speed of moving water resulted in the pressure needed to deliver it to its destination over long distances.

In the Hellenistic period, sophisticated hydraulic engineering combinations of piping, siphons, settling, and distribution tanks delivered water more efficiently (Hodge 2000a:42–43). In addition to those mentioned from Mesopotamia, ceramic pipes have been found throughout Canaan/Israel at sites such as Banias, Caesara, Dor, and Ugarit.

Channels

Channels, as opposed to pipes, canals, or aqueducts, were conduits that delivered water to basins, pools, fountains, transfer stations, and into buildings. Channels form an important component in the water system and should therefore be considered independently. Channels are generally constructed from stone or mudbrick, are U-shaped, and are covered with a thick mud-clay coating then sealed by a thick limestone plaster to make it waterproof. Channels were open on the top, covered with stone or clay slabs, or lined with pipes (Figure 12.3).

Although channels were utilized earlier, such as at Gezer, where the tenth century gate complex contained a channel and basin, from the Hellenistic period onward, the use of channels was ubiquitous, especially in the Roman period. Channels have been discovered at Qumran, Caesarea, the Cypros fortress, Dor, and Petra to name a few. Some channel systems were quite complex such as those at Qumran and Petra (Ortloff 2005, 2009). Some systems are so complex that scholars have theorized as to their purpose: utilitarian, decorative, or ritualistic (Bedal 2004).

Water tunnels

Extensive water systems were hewn directly into bedrock to deliver spring water or rainwater to settled areas (Figure 12.4). These systems were massive and could handle a large amount of water. Engineering and survey techniques were established early,

FIGURE 12.4   Western Wall Tunnel, Jerusalem, Israel. Second Temple Period. Water
channel leading to large cistern

Photographs by Jill L. Baker.

and it was with impressive precision that these conduits were constructed. In the
tenth and ninth centuries BCE, a complex sequence of tunnels, shafts, basins, and aqueducts were devised to deliver water from the Gihon spring east of Jerusalem in the
Kidron Valley into Jerusalem. The construction of it is attributed to King Hezekiah in
the eighth century BCE. Hezekiah constructed this system to deliver water directly
into the pool of Shiloah, inside the walls of Jerusalem, so that there would be ample
water in time of attack. This proved useful during the siege of Jerusalem by Sennacherib
ca. 701 BCE (2 Kings 20.20; 2 Chronicles 32.30; Isaiah 22.9, 11).

   Hezekiah is credited with the construction of this tunnel in the eighth/seventh
century BCE. Also known as the Siloam Tunnel and the Pool of Siloam, it curves and
measures some 533 meters (1750 feet, 0.33 miles) long, has a 6 percent gradient or
an elevation drop of ca. 2 feet, and there is a 30-centimeter difference in elevation
between the entrance and exit. The tunnel measures 5.5 to 6.5 meters in height.
(Wikander 2000:620). An inscription inside the tunnel says the tunnel was constructed by two teams, each beginning at opposite ends, and meeting in the middle
with only slight deviation—a feat that remains a tribute to the engineering and

surveying skills of those who built it. This tunnel was discovered in 1652 by Franscicus Quaresmius and was explored by Edward Robinson in 1838 and Charles Warren in 1865. Prior to this, in ca. 1800 BCE, Canaanites had already erected a tower and wall around the spring and cut a tunnel diverting the water through bedrock into a reservoir; however, it remained outside the city wall. Hezekiah brought that water into the city. Other water tunnels combined techniques, such as the water systems at Gezer from the Early Bronze Age and Sepphoris from the second to the seventh centuries BCE. Engineers combined aqueducts, channels, pools, and a very large rock-hewn reservoir.

Aqueducts

When considering the artificial movement of water from one place to another, aqueducts may be the first system of hydraulics that comes to mind. However, as can be seen, this was only one of numerous methods. Nevertheless, the hydraulic engineering behind aqueducts is impressive and surprisingly simplistic. The word aqueduct comes from two Latin words, *aqua* meaning "water" and *ducere* meaning "to lead." The overall meaning of the word aqueduct, leading water, can apply to numerous types of artificial systems including channels and pipes, ditches and canals. Here, the term aqueduct will refer to the system that employs bridges with incorporated channels and piping.

The earliest known aqueduct was the one mentioned earlier by the Assyrian king Sennacherib (ca. 704–681 BCE) who harnessed the Atrush and Kohar rivers, diverting their waters into Nineveh via a 55-kilometer canal. The system included a 300-meter dike, cut limestone blocks and a channel that was 12 meters wide (Hodge 2000b:40). The pre-Hellenistic Greeks also utilized aqueducts though these were mostly underground conduits made of clay pipes. However, with the dawn of the Hellenistic period and new scientific and engineering advances, aqueducts employed new techniques. Although the Greeks never used arches, they did employ embankments and causeways to carry the piping over uneven terrain. They also cut tunnels through mountains, such as the one on the island of Samos, carved in the sixth century BCE, engineered by Eupalinos of Megara. This tunnel was constructed by two teams digging simultaneously, each from a different end (Hodge 2000b:43). The Samos tunnel was ca. 1.8 x 1.8 meters wide and over 1 kilometer long. This is much like Hezekiah's Tunnel in Jerusalem, which was constructed in the same way (ca. 715–696 BCE) (2 Chronicles 32.30). Herodotus described the construction of the Samos tunnel and provided the date and method of construction.

Finally, Hellenistic Greeks also employed the siphon. This technique involved a closed pipe system that ran down one side of a hill or mountain, across the bottom, and up the other side forming a U-shape. Hydraulic engineering describes this as an inverted siphon.

The Romans adopted and adapted what was already known about water systems and improved known techniques by incorporating the use of arched bridges, retention pools, and filtration. Roman engineers first had to find a perennial source of water, which usually came from mountains some distance from the city. The spring had to be clean and produce enough water to fill the city's needs. The key to a successful aqueduct was the gradient. Since Roman aqueducts traveled great distances, the gradient had to be calculated to keep the water moving. For example, the water source for Marcia was located 91 kilometers away, and the gradient of its aqueduct was 2.7 meters per kilometer. In another example, the aqueduct serving Trier in Germany was 13 kilometers away with an average slope of 0.6 meters per kilometer. Thus, the gradient for each aqueduct depended on distance and terrain. The gradient not only determined whether enough water reached the desired destination but also the speed of the current. If the current was too slow, there was risk of clogging. If the current was too fast, flooding occurred.

Once the water source had been chosen, the course of the aqueduct had to be established. This was accomplished using known survey techniques and instruments such as the *groma*, *dioptra*, and *chorobates*. These instruments are discussed in another chapter. The construction of the aqueduct itself comprised a combination of underground as well as ground-level channels and raised bridges with channels on top. Underground and aboveground conduits were constructed of brick and/or stone and cement, forming a U-shaped channel, which was then plastered, making it waterproof. The channel was covered with an arched or peaked roof with manholes every 75 meters to allow for maintenance access. The conduit was usually 0.50 to 1 meter underground to avoid pollution or tampering. It usually measured ca. 0.8 to 0.9 meters wide by 1.7 to 2.4 meters high (Hodge 2000b:57). Along the route, settling tanks were inserted to allow sediment and impurities to work their way out of the water by the time it reached the city. Once in the city, a series of tanks allowed for collection and distribution to various sectors of the city.

With the expansion of the Roman Empire, hydraulic technology reached the Near East. Numerous aqueducts have been discovered; however, one of the most impressive is that of Caesarea in Israel. Sophisticated hydraulic technology can still be observed at Petra in Jordan. The water supply and distribution system of the Nabateans that inhabited the city employed numerous components to deliver a reliable steady supply of water to its inhabitants. Perhaps borrowing engineering knowledge from neighboring Mesopotamia, Greece, and Egypt, these components included pipes, canals, channels, and collection and distribution basins to deliver water from distant sources and to collect rainfall. Evidence of this system can still be seen throughout the ruined ancient city (Ortloff 2005).

Water usage

Water was important not only for its life-giving qualities, for drinking and agriculture, but also for industry. As industries advanced, so too the need for water in large quantities. Some industrial uses included textiles, metallurgy, the making of ceramics, and food production. Non-industrial uses included baths, timekeeping, drainage and sanitation, and fountains and pools, some of which will be briefly discussed later.

Textile industry

As discussed earlier, the three most common materials used to make textiles included wool, flax, and cotton. Before these materials could be woven into fabric, the raw material had to be prepared, and water was an integral part of the process (though cotton did not require water for processing). After shearing wool from sheep, it needed to be cleaned. The raw fibers were washed using soap and water to remove the dried suint and excess lanolin and dirt before dyeing. Washing raw wool could decrease its weight by 30 percent. At Dura Europos (Syria), merchants' records of sold wool indicate it was marketed as degreased and washed, and sorted by weight. Once washed, the wool was combed then prepared for dyeing. This process involved using alum as a mordant for cleaning. One recipe for this process includes 3 oz. of potassium aluminum sulfate, for fine textured wool, or 4 oz. for heavy textured wool; 1 oz. cream of tartar; 4 gallons of water, and 1 pound of wool. The alum was dissolved in warm water and then added to the woolen bath, which was heated to 160° F. The cream of tartar was dissolved in another pan and added last. The entire solution was boiled for 45 minutes for fine wool and one hour for heavy wool. After this process the wool could be dyed, which also used a mixture of water and pigment (O'Kelley 1975; Humphrey et al. 2006:357–358). Producing the dye and the process of dyeing also required large quantities of water. Dyes were produced from plants, minerals, and sea snails such as the murex, which produced purple dye. In his work *Natural History* (35.175, 196–198, Henderson and Rackham 1952), Pliny describes preparation of the purple dye, which involved heating in saltwater (Wilson 2000a:143–144). Evidence for such activities has been discovered at Philistine sites such as Ashkelon and Tel Miqne-Ekron, as well as basins used for processing wool (Mazow 2013). Assyrian records indicate fullers' activities at palace workshops. Additional textual evidence may be found in correspondence between the women who ran the textile industry in Mesopotamia and their customers and husbands and family members who marketed the finished products in Anatolia.

Flax, from which linen is produced, had to be soaked in water for several weeks to loosen the fibers from the stalk. Additionally, spinning flax into yarn is easier when damp (Pliny, *Natural History* XIX 3.16-18; Wilson 2000a:143). Soaking flax, or retting, was done in tanks or ponds, or left under running water (Vogelsang-Eastwood 2000:271). The stalks were then dried and broken with a wooden mallet, then scotched with a wooden blade to remove the bark and core (Oleson 2008: 468–469; Humphrey et al. 2006:353).

Mining and metallurgy

Water was used to separate the metal ore from the rock that encased it. Once the ore was removed, it had to be fired to separate the metal from the rock and then washed to further remove the smaller impurities. This was done prior to smelting, which further refined the metal's purity. Gold washing has been depicted in tombs, such as the sixteenth century BCE tomb at Beni Hasan depicting the extraction of gold from crushed ore using water (Neuburger 1930:8–9, Figure 8), and the tomb of Kha'y at Saqqara (Ogden 2009:162, Figure 6.4).

Another example comes from Timna where copper was mined, processed, and fashioned into ingots. Once the copper ore was obtained, it was crushed and placed into a fire pit with charcoal then set aflame. The chemical reaction between the charcoal and the copper ore is what changes the copper ore into metal. Once complete, the charcoal and copper were placed into a large wide bowl of water where the copper was further separated from impurities. The final stage was to smelt the copper in a crucible to refine it. Judging from the slagheap, also known as Slaves' Hill at Timna, extensive mining and refinement took place in the Bronze and Iron Ages. The amount of water needed for this activity would have been extensive, and would have been obtained by runoff and rainwater collection, by drawing water from a well, or by bringing in water from a distant source (Sapir-Hen and Ben-Yosef 2014).

Ceramic production

The preparation of clay requires an extensive quantity of water. Clay was first dried so that it could uniformly absorb water for cleaning. This process is called aging. By the sixth millennium BCE, potters realized this was a necessary step in clay preparation. Once dried, intrusive inclusions were removed and the clay was set into a pit or vat of water. This is known as slaking. After a few hours or days of slaking, more water was added to completely saturate it. At this time, the potter stirred, kneaded, and churned it with hands and feet or a paddle. This way the larger, heavier particles sank and the lighter ones floated. The unwanted inclusions could then be removed, thus making the clay finer. As the slip settled, it could be removed and sieved even further to obtain materials for wash and paint to be used as decoration (Wilson 2000a:128–129). Pottery workshops evidencing pooling were found at Ur from the Jamdat Nasr period, ca. 3100–2900 BCE.

Food processing and production

Just as today, water was an essential element of food processing and production. Raw foodstuffs, fruits, vegetables, and even meat must first be washed before processing or preparation can begin.

To make wine and beer, copious quantities of water were required to process and mix the ingredients. When brewing beer, for example, one stage involves the transformation of grain starch into maltose sugar, which requires germination by the application of moisture and heat in a full vat of water (Wilson 2000a:146).

Milling of grain to produce flour from which bread was made required a constant source of energy to turn the millstone. Water wheels were an efficient way to turn the grinding stones. This required a river or stream with a strong and reliable current whose energy could be harnessed.

Olive pressing required water to wash the baskets after pressing and to soak the pulp after the first and second pressings.

Finally, most recipes required some water to combine ingredients.

Timekeeping

Tracking time during hours of daylight was relatively straightforward. One only had to look at the sun's position to know the time of day. However, at night or when there was significant cloud cover, keeping time was not as easy to do. To compensate for this, Amenemhet, an Egyptian court official ca. 1500 BCE, invented the water clock, according to an inscription in his tomb. During the reign of Amenhotep III, ca. 1391/1388–1353/1351 BCE, water clocks were used in the Temple of Amen-Re at Karnak. Water clocks were useful especially for priests who had to perform rituals at specific times of day and night. In Babylon, ca. 2000–1600 BCE, simple outflow water clocks were also used. These were cylindrical in shape and aided astronomical calculations. The Enuma-Anu-Enlil (ca. 1600–1200 BCE) and the MUL.APIN, seventh century BCE, reference water clocks as payment to night and day guards. Water clocks are discussed in greater length earlier/later.

Drainage and sanitation

Public water works were an integral component to a well working and managed city. The removal of unwanted water was crucial to business and quality of life. Unwanted water comes in two forms: rainwater and wastewater or sewage.

Managing and removing water from rainfall was surprisingly important. In cities (and villages) where the majority of the buildings were constructed from mudbrick, mud plaster, and limestone plaster, excess rainfall and water runoff can cause unwanted erosion. The exterior of most buildings, walls, and installations were covered with a thick limestone plaster, which had to be regularly maintained; however, they remained susceptible to erosion and expeditious removal of excess water was imperative. Removing wastewater was equally important. Consequently, early drainage systems can be found in Mesopotamia and Syria. At Šagar Bazar and Byblos in Syria stone drain channels were used in the sixth and fifth millennia BCE and at Tepe Gawra in Mesopotamia Tell Mudhar and Uruk mudbrick drains were used in the fourth millennium. In the sixth millennium BCE at Tell Hassuna in Mesopotamia, clay pipes and channels were introduced (Wilson 2000b:152).

In Early Bronze Age Canaan, city planning incorporated drainage, as, for example, at Arad. These channels were constructed of fieldstone and may have been plastered. In Mesopotamia during the First Dynasty, at Ur, Ubaid, and Kish, houses were equipped with soakaways. Soakaway systems have also been discovered in Egypt at Saqqara from the Second Dynasty (ca. 2890–2686 BCE) and Eighteenth Dynasty El-Amarna elite homes (ca. 1350 BCE) where in upper class private homes lime-stone seats with keyholes have been discovered. A soakaway consists of a deep shaft dug into the ground lined with wide ceramic rings perforated with holes. Water, whether runoff or waste water from baths and toilets, was directed into the soakaway by clay pipes. The water was then allowed to seep into the surrounding earth via the holes in the rings. This basic system remains in use today for diverting water away from structures and is similar to a septic tank system. Soakaway systems allowed wastewater to remain within the boundaries of private individual homes without disturbing neighbors. Later, as urban centers became more sophisticated, waste water systems became public and civil citywide infrastructures carried away every dwelling's waste via public sewers. Public drainage systems were in use as early as the Middle Bronze Age as evidenced at Ashkelon with the discovery of a mudbrick drain that went through the northern city gate (Stager et al. 2008:221–234), and the tenth century BCE gate at Gezer.

In Neo-Assyrian Mesopotamia at Assur, houses incorporated channels that drained into the street or exterior seepage pits. The Governor's Palace in Nimrud, built by Shalmaneser III, ca. 859–824 BCE, contained a bathroom, with ablution slabs and drain holes as well as an arched entryway to the sewer for maintenance. The Palace of Sargon II at Khorsabad, ca. late eighth century BCE, was very sophisticated. It contained large mudbrick drains with vaulted ceilings. Ceramic chutes allowed the constant outflow of wastewater. One drain configured with an oval vault measured 1.40 meters high by 1.12 meters wide and was over 66 meters long (Wilson 2000b:161). These examples illustrate the need for removing the overflow of rainwater, wastewater, and human waste from living areas.

Bathrooms and bathhouses

Personal hygiene was as important in the ancient world as it is today, as evidenced by en-suite bathrooms in private dwellings and palaces. These rooms often combined bathing and toileting facilities, just as bathrooms do today.

Private dwellings of First Dynasty (2600–2450 BCE) Ur, Ubaid, and Kish contained rooms for bathing as evidenced by mudbrick floors sealed with bitumen to prevent erosion. The private houses of Tell el-Amarna (ca. 1350 BCE) contained bath or toilet rooms that were connected to drainage channels. Limestone toilet seats with a keyhole-shaped opening were discovered there (Amarna Project, http://amarnaproject.com/, accessed 18 June 2017).

The Greeks incorporated bathing rooms and bathhouses into their lifestyle, but theirs were not as elaborate as the Romans'. Domestic bathing rooms were located near the kitchen, probably so that heated water could be transported easily and quickly before it cooled. Bathing consisted of a tub or a trough whereby one stood next to the water filled vessel and cleaned oneself. Some tubs/troughs may have been large enough for a person to sit in while another person poured water over them. Public bathhouses likely operated similarly. These are often referred to as hipbaths. Disposal of bathwater was probably done by bailing the water from the tub or trough and pouring it onto the sealed bathroom floor so that the water could drain into a soakaway or the public drainage system.

Roman baths were much more elaborate and required a substantial amount of water, which was obtained from a spring, river, well, or rain collection, or from a distance by a public supply system such as an aqueduct. Initially the water went into a collection tank, and from there it was delivered to the bathhouse.

As mentioned earlier, Roman baths included a labyrinth of rooms: frigidarium, tepidarium, caldarium, fountain, latrine, thermopolium, pools, and a sewer system. Water had to be heated, which consumed a large amount of fuel for the fires. Hot and cold water were delivered to their respective rooms via pipes, and hot rooms were heated by the hot water that flowed through pipes in the walls and floors. Although bathhouses utilized ingenious hydraulic technology, they required a very large amount of energy to operate.

With the spread of Graeco-Roman culture throughout the Near East, bathing and bathhouses quickly became popular, especially with elite members of society. Bathrooms were incorporated into palaces such as Herod's palace at Masada. Elaborate bathhouses were built in cities such as Sepphoris and Beth Shean (Manderscheid 2000).

Fountains and pools

With the Romans also came fountains, pools, and ornamental water features. Fountains, while also ornamental, also provided a supply of water to those who could not afford to connect public water pipes to their homes. Communal fountains allowed a person to bring their vessel to the basin and fill it. These functioned much like perennial springs, rivers, or public wells where people collected daily water.

Other cities incorporated channels to deliver water. Qumran, for example, boasts an elaborate system of channels, pools, and storage basins throughout the settlement, though the exact purpose for these water features remains unclear (Galor 2002). At the Nabatean city of Petra, numerous pools, gardens, channels, fountains, baths, and fishponds were fed by aqueducts and cisterns. Throughout the city, water played a prominent role. Some water features were associated with a deity in the form of a statue, stele, graft, figurine, or shrine. However, aside from utilitarian reasons, the overall purpose of incorporating water features throughout the city is not entirely understood. Speculation ranges from ornamental to sacred to luxury (Bedal 2004).

Water management

In Canaan the earliest evidence for water management may be found at Tel Arad, when in the Early Bronze Age, a well appears to have been associated with a large structure (Aharoni 1993:78–79). It is assumed the large structure housed the person who managed access to the water, the water administration and/or maybe his/her family. The Babylonian King Hammurabi (ca. 1792–1750 BCE) introduced a series of laws known as the Law Code of Hammurabi, some of which addressed water control. Articles 53–56 of the Law Code states:

> If a seignior was too lazy to make [the dike of] his field strong, and did not make his dike strong, and a break has opened up his dike, and he has accordingly let the water ravage the farmland, the seignior in whose dike the break was opened shall make good the grain that he let get destroyed. (54) If he is not able to make good the grain, they shall sell him and his goods, and the farmers whose grain the water carried off shall divide (the proceeds). (55) If a seignior, upon opening his canal for irrigation, became so lazy that he has let the water ravage a field adjoining his, he shall measure out grain on the basis of those adjoining his. (56) If a seignior opened up the water and then has let the water carry off the work done on a field adjoining his, he shall measure out ten *kur* of grain per eighteen *iku*.
>
> *Meek 1992:168*

Later, the Romans imposed strict management of water in cities. The first Roman aqueducts were constructed by Appius Claudius (340–273 BCE). These monumental waterways transported water long distances for distribution within Roman cities for public and private consumption. In Republican times, waterways were operated by private contractors and overseen by censors. It is not surprising that people secretly and illegally tapped into the water system to obtain water for private use. Under Augustus the system was overseen by an imperial water commissioner who could determine the amount of water allotted to public structures, such as bathhouses, and to public fountains and private users; he also determined who paid for water and how much. Marcus Agrippa was the first water commissioner to standardize pipes sizes and stamp them with the seal of the imperial government to regulate use and to equitably charge for water use. Sextus Julius Frontinus (35–103 CE) was a water commissioner who wrote *The Aqueducts of Rome*, which studied the water supply, aqueducts, pipes, the location of pipes, leaks, water quality, and much more. His work drastically reduced waste and fraud (Richard 2011:58–62). When the Romans controlled portions of the Near East, it is likely that these same management techniques were employed.

Water purification and filtration

As early as 2000 BCE (approximately), the *Sus'ruta Samhita*, an Indian Sanskrit medical text and Egyptian sources describe water purification methods, including boiling water over fire, heating water in the sun, inserting heated iron into water, filtration through gravel and sand, and use of *Strychnos potatorum* seed and *gomedaka*, a stone. In Egypt, a water purification device is depicted in the tombs of Amenophis II (fifteenth century BCE) and Rameses II (thirteenth century BCE) (www.freedrinkingwater.com/resource-history-of-clean-drinking-water.htm, accessed 9 June 2016). Water was passed through a filtration system using sand, gravel, and/or charcoal, as well as ceramic fragments and shells. Alum aided in particle settlement (Hodges 1992:123–124). Hippocrates (ca. 460–370 BCE) advised boiling water to improve the taste and to filter it through a cloth bag, which came to be known as the Hippocrates Sleeve.

The cloth bag trapped sediment that caused bad taste and odor. Finally, by routing water through canals, tunnels, and aqueducts, and through catch basins and settling tanks, any impurities in the water were filtered before the water reached its intended destination.

Biological filtration is a simple yet effective method that passes water through sand and gravel to strain and retain particles too large to pass through the sand. As the water passes through the sand, other impurities such as bacteria are caught. The addition of nutshells such as pecan or almond aid in the process and may help improve the water's taste. This system is not only simple but can be easily built and employed anywhere. Campers and outdoor enthusiasts will recognize this system from their personal water filter gear.

A nineteenth-century example of the successful use of sand filtration comes from John Gibb of Paisley, Scotland, who in 1804 used a slow-sand filtration system, also known as biological filtration, for his bleachery. He sold access to filtered water to the public for half a penny per gallon. By 1829, this system was improved and this method was adopted for the public water supply by James Simpson, who installed a treatment plant for water supplied by the Chelsea Water Company in London. By 1852, this was the standard water technique, and the Metropolis Water Act required all water taken from the River Thames within five miles of St. Paul's Cathedral to be filtered in this manner before being distributed to the public. Later, from the 1850s to the 1870s, better knowledge of bacteriological organisms allowed for more effective filtration of drinking water, and those who consumed filtered water did not catch diseases as opposed to those who drank non-filtered water.

In antiquity, water was needed to prepare food; to wash oneself; to prepare raw materials before making them into clothing, such as wool; to smelt and purify metals; to facilitate drainage; to aid in the process of leather tanning; to water crops; to cool drinks and foodstuffs; and to cool room temperatures. Water management and consumption in early societies was demanding and extensive. Today, water consumption not only rivals earlier needs but has no doubt surpassed those. Some would argue that the Earth's freshwater supply is running out while others argue there will always be plenty of it. Whatever the fate of the water supply, there are ways to manage it and keep it clean.

Some of the collection and purification systems discussed here could be efficiently and effectively employed today. For example, in areas where rainfall is high, water could be collected from rooftop systems that employ gutters and basins. This water could be used to water lawns and gardens. Bio-filtration systems could be utilized instead of chemicals for purification, which would improve the use of recycled water. Most water systems use water once then flush wastewater downstream with less than 3 percent reuse. There is a perception that all water must be brought up to drinking standards, including water used for lawns, gardens, toilets, and manufacturing. Less than 20 to 30 percent of used water needs to be potable, and non-potable water could be used for car washes and for watering lawns. Already some companies are creating and using bio-filtration systems that filter wastewater through a series of bio-systems and return it to use in sanitation systems and even back to drinking water. These bio-systems (see Living Machine®, www. livingmachines.com/Home.aspx) send wastewater through a series of tanks that contain soil, gravel, and plants that filter out impurities, making water safe for human use and consumption. These tanks can be imbedded outdoors or inside a green-house-type space. Such systems have been installed at schools and universities, government buildings and complexes, and at interstate rest stops, such as one located on Interstate 91 in Sharon, Vermont (July 2016). To incorporate such systems into residential, business, and industrial zones would go a long way to improving and maintaining water resources.

13
MEDICINE

The art of healing is ancient, instinctual, and natural. People have been aware of the cycles of birth, life, and death, and biological changes such as childhood into puberty into adulthood, for as long as humankind has existed. People have also been aware of illness, abnormalities, and injury. To address these, humankind devised remedies, often combined with ritual, to aid good health and combat ill health. Today the medical and pharmaceutical industries are mega-businesses in which numerous resources are invested, including research, technology, and money.

To some, medicine is more science than technology, and to include a discussion about medicine in this work may seem out of place. Indeed, medicine is defined as "the science or practice of the diagnosis, treatment, and prevention of disease" and "a drug or other preparation for the treatment or prevention of disease" (*Oxford Dictionary*, https://en.oxforddictionaries.com/definition/medicine). Yet, whether ancient or contemporary, the importance of one's medical well-being cannot be overstated. Health and healing held an essential role in the ancient world, into which numerous resources and much energy were invested. Given medicine's significance and in keeping with our working definition of technology as the practical application of knowledge, scientific or otherwise, to resolve a problem, achieve a goal, satisfy curiosity, make life easier, or to accomplish change, it is appropriate to discuss the medical practices of the ancient Near East.

Medical literature first appeared in Mesopotamia and Egypt in the form of long medical treatises and short practical handbooks. The earliest known Mesopotamian medical text, a therapeutic text, dates to the Ur III period (ca. 2112–2004 BCE) and was written in Sumerian (Scurlock and Anderson 2005:2). Early Egyptian medical papyri include the Papyrus Turin, Papyrus Kahun, and Papyrus Ramesseum IV and V, and date to the Middle Kingdom (Weeks 1995:1793). Doctors and chemists wrote theories, methods, and remedies, and shared them with the medical community. These treatises and manuals were copied, recopied, and handed down from one generation to the other. Ancient medicine, like modern medicine, was an art, a combination of research, trial and error, and ritual. In an atmosphere where the gods infiltrated every aspect of life, one's spiritual healing was equally important to one's physical healing, so ritual and medical healing went hand-in-hand. To the ancients, the physical and spiritual were inextricably interwoven, even as the practical, scientific aspects of medicine advanced.

A typical day in the life of a healer is best illustrated from Graeco-Roman Egyptian papyri dated from the second to the sixth century CE. Healers were summoned to inspect injuries or to diagnose illnesses. They declared a prognosis and prescribed remedies and treatments. They ran family hospitals and kept their own records and financial accounts. Occasionally, especially in later periods in Rome, doctors were called upon to resolve plagues and epidemics. For example, an epidemic recorded in 278–276 BCE occurred only in Rome and Latium due to an exceptionally cold winter (Nutton 2013:24–25). The ancient medical community addressed issues such as kidney and bladder problems, cancers, sexually transmitted diseases such as syphilis, arthritis and other joint afflictions, eye disease such as glaucoma and cataracts, headaches, gout, malaria, heart disease, skin problems, and dental issues. Ancient medicine was surprisingly advanced and can still influence modern medicine.

Mesopotamia and Egypt are among the earliest peoples to practice medicine. In Mesopotamia, cuneiform texts recovered from the library of Ashurbanipal (ca. 668–627 BCE) in Nineveh address medical issues. The earliest known texts date to ca. 2000 BCE. Some 660 tablets were discovered in Ashurbanipal's library in Nineveh and some 420 from other sites; hundreds of medical tablets were translated first by F. Kocher and the project was later finished by R. Biggs and M. Stol (eds.) after Kocher's death in 2002 (*Die Babylonishch-Assyrische Medizin in Texten und Untersuchungen,* Volumes 1–10). An important text, the *Treatise of Medical Diagnosis and Prognoses*, dates to ca. 1600 BCE and consists of forty tablets. The information in this text appears to summarize multiple centuries of medical knowledge into one work. Subjects were organized from head to foot, including gynecology, pediatrics, convulsive disorders, fevers, worms, and skin diseases, to name a few. The treatise describes the ailment and the prescribed treatment. The reason for disease and ailment were generally credited to gods, spirits, and ghosts, and were usually the result of the person having angered the entity in some way.

In Mesopotamia, there were two types of medical practitioner: *ashipu* or *mašmaššu* and the *asu*. The *ashipu* or *mašmaššu* were sorcerers or magicians. This type of sorcerer-physician addressed the spiritual aspect of illness. The *ashipu* first diagnosed the malady then identified the god or demon causing it. The *ashipu* determined whether the illness was due to a sin or an error, and cured the patient with spells and charms that were meant to drive out the demon or spirit causing the illness. The second type of doctor was an *asu*, a physician who treated the body rather than the spirit. An *asu* focused on the physical, scientific aspect of medicine and treated disease, wounds, and illness with prepared herbal remedies; an *asu* also washed, bandaged, and plastered wounds. (Plasters were made of medicinal ingredients such as plants or animal fats held onto the wound with a bandage.) Although the *ashipu* and *asu* treated different aspects of the body, both worked in concert to heal the whole person (Biggs 1995; Scurlock and Anderson 2005; Scurlock 2014; Yamauchi and Wilson 2016 vol. III:252–256).

In the Law Code of Hammurabi (ca. 1754 BCE, 215–227, Meek 1992:175–176), physicians were held responsible for the errors and failures caused by "the use of the knife." If the surgeon's patient lived, he received two shekels in payment. However, if the patient died, the surgeon could have his hand cut off, in extreme cases. If a slave died under the surgeon's care, the surgeon had to pay for a replacement slave. Hammurabi's law code also established rates for general surgery, eye surgery, setting fractured bones, curing diseased muscles, and much more. Fees were commensurate with the patient's ability to pay. Slave owners were responsible for the health and care of the slaves whom they employed, and their care had to meet a certain standard of quality. Medical data were collected and evaluated, and patients' rights were published and publicly displayed. Although health care was provided and made available to all Babylonians, not all received equal treatment.

A diagnostic handbook was written by Esagil-kin-aplt of Borsippa, a practicing physician at the time of Adad-apla-iddina (ca. 1069–1046 BCE). This handbook discussed methods of therapy and etiology, as well as the use of logic and rationality and the empirical senses to make a diagnosis and describe the treatment (Scurlock 2014:7–9; Yamauchi and Wilson 2016 vol. III:253). Concurrently, hepatoscopy, divination of a sheep's liver, was practiced through the Roman period. The liver was considered the source of blood and the giver of life. Special Babylonian priests, *baru*, examined the liver of a selected sheep to interpret the signs to determine omens. By examining the liver, the exact disease could be determined, the reason for the disease surmised, and the outcome of the patient's illness predicted. This practice was also mentioned in the Hebrew Bible by the prophet Ezekiel (Ezekiel 21:21).

In Egypt, great advances were made during the Old Kingdom from the Third to Sixth Dynasties (ca. 2686–2181 BCE), including construction of the Giza pyramids, mathematics, stonework, astronomy, transportation, administrative organization, and medicine. Nearly half of the known pharaonic doctors practiced during the Old Kingdom, with specializations already well developed. According to Herodotus, Egyptian medicine had become too specialized:

> …each physician is a physician of one disease and of no more; and the whole country is full of physicians, for some profess themselves to be physicians of the eyes, others of the head, others of the teeth, others of the affections of the stomach, and others of the more obscure ailments.
>
> *Herodotus 2.84; Strassler and Purvis 2007:152*

Most of the known medical papyri, such as the Edwin Smith Papyrus, were written during the Old Kingdom. The medical papyri as a corpus show the progression of medical practice beginning with the incorporation of magic in earlier writings to a decreased use of magic as a result of medical knowledge and greater trust in science. This suggests confidence in the achievements and abilities of medical science (Nunn 2002; Yamauchi and Wilson 2016 vol. III:256–259).

The earliest known physician is Imhotep (ca. 2650–2600), who was not only a physician but a priest, an architect, and an engineer. Imhotep, whose name means, "one who comes in peace, is with peace," was an official serving Pharaoh Djoser and was the architect of the pyramid of Djoser at Saqqara, ca. 2630–2611 BCE. He was also the likely author of the Edwin Smith Papyrus, a medical treatise. This papyrus presents a rational approach to medicine but acknowledges that as a priest he could invoke magical healing when necessary. From this papyrus, it is clear he knew the medicinal uses of plants. Aside from Imhotep, several other physicians are known, mostly by the discovery of their tombs. Unless otherwise noted, these tombs were found at Saqqara:

Hesy-Ra (ca. 2670 BCE) practiced during the reign of Djoser, was Chief of Dentists and Physicians, and Chief of the King's Scribes.

Merit–Ptah (ca. 2700 BCE), a female who was Chief Physician.

Penthu (ca. 1350 BCE), Chief Physician to Akhenaten, Amarna Tomb 5.

Peseshet (ca. 2500 BCE), Fourth Dynasty, Lady Overseer of the Female Physicians.

Iwti (ca. 2500 BCE), Nineteenth Dynasty, Chief Physician.

Qar (ca. 2350–2180 BCE), a royal physician in the Sixth Dynasty. His mummy was in a limestone sarcophagus with twenty-two bronze statues of different deities including a statue of Imhotep. Also included were the oldest bronze surgical tools discovered. He died at the age of 50.

Psamtikseneb (ca. 664–525 BCE), Twenty-sixth Dynasty, Head of Physicians, and a dentist. Tomb at Heliopolis.

Udjahorresenet, Twenty-sixth Dynasty, Head of Physicians, supervisor of medical schools called Houses of Life. Tomb at Abu Sir.

Harsiese, son of Ramose (ca. 550 BCE), Head of Physicians, Chief Physician of Upper and Lower Egypt, Leader of Aegean foreign troops and admiral of the royal fleet.

Petuaneith, Twenty-sixth Dynasty, Chief Physician.

Shepseskaf-Ankh, Old Kingdom, Fifth Dynasty, ca. 2465–2325 BCE. His tomb was located at Abu Sir, and he was Head of the Physicians of Upper and Lower Egypt. He was a priest of Ra in the Temple of the Sun, a priest of the god of Khnum, and a priest of magic.

From these eleven ancient Egyptian physicians and medical papyri, we learn several things: the medical field was vibrant, knowledge was shared, physicians incorporated magic and religion into their healing, and women were respected medical professionals.

Homer in the *Odyssey* (Book IV) and Herodotus (2.84; Strassler and Purvis 2007:152) note that the Egyptians were more skilled in medicine than any other peoples, and they were skilled in medicine more than any other art. This knowledge and skill is made apparent in the medical papyri, of which ten are known.

Each describes medical procedures and practices including details regarding disease, diagnoses, and remedies. Usually a combination of herbal mixtures, surgery, and magical spells are prescribed. Illness was considered to have been inflicted by deities in retaliation for bad behavior on the part of the patient. To be rid of the illness, the patient was treated with a medicinal remedy by a physician and instructed to use magic spells, charms, and amulets and to take certain actions prescribed by the priest; or, a physician-priest could perform both functions (Nunn 2002). Following is a discussion of the ten medical papyri.

Edwin Smith Papyrus (ca. 1550 BCE)

An Egyptologist named Edwin Smith purchased this papyrus in Luxor, Egypt, in 1862. It primarily discusses surgical remedies related to trauma. Magic is rarely referenced; instead, rational methods of diagnosis and treatment are described in detail. It was purchased from a local man who was a merchant, dealer, and consular agent, so its original context remains unknown. It is assumed to have come from the tomb of a physician in the Theban necropolis. There are seventeen pages, or 377 lines, on the recto and five pages, or 92 lines, on the verso. The entire work appears to have been written by the same person in hieratic, which suggests a date of 1550 BCE; however, this text is considered a copy of an earlier text, one possibly written by Imhotep. The recto or front side of the scroll includes the surgical papyrus and is divided into seventeen pages that discuss forty-eight cases, mostly trauma victims. It appears to be an instructional book rather than a compilation of remedies. The examination and diagnosis process is described, and each injury, diagnosis, and treatment is detailed. These are presented in anatomical order. The text discusses closing wounds with sutures, bandaging splints, making and applying poultices, preventing and curing infection with honey, and stopping bleeding with raw meat. It also discussed spinal injuries, immobilization, fluids, as well as the brain and its influence and related injuries. This papyrus appears to contain more advanced medical knowledge than that of Hippocrates and his colleagues more than a thousand years later (Nunn 2002:26–30).

The Papyrus Ebers (ca. 1500 BCE)

This is the longest of the medical papyri and seems folkloric, possibly reflecting traditions from an earlier time due to the archaic terms used within the text. It was probably found in a Theban tomb and later purchased by George Ebers 1873/1874 in Luxor (Thebes). It now resides at the University of Leipzig, Germany. It was probably copied from a text that may date as early as 3400 BCE. It is 110 pages in length and ca. 20 meters long. It was written in Hieratic Egyptian. It contains 700 magical formulae and remedies, including incantations to remove demons that cause disease. It notes that the heart is the center of the body's blood supply with vessels that carry fluids to every part of the body. It also discusses disorders such as dementia and depression; contraception; pregnancy and gynecology; tumors; bone setting; parasites and intestinal disease; abscesses and surgical treatments (Nunn 2002:30–34).

Kahun Gynecological Papyrus (ca. 1800 BCE)

This papyrus was discovered by Sir W. M. F. Petrie in 1889 at El-Lahun near the Fayyum. It was translated by F. L. Griffith in 1893 in the Petrie Papyri: Hieratic Papyri from Kahun and Gurob. The papyrus dates to the twenty-ninth year of Amenemhat III (ca. 1825 BCE) based on a notation. The subject matter is women's health: the diagnoses and treatment of gynecological disease, fertility, pregnancy, contraception, and other women's health concerns. There are thirty-four paragraphs, each discussing a specific problem, divided into sections by subject. Each line begins with "Instructions for a woman suffering from..." (Nunn 2002:34), followed by a list of symptoms and specific questions to ask the patient, followed by a diagnostic prognosis. Interestingly, most treatments are not surgical (Nunn 2002:34).

Hearst Papyrus

This papyrus was discovered by a villager in 1901 and given to the Hearst Egyptian Expedition near Deir el-Ballas. It dates to the Nineteenth Dynasty, around the time of Tuthmosis III (ca. 1479–1425 BCE), but it may have been written earlier, ca. 2000 BCE. It was written in hieratic, and there are eighteen pages divided into 260 paragraphs. This papyrus discusses the urinary systems and the *metu* (the vascular system), as well as blood, teeth, bones, hair, bites, and remedies for ailments that remain unidentified (Nunn 2002:35). One section discusses the "Canaanite Illness," which is when coal-black spots cover the body. This may have been tularemia, a plague that afflicted the Hyksos. Some 100 paragraphs are very similar to the Ebers Papyrus (Nunn 2002:35).

Chester Beatty Papyri

Sir Alfred Chester Beatty (1875–1968) owned nineteen Egyptian papyri. These were found at Deir el-Medina, the workmen's village associated with the Theban necropolis. These were part of a family's archives written by a scribe named Qen-her-kepeshef in the Nineteenth Dynasty. The archive was passed down through his wife, Niut-nakht, and through the children of her second marriage (Nunn 2002:36). These contain magical incantations against headaches. This corresponds with the Greek "hemi-cranid" or half head, from which our term migraine is derived (Nunn 2002:37). It also contains eight pages divided into forty-one paragraphs that deal with anal disease (Nunn 2002:36).

Berlin Papyrus

Also known as the Brugsch Papyrus, this papyrus was acquired by Giuseppe Passalacqua in Saqqara then sold to Friedrich Wilhelm IV of Prussia for the Berlin Museum in 1827, where it remains today (Nunn 2002:37). It dates to the Nineteenth Dynasty, ca. 1350–1200 BCE. This papyrus is magical and religious in nature. It includes twenty-four pages and 191 paragraphs. It parallels the Ebers Papyrus in part with a duplication of the paragraph on the *metu*. It discusses fertility tests and contraception (Nunn 2002:37–38).

London Medical Papyrus

It was acquired by the British Museum in 1860; however, nothing more is known of its provenance or chain of possession. It probably dates to Tutankhamun (ruled ca. 1332–1323 BCE) in the Eighteenth Dynasty. It consists of nineteen pages of sixty-one paragraphs of which twenty-five are medical and the rest magical. Seventeen paragraphs parallel the Ebers Papyrus, and the medical foci include eyes, skin, burns, and healing, predominantly dealing with gynecological issues (Nunn 2002:38–39).

Carlsberg Papyrus

The origin of this papyrus remains unknown. It likely dates to the Nineteenth or Twentieth Dynasty; however the style suggests Twentieth Dynasty. It was written recto-verso (front and back sides of the paper) and by two different people. The recto side discusses diseases of the eyes and is an almost exact copy of the Ebers Papyrus. The verso side, while damaged and difficult to read, appears to deal with the detection of pregnancy, sex of the unborn child, and ability to conceive. It was written in hieratic, demotic with some parts in Greek and hieroglyphics (Nunn 2002:39).

Ramesseum Papyri III, IV, and V

These consist of seventeen papyri, which were discovered in 1896 by Quibel in a wooden box at the bottom of a shaft under a brick mastaba next to the Ramesseum temple in Thebes. These belonged to a magician and medical practitioner. They probably date to after 1854 BCE because papyrus VI mentioned Amenemhat III, Twelfth Dynasty ca. 1860–1814 BCE. These were written in vertical columns, and Papyrus V was uniquely written in cursive hieroglyphs like the Kahun Veterinary Papyrus (Nunn 2002:38).

Brooklyn Papyrus

This papyrus dates to either the Thirtieth Dynasty (ca. 380–343 BCE) or to the early Ptolemaic period (ca. 305–30 BCE). It was written in Middle Egyptian (ca. 2000–1300 BCE), a type of hieroglyph that could be written in cursive form and related to hieratic. The papyrus was divided into two parts and written recto side. It primarily discussed snakebites and their treatment. It contains medical remedies and magical spells (Nunn 2002).

The Egyptians believed that the combination of magic and medicine united "the whole set of forces necessary to the protection of life and to its increase"

(Francois Dumas quoted in Halioua and Ziskind 2005:8). They further contended that magic maintained harmony between the body and the cosmos so that the body could function as a receptacle for the "vital forces that created the universe" (Halioua and Ziskind 2005:8). Magic was used to treat internal illnesses such as fractures and wounds, malevolent spirits, and evil divinities. The magician-physician, therefore, held particular powers, though many scholars feel the magical aspect restricted the medical. As rational thought and scientific method and theory progressed, magic and medicine diverged, ultimately resulting in a rational scientific approach to medicine without the hindrance of magical or religious overtones (Nunn 2002:96–112).

Egyptian physicians were trained at "houses of life" located within temple complexes, though a separate institution from them. However, since much of medicine overlapped with magic and religion, associating houses of life with temples seemed appropriate. Scribes specific to medical practice were associated with houses of life. These specially trained scribes copied medical papyri and recorded new information. It is possible that information dictated in individual houses of life were assembled into what was found in the above-mentioned papyri to become a large and well-distributed corpus of medical knowledge (Halioua and Ziskind 2005; Nunn 2002:113–135).

In addition to recitation of ailments and remedies, practitioners' methods can be observed. Like today, physicians examined the patient, gave a diagnosis and prognosis, and prescribed a treatment. The examination consisted of a series of questions and dialogue wherein the patient disclosed the symptoms s/he suffered, which gave the physician clues as to the malady and thus an accurate diagnosis. Next was an examination of the face, urine, excrement, and expectoration as well as the skin and rest of the body for abrasions or any additional indications of sickness. Physicians also took note of any odor that may be present. It is not clear whether early physicians took their patients' pulse rate; however, some argue they did and used a clepsydra (water clock) to aid in counting. Once all the data were gathered and in consultation with medical papyri, a diagnosis and treatment was pronounced. Physicians were acutely aware of their limitations, especially in the case of the terminally ill. Thus, the physical and spiritual aspects of a person were treated with the hope of full recovery (Nunn 2002:113–135).

Physicians were employed by pharaohs to serve the royal family and court, but they also practiced outside the court. In both realms, there was a strict hierarchy among professionals. Physicians were compensated for their services; however, in pre-monetary Egypt payment was in commodities, a barter system regulated by the state. Physicians were civil servants whose housing and provisions were provided by the government, especially if on military campaign or when traveling the countryside. All Egyptians received medical treatment and did not necessarily have to pay the physician because s/he was paid from public funding, according to Diodorus. Based on documents found at Deir el-Medina, payment to physicians consisted of what was needed for one's daily sustenance: cereal (wheat and barley), bread, and beer. A Twentieth Dynasty ostracon indicates that physicians received one-quarter khar (grain) and one khar barley. This was less than what other workers received, and another document, the Turin Canon, suggests that doctors were paid less than scribes or porters (Halioua and Ziskind 2005:19). Private patients may have remunerated with cattle, copper, slaves, and anything of value, though if a person needed medical attention, s/he likely received it whether s/he could afford to pay for the service or not. It is likely that the Egyptian rulers realized it was advantageous to have a healthy population.

Anatomy

It is clear that the Egyptians were keenly aware of most of the major organs and their function. They also appear to have had a basic understanding of blood and the brain. It is likely physicians gained their understanding in concert with embalmers, who routinely removed certain organs for mummification. It is also likely that in times of war, physicians examined wounded bodies, and in so doing, learned how body parts worked (Nunn 2002). Manetho (ca. 241–200 BCE) was an Egyptian historian and priest from Sebennytos during the Ptolemaic period. Manetho, quoting Africanus, who was another historian writing about Egypt's First Dynasty, discussed Pharaoh Athothis' (Djer's) son who lived ca. 3000 BCE and ruled for twenty-seven years (Nunn 2002:42, 121–122). The pharaoh's son built a palace at Memphis where he practiced medicine and wrote anatomical books. This is the earliest known reference to the study of anatomy. This is important because despite all the knowledge the Egyptians appear to have gained about the anatomy of the human body, mutilation of the body was taboo. Early Egyptian law would not have allowed the dissection of a corpse. They believed that one's body had to be whole, or as whole as possible, to enter heaven (Nunn 2002:42). It was probably not until the Hellenistic period that the Egyptians were able to fully investigate the inner workings of the human body. One of the first to do so may have been Herophilus, a Greek physician from Chalcedon, who worked at a medical school in Alexandria in the Ptolemaic Period. His works did not survive, but they were referred to by Celsus, Galen, and others, and indicate that he was allowed to work on human cadavers for dissection and possibly for vivisection on condemned criminals who remained alive (Nunn 2002:42). This work established a basis for the study of anatomy.

Pharmacology

Pharmacology, from pharmacopoeia, from which the word *pharmakon* was derived, means "he who brings security." It is likely that, at first, physicians' assistants prepared remedies. As time progressed, those who gathered and prepared the drugs probably developed into a specialized field within the overall practice of medicine. According to the Egyptian papyri, remedy recipes were prepared with exact, precise, and well-organized instructions. There were a multitude of recipes, some of which seem obscure as to their use or intended cure: "eye of the sky," "costly ointment," "tail of rat," and "tooth of hog" (Halioua and Ziskind 2005:31). In Babylon and Assyria, *pasisu*, "preparers of medicine" were an important group in the development of medicine and pharmacology. During the time of Hammurabi (ca. 2111 BCE), pharmacists appear to have established shops on one street in Sippar (Sonnedecker 1976:5). It is also from Mesopotamia (Babylonia and Assyria) that the gods Ea and Gula are frequently mentioned in incantations when drugs were dispensed. Additionally, a serpent cult and the use of serpents as healers became prevalent during this period (Sonnedecker 1976:5).

Pharmacology may have developed as a specialized practice in Mesopotamia, but Egypt refined the role. Pharmacy technicians ranked just below physicians and included titles such as Chief of the Preparers of Drugs, Conservator of Drugs, and Priest-herbalist (Sonnedecker 1976:10). There were also Collectors of Drugs and Laboratory Aides. By 1500 BCE the Egyptians utilized mouthwashes, snuffs, inhalations, suppositories, fumigations, enemas, poultices, infusions, pills, ointments, lotions, and plasters (bandages), just as we do today. Some 700 drugs and 800 formulas are described in the Ebers Papyrus alone (Sonnedecker 1976:9; Nunn 2002:136–162).

Most drugs were plant-based, derived from animals or animal by-products, or from minerals. Water, oil, wine, milk, and beet functioned as the vehicle by which medicines were delivered to the patient's body (Nunn 2002:134–140). Some of the most frequently used plants were acacia, date, fennel, fig, garlic, castor bean, wormwood, and poppy seeds. Minerals included alum, iron oxide, limestone, sodium carbonate, salt, and sulfur. From animals, honey was used as a binding agent in many formulas (Sonnedecker 1976:9) because of its antibacterial properties. The preparation of drugs included pressing, grinding, or mashing using a strainer in a copper plate (Nunn 2002:139). This would extract the active properties of the substance being mashed. Egyptian medicine did not change much from its beginning until the Ptolemaic period when Greece came into contact with Egyptian medicine. Some recipes and remedies probably did nothing at all except to provide assurance to the patient and act as a placebo, which can be beneficial to the healing process.

Below is a description of some of the herbs, plants, and minerals used in remedy recipes or taken alone. They are in no particular order.

Honey: its use was considered magical and medicinal. Honey relieved persistent cough, aided in digestion, and reduced swelling. It is antibacterial because of an enzyme, inhibine, secreted from the pharyngeal glands of bees. Effective against staphylococcus, salmonella, and candida bacteria. Used to treat wounds, ulcers, and burns. Was used widely and liberally in antiquity in numerous cultures (Nunn 2002:148).

Onion (common): an antibiotic, diuretic, and expectorant. Egyptians may have believed the onion symbolized eternal life due to its shape and concentric circles.

Garlic: contains amino acid, allium, which releases the enzyme allinase. Its antibiotic properties are 1 percent the strength of penicillin. Used for treating wounds and as an antifungal against candida. Also contains methylallyltrisulphide, which dilates blood vessel walls and thins blood, lowers blood pressure, and helps prevent heart attack.

Malachite: contains cupric carbonate/hydroxide, effective in preventing the growth of staphylococcus aures and pseudomonas aeruginosa. Used extensively for eye disease. Malachite was used in kohl, an eye paint, which helped prevent eye disease. Malachite was mixed with oil or animal fats, soot, and gum resins to make the eye paint. It was also effective in treating burns (Nunn 2002:147).

Cannabis: known as qunnabu in classical Rome. Herodotus (ca. 484–425 BCE) mentions the Scythian use of cannabis in steam baths. He says that hemp seeds were thrown onto hot stones, which "gave out such a vapor as no Grecian vapor-bath can exceed" (*Histories*). The cannabis plant was used for hemp (rope), oils, medical purposes, and for recreational use. It was used as a painkiller, anesthetic, and as an intoxicant. It reduced nausea and vomiting. It reduced muscle spasms and seizures. It was also used as an antidepressant.

Opium: the dried latex from the opium poppy contains ca. 12 percent morphine and codeine. It has been used since the Neolithic period in Samaria, Assyria, Egypt, India, Greece, Cyprus, Rome, and Persia. Germany, Switzerland, and Spain also exhibit remnants of opium use. Opium was most commonly used to relieve pain, but it was also used recreationally. The Sumerians referred to it as the "joy plant." It is mentioned in the Egyptian Ebers Papyrus (ca. 1500 BCE) to stop a crying child, among other uses. On Cyprus, opium plants were cultivated and traded by the Phoenicians and Minoans around the Mediterranean. Some historians believe that Base Ring Ware from Cyprus—bowls, juglets, and jugs referred to as bilbils—contained opium or an opium product. The juglets in particular appear to resemble the opium poppy in shape, which accounts for their association with opium (Merrillees 1962). Bilbils have been found not only in Cyprus, but also in Egypt and Canaan in great quantities. Opium was used in Egypt as pain relief for wounds, abscesses, scalp exanthema, and to soothe a crying child (Merrillees 1962:292). When considering ceramics vessels as packaging and labeling for commodities, it is safe to assume the bilbil's shape betrayed the substance within. Finally, Philostratus, the Greek writer, describes how the priests of Asclepius, the god of medicine, learned their arts through divination. Oracles used opium and cannabis to induce their visions.

Cinnamon: obtained from the inner bark of the genus *cinnamomum*, cinnamon was used as a sweetener and a germicide. In the Hebrew Bible, Moses uses cinnamon and cassia in the anointing oil (Exodus 30.22–26). Chewing on cinnamon root or drinking ginger tea alleviates sore throat, colic, and flatulence, and stimulates appetite.

Myrrh: from the Aramaic *murr* and Arabic *mur*, which means bitter, myrrrh is a resin or natural gum or essential oil. The tree sap bleeds a resin gum like frankincense. Used in perfumes, as medicine, and as flavoring, myrrh is good for the heart, liver, and spleen, and it safely purges blood clots. It is also very good for rheumatoid arthritis, circulatory problems, and uterine tumors. Egyptians used it for embalming. In the First and Second Temple periods in Israel, it was used as incense. The Nabaateans traded it with southern Arabia. Myrrh was one of the three gifts brought by the Magi from the East to present to the child Jesus.

Frankincense (Boswellia): the tomb of Queen Hatshepsut (ca. 1458 BCE) depicts sacks of frankincense traded from the Land of Punt. The Hebrew Bible mentions that frankincense was traded with Sheba (Isaiah 60:6; Jeremiah 6:20) and that it was used in the Temple as incense (Exodus 30:34; 1 Chronicles 9:29). Its resin comes from the Boswellia tree, which is considered the best of all the frankincense species. Herodotus said that frankincense was harvested from trees in southern Arabia and was dangerous to collect due to venomous snakes that lived in the trees. Frankincense is very effective in treating arthritis, healing wounds, improving the female hormonal system, and purifying the air. Several modern medical studies have found boswellia to be excellent in treating ulcerative colitis, asthma, and rheumatoid arthritis as well as depression and anxiety. The chemical compound incensole acetate helps to reduce depression and anxiety (Moussaieff et al. 2008).

Willow Tree: in the third and second millennia, Assyrian, Sumerian, and Egyptian texts reference the bark and leaves of the willow tree as remedy for aches and fever. The Ebers Papyrus (ca.1500 BCE) mentions willow and myrtle (both salicylate-rich) as effective analgesics and antipyretics, and both have anti-inflammatory properties. Hippocrates (ca. 460–377 BCE) describes how the powder made from willow bark and leaves helps to alleviate headaches, pain, and fever. Willow was used in the Americas by the indigenous peoples and by several European physicians such as Rev. Edward Stone in England, who observed the willow's medicinal properties and reported it to the Royal Society in 1763. In 1853, Charles Frederic Gerhardt, chemist, treated acetyl chloride with sodium salicylate to produce acetylsalicylic acid, and in 1897, Bayer established the standard for acetylsalicylic acid and called it Aspirin.

Chamomile (anthemis nobilis): Egyptians used it to calm nerves, induce rest, soothe upset stomach, and ease menstrual cramps. Helps with muscle pain and relieves depression and anxiety.

Celery (opium graveolens): found in Tutankhamen's (ca. 1332–1323 BCE) tomb. Lowers blood pressure, reduces inflammation due to bladder infections, gout, and arthritis. Known as a pain reliever since ca. 30 CE. External application as an anti-fungal.

Hyssop (hyssopus officinalis): has purification properties. Known from the Hebrew Bible, Psalm 51, "You shall purge me with hyssop, and I shall be clean." The New Testament describes its purification properties. The Greeks and Romans used hyssop water to purify a corpse. It also treats lung infections, bronchitis, relieves nasal congestion, coughs, colds, and sore throat. It also stabilizes blood pressure and prevents dizzy spells for people with low blood pressure. It can also be used for minor cuts and bruises.

Anesthetics: aside from wine, beer, opium, and cannabis, other plant-based anesthetics were effective in later periods. Henbane contains scopolamine, which is still used as a pre-anesthetic today. It induces sleep and amnesia. It is also a psychoactive drug used in "magic brews" to induce visual hallucinations and the feeling of flight (Long et al. 1999). The Romans also used mandrake because it contains hallucinogenic tropane alkaloids. It was used in magical ritual as well as an anesthetic. Finally, Datura contains atropine and hyoscine, which slows the heart rate and can dull pain and reduce trauma experienced during surgery. The Romans combined opium, mandrake henbane, and hemlock to produce an anesthetic, which was administered via a soporific sponge from the ninth to fifteenth century CE. The dried sponge was soaked with the mixture and held over the patient's mouth. As the fumes were inhaled, the cocktail of drugs made the patient insensible. Although effective, this concoction could also be dangerous.

Bacteria and antibiotics

Even though the ancients had no terminology for bacteria, they knew how to combat them. The Egyptians knew that an untreated wound, for example, could get infected (Nunn 2002:73–77). To prevent infection, the Egyptians applied moldy bread as a poultice (Keyes et al. 2003:45). Sumerian doctors used beer soup mixed with turtle shell and snakeskin. However, the most effective treatment appears to have been the use of mold. The Romans were also aware of bacteria. Varro (116–27 BCE), in his book *Agricultural Topics in Three Books*, 1.12.2, suggests that:

> precautions must also be taken in the neighbourhood of swamps . . . because there are bred certain minute creatures which cannot be seen by the eyes, which float in the air and enter the body through the mouth and nose and there cause serious diseases.
>
> *Henderson and Hooper 1935:209*

The "discovery" of bacteria is credited to Antony van Leeuwenhoek in 1632 in Delft, Netherlands. He discovered protozoa, single-celled organisms, and called them animalcules. Later, Sir Alexander Fleming, a Scottish biologist, discovered the enzyme Lysozyme in 1921 and Penicillin in 1928 from the fungus penicillium notatum, which proved to be more effective in battling bacterial infections such as syphilis, gangrene, and tuberculosis.

Surgical instruments

As early as the Neolithic period people have been using obsidian knives to remove thorns, splinters, arrowheads, and other shards that pierce the skin. The domestication of animals required minor surgeries such as castration, the birthing of calves, and the setting of broken bones. Obsidian is so strong, sharp, and precise that some surgeons continue to use scalpels made of obsidian blades today.

The first surgical instruments dated to as early as 2600 BCE, as depicted by the Egyptians. Their instruments, however, were made from copper, which they used for procedures such as circumcision. The Egyptians also used copper sewing needles. The Babylonians and Assyrians used obsidian and copper for their surgical instruments. They also used saws, trephines, forceps, drills, and scalpels.

The Temple at Kom Ombo in Egypt depicts the most complete set of surgical instruments known in the ancient world and dates to ca. 180–147 BCE. Depicted are a probe, forceps, saws, a retractor, a burning iron, bandages, a flask, scales, medical plants, shears, a sponge, scalpels, instrument case, and cupping vessels (James and Thorpe 1995:13).

Procedures

Trephination or trepanning

One of the earliest known surgical procedures was trephination, performed as early as 100,000 years ago in Europe, the Near East, North Africa, Egypt, and the Americas. This practice continued well into the eighteenth and nineteenth centuries. Trephination was performed with surprising frequency. For example, at a Neolithic site (ca. 6500 BCE) in France, one-third of the skulls recovered from graves showed signs of trephining (Irving 2013), and three individuals at Jericho, one in Tomb G88, show signs of trephining operations; one was well-healed, and the others show signs of slight healing (Kenyon 1965:60, Plate III:1, 2; Zias 1982). Trephination is drilling a hole into the skull to release fluid to relieve pressure. The survival rate was variable; however, the Maya appear to have achieved an extremely high rate of success with nearly all individuals healing from the surgery and living several years thereafter. It was thought that trephination relieved migraines, seizures, and mental disorders, and it was used to heal battle wounds and to remove parasites. Early tools included wooden shafts with hard tips made of flint, obsidian, or bronze. The hole could have been made with a knife or a hollow drilling tube to bore into the dura matter of the brain. The bone was sometimes kept for good luck or to ward off evil spirits (James and Thorpe 1995:24–32; Nunn 2002:168–169).

Bloodletting

Bloodletting is the removal of small quantities of blood from a patient for the purpose of curing or preventing illness and disease. The physician made an incision in the patient's vein with a scalpel and applied a bleeding-cup to the wound. The bleeding cup formed a vacuum, which gently sucked out a small measure of blood. After the desired amount of blood had been drained, the wound was bandaged. The cups were made from glass, horn, or bronze. Bloodletting was utilized from the earliest times until the nineteenth century and was a kind of cure-all. Erasistratus (ca. 304–250 BCE) discussed the overabundances in blood caused by disease and the need to purge. The Talmud discussed specific days of the week/month for bloodletting. Christians discussed the best saints' days for bloodletting. Specific points in the body were identified for letting. As new medical knowledge was acquired, the practice of bloodletting was eventually replaced with procedures and cures specific to the illness or disease (Nutton 2013:93; James and Thorpe 1995:13–15).

The purpose of bloodletting was to remove impurities from the body to allow the body's fluids, or humors as they were called, to attain proper balance for good health. The Egyptians practiced bloodletting as early as 1000 BCE, a practice that was later adopted by the Greeks and Romans. Bloodletting cups are among the surgical instruments depicted at the Temple in Kom Ombo. In addition to cupping, leeches were also used to induce blood flow. Today, bloodletting continues to be used in some parts of the world, and in surgery leeches are used to restore blood circulation and promote healing in skin grafts.

Disability and prosthetics

Ancient disability studies have advanced over the last thirty years and have received renewed attention (Draycott 2016). Comparatively speaking, the number of disabled individuals found in the archaeological record is less than those with normative bodies; however, there is a growing corpus of data in and beyond the Near East of disabled individuals living to adulthood and receiving a proper burial. Some of these include a Neanderthal male from Shanidar 1 (Crubézy and Trinkaus 1992); a Neolithic adult male, M9, from Man Bac, Vietnam (Oxenham et al. 2009); a teenage boy known as Romito 2 found in Italy, who dates to ca. 10,000 years ago (Frayer et al. 1988); a young woman, 18 to 23 years of age, from Dilmun (ca. 2050–1800 BCE), in present-day Bahrain, whose deformity included shorter than normal oddly angled right humerus, which caused problems for the shoulder and neck, and knocked knees (Boutin and Porter 2014). Although the bodies of these and other ancient individuals differed from what would have been considered "normal," they lived to adulthood and were given proper burials, if not elaborate as in the case of the Dilmun woman. This would suggest that even though some individuals suffered from physical abnormalities, they were likely accepted and productive members of their communities.

As has just been discussed, the people of ancient Egypt and Mesopotamia possessed well-developed and researched medical knowledge, which was thoroughly documented. According to the Egyptian medical papyri, doctors were keenly aware of deformities, amputations, and the replacement of limbs (Zaki et al. 2010; Binder et al. 2016; Nunn 2002). Amputations were performed for medical reasons, such as gangrene or due to battle or work-related injury as early as 2000 BCE, and as a form of punishment (Binder et al. 2016:29).

Artifactually, prosthetics have been found in Egypt, Mesopotamia, and China. In some cases, the prosthetic was for practical reasons, and, in others, mainly for aesthetics. Additionally, it was important for the body to be as whole as possible when buried to ensure its journey into the afterlife. Numerous individuals were buried with replacement eyes, ears, noses, and other body parts. Two examples of prosthetic toes have been discovered in Egypt, one made of wood and leather and the other made of cartonnage, a combination of linen or papyrus, glue, and plaster.

The wood and leather toe dates to ca. 950–710 BCE and was found in a tomb in Thebes, belonging to Tabaketenmut (ca. 1065–710 BCE; Nerlich et al. 2000), and was still attached to her foot. The individual was a female, 50 to 60 years of age, who is thought to have lost her toe to gangrene due to diabetes. Tabaketenmut was the daughter of a priest, and her prosthetic toe shows signs of wear. It consists of three parts or joints and includes holes for lashing it to the foot. The other toe is known as the Greville Chester Great Toe and lives in the British Museum. This prosthetic toe was made of cartonnage and also shows signs of wear. It is in the shape of the right toe and part of the right foot. It is less flexible than the other one and probably dates to 1295–664 BCE (Choi 2007; Lorenzi 2012). Tests conducted by Dr. J. Finch show that these toes were actually functional rather than simply ornamental. Replicas of the toes were made, and volunteers missing their right toes were fitted with the replicas. They were asked to walk barefoot and with sandals to see how effective the prosthetics were. The data revealed that the volunteers were able to walk comfortably using these prosthetics (Finch 2012).

In a necropolis in Shahr-i-Sokhta (Burnt City) in the Sistani Desert, Iran, a female skeleton was found with a prosthetic eye. Presumed to be a priestess, this female was 1.82 meters (6 feet) tall, and lived between ca. 2900–2800 BCE, and wore the ocular prosthetic in her left eye. She was ca. 25 to 30 years of age when she died; however, a cause of death could not be determined. The prosthetic eye was made of a kind of bitumen paste, a mixture of animal fat and natural tar. Lines were etched into it mimicking the iris with lines radiating from it. A thin layer of gold was applied to the surface and a very small hole was drilled on each side of the eye so it could be fixed to the head. The eye measured ca. 2.5 centimeters (1 inch). Based on microscopic examination, the priestess wore the eye throughout her life; it was not merely put into her eye socket for burial. There were marks on the eye socket from wearing the eye as well as marks from the thread. She may also have suffered an abscess due to prolonged use of the prosthetic eye (Moghadasi 2014).

In Turfan, China, a male, 50 to 65 years of age, ca. 170.4–178.2 centimeters tall, from the third/second century BCE was buried with his prosthetic leg. His left knee, the femur, patella, fibula, and tibia, had completely fused "with fixation at 135° flexion and 11° internal rotation" (Li et al. 2013:337). The peg-leg was comprised of three components: "a flat, lateral thigh-plate stabilizer," "a round distal peg (diameter 3.6 cm)" made of one piece of soft wood, possibly poplar, and "robust sheep/goat horn to reinforce the tip of the peg; and a horse or Asiatic ass hoof as sink resistance" (Li et al. 2013:339). Holes pierced into the thigh plate allowed the device to be strapped to the man's thigh. Additionally, during the Second Punic War (218–201 BCE), Marcus Sergius Silus lost his right hand in battle and was wounded numerous times. He was taken hostage by Hannibal and managed to escape. His right hand was replaced by an iron prosthetic, and he learned to wield a sword with his left hand, enabling him to continue to serve in battle (Pliny HN 7.28.104–5 from Draycott 2016:192).

These represent some of the earliest known examples of prosthetics used by people who lost limbs yet continued to be productive members of society. Certainly, some prosthetics functioned so practically that they completely assumed the respon-sibility of the lost body part. It may also be that they held aesthetic value, as a way to hide the deformity, and to make the body appear whole again, especially important for afterlife scenarios. The majority of the abovementioned individuals are known from their burials, which appear to have been conducted according to local cultural tradition. This suggests that these individuals were considered "normal" even if their bodies were not, and they were accepted and treated as full members of their community.

There are, however, accounts of impaired individuals who were treated poorly. In her article, Draycott (2016) focuses on one Gaius Germellus Horigenes who lived in Karanis, Egypt during the Roman period. Born ca. 171 CE, Gaius was 26 years of age when he was first mentioned in the family records, and 43 years of age when last mentioned. Gaius was blind in one eye and had a cataract in the other, which severely limited his sight. Based on the family archives, Gaius was not well treated by his brothers or other members of the community, and he remained unmarried. Whether this was due to his blindness or his behavior is not known; however, Gaius' experience offers another aspect of how the disabled were treated in antiquity.

Eye surgery: cataracts

Ophthalmic surgery was one of the most advanced surgeries in the ancient world because eye disease was one of the most common problems (Nunn 2002:201–202). The Babylonians were performing ophthalmic surgery as early as the eighteenth century BCE. The law code of Hammurabi mentions the "opening of the Nakkaptu" with a bronze lancet as a way of curing blindness (Meek 1992:175). In Upper Egypt, flat copper needle knives, a "needling for cataract" (Nunn 2002:200–201), were found in the tomb of Khasekhemwy, ca. 2700 BCE. The surgeon inserted the flat needle knife into the edge of the cornea and pushed the lens away from behind the iris into the vitreous gel where it meets the lowest part of the eye. The pupil was left unfocused, and the lens was broken up and removed.

This surgery could also be accomplished by couching, a procedure in which the opaque cataract was pinched by strong finger pressure on the eye to dislodge it from its supports. While both of these surgeries restored some sight to the patient, there was risk of infection, and vision was blurred thereafter (www.medicinenet.com/script/main/art.asp?articlekey=6886, accessed 30 April 2018).

Urology

Five of the ten Egyptian medical papyri discuss urology. One specialist noted among the physicians is Irenakhty, whose title was Interpreter of the Liquids in the Netnetet. The word netnetet means an organ in the shape of a sac, or the bladder. In the Ebers Papyrus, ca. 6.8 percent of the medical disorders discussed within refer to urological problems. To treat urinary problems, physicians used dates, gum, grapes, wheat, celery, rush-nuts, figs, carob, and yellow ochre. To address impotence and priapism they used carob, juniper, hyoscyamus, pine, salt, oils, watermelon, and flax. Additionally, honey was the most prescribed remedy in the Ebers Papyrus (Gordetsky and O'Brien 2008).

Schistosomiasis, a disease from the parasitic worms Schistosoma that infect the urinary tract, was mentioned in the Kahun Papyrus ca. 1900 BCE, called the *ā-a-ā* disease, and the worm itself was called *hr wt*. This disease was mentioned fifty times in the medical papyri: twenty-eight in the Ebers Papyrus; twelve mentions in the Berlin Papyrus; nine in the Hearst; and one mention in the London Papyrus. Symptoms associated with this condition were maematuria, frequency of micturition, painful micturition, effects on the anus, abdominal pain, diarrhea, bloody stool, cardiac disturbances, and mental weakness. The cardiac and mental weakness may reflect anaemia. Reliefs in the tombs of Pta-Hotep and Ankha-ma-hor at Saqqara depict patients with extended abdomen, umbilical hernia, and scrotal swelling. The remedies for schistosomiasis included sedatives using hyoscyamus; antispasmodics, ammi-visnaga; diuretics such as juniper and beer; colon evacuation with castor oil; and antimony. Physicians also suggested preventive measures including encouraging people to stop polluting their water and to stay away from water that was already polluted (Shokeir and Hussein 1999).

Egyptians were among the first to identify bladder tumors. The Edwin Smith Papyrus mentions *bn wt*, a urinary bladder tumor. This was mentioned twice in the Chester Beatty Papyrus as *dyjt*, a lower urinary tract disturbance, and *hdbw*, or burning micturition, and as *nnw* to describe dysuria in males (Nunn 2002).

Egyptian physicians also conducted urological surgeries. It appears that they allowed the kidneys to remain in the body; however, scars on some mummified bodies suggest physicians may have had to correct hernias. Circumcision appears to have been a regularly performed minor surgery some 2000 years prior to the rein of Rameses II (ca. 1279–1213 BCE). Circumcision was at first restricted to the priestly class, then extended to royalty and nobility, and eventually to the general population. Males were usually circumcised at the age of puberty. Reliefs in the temple of Ankha-ma-Hor at Saqqara, Fifth Dynasty, ca. 2400 BCE, depict preparation for circumcision and the actual procedure. It is not clear what anesthetics were used; however, it is speculated that Memphis stone was used for the procedure because when the stone cut into the skin, it released carbonic acid, which functions as a local anesthetic (Shokeir and Hussein 1999; Nunn 2002).

Dentistry

One of the earliest references to tooth disease comes from a Sumerian text dated to ca. 5000 BCE. It describes the tooth worm as being the cause for dental caries (cavities) and was blamed for tooth decay in Egypt as well. The Egyptian papyrus Anastasi IV discussed the tooth worm and credits it with being the cause of toothache. The tooth worm was mentioned by Homer, and was known as the cause of tooth decay in numerous cultures, a belief that continued until the eighteenth century.

In Mesopotamia, dentistry was not a specialized profession. The *āšipu* appear to have treated oral problems as well as those associated with the body. Among the oral problems were seized mouth (stuttering), drooling, red/black mouth, general pain, shriveling of the tongue or off-color tongue, and enlarged tongue (Scurlock and Anderson 2005). General oral hygiene included keeping the teeth and mouth clean. The Mesopotamians chewed on the branches of the "toothbrush tree" (Salvadora perisca), the margusu plant, to freshen their breath and make their teeth shine (Scurlock and Anderson 2005). There is no evidence for the pulling of teeth, even though there is evidence of tooth decay, gum disease, abscessed and loose teeth. In the case of cavities, the tooth worm was perceived as sucking the blood of the tooth and feeding on food particles in the mouth; remedies seem to suggest these teeth were extracted, but it is not clear (Scurlock and Anderson 2005).

In Egypt, dentistry was a specialization among physicians. Nine individuals, of the ca. 150 medical professionals thus far identified, were credited with being dentists. Their titles included One Who Is Concerned with Teeth and One Who Deals with Teeth. There were also Chief of Dentists and Chief of Dentist of the Palace. Perhaps even within the specialization there were sub-specialists or a hierarchy. As mentioned earlier, the earliest known dentist was Hesy-Re, ca. 2670 BCE, known from six carved wooden panels from his tomb at Saqqara. His titles included Chief of Physicians, Dentist, and Elder of the Physicians of the Palace (Forshaw 2009).

The teeth of numerous mummies and other human remains show signs of extreme wear. This is due to the coarse nature of foodstuffs, especially bread, made from grain that was ground with grindstones, which left tiny bits of stone and sand in the flour. Many teeth were ground down to the pulp, which caused abscesses. As early as 2500 BCE, some teeth show signs of drilling in an attempt to drain abscesses and infections. Some scholars argue the holes were not the result of drilling but the condition itself dissolving the tooth in a clean hole (Forshaw 2009).

Some mummies were discovered with wire wound around teeth. On a mummy at Giza in a burial shaft dating to ca. 2500 BCE, a mandibular second molar was connected to the third molar by gold wire. The original assumption was that an attempt was made to preserve a tooth or to insert a bridge between two good teeth. Further study revealed the prosthetic tooth did not belong to the individual but to somebody else and was inserted after death so the person's body would be as whole as possible in the afterlife. However, a second example from el-Quatta, near Cairo, also dating to ca. 2500 BCE, exhibited use of bridges during the lifetime of the person who received them. A third example comes from Tura el-Asmant and was attached to the skull. This example dates to the Ptolemaic period, ca. 32–330 BCE. This bridge was attached to a right maxillary central incisor. One silver wire passed through two holes drilled into the crown of the tooth. The tooth was prepared outside the body and placed into it once the socket had healed (Forshaw 2009). Early in Egypt's dental history, it is unclear whether teeth were extracted. Thus far, no instruments for extraction, such as forceps, have been found prior to the Kom Ombo relief, which dates to a later period.

Remedies or prescriptions for oral conditions can be found among the medical papyri. These address tooth decay, tooth loss, and gum disease. One remedy includes placing a paste around the tooth and gum, which would harden and provide stability to the tooth. A prescription in the Ebers Papyrus includes flour made from emmer seeds, ochre, and honey. This was made into a mass and packed into and around the tooth. Ochres contain iron oxides, which contain mild astringent and antiseptic properties; honey is used for binding but also for its antibacterial properties (Forshaw 2009). Other compounds for packing teeth include malachite and terebinth resin, and beeswax; all possess antiseptic properties. A third recipe used for ulcers or abscesses of the gum or infection includes cumin, terebinth, and carob ground into a powder and applied to the tooth. Cumin is a carminative with antiseptic and local anesthetic properties; terebinth resin is an antiseptic; carob is a stabilizer, astringent, and demulsifyer. This compound would have disinfected and soothed the infected area (Forshaw 2009).

Forshaw concluded that early dentists in Egypt, much like those of Mesopotamia, did not perform surgery on teeth and gums, but instead treated them with medications. It is also evident that they attempted to keep movable teeth or teeth that had fallen out in the mouth by wiring them to teeth that were still rooted.

By the time of the Etruscans and the Romans, false teeth were attached to healthy teeth with the aid of metal bands. By the seventh century BCE, Etruscan dentistry had reached a very high level of sophistication. Several examples of appliances have been discovered. These include gold bands that were fitted over remaining teeth, and the lost teeth were replaced by one fixed into the band. Replacement teeth were usually human, though in one case an ox's tooth was used. Such dental work was reserved for the wealthy and was quickly adopted by the Romans (Bonfante 1986:251).

Ancient medicine does not mean obsolete practices or ineffective pharmaceuticals. Greek, Roman, and modern medical procedures and medicines were based on those developed millennia ago in Mesopotamia and Egypt. Ancient human bodies were susceptible to disease, deformity, and injury just as they are today. The desire to maintain health and regain it from malady has always been a driving force in finding practical medical solutions. It is not surprising that ancient peoples devised methods to ensure the health and well-being of their communities. It is important and impressive to note that Mesopotamian and Egyptian rulers realized the importance of a healthy population and made health care available to all citizens no matter their rank in society.

In the main, if a person ate a balanced diet and led an active life, good health was the norm. However, human nature being what it is, and the body being susceptible to disease and infection, extra care was needed in the form of medical intervention. Knowledge of the healing properties of plants and animal by-products formed the basis for early and modern pharmaceuticals. That which was necessary to sustain human life could be found in nature. Even today, countless books on herbs, spices, and natural remedies extol the virtues of natural healing as a way to maintain daily health and well-being. Honey and its antibacterial and healing properties is being rediscovered by veterinarians and animal rescue hospitals. For example, the Turtle Hospital in Marathon, Florida, uses honey and honeycomb casts to heal turtles injured by boat propellers, rope, and fishing line (www.turtlehospital.org/). From the author's experience, honey helps to quickly heal an adventurous dog's paw when cut on coral rocks! In today's modern world, we forget that humans are animals and members of the natural world. It is only fitting that we should embrace the medicines found in nature, which are much less toxic than synthesized pharmaceuticals.

Although today most use a toothbrush to clean teeth, toothbrush sticks remain in use in some parts of the world. Known as a miswak stick, this natural toothbrush works really well and is available online (www.miswakstick.com/miswak.html). The nutrients from the stick include fluorine, silicon, vitamin C, Salvadorine and Trimethylamine, as well as potassium, sodium, chloride sodium bicarbonate and calcium oxides. Although seemingly primitive, the miswak is a much healthier and beneficial way of cleaning teeth and, according to studies, reduces plaque and gingivitis. Similarly, African chew sticks, or licorice root, can help make teeth whiter (Beauchemin 2016).

Knowledge gained by ancient physicians and pharmacists remains useful today, and the rediscovery of that knowledge can be used in concert with modern medical and pharmaceutical practices. Many have already been doing this as an alternative to modern Western medicine; however, greater incorporation of ancient medical practices could be beneficial in areas where medical care is scarce or unaffordable.

14

DAILY LIFE

Our daily routines utilize many objects, substances, and products, about which we rarely consider the research, development, or technology that produces them. Scientists, chemists, engineers, and artists have invested considerable time, energy, and money into developing products such as wigs, make-up, perfume, and soap, and consumers spend billions of dollars on them; however, the technology behind these items remains overlooked. Such technologies were an integral component of sophisticated ancient societies, the use of which established the foundation for our own. This chapter will focus on daily items and personal maintenance, and the overlooked technologies that went into producing seemingly unremarkable goods. There may be some overlap with other chapters; however, the focus of this chapter will serve to illustrate how some items have multiple uses in a variety of settings. To that end, in addition to those mentioned above, this chapter will discuss bathing, false teeth, hair coloring, tattooing, shaving, footwear, and laundering, to name a few. Realizing that so many of the things we use in our daily lives were employed so long ago, we are reminded of the truth and wisdom of Solomon's words in the book of Ecclesiastes in the Old Testament: "Is there a thing of which it is said 'See, this is new'? It has been already in the ages before us" (Ecclesiastes 1:4–11).

Bathing

When considering bathing in the ancient world, Roman bathhouses immediately come to mind. After all, the Romans were famous for their attention to cleanliness, indoor plumbing, sewer systems, aqueducts, and bathhouses. The practice of routine bathing developed in Greece and had become a widespread custom throughout the Mediterranean region by the Hellenistic period. As with many things, the Romans adopted and adapted this practice from the Greeks, and constructed elaborate bathhouses, private and public. No matter the size, bathhouses consisted of several components: apodyterium, frigidarium, tepidarium, and caldarium; sub-floor ducts heated floors and pools of water, while other basins contained cold water. The warm rooms were meant to cause sweating, which opened the pores, thus making the removal of dirt from the skin using scrapers an easier task. At bathhouses, members could exercise or receive massages (Fournet 2012).

By the time the Romans built these elaborate facilities, bathing had reached a sophisticated level, thanks in part to the Mesopotamians, Egyptians, and Canaanites/ Israelites before them. Archaeological evidence for bathing can be found as early as the eighteenth century BCE from Mari, on the Euphrates River. Here, terra cotta bathtubs have been recovered from the palace as well as bronze tubs from the first millennium BCE. Most upper class residences in Mesopotamia contained a bathroom, which could include a tub, a fired-brick floor sealed with bitumen and powdered limestone, and a drain that allowed water to flow into a sub-floor sump or drain pipe. These rooms also contained a toilet in the form of a small hole in the floor leading to a sewer and a fireplace with flues. Bathrooms were located near the main room of the house (James and Thorpe 1995:456; Killebrew 1997:283).

Egypt also employed bathrooms, most commonly found in palaces, temples, and tombs, though some private residences also exhibit use of them. Several sites, such as the palace of Amenophis III in Thebes and residences at Lahun and Tell el-Amarna, the latter of which Akhetaten, Pharaoh Akhenaton, established as the capital city in the middle fourteenth century BCE. The private homes of noble people and common citizens also included bathrooms. In private dwellings, the bathroom was located next to the main bedroom near the dressing room and toilet. The floor of the bathroom was constructed of a stone slab with a slight slope and other stone slabs set vertically against the mudbrick wall to protect the walls from water. The floor slabs contained a shallow channel that guided water to a spout at the lowest point of the slab leading into a drainage channel, which deposited wastewater into a vessel or a drain that removed it from the house. A low wall separated the bath from the toilet (James and Thorpe 1995:456; Killebrew 1997:283).

In addition to bathing in a tub, ancient Egyptians also showered with water poured from a vessel by attendants (Figure 14.1). A painting from a Theban tomb depicts a woman being showered with water in this manner. The woman and one attendant sit on top of a stone slab while the other three stand next to it. One pours the water on the woman's head, and one washes her arms and body, while the third removes her jewelry and clothing (Wilkinson 1837b:388–389).

Bathing was also practiced among the Canaanites and Israelites. Installations found at Tell el-'Ajjul and Beth Shean have been interpreted as baths because they contain pebble-paved, plastered, or shell flooring. Textual references to bathing can be found in the Hebrew Bible, such as Exodus 2:5, 2 Samuel 11:2, Job 9:30, Song of Solomon 4:2, 6:6 (sheep), suggesting bathing was already part of one's daily routine.

Bathtubs have been found at Minoan sites on Crete. Bathrooms at the palace of Knossos, ca. 1700 BCE, consisted of a sunken tile floor with descending steps, a drainage system, and a bathtub. The tubs were made of terra cotta and were elegantly decorated. They contained a drain and handles, presumably so the tub could

FIGURE 14.1 Woman being showered by attendants

Adapted from Wilkinson 1837b:389 (Public Domain, PD-1923).

be taken out for draining (Evans 1921; Corrigan 1932; James and Thorpe 1995:456; De Feo et al. 2014:173–174). Bathing tubs were also found on Cyprus during the Late Cypriot II period, ca. thirteenth–fourteenth century BCE, growing in use during the Late Cypriot IIIA period, ca. twelfth century BCE. Terra cotta tubs have been discovered at Ayios Iakovos, Enkomi, Maa Palaeokstro, and Kalavasos Ayios Dhimitrios (Killebrew 1997:283). The Mycenaeans also incorporated bathrooms into the palaces at Tiryns and Pylos in the fourteenth to thirteenth century BCE. The bathroom at Tiryns includes a floor made from one large stone slab that slants from the tub to a gutter and drain, allowing excess water to flow out of the room. Homer mentions bathing in tubs in the *Iliad* and *Odyssey* (10.165) (James and Thorpe 1995:456; Killebrew 1997:283).

Terra cotta or stone basins, often referred to as bathtubs, have been discovered at Tell Qasile, Ashdod, Ashkelon, Tel Miqne/Ekron, Tell Abu Hawam, and Tell Dan. These large vessels remind us of the bathtubs we use today, hence the reference and (mis)interpretation of them as bathtubs. Recent research has shown that these were likely used as dyeing or fulling basins. These tubs were situated in rooms associated with weaving activities based on the presence of loom weights and yarn fibers (woolen and linen). Thus, it can be assumed these tubs were used for dyeing wool, and the architecture of the tub was useful not only for bathing but also for processing textiles (Mazow 2013).

Bathing was practiced for two purposes: personal hygiene and ritual purification. It goes without saying that personal grooming is necessary to maintain one's health. Regular washing helps one's skin and body retain essential nutrients, maintain certain ph. balance, remove dirt and old skin cells, and combat harmful germs. Even cats, dogs, birds, squirrels, and primates are aware of the benefits of bathing and grooming. However, recent studies have shown that the soaps and chemicals we use today could actually create an unhealthy environment on our skin. Prior to developing harmful soaps, Nitrosomonas eutropha, ammonia-oxidizing bacteria (AOB), lived on our skin, helping to maintain a balance between good bacteria and bad. By using today's soaps and shampoos, these harmful chemicals wash away the beneficial bacteria along with the bad instead of allowing the good bacteria to combat and triumph, thus creating an unhealthy environment for the skin. AOBiome, a biotech company in Cambridge, Massachusetts, has developed a spray that eliminates the need to shower. By spraying the AOB onto the skin, the beneficial bacteria feed on the ammonia found in sweat and convert it to nitrite and nitric oxide, acting as cleaning, deodorizing, anti-inflammatory agents, and immune boosters (Scott 2014; AOBiome, www.aobiome.com). Regular use of this sort of substance keeps the skin healthy and eliminates the need for conventional showering or bathing.

In antiquity, bathing could be accomplished with or without soap (discussed later). In the absence of soap, the heat of a bath or shower combined with olive oil and a scraper also provided an efficient way to cleanse one's body. The warmth of hot water opened the skin's pores so that the dirt could be trapped in the oil and scraped away with a scraper or *strigil*. Illustrations from Greek vases depict bathers with a strigil, oil pot, and sometimes a basin presumably holding water (e.g. Foundry Painter, ca. 480 BCE).

Washing was also performed for the purpose of ritual purification. There are numerous references in the Hebrew Bible to washing of garments, body, feet, and hands (Genesis 19:2, 24:32, 43:24, 49:11; Exodus 19:10, 29:4, 29:17, 30:19–21, 40:12 and 31; Leviticus 1:9 and 13, 6:27, 11:25 and 28, 13:6). Cleanliness laws in Leviticus describe numerous circumstances for which people must wash, which appear to be for ritualistic reasons as well as practical ones. Canaanite, Egyptian, Mesopotamian, and Israelite temples contained basins of fresh (holy) water for washing before entering the temple. These basins were usually placed at the entrance to the temple precinct or in the outer courtyard as well as perhaps the inner courtyards and chambers so that worshippers and priests could clean their hands and feet before entering the holy space.

Soap

Pliny the Elder described soap as having been invented in the Gallic provinces and was used to dye hair red. He described it as being made from suet and ash, with the best suet being from goat and the best ash being from beech trees. Soap was available as a liquid and solid, and used by German men and women (Pliny *Natural History* 28.51; Henderson 1963:130–131). Galen (ca. 129–200 CE), a well-known Greek physician, claimed that the best soaps came from Germany and the second best from Gaul. He claimed that *sapo* was a better cleaning agent than soda, and prescribed German soap for body washing because it was the most pure (*Method of Medicine* VIII:569K; Johnston and Horsley 2011:404–405; James and Thorpe 1995:261). According to unsubstantiated legend, *sapo* (soap) originated from Mt. Sapo, the fictional mountain where the Romans sacrificed animals as burnt offerings.

During animal sacrifices, fats mixed with ash and trickled down to a stream nearby. When people went there to wash their clothing, the mix of fats, ash, and water produced sapo, thus helping to clean their clothing. It is from the Latin word *sapo* that the modern English word soap is derived.

However, much earlier, in Mesopotamia, the Babylonians applied their knowledge of chemistry to create cleaning substances. Artifactual evidence for soap dates to ca. 2800 BCE from a vessel containing a soapy substance, and from textual evidence dating to ca. 2200 BCE. A recipe found on a tablet describes a soap formula consisting of water, alkali, and cassia oil. Chemists boiled these together to produce a residue with which people washed themselves and their clothing. They also mixed animal fats (e.g. goat) and/or vegetable oil and/or olive oil and/or coconut oil with wood ash (e.g. beechwood) and water. Alkali can be derived from burnt plant ashes soaked in a pot of water, also known as potash. Alkali can also be mined as a mineral and heated with calcium hydroxide (slaked lime), which results in caustic potash or potassium hydroxide. Caustic potash, combined with fats or oils (plant or animal), produces soap, and when combined with other fruits and vegetables, can be beneficial to one's skin and hair. The soap was pressed into balls or blocks, much like we do today. The chemical reaction of the alkali (or lye) breaks down the triglycerides found in oils, and it is through saponification, the reaction between fatty acids and lye, that the soap is produced (Cable 2017). Soap allows otherwise insoluble particles like grease to become soluble in water so they can wash away (James and Thorpe 1995:261–263).

In Egypt, the Ebers Papyrus (ca. 1550 BCE) discusses regular bathing with animal and vegetable oils mixed with alkaline salts that were combined and formed into soap. Neo-Babylonian King Nabonidus (ca. 556–539 BCE) discussed a soap recipe using uhulu (ashes), sesame oil, and cypress oil (Levey 1958). The Canaanites, Phoenicians, Greeks, and Romans (second century CE) adopted soap soon after the Mesopotamians and Egyptians. The Canaanites and Israelites used soda to clean their hands. Several passages from the Hebrew Bible mention washing one's body with soap and one's hands with soda. Job 9:30 and Jeremiah 2:22 are two examples.

Soap was not just used for personal hygiene. It was also used to clean wool, eating utensils, dishware, drinkware, and clothing. Once a sheep had been sheared, the wool (and the animal) were washed. Fleece was washed to remove suint (dried perspiration), excess lanolin, and dirt before dyeing. At Dura-Europos (Syria), records of sold wool were discovered, describing wool that had not been degreased, wool that had been washed, and the separation of these according to weight. Washing wool decreased the weight by ca. 30 percent. To clean wool, alum, the easiest of all mordants, was used. A mixture of potassium aluminum sulfate was used for fine textured wool: 4 oz. for heavy textured wool mixed with 1 oz. cream of tartar, 4 gallons of water, and 1 pound of wool. The alum was dissolved in warm water and added to the bath, which was then heated to 160°. The addition of cream of tartar produced brighter, clearer colors. Once clean, the wool was ready for dyeing.

Toothpaste and toothbrushes

A toothpaste formula has been discovered among a collection of papyrus documents in the National Library in Vienna, Austria, that date to the fourth century CE. The name of the recipe is "for white and perfect teeth," and it was written in Greek (Catchpoole 2014). Although late, this provides an early example of toothpaste, which should be noted. The recipe for this toothpaste is 1 drachma of dried iris flower, 2 drachmas of mint, 1 drachma of rock salt, and 20 grains of pepper, all crushed and mixed together (1 drachma = 1/100 ounce). Recent research suggests that properties in the iris flower are effective in fighting gum disease (Catchpoole 2014; Zoech 2003).

Toothbrushes were effective but primitive. The Babylonians appear to have used a brushing tool as early as 3500–3000 BCE, which was little more than a stick or twig with a frayed end. These are often referred to as chew sticks or toothsticks. Toothsticks such as these have also been found in Egyptian tombs. Toothsticks, or toothbrush sticks, remain in use today in some Eastern regions such as the Arabian Peninsula, India, and Malaysia. Known as a miswak, miswaak, or sewak, wooden sticks are used to clean teeth in conjunction with a toothpaste made from activated charcoal. Miswak stick comes from the Salvadora Persica tree, also known as the arak tree. When the thin outer bark is removed at the tip of the stick, the underlying wood can be mashed with one's teeth to form a brush. The oils help combat bacteria and plaque. Recent studies indicate that the miswak is an effective method of oral hygiene. Having purchased miswak for personal use and incorporated it into my own routine, I can confirm that it is amazingly successful at cleaning teeth and gums (www.miswakstick.com/miswak.html).

Shaving

Exactly when people first shaved is not known; however, based on cave paintings that depict clean-shaven men, one can assume that shaving, or plucking, has been practiced since prehistoric times. The Egyptians are perhaps the best-known shavers in the ancient Near East. Egyptians maintained very short haircuts or shaved their head as well as their entire body for general cleanliness and due to the very hot climate, and priests followed this practice for ritual cleanliness. Short or no hair also helped prevent infestations of lice or other parasites. To the Egyptians, facial hair was a sign of personal neglect or of a barbarian. The word barbarian, Greek βάρβαρος, "barbarous" or "barbarian," may have referred to a bearded individual or cultures that did not shave. However, close-cropped, well-manicured beards, trimmed mustaches, or a small goatee were acceptable in Egyptian society. Another reason to shave or maintain close-cropped facial hair may have been to prevent it from being grabbed during hand-to-hand combat, though some dispute that theory.

A principal profession in Egypt and Mesopotamia was that of the barber. The royals and the wealthy included personal barbers among their household staff. Every village had at least one barber, as described in the *Satire on Trades*, ca. 1700 BCE:

> The barber barbers till nightfall,
> He betakes himself to town,
> He sets himself up in his corner,
> He moves from street to street,
> Looking for someone to barber,
> He strains his arms to fill his belly,
> Like the bee that eats as it works.
> *Lichtheim 1975:186*

Mesopotamian barbers were organized into guilds, and every city-state boasted one or several barbershops. These were open to the public and could be found on most main streets. Later in Egyptian history barbers also worked from a shop as evidenced by Ctesibius (ca. 385–222 BCE) who ran a barbershop in Alexandria.

The earliest razors were made from flint, obsidian, sharks' teeth, or clamshells, and ranged in size. By the third millennium, men and women in Egypt and the Near East were using copper and bronze blades and pumice. Some ancient razor blades could measure 5 centimeters wide and 17 centimeters long. They were usually oblong, rectangular, or crescent in shape and contained a handle made of ivory, bone, wood, or metal. Some razor blades and/or handles were decorated. Upon completion of shaving, the barber rubbed his client's skin with oils and perfumes, presumably to prevent bleeding and infection. The menfolk of some peoples did grow beards; however, most were well manicured, which was a sign of attention to personal grooming. A straggly, unkempt beard was a sign of personal neglect and disrespect. Scissors and blades were used to crop facial hair. A much-referenced example of facial hair is that of the "Asiatics" from the tomb painting of Khnum Hotep at Beni Hasan (Cohen 2015). One of the characteristic features of the "Asiatics" was their distinctive beard and short hair, along with their brightly colored garments. Mesopotamians cultivated their beards, fastidiously oiling and dressing them with tongs and curling irons to create waves, patterns, and curls. The Assyrians used black dye to color their hair, eyebrows, and beards. The Persians dyed their hair an orange-red color using henna as early as 1900 BCE. On festive occasions, gold dust and thread were woven into the beard. Scissors, in the form of shears, were known from ca. 1500 BCE, if not earlier. Early scissors consisted of two bronze blades connected by a thin, flexible bronze band that fixed the blades in place and provided springing action, which kept the blades open while also allowing the user to squeeze the blades closed when cutting (Wilkinson 1878).

Hairstyles

Just as today, much attention was given to the styling of one's hair. The haircut one chose could be for practical purposes, to mark one's status, or to make a statement.

Although most men shaved their heads in Mesopotamia, some maintained long hair. Women's hairstyles during the Early Dynastic Period (ca. 2900–2350 BCE) were long, consisting of elaborate plaits and hair piled up on top of the head with a scarf, net, or headdress holding it in place (Nemet-Nejat 1998:155). Women also adorned their hair with jewelry. The Royal Cemetery at Ur (ca. 2600 BCE) reveals that women wore strands of gold willow leaves with beads of lapis lazuli, gold, and carnelian in their hair. They also wore hair nets made of gold ribbon, and hairpins of silver with red and blue flowers made of lapis lazuli and limestone.

Men's hairstyles were also reflected on their helmets. From the Royal Cemetery a gold helmet depicted thick braiding "wrapped around the head, coiled in a chignon at the nape of the neck" (Nemet-Nejat 1998:155). If not bald, men fashioned their hair and beards into elaborate and well-maintained waves. Men's beards were full with a mustache, each having curls and ringlets at the ends. Professional men, such as priests and doctors, wore hairstyles commensurate with their profession, ceremonial function, and status. Gray hair was treated with dye and incantations (Nemet-Nejat 1998:155).

In the wall painting from the tomb of Knumhotep at the necropolis of Beni Hasan in Egypt, "Asiatic" (Canaanite) men were depicted wearing short-cropped hair with sculpted beards, and women wore their hair long, just below the shoulder with a headband. Numerous other ancient Egyptian paintings depict men with shaved heads, close-cropped hair, or with short hairstyles. Women were often depicted with shoulder-length hair, though these could have been wigs.

Wigs

Ironically, even though Egyptians fastidiously removed most or all of their hair, they were also careful to save it to make wigs (Figure 14.2). Men and women of the upper class appeared in public, at ceremonies, and when buried (mummified) wearing a wig, and men's wigs were often much more elaborate than women's. Hair and wigs were considered a very valuable possession (Fletcher 2009:495). The earliest known wigs have been found at Hierakonpolis cemetery HK.43 dating to ca. 3500 BCE, and at Lisht cemetery dating to the Twelfth Dynasty where the wigs remained inside their storage boxes.

To make a wig, hair was obtained from the wearer or from a stockpile of hair. The hair was sorted according to length then combed to remove tangles, lice, and any other parasites, and washed with soap (solid soda). Once prepared, the strands of hair were woven into a wig and fashioned into a series of braids, curls, and plaits depending on the desired style. To hold the hair in place, a resin or beeswax or a mixture of both was applied to the hair. The hair was woven into a net, which was then fixed directly onto the head. The net could be made from date palm fiber and could be padded. The hair could also be made into locks, clumps, or braids, which could also be woven into the net. Locks were also used as hair extensions, being woven into the wig to provide length or even into the person's own natural hair to provide length and volume (Fletcher 2009:496). In the cemetery at Amarna, the

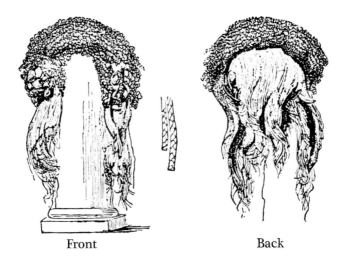

Front   Back

FIGURE 14.2 A man's double-style wig, said to have been found in its storage box in Thebes, Egypt. This wig consists of two parts: the top part of naturally curly hair with several hundred plaits extending below the neck of the wig. The curls were treated with a mix of beeswax and resin. The hair was waxed on the ends and attached to the wig by twisting and pressing back the strand. This example is from the British Museum (Museum number EA2560).

Adapted from Wilkinson 1878:329, No. 440 (Public Domain, PD-1923).

capital city established by Akhenaten (ca. 1353–1335 BCE), a mummified woman was discovered whose hair contained 70 extensions (Jarus 2014). The Egyptians also used hair gel to help the wig-hair keep its intended shape, especially for mummies. N. McCreesh, of the KNH Centre for Biomedical Egyptology at the University of Manchester, UK, analyzed hair samples from eighteen mummies ranging in date from 3500 to 2300 years ago from the cemetery at the Dakhleh Oasis in the Western Desert from the Graeco-Roman period. The gel appears to have been fat-based, a different substance than that used for embalming (Merchant 2011).

Wig styles were commensurate with age, sex, and social status. As paintings, reliefs, and the wigs themselves attest, style, and complexity revealed one's status within the community and signified royalty. While removing body hair was a practical matter, warding against lice, dirt, and providing relief from intense heat, wigs may have provided some protection from the sun for a shaved head.

Combs

As was mentioned earlier, combs were used to prepare hair for wigs; however, combs were also, and more regularly, used for personal grooming of hair, especially in cultures that did not shave their hair (Figure 14.3). One of the oldest combs thus far discovered comes from Canton of Bern, Switzerland, and dates to the Neolithic period. It is made from wood and measures ca. 10 centimeters. Combs were often

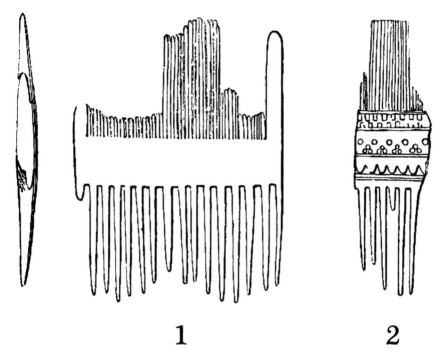

FIGURE 14.3   Two Egyptian combs, one decorated

Adapted from Wilkinson 1878:347, No. 450 (Public Domain, PD-1923).

rectangular and consisted of a shaft with tapered teeth extending from each side, with the teeth on one side being finer or closer together than on the other. The purpose for tooth positioning was practical: the finer toothed side was used to remove parasites and bugs (Zias 1991; Zias and Mumcuoglu 1996) while the other was used to remove snarls and tangles. Combs were made from various materials: ivory, bone, wood, tortoise shell, gold, and silver, and could be elaborately decorated. While some combs were used for practical purposes, others were merely for adornment.

Modern combs look much like ancient ones and perform similar functions. Although made from synthetic materials and sometimes larger than ancient ones, present-day combs still possess a finer toothed side and a wider side, and decorative combs continue to adorn people's hair.

Scented oil (perfume)

At least as early as 2900 BCE, the dead were buried with perfume in Egypt, Canaan, Mesopotamia, and on the island of Crete in Greece. Bodies were anointed and buried with perfumed oils, unguents, herbs, and spices to hide the odor of a rotting corpse and for medicinal purposes for those performing burial rituals around the body and within the tomb. Prior to burial, the corpse was washed and perfumed oils applied; however, perfume was for the living as well. The Egyptians were especially captivated by perfume as evidenced by Hatshepsut's voyage to Punt to obtain a frankincense tree so that Egypt could grow its own without having to travel such a great distance for the substance. Unfortunately, the frankincense tree would not grow in Egypt's soil or climate so the expeditions continued. Throughout the ancient Near East, perfume was used for ritual purposes in temples as well as for daily needs (James and Thorpe 1995:266–267; Serpico 2009:460–464).

In Mesopotamia, two of the earliest chemists to make perfume were Tapputi-Belatekallim and (...)ninu, women described as "mistress of a household and in charge of manufacturing perfume" according to a tablet dated to ca. 1200 BCE (Miller 1993:301). Tapputi combined flowers, oil, and calamus with other aromatic substances; then she distilled and filtered the mixture several times (Levey 1956, 1960). It has been noted that in Mesopotamia, chemical equipment appears to have originated from kitchens, and many kitchen utensils evolved into those used in chemistry and alchemy. Women held a vital role in science and chemistry; however, after the scientific revolution in the time of Galileo and Newton, women became relegated to the position of assistant.

In 2003, a perfume factory was discovered at Pyrgos on the Mediterranean island of Cyprus, which was destroyed by an earthquake ca. 1850 BCE. A 300-square-meter (3230 feet) factory was excavated, which was part of the larger perfume-making complex. Some of the artifacts include perfume bottles, mixing jugs, and extracts of anise, pine, coriander, almond, parsley, and bergamot. Four recipes also were discovered in this building. The clay mixing jugs support texts describing perfume manufacturing, one written by Theophrastus (ca. 270–285 BCE) entitled *On Odors*, and in Pliny the Elder's *Natural History* (Book XIII; Henderson and Rackham 1968). Perfume recipes and instructions were also recorded at Edfu, the Temple of Horus, and at Dendara in the time of Ptolmey III, ca. 237 BCE (Serpico 2009:460–461; Roach 2007).

Although Pliny mentions distillation, it is clear that this method was in its infancy (Lucas 1930:44–47). Originally, "perfume" was actually scented oil and/or animal fat in the form of an ointment or unguent. Perfume as we know it today is the product of a process known as distillation, a process that was not known until Aristotle (ca. 384–322 BCE) at the earliest but certainly by ca. 200 CE from Alexander of Aphrodisias who described the distillation process. Concurrently, the process of distillation was known in China during the Eastern Han Dynasty (ca. first to second centuries CE). The distillation of rosewater and other scented perfumes was known to the Islamic world in the ninth century CE, and large quantities of perfume were exported from Damascus (James and Thorpe 1995:266–267). The ninth century chemist Al-Kindi wrote *Book of the Chemistry of Perfume and Distillations*, wherein among other recipes he describes 107 recipes for making perfume, and the equipment needed for that process (Levey 1956). Prior to the discovery of distillation, there were two ways to make perfume: enfleurage and maceration. Enfleurage is a cold steeping process, wherein layers of animal fat were smeared onto a wooden board with flower petals spread over it. A second board was placed over the first, and

FIGURE 14.4   The tomb of Nakht in Thebes. Perfume cones atop the head of female guests and the blind harpist at a banquet in honor of the deceased

Adapted from Davies 1917 Plate XVII (Public Domain, PD-1923).

the two were allowed to steep for twenty-four hours. After steeping, the old petals were replaced with new ones, and the process was repeated until the desired scent had been transferred to the fat. Maceration was a process of hot steeping. The flowers or herbs were mixed with oil or fat then heated in a vessel that was situated over a second vessel of boiling water, similar to a Dutch oven. Once heated to the correct temperature, the mixture was allowed to steep for several days. Maceration appears to be the technique described at Edfu and Dendara. A third technique may have employed a press, similar to one used to press grapes and olives (Serpico 2009:460–461).

Once the desired fragrance was obtained, it was delivered to the wearer via oil or animal fat (Figure 14.4). One of the Egyptians' methods of delivering the fragrance was to infuse perfumed oil into fat, then build a cone of scented fat layers and set the cone on top of the person's head, directly onto the hair or wig. As the fat melted, the scent(s) spread over the hair/wig, clothes, and body, producing the desired aroma that lasted a desired period of time (Serpico 2009:462–462; James and Thorpe 1995:267). Knowing this, Psalm 133 makes much more sense:

> Behold, how good and how pleasant it is for brothers to dwell together in unity! It is like the precious oil upon the head, coming down upon the beard, even Aaron's beard, coming down upon the edge of his robes. It is like the dew of Hermon coming down upon the mountains of Zion; for there the Lord commanded the blessing—life forever.
>
> *New American Standard Version*

The perfumer's task was complicated. A skilled perfumer could create a fragrance from one or several sources combined. The order, quantities, and substances had to be perfect; otherwise, the perfume would be too strong, too weak, or simply smell horrible! A perfumer had to make the fragrance last and had to know exactly how to mix the ingredients to do so. The fragrance had to last while on the wearer as well as in storage. For example, the abovementioned cone had to be layered with perfume perfectly so that the scent remained strong for as long as was required by the wearer. Ingredients such as roots, barks, resins, flowers, leaves, and grasses were collected from around the ancient world so the perfumer could make just the right concoction. The profession of perfumer should not be taken for granted or dismissed as frivolous. This delicate profession required highly skilled precision with perfection as the goal, especially given the value placed on the use of fragrance in temples, royal courts, and in homes. At Edfu in the Temple of Horus, dated to the time of Ptolmey III, ca. 237 BCE, wall inscriptions describe a perfume laboratory and recipe. The laboratory was kept dark and mysterious. Some recipes could take up to six months to mature. One famous recipe, balanos, was made in the city of Mendes in the Nile Delta, and was exported to Rome. This perfume was made from the balanos tree, or "false balsam" tree mixed with myrrh and resin. Today, the importance of the perfume industry can still be seen when walking through Cairo's Old City market as well as other marketplaces throughout Egypt, not to mention through any major department store.

Mirrors

Self-awareness and gazing at one's appearance is an essential component to personal grooming, and is facilitated by mirrors (Figure 14.5). One's attire and coiffed hair were just as important to our distant ancestors as to us today. Initially, people probably first observed their reflection in pools of water, in water vessels, and from shiny objects such as obsidian and mica (Aston et al. 2000:45; Enoch 2006), which later transformed into the manufacturing of mirrors.

Mirrors have been discovered at the Anatolian (Turkey) Neolithic site of Çatal Hüyük from ca. 6000 BCE (James and Thorpe 1995:248). The reflective face was

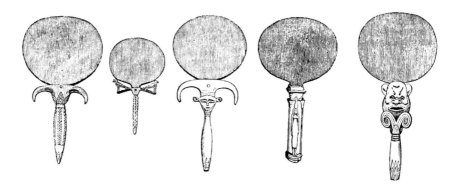

FIGURE 14.5   Selection of Egyptian mirrors. Metal mirrors with wooden handles in the shape of a papyrus scepter, braided hair with flanking hawks, papyrus scepter with face of Hathor, the goddess Neneb, and lotus with the face of Bez

Adapted from Wilkinson 1878:350–351, Nos. 453–455 (Public Domain, PD-1923).

made from ground and polished obsidian, and the surfaces of the mirrors were slightly convex. The mirrors had a diameter of ca. 9 centimeters, and some were conical in shape, easily held with one or two hands. One mirror stood vertically on a small, flattened base. Another was set into a lime plaster (Enoch 2006). Egyptians also utilized mirrors, some argue as early as the Predynastic periods with the discovery of ceramic bowls found at El Badari, which have been interpreted as mirrors. The bowls were probably filled with water, which provided the reflective surface. However, mirrors as we recognize them were discovered in abundance in the Dynastic periods. From ca. 4000 to 3000 BCE onward, disc-shaped mirrors were used throughout Egypt and in Mesopotamia (Albenda 1985; Enoch 2006). These mirrors were generally handheld, round or oval in shape, and made from flat or slightly convex (for magnification) discs of highly polished copper, bronze, or stone. The reflective piece was fixed to a handle, which was made from the same material or a different one such as wood, ivory, bone, metal, or stone. Occasionally the reflective piece was set into a frame, also attached to a handle. The frame and handle could be plain or fashioned in the shape of an animal, deity, or plant. The reverse side of the mirror could also be highly decorated with geometric designs, mythological scenes, creatures, or deities (Albenda 1985; Enoch 2006).

Aside from providing a reflective surface on which to see one's self, mirrors may also have held magical or ritualistic qualities. They may have been symbols of the sun or moon, or represented the setting or rising sun to symbolize one's inner self. The Egyptians may also have believed that the reflective side warded off evil spirits. Practically speaking, one could use a mirror to see what was behind. Finally, some scholars suggest mirrors were used to shine light into passageways of tombs, especially during the construction and decoration of them, and into mines (Aston et al. 2000:45).

Mirrors have been found in numerous graves beginning in very early periods. Some of the mirrors from Çatal Hüyük were found in graves thought to be those of females. In Canaan at Deir el-Balah, mirrors were found in several of the anthropoid coffin burials. The mirror was usually located near the upper torso. These burials date to approximately the thirteenth century BCE (Dothan 1979). Etruscan (modern-day Tuscany, Umbria and Lazio, in Italy) burials dating to the fourth to second centuries BCE contained mirrors. These were handheld mirrors made of gold or silver, and the backing was engraved with banqueting scenes, mythological creatures, or decorative designs. These were usually found on or next to a corpse in the leg region and were generally found with the obverse side, or reflective side, fading upward. The presence of these mirrors, together with their position, has caused scholars to speculate that the mirrors may have been thought to deflect harm or evil from the deceased, or were receptacles for the soul, or somehow preserved the individual's soul for eternity (Carpino 2008; Baker 2012:140–141).

Numerous texts, paintings, reliefs, and statues depict queens, kings, and deities gazing into handheld mirrors. For example, a stele discovered at Carchemish in northern Syria dating to ca. 1000–700 BCE depicts a goddess standing and holding a mirror in her hand (Albenda 1985; Enoch 2006). It is assumed that mirrors were predominantly placed with female graves (Albenda 1985); however, in Etruscan graves, mirrors were placed with the deceased without sex or gender bias (Baker 2012:141).

The ancient Near East was not the only place to develop a use for mirrors. The production of mirrors began in China in the Shang Dynasty (ca. 1500–1000 BCE); however, the best-known mirrors date to the Han Dynasty (ca. 202 BCE to 220 CE). Early Chinese mirrors were ca. 6 to 12 centimeters in diameter and consisted of a handle or knob on the reverse for holding it or suspending it with a rope. These mirrors were nominally decorated with raised ridges that formed patterns, and were made from copper or bronze. To the Chinese, mirrors held magical qualities that allowed the observer to look back in time (Enoch 2006; James and Thorpe 1995:248–254). Pre-Columbian South American peoples also used mirrors. The Olmec, Maya, Teotihuacan, Calvo, and Moche are among the many peoples who made use of them as early as 1925 BCE. Frames were made from gold, various stone types, and copper. The reflective lenses were made from crystal, obsidian, iron pyrite, and hematite. These ranged from 5 to 80 centimeters. In addition to gazing at one's reflection, mirrors were used to reflect the sun's rays to make fire, to aid in surgeries, for divination, and for astronomy (Enoch 2006).

Cosmetics

One has only to look at a few Egyptian paintings to realize that men and women applied makeup to their faces and bodies (Figure 14.6). Artifactually, cosmetic pallets from Egypt and a cosmetic case found in a tomb from the Sumerian city of Ur attest to the use of makeup. The Hebrew Bible also mentions the use of eyeliner (2 Kings 9:30 and Ezekiel 23:40). Jezebel, a foreign princess, painted her eyes and arranged her hair, and the women in the Ezekiel passage used eyeliner to beautify themselves. Women applied rouge to their cheeks, painted their lips, enhanced their eyebrows, and used eye shadow. They also colored their nails and applied elaborate henna decoration to their hands, wrists, and lower arms. Cosmetics were used not only for beautification but also for ritual purposes and were considered to hold magical power. However, men wore makeup as well, especially around the eyes. People were likely using makeup as early as 4000 BCE based on artifacts from the Predynastic periods.

Women and men applied kohl, black galena, or green malachite around their eyes. Kohl was usually applied in an almond shape around the eye. This emulated the eye of Horus, a falcon-headed deity and a god of sun, war, and protection. Eyeliner was made from green malachite or black galena. Green malachite was the first to be used but later replaced by black galena. Malachite was mixed with lead carbonate, copper oxide, brown ochre, magnetic iron oxide, manganese oxide antimony sulfate, and chrysocolla (Lucas 1930). This compound was mixed with animal fat, oils, gum resins, milk, and/or water and applied to the eyes. Black galena used galena, cerussite, phosgenite, laurionite, lead oxide, rock salt, natron, and water (Lucas 1930; Kreston 2012).

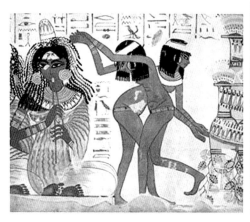 

FIGURE 14.6   Musicians and dancers, Tomb of Nebamun, Thebes and kohl container. Left: Tomb of Nebamun, Thebes, ca. 1420–1375. Musicians and dancers adorned with makeup. Right: Kohl container inscribed for Queen Tiye, (ca. 1410–1372 BCE) Eighteenth Dynasty. Measures 8.2 cm high, 5.4 cm wide, 1.3 cm deep (3 1/4, 2 1/8, 1/2 inches). LACMA M.80.198.89"

In addition to vanity, ritual, and mythological purposes, kohl also had practical and medicinal properties. Practically speaking, kohl repelled flies and other bugs, and it deflected sunlight. It has long been held that the Egyptians initially applied eyeliner to their lids for medicinal purposes. Recent research has revealed that the lead sulfates in kohl caused a "profound immunological response." Tests show that:

> the cultured cells released one of the most important messaging molecules in the immune system, nitric oxide gas (NO); this gaseous molecule serves an activating messenger to bacteria-eating macrophage cells and stimulates blood flow by increasing the diameter of capillaries, encouraging rapid immune cell movement within the bloodstream.
>
> *Kreston 2012*

This would help to combat eye infections by activating the immune system to kill harmful bacteria. The results of this study suggest that the ancients were actually protecting their eyes from infection due to harsh environmental conditions caused by sand in the wind, bugs, and general infectious germs encountered daily.

   Makeup kits consisted of the cosmetic, jars or linen or leather pouches, palates, and sticks. Sometimes all of these were kept in a box or chest. The cosmetic could be kept as powder or in a lump wrapped in leather or linen. To use it, the powder or lump was mixed on the palate with water or oil and then applied to the eyelids with a stick. Cosmetic kits and palates have been discovered in numerous tombs and in other contexts. Early palates were rectangular and date to ca. 4000 BCE. Later, palates could be rounded or other shapes such as fish. Some were decorated, such as the Narmer palate, which depicted the king smiting Egypt's enemies and unifying Upper and Lower Egypt. It also contained a well for mixing. There were also kohl pots in various shapes, from alabaster vases to stylized jars in the shape of deities, such as Bes, or baboons. Kohl tubes could be made from wood, stone, alabaster, or glass. The application of makeup was enabled by the use of mirrors as well as attendants. Some Egyptian cosmetic chests also included a mirror.

In Mesopotamia, evidence for cosmetics has been found at the Royal Cemetery of Ur, and some texts seem to refer to the use of cosmetics. The Sumerian goddess Inanna (Ishtar) was described as "... daub[ing] her eyes with ointment" in preparation for her descent into the underworld. Cosmetics were made into a paste and applied with an ivory stick (Nemet-Nejat 1998:158).

Tattoos

It is not known exactly when people began tattooing their bodies; however, people have been practicing the art of tattooing for millennia. Tattoos have been used for the purposes of ritual and ceremony, as symbols of status, tribal markers, group affiliations, control, for medical reasons or for pure artistic expression. Some of the earliest evidence for tattoos found thus far has come from Europe. Figurines of the Pre-Cucuteni culture (a Neolithic culture found in Eastern Europe) dating to ca. 4900–4750 BCE depict females with tattoos of bands, dots, dashes, lozenges, and other shapes on their bodies (Lobell and Powell 2013). The graves of an Ukok Princess and a warrior found in the Altai Muntains on the Ukok Plateau yielded kurgans whose mummified bodies included elaborate tattoos depicting animals (The Siberian Times reporter 2012). These individuals were probably members of the Pazyryk people who were nomadic and mentioned by Herodotus in the fifth century BCE as having the most elaborate tattoos of any known people.

Ötzi (ca. 3400–3100 BCE), the male mummy found in the Ötzal Alps, South Tyrol, Italy in 1991, had sixty-one tattoos on various places on his body. Ötzi's tattoos were in the form of lines, groups of lines, or crosses. It is thought that these were not intended for symbolic, artistic, or ritual purposes but rather to function as therapeutic markers for pain-relieving treatment such as acupressure or acupuncture (South Tyrol Museum of Archaeology, www.iceman.it/en/the-mummy/#tattoos). Vertical lines were located on both sides of the spinal column, left calf, right instep and on the inner and outer ankle joint and on the chest at the lowermost right rib, and two lines were located across the back, left wrist. Cross-shaped tattoos appear on the right knee at the back and on the left Achilles tendon. These seem to correspond to known pressure points in acupuncture. The tattoos were applied in an unconventional manner. Rather than using needles, fine incisions were made and charcoal was rubbed into the incisions (South Tyrol Museum of Archaeology, www.iceman.it/en/the-mummy/#tattoos).

In Mesopotamia, it appears that women wore tattoos as early as 4500 BCE based on a figurine that depicted dots on the shoulders and stomach suggesting tattooing that may have symbolized sexuality or fertility. A contemporaneous male figurine depicted similar dotted tattooing in similar areas of the body (DeMello 2014:315). Tattoos were used to identify the deity that temple slaves served by tattooing a symbol of the deity onto the back of the hand. For example, a spade referred to Marduk and a star to Ishtar. Temple slaves were also marked with their name and their father's name (Nemet-Nejat 1998:194). Tattoos, as well as brandings or incisions, were used to mark slaves so they could be returned to their master (Huehnergard and Liebowitz 2013:72).

In Egypt, tattoos have been predominantly associated with women: on dancers, slaves, and even women of high rank. Tattoos adorned the legs, arms, and torsos (Huehnergard and Liebowitz 2013:73). Some of the earliest known tattoos date to the Eleventh Dynasty (ca. 2160–1994 BCE), from Deir el-Bahri, Thebes, from a mummified woman identified as Amunet, priestess of Hathor. Her tattoos consisted of parallel lines on her thighs and arms and an elliptical pattern in the pelvic region, just below her belly button. These tattoos may be related to fertility or may have been used to indicate specific medical conditions. Egyptian figurines, decorated vessels, paintings, and reliefs depict individuals, men and women, with tattoos. In the Middle Kingdom, female faience figurines referred to as Brides of the Dead were decorated with dotted patterns in the form of bands and diamond shapes in the region of their pelvis, stomach, and chest. These tattoos are interpreted to represent fertility or to identify their sex (Lobell and Powell 2013). A faience bowl dated to ca. 1400–1300 BCE depicts a female lute player with a tattoo on her right thigh. Her tattoo is of Bes, protector of household and family, and is associated with music and dance (Vandenbeusch 2014). The tomb of Seti I, ca. 1279 BCE at Abydos, depicts Lybian figures with tattoos on their arms, legs, and torsos. Faience tiles from Medinet Habu, the mortuary temple of Ramesses III, depict a Canaanite, Nubian, Lybian, Syrian, Shasu Bedouine, and a Hittite man. The figure representing the Canaanite shows tattoos on his arms and left leg. The tattoos appear to be in the form of parallel lines. In the Hebrew Bible, Leviticus 19:28 prohibits the Israelites from "… cut[ting their] bodies for the dead" and from putting tattoo marks upon themselves. The very existence of a prohibition suggests regular practice of said prohibited practice. Thus, a prohibition against tattooing among the Israelite community suggests that they or their Canaanite neighbors were tattooing themselves, and this practice was to stop among the Israelites. Although some scholars have used this passage to associate tattooing with mourning practices, it is more likely that tattooing was a practice among the living (Huehnergard and Liebowitz 2013).

Tattooing technique is the application of color by means of a puncture just below the subcutaneous layer of the skin. The ink is transferred via a hollow tube inserted into the skin. Once the ink is below the skin, pressure is applied so the skin does not bleed and the ink does not escape. Instruments considered to have been used for tattooing were discovered at Abydos dating to ca. 3000 BCE, and at Gurob in Northern Egypt dating to ca. 1450 BCE by W. M. F. Petrie. These instruments were made of bronze, and those from Gurob could have been bundled together to provide a pattern consisting of multiple dots (Lineberry 2007; DeMello 2014).

Tattooing tools could also range from bamboo sticks, fish teeth, fish bones, or old nails. The ink could be made from soot mixed with oil or water. Other colors may have come from indigo, or red and yellow ochre. Both soot and indigo have antibacterial properties. Another method used to deliver the ink into the skin was a sewing method. It could create up to forty stitches in a line of ca. 5 centimeters in length. An eyed needle was threaded with twine that was blackened with soot. The needle and twine were threaded through the skin in short but deep stitches. As the twine passed through the skin, pressure was applied to embed the pigment. When finished, oil was rubbed into the skin, and herbs such as cloves or white beet leaves may have been applied to the skin as well (Tassie 2003).

Beyond the Mediterranean, in the Altai Mountains of Siberia, several tombs of the Pazyryk Nomads have been discovered. A Pazyryk chief dating to ca. 600–300 BCE was found in his wooden chamber, which was lined with felt. His body boasted numerous elaborate tattoos depicting a stylized donkey, a mountain ram, a highly stylized deer with long antlers, an imaginary carnivore on the right arm, two griffins on the chest, and two deer and a mountain goat on the right arm. On the right leg was a fish, and a monster was crawling over the right foot. Four running rams were on his inside shin. The left leg had indistinguishable tattoos. On his back were a series of small circles in line with the vertebral column, presumably for therapeutic purposes. Herodotus, ca. 484–425 BCE, wrote that tattoos in Thrace were a mark of high birth, and the absence of tattoos signified low birth rank (*Histories* 5.6.2; Strassler and Purvis 2007:368).

Family planning

Children were a vital component of the household and family legacy, just as they are today. Children helped maintain the household, run the family business, and provide proper burial and ongoing funerary rituals for parents. Female children often helped foster alliances between clans or nation-states through marriage; acquired property or wealth for the family through marriage; and provided heirs to the family fortune. However, too few or too many children could be as much of a burden as a potential blessing. Too many female children could be expensive, and too few male children could have a negative economic effect on a family. So, the quantity and sex of children helped determine the future of a family. Hence, family planning played a significant role in the ancient world.

Numerous effective contraceptive methods were available to prevent or abort a pregnancy. Contraceptives were used in Egypt, Mesopotamia, and Canaan very early in their history. Recipes for contraception can be found in the Egyptian Ebers

Papyrus, ca. 1550 BCE, and the Kahun Gynecological Papyrus, ca. 1850 BCE (Nunn 2002:196). Certain herbs and other substances were proven to block or kill sperm. One of the most effective methods was to block sperm from entering the uteris by plugging the "mouth of the uteris" or the cervix (Nunn 2002:196, 47). Plugs usually consisted of a gum mixture of honey and sodium carbonate, or honey and acacia leaves and cotton lint, or a sponge placed into the vagina to "mouth of the uteris" or the cervix (Nunn 2002:196, 47). Pessaries of acacia gum also prevented pregnancy because acacia leaves contain lactic acid, a very effective spermicide. Other mixtures included olive oil mixed with frankincense and white lead, olive oil mixed with cedar and balsam resin and white lead, or a paste made of crocodile dung and sour milk. In addition to plugs, gums and jellies were placed at the "mouth of the womb" or the cervix. Aristotle, ca. fourth century BCE, describes a mixture of cedar oil, lead ointment, or frankincense mixed with olive oil to be used as a contraceptive. A study conducted by Marie Stopes in the 1930s concluded that olive oil was a natural contraceptive with a zero percent failure rate (Stanley 1995:251; James and Thorpe 1995:185–191). Other contraceptive methods included breast-feeding for up to three years, *coitus interruptus*, and the use of condoms made from sheep's intestines.

There were also oral contraceptives, though these methods were abortatives rather than preventative and are known from later Greek sources (Riddle 1992). Abortion in the ancient world was a widely accepted practice since, as mentioned earlier, too many children could be detrimental to the survival of a family. Interestingly, in the Law Codes of Hammurabi, ca. 1728 BCE, and in Egypt, and among the early Jews, there were penalties for abortion in the event of miscarriage or violence. In cases where the life of a fetus was wanted and birth expected, but the life of the developing fetus was abruptly ended due to assault, for example, compensation had to be paid. However, if a conscious decision was made to terminate the pregnancy, then no compensation had to be paid and no feelings or judgement of condemnation or immorality were assigned to the parents (Bullough 2001). It was not until the second and third centuries CE, when Christianity had taken hold that a debate regarding spiritual and ecclesiastical morality of abortion arose and influenced civil law (Bullough 2001; Riddle 1992).

Plants and herbs served as natural abortifacients, such as pennyroyal, juniper, and wild carrot, also known as Queen Anne's lace. Dioscorides, ca. 40–80 CE, and Galen, ca. 129–199 CE, listed numerous plants with contraceptive properties: asafetida, juniper, pennyroyal, and Queen Anne's lace, to name a few. Taken orally, these remedies had dangerous side effects; nevertheless, they were utilized, and modern research supports their potency. Some herbal books even cautioned readers to avoid juniper if pregnant (Webb and Craze 2004:267). Queen Anne's lace was described and prescribed by Hippocrates as an effective abortifacient with few or mild side effects. Queen Anne's lace blocks progesterone synthesis, thus disrupting implantation, and can be taken as an emergency contraception within eight hours of sexual intercourse. One problem with this herb, however, is that it looks quite similar to hemlock, which is poisonous, so when looking for it in the wild, one had to choose carefully the proper plant. The Greeks and Romans used pennyroyal to induce abortion, as described by Dioscorides. Pennyroyal was also used to flavor wine, and was boiled into a tea and drunk; however, too much could lead to organ failure. The Native Americans used blue cohosh because it contains two abortifacients. One mimics oxytocin, a hormone produced during childbirth that stimulates contractions, and the other, caulosaponin, unique to blue cohosh, also produces contractions (http://listverse.com/2010/11/14/10-ancient-methods-of-birth-control/). Soranus, a second century CE Greek gynecologist, described rue as a potent abortifacient when eaten regularly or taken as a tea because it decreases blood flow to the endometrium, making the uterine lining incapable of providing nutrition to a fertilized egg. For centuries, Rue has been a regular part of the South American diet used in salads and drunk as an emergency tea. Lemons were thought to have spermicidal properties, so lemon juice was used as a pessary, or the rind was placed in the cervix as a barrier. This was practiced among the early Jewish community (Nunn 2002).

Pregnancy tests were as important in the ancient world as they are today. Babylon and Egypt devised methods to determine whether a woman was pregnant. A Babylonian tablet from 700 BCE describes a method by which a wad of wool was saturated with the juices of the "white plant" (the species of the white plant is not known to us today) mixed with alum (a salt mineral) and inserted into the woman as a plug for three days. Once removed, the color revealed whether the woman was pregnant. The reaction of this mixture with changing hormones produced a color that suggested impregnation. In Egypt, midwives performed pregnancy tests, described in the Berlin Papyrus, ca. thirteenth century BCE. A woman's urine was poured over bags of wheat and barley, which were left to sit for three days. The hormones present in the urine were known to accelerate the growth of the grain. If after three days the grain grew, the woman was pregnant. Furthermore, if the barley grew, the child was a boy, and, if wheat, a girl. In the 1930s, tests showed that in 40 percent of the cases, growth was stimulated by a pregnant woman's urine (James and Thorpe 1995:192–193; Nunn 2002:191–194). A student in my 2016 class became intrigued with this and decided to test the theory herself. After gathering samples from two pregnant women, one early in her pregnancy and the other in the last trimester, the early-term sample caused the barley seeds to grow, indicating the child was male. The donor knew from ultrasound that her child was indeed a male.

Finally, infanticide or exposure was another effective method used to control the birth rate. Infanticide is the intentional termination of a child's life in the first twelve months, before one year of age. This practice was considered normal in numerous ancient societies to control the population and family size. Child sacrifice was also practiced in many ancient societies. Ancient Carthage, in Tunisia, originally a Phoenician city, contained a tophet, a term from the Hebrew Bible meaning a place of burning and can be used to refer to a place of burnt sacrifice, in this case a place where children were sacrificed to deities such as Ba'al and Tanit. Although disputed, many support the notion that the Carthaginian Tophet was where children were sacrificed, and the graves appear to attest to that practice (Stager and Wolff 1984;

Brown 1991). Child sacrifice at Carthage is mentioned by Plutarch (ca. 46–120 CE), Tertullian, Diodorus Siculus, and Philo. The Hebrew Bible also mentions child sacrifice in a Tophet by the Canaanites (2 Kings 23:10; Jeremiah 7:31–34).

Infanticide via exposure was practiced throughout the Middle and Near East and beyond, including the Graeco-Roman world. Often it was selective, keeping one sex over and above another depending upon needs and desires. A vivid example comes from Ashkelon, Israel, where a late Roman/early Byzantine sewer yielded hundreds of complete or near complete baby skeletons. Above the sewer was a building thought to be a brothel/bathhouse dating to ca. 400–500 CE. Based on the DNA analysis of forty-three infants' left femurs, reliable DNA was extracted from nineteen individuals. Of those, fourteen were male and five female. This has led some to conclude that the bathhouse prostitutes were allowing pregnancies to come to term, keeping the females but discarding the males. The females, then, were brought up to become part of the employee base of the brothel (Rose 1997). Recently, in England, the remains of 103 individuals from a Roman villa were discovered in the Buckinghamshire County Museum. These individuals were originally excavated in 1912 by Alfred Heneage Cocks, curator of the museum. Of the 103 individuals, ninety-seven were infants, three children, and three adults. Jill Eyers, director of the Chiltern Archaeology in England and an archaeologist, discovered the remains in an archive and analyzed them. Thirty-five were intact and yielded useful information. S. Mays, who examined the bones, determined that most died at or around the time of birth. These individuals date to ca. 150 and 200 CE. This has led researchers to conclude that the structure could have been a villa or a brothel; however, the killing of unwanted babies parallels those from Ashkelon (Perry 2011). Although a widespread practice well into the Middle Ages, infanticide became a capital offence in 374 CE under Roman law. However, those who practiced infanticide were rarely ever punished.

Interestingly, in Egypt, children of each sex and irrespective of social status were valued, and infanticide was forbidden. When the Greeks and Romans overtook Egypt, bringing with them their practice of infanticide by exposure, the Egyptians often adopted these infants as foundlings or raised them as slaves. According to Diodorus, infanticide was a punishable offence in Egypt (Diodorus Siculus, *Library* I.77.7; Henderson and Oldfather 1933:266–269).

15

TRANSPORTATION

Humankind is mobile, and has been since the days of hunting and gathering. When people began producing tools and foodstuffs, and accumulated surplus and tradable inventories, methods by which goods could be delivered to customers had to be devised. The transportation of raw materials and finished goods, as well as food, animals, and people, was essential to survival and vital in supporting a stable and growing economy. For these reasons, humankind devised ways to move these things from one place to another and over long distances. This chapter will discuss the ways in which early peoples resolved the problem of transportation and the timely movement of people and commodities. There were two forms of transportation: by water and by land. Each shall be discussed separately.

Maritime transportation

It remains unclear when humankind developed nautical skills; however, by the time the Mesopotamians and Egyptians included nautical scenes in their reliefs and paintings, their maritime vessels and abilities were well developed. The use of flotation devices probably began when the first person needed to cross a large body of water, be it a stream, river, lake, or sea. Going around large bodies of water could take a long time or prove impossible, particularly in the case of rivers such as the Tigris, Euphrates, and Nile. To solve this problem, efficient forms of marine transportation were devised.

Rafts

The earliest type of water vessel was probably a raft. Perhaps at first, one or several logs or a large bundle of reeds were lashed together to form a raft. This, together with a pole or paddle, proved efficient for crossing water and was easily constructed.

Reed boats came to be used by the Mesopotamians and the Egyptians from early in human history and continued in use for millennia (Casson 1995:3–5; Wachsmann 2009:9).

A very clever raft made by the Assyrians was the *kelek* (see Figure 9.5, middle). Depicted on an Assyrian relief from Nineveh (ca. 700 BCE), keleks consisted of a wooden frame supported by pigskins that were sewn up, except for the neck or one of the feet, and inflated. Then they were bundled under the flat surface of the raft, thus making it floatable. Keleks were used for transportation of goods as well as an army and its equipment. Keleks continue to be used and can measure 50 square feet floated by approximately a thousand inflated pigskin (Casson 1995:4). The inflated pigskin could also be used as a personal flotation device, as depicted in the relief. A person could use it for floating or as an underwater breathing apparatus.

Another simple boat was a *quffa* or coracle (Figure 15.1), a round boat made of a wooden frame of interwoven branches much like a basket, with animal skins stretched over the frame made waterproof by pitch (bitumen). Today these are often referred to as coracles and remain in use in some places. According to Herodotus, the Mesopotamians made the frame from willow branches and stretching hides

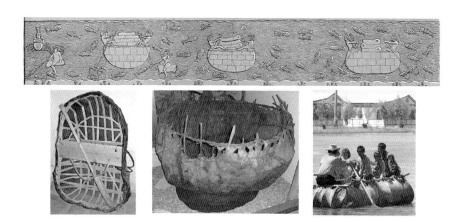

FIGURE 15.1 Examples of coracles. Top: Sennacherib's palace at Nineveh. Relief depicting people rowing coracles to transport materials, with individuals on inflated skins. Bottom, left: Coracle from Old Parish Church, Manordeifi, Pembrokeshire, Wales. Middle: Ku-Dru from Tibet, in the Field Museum of Natural History, Chicago, IL. Right: A Yak-skin coracle from Tibet (2006)

across the exterior hull. To Herodotus they looked like a shield and could be quite sizeable, carrying ca. 5000 talents, which is ca. 125 tons. Coracles remain in use today and can be 13 feet in diameter and 7.5 feet deep (Casson 1995:6; Landels 2000).

In 2014, Dr. Irving Finkel of the British Museum translated a 3700-year-old Mesopotamian tablet. The tablet describes building an ark that was a coracle some 3600 square meters in dimension, constructed like a "giant rope basket strengthened with wooden ribs, and waterproofed with bitumen inside and out" (Kennedy 2014). The instructions for building the ark were specific, including the use of two types of bitumen and the amount of rope needed for the project. Finkel describes this vessel as being quite familiar to local Mesopotamians and the more logical type of vessel that would have been built by Noah, as described in this tablet, now the earliest known account of the ark story (Kennedy 2014). Coracles continue to be used in many parts of the world today and have captured the fascination of enthusiastic hobbyists (The Coracle Society, www.coraclesociety.org.uk/).

Boats

Soon after rafting, the rigors of maritime travel probably led to the development of proper boats made from timber. The jagged rocks and shoreline probably damaged reed-built rafts and their inflated skins, thus requiring a durable material, such as timber, for a more dependable vessel. Here, the term boat will apply to vessels made from timber powered by oars, paddles, poles, or sails. The first wooden boats may have been dugout canoes. These are made from a tree trunk with chisel and hammer. This type of boat was utilized in numerous regions of the world and by numerous cultures.

Little is known of early Mesopotamian boats other than representations on seals and in reliefs (Figure 15.2). Several seals depict Mesopotamian boats as sickle boats.

FIGURE 15.2   Reed boats used in the conquest of a marsh village. Reliefs from the Palace of Nineveh

Adapted from Layard 1853, Plates 27, 28 (Public Domain, PD-1923).

Shown in profile, sickle boats are long, flat in the middle, and have a raised vertical bow and stern. Some include a shelter on board. Similar to a gondola, sickle boats are maneuvered by paddles or poles. They transported people and cattle, and one official seal depicts a dignitary on board.

More is known about Egyptian boats because many of them have been excavated, and there are numerous textual references, models, and depictions in reliefs and tomb paintings. The Egyptians employed several types of boats: ceremonial barques, planked boats, barges, and sailboats.

From the tomb of Meketre (TT280) from the Middle Kingdom, Twelfth Dynasty, ca. 1981–1975 BCE), a wooden boat model with figurines was discovered. This boat contains at least sixteen people, twelve of whom are oarsmen; one attends the rudder, one appears to navigate, and one or two are probably attendants to the pharaoh who is riding inside a covered structure near the stern of the boat. It is spoon-shaped and has a very low bow and stern. It is likely this boat was used to transport the pharaoh in life and perhaps in death as well.

Planked boats appear to have been square-ended with a tapered bow and stern, a wide midsection, and a flat bottom (Casson 1995:14–15). This shape and construction style was probably chosen because it was stable and easy to build. This barge-type boat was useful for transporting large objects, animals, people, or cargo on the Nile River. This shape was so useful that it remained in use from 2000 BCE, evidenced by the Dashur boat, through the fifth century BCE. Herodotus described how planked boats were built (Herodotus, *Histories*, 2.96; Strassler and Purvis 2007:156; Humphrey et al. 2006:447–448).

Acacia was the timber of choice. Planks were cut to ca. 2 cubits long (ca. 45.72 centimeters or 1.5 feet) and were laid like courses of brick with alternating joins. The boat builder started with the keel plank, consisting of several planks dovetailed together, which formed the centerline of the hull. On each side of the keel, short planks were fastened edge-to-edge using dowels (wooden pegs), mortise and tenon, wooden clamps, or a combination of these. Once the shell of the planks reached the desired height, the edge was finished with gunwales and a series of crossbeams at gunwale level. Gunwales provided lateral stiffening, carried the deck planking, and kept the sides from sagging outward. A stringer was inserted from stem to stern under the crossbeams supported by stanchions that stood on the keel plank. Seams were caulked with papyrus resin, beeswax, or pitch from the interior. Planks were sewn together with halfa grass. The entire structure was sewn from edge to edge by transverse sewing, the stitching being internal not external. The combination of dovetail, pegs, sewing, and caulking made the vessel watertight. Mortise and tenon joins, planked hull, and ribbing provided strength (Humphrey et al. 2006:447–448; Casson 1995:14–15).

The decks of planked boats and barges were movable to accommodate cargo of various types, sizes, and shapes. Cabins were sometimes added to the upper deck to accommodate passengers. The deckhouse was generally made from a wooden frame covered with mats, and was usually either amidships or aft. Another favorite boat-building timber was the prized cedar from Lebanon. Barges could be ca. 150–200 feet in length, and were powered by paddles, oars, or poles. Paddleboats, like modern tugboats, may have aided larger ships with maneuverability. Oarlocks, which were loops of rope, passed through holes in the gunwale. Rowing strokes had to be simultaneous and strong, so a rhythm had to be maintained. Steering with oars could include one or multiple oars. Later, sets of four—two on each side—became standard. These also helped with steering. The barge depicted in Queen Hatshepsut's tomb ca. 1479–1458 BCE is transporting two obelisks, has two sets of oars, a covered wooden shelter on deck, possibly for seating dignitaries, oarsmen, and a smaller barge that helped with navigation (see Figure 3.5). Barges like the one depicted in Queen Hatshepsut's funerary temple carried obelisks that were 29.6 meters long and 323 tons.

Sailing ships

Based on depictions from Hatshepsut's tomb, Egyptian sailing ships were elaborate, majestic, and well developed (Figure 15.3). Early sailing ships consisted of one pole or mast; these as well as two-legged masts were used until the end of the Sixth Dynasty, ca. 2200 BCE. Through the third millennium BCE, masts were very high to support the tall oblong sail and rigging typical of these ships, a construction style intended to catch the upper breezes, especially between high-rising cliffs.

The mast and sail could be dismantled and carried on deck if necessary. The mast was supported by numerous lines running aft that served as shrouds and backstays. Forestays appeared by the Fifth Dynasty, ca. 2400 BCE. Mast position shifted early: at first the mast was forward of amidships. Gradually it moved aft, so that by 1500 BCE the mast was at the center of the vessel, where it remained. A mast at amidships

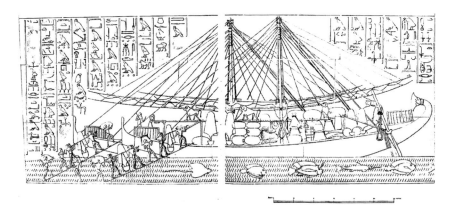

FIGURE 15.3 Line drawings made from reliefs found in Queen Hatshepsut's funerary temple at Deir el-Bahri, Egypt. These scenes record Hatshepsut's expedition to Punt, ca. 1493 BCE

Adapted from Naville 1908, Plate LXXIV (Public Domain, PD-1923).

provided greater stability and the ability to sail in winds coming from different directions (Casson 1995).

The sail hung from a yard and was stretched by a boom at the foot. Sails were made from papyrus. The boom remained fixed, and the sail was raised and lowered by the yard via a series of lifts. Block and tackle had not yet been invented, so raising and lowering was done by pure muscle power. The lines were made of palm fiber, papyrus, and grass fiber. Originally, the sails were tall and narrow; however, they were replaced by wider sails, probably because those were easier to handle. Eventually, oarsmen were added to the sailboat, which increased speed and enhanced maneuverability. Rudders were added, extending from the stern, to allow better control in steering the ship (Casson 1995).

There were two types of sailing vessels: river and sea going. The riverboats were spoon-shaped and had a very high fore and aft hull. Seagoing boats were long, slender, and narrow, and often had a pole or truss with heavy cable and loop for steering. Seagoing vessels had cleaner and more graceful lines and more complex sails and rigging (Casson 1995).

Recently, a boat burial was discovered in the tomb complex of Senwosret III of the Twelfth Dynasty at Abydos in southern Egypt. Dating to ca. 1840 BCE, this subterranean mud brick tomb at one time housed a wooden boat, which was integral to Egyptian funerary practices for pharaohs. Although the wooden boat was removed in antiquity, the etched, whitewashed walls still depict some 120 boats of varying size, shape, and design. Boat types include sailing vessels, ships with sails and paddles, and pole-operated boats (Williams 2016).

Phoenician and Canaanite ships

In the Late Bronze Age, Canaanites were already heavily involved in trade with Egypt and Ugarit. Textual and iconographic evidence provide descriptions of the ships. Canaanite culture can be found throughout Canaan (modern Israel), Lebanon, Syria, and Anatolia (Turkey). Although there is evidence that the Canaanites participated in maritime trade, they were not considered to possess the same maritime prowess as the Phoenicians. The Canaanites were merchants who transported heavy cargo from one place to another, probably under the instruction of their Egyptian overlords, especially in the Late Bronze Age. In a textual reference by Kamos regarding his expulsion of the Hyksos from Avaris, he describes the captured merchant ships and the valuable cargo they carried, including cedar, gold, lapis lazuli, turquoise, silver, battle-axes, honey, fat, incense, and Maringa oil (Wachsmann 1998:39).

In another account, Thutmose III describes his capture of two Syro-Canaanite ships filled with cargo in his fifth campaign, ca. 1450 BCE. These ships carried wide-ranging cargo, including male and female slaves, copper, lead, and emery. The Amarna texts also describe cargo carried on Canaanite ships in the mid-fourteenth century BCE. References from Ugarit describe merchants stationed there who did regular business with the cities of Ashkelon, Ashdod, Acco, Tyre, Beirut, Byblos, and Arwad. This was only part of an extensive ancient trade network

(Wachsmann 1998:40). These ships were depicted as being crescent-shaped with a steep angle. The ships contained much detail including butt joints, planks, vertical stem and stern posts, lacing, two rudders, mast, booms, sail, rigging, and screens (Wachsmann 1998:44–45). Although detailed in appearance, a knowledgeable sailor will note the inaccuracies and missing items. Nevertheless, the depictions contain enough details to identify the ships' origin (Wachsmann 1998:42).

The Phoenicians were best known for their ship making and maritime prowess, and are sometimes considered the more professional seafaring branch of the Canaanites. They were cunning merchants, transporting their goods to distant lands around the Mediterranean, and formidable maritime warriors. For these purposes, the Phoenicians are known to have had at least two types of ships: one for transportation of goods and people, and another that functioned as a war ship (Figure 15.4).

The earliest reference to Phoenician ships comes from Egypt, ca. 3000 BCE, discussing forty merchant ships delivering cedar to an Egyptian port. Another comes from the Egyptian tomb of Kenamon (Tomb 162) at Thebes, ca. 1400 BCE. This scene depicts Phoenician ships unloading at an Egyptian port. The Egyptian tale, The Journey of Wen-Amon to Phoenicia (ca. eleventh century BCE) describes Phoenician merchant ships (Wilson 1992a:25–28). A later (Iron Age) scene comes from Sargon's tomb depicting oared vessels with high-rising stem and sternposts decorated with figureheads in the shape of horse heads.

Finally, a well-known scene comes from the palace of Sennacherib in Nineveh, carved ca. 701–681 BCE, depicting two types of Phoenician galleys, an asymmetrical two-banked galley with a low bow, high curved stern, straight sheet line, and a curved battering ram (Figure 15.4). There is also a symmetrical galley without a ramming bow, probably also a merchant ship. By the Iron Age, Phoenician ships had evolved into asymmetrical two-banked galleys. The hull of the merchant ship remained crescent shaped with two vertical posts, in the shape of a horse's head or a bird at bow and stern, with a mast and sail at midship, and one or two rudders for steering. However, sometime from ca. 1500 to 1000 BCE, rowers were added to each side of the vessel, a type of ship known as a bireme. The hull of the merchant ship was deep and rounded. It was not built for speed, but rather to accept a large load of cargo (Casson 1995).

The bireme also functioned as a warship with slight modifications. Its hull was straighter, shallower, and built for speed. The sternpost curved up and inward, and the bow, which functioned as a battering ram, was a very solid piece of wood covered with bronze. The bireme included two banks of oars, upper and lower, and was introduced by the Phoenicians ca. 700 BCE. This became the leading warship design in the eighth century BCE. The Phoenicians also introduced a locking joint known as the Phoenician joint (Oleson 2008:615). Wood planks were joined by locked mortise and tenon fastenings. Although the Egyptians introduced this type of join, the Phoenicians improved its design and made it waterproof. This type of join was also used in the vessels found in the Uluburun and Cape Gelidonya shipwrecks (Institute of Nautical Archaeology). Locking joints were also described by Homer in the *Odyssey* (5.259–287). Herodotus mentioned biremes and penteconters, 50-oared ships, in his work *Histories* (7.89, 184.1–2).

FIGURE 15.4 Phoenician merchant ships and warships. Drawings from the reliefs found at Sennacherib's palace in Nineveh

Adapted from Layard 1849, Plate 71 (Public Domain, PD-1923).

In the fifth century BCE, the Phoenicians introduced the trireme. It was light, fast, and maneuverable. This became the Phoenicians' principal naval vessel as well as that of the Persian and Greek city-states. It consisted of three tiers that included 170 oarsmen: 62 *thranitai* in the top tier, 54 *zygitai* in the middle tier, and 54 *thalamitai* in the third. The hull was made of thin planks joined edge to edge, strengthened by a keel and transverse ribs. This trireme displaced only 40 tons and measured ca. 120 feet (37 meters long with a beam of 18 feet, or 5.5 meters). There was no ballast. It could reach 7 knots (8 mph/13 kph). The sail was square-rigged and used for power when the ship was not engaged in battle. The battering ram was more elaborate and was bronze-clad (Aubet 2001).

In the *Iliad*, Homer described ships from the late eighth century BCE. They were hollow (below deck), swift, and sleek. They were long, narrow, and low for maneuverability and for beaching overnight. There was a small forward deck for a lookout and a slightly larger aft deck where the captain and one or several passengers could operate the rudders and give commands. The crew slept on benches if they could not pull ashore at night. Gear and provisions were stored below decks. Cargo included leather sacks, wine, water, clay jars, and animal skins. Several standard styles included the 20-oared, the smallest vessel; the 50-oared, the penteconter, the most commonly used for troop transport; and the tricoter, or 30-oared. The hull was painted black or coated with pitch, and comprised the keel, stem post, sternpost, frames, planks, gunwale and beams, as well as the rowers' benches. It was held together with wooden pegs and joints. There were massive through-beams, one behind the fore decking and the other forward of the after-decking. The timber was of oak, poplar, pine, and fir. Masts and oars were made of fir. The rigging consisted of one sail amidships on a mast, which could be raised or lowered. The sail was square, bent on a yard. Two forestays ran to the bow, and there was a single backstay. Rigging included braces, sheets, and brails to shorten the sail. Gear included mooring lines, stern lines, stone anchors, a drain plug to empty the bilge, punting holes, pikes for fighting, side screens to close the waist in heavy weather, and provisions for the crew. Depictions of penteconters appear on Attic black figure vases from the sixth century BCE. They appear as warships and as merchant ships (Casson 1995).

Ancient shipping industry

By the Late Bronze Age, the shipping industry was well established. Maritime trade routes were routinely traveled from Ugarit to Egypt, and throughout the Mediterranean, with regular stops along the coast. Perhaps one of the best known and largest of the commodities transported was Cedar from Lebanon. The Palermo Stone describes Sneferu's (Fourth Dynasty) importation of cedar wood on forty ships filled with cedar logs, for the purpose of shipbuilding. Another Egyptian pharaoh, Thutmose (ca. 1448 BCE), during his seventh campaign, utilized ships to move troops and supplies from Egypt to the Canaanite coast. This vastly improved logistics and the ease with which supplies could be delivered to Egyptian troops in Canaan (Wachsmann 1998:10).

Moving commodities via ship was preferred to overland routes. Ships could hold greater quantities of cargo than could donkeys and carts. Additionally, travel by sea was more direct than some overland routes with high mountain passes and rivers, for example. Furthermore, ships did not need regular feeding, water, or rest as their donkey and human counterparts did. Therefore, whenever possible, merchants and traders chose to send their goods via water. Travelers often chose to go by sea rather than by land. For example, WenAmun (Wilson 1992a) chose to flee Egypt by boat to get as far away as possible as quickly as possible. Maritime trade also made it possible to exchange commodities with distant lands. Canaan and Egypt were trading with Cyprus, Crete, Mycenae, Greece, and beyond throughout the Mediterranean basin.

This is but a very brief summary of some of the nautical crafts that were in use in the ancient world. A more thorough treatment of vessels in the ancient Near East, as well as their construction and rigging, can be found in Casson's work, *Ships and Seamanship in the Ancient World*. Casson's excellent research revealed an extensive shipbuilding and shipping industry, which need not be repeated in detail here. The purpose here is to make the reader aware of the technology as a first step to a more thorough investigation.

Maritime navigation

It has long been thought that sea routes hugged the coastline to avoid open seawaters. Certainly, the Mediterranean could be a treacherous sea to travel. There were very strong winds, currents, and storms to contend with. The best time for sailing was from March to November. The wind direction was more favorable to sailing, especially given the type of sails in use during that period (Wachsmann 1998:295). In light of the tumultuous sea, hugging the coastline between ports of call makes perfect sense, especially because a merchant ship needed to make numerous stops to unload or load goods and passengers from various ports; however, this may not have been the norm based on recent discoveries. Shipwrecks found in the Mediterranean suggest that navigation of the open water may actually have been commonplace.

In 1999, the Leon Levy Expedition to Ashkelon, the Institute for Exploration, and a team from Woods Hole Oceanographic investigated two Iron Age Phoenician ships that sank in antiquity off the coast west of Gaza at a depth of 400 meters. The two ships were named the Elissa and Tanit and date to ca. 750 BCE. Each wreck carried numerous amphora, jugs, juglets, jars, and cooking pots. While some artifacts were retrieved, these wrecks await proper excavation. Nevertheless, from these two ships it can be concluded that the vessels carried a massive and heavy cargo and were traversing open sea, not hugging a coastline (www.whoi.edu/sbl/liteSite.do?litesiteid=2740&articleId=5018).

The Uluburun shipwreck, located off the coast of Turkey, ca. six miles southeast of Kaş, ca. 50 meters (160 feet) off the coast, was likely *en route* to Mycenae with a full cargo when she went down. Discovered in 1982 by a sponge diver, this ship dates to the Late Bronze Age, ca. 1305 BCE, based on dendrochronology, pottery, and other artifacts. This is the Amarna Period in Egypt. She appears to have been sailing from Cyprus or from a Syro-Canaanite port headed west of Cyprus for the Aegean or Mycenaean Greece. The vessel was ca. 16 meters long, built in a shell-first method, with mortise and tenon joints. The keel seemed to be rudimentary. The wood was Lebanese cedar planks and oak tenons. There were twenty-four stone anchors made from stone that is common to the Levant. It settled at a depth of 44 to 52 meters. It had a vertical post bow upper decking, booms, and rigging for sail; the rigging was intact, but the sail had disintegrated. The cargo she carried included 354 copper ingots weighing 10 tons; 149 Canaanite jars containing glass beads, olives, pistachio (terebinth) resin; 175 glass ingots of cobalt blue, turquoise, and lavender; blackwood logs from Africa (ebony); ivory tusks from elephants; hippopotamus teeth; tortoise shells; murex opercula for dye; Cypriot pottery and oil lamps; arrow and spear heads; daggers; swords; almonds; pine nuts; olives; black cumin; sumac; and many other commodities (see Institute of Nautical Archaeology, https://nauticalarch.org/projects/uluburun-late-bronze-age-shipwreck-excavation/). This ship is nearly completely intact. It is a living example of an ancient sailing vessel from the Bronze Age, which verifies the iconographic and textual references known thus far.

To successfully navigate the seas, sailors utilized several tools: a lead line, time-keeping, a cross-staff, an astrolabe, and the stars. The lead line was a long rope attached to a weight with knots at regular intervals (Herodotus *Histories*, 2.5; Strassler and Purvis 2007:118–119). By lowering the line, sailors knew the depth of the water at the given position, which helped them determine their position on the sea. The Egyptians used this device at around 3400 BCE, and it remained in use into the Greek period, as mentioned by Herodotus. In 1600 CE, the English continued its use marking out the fathoms at regular intervals. By keeping track of time onboard ship, the sailors could estimate the position of the sun relevant to their position, and determine how long and far they traveled by keeping track of their speed. To aid in all this, sailors used several sand glasses, known to us as an hourglass. A cross-staff dates to ca. 400 BCE and was a long cross bar with a shorter cross bar attached at a right angle in the middle of the longer one. The long part of the cross-staff was placed below the user's eye with the other end pointed toward the sun or Polaris so that the observer could position the upper end of the crossbar to the sun or Polaris and the horizon. The crossbar became the transom, and the long end the staff. Once the sun/Polaris and the horizon were aligned with the cross-staff, one's angular altitude could be calculated. An astrolabe, Greek for "star taker," was an inclinometer, which was used to locate and predict the positions of celestial bodies, calculate a local time at a given latitude, and was used in surveying and triangulation. This device is considered to have been a Hellenistic invention by Apollonius of Perga or Hipparcus around ca. 220 BCE/150 BCE. It was originally used in astronomy and astrology and adapted for maritime navigation. Finally, the stars and planets themselves provided navigational aid to sailors. The Phoenicians kept land in sight while also keeping track of the stars, specifically Polaris, the North Star, also called the Phoenician Star (see Mariners Weather Log, www.vos.noaa.gov/MWL/aug_08/navigation_tools.shtml).

In 1901 sponge divers discovered a shipwreck that contained a device that has come to be known as the Antikythera mechanism, named for the Greek island of Antikythera where the wreck was located. A complex network of thirty interacting bronze gears, this device was likely built between 150 and 100 BCE. After extensive study, it has been determined that this device was used to track or predict the positions of celestial bodies, eclipses, and other astrological phenomena (The Antikythera Mechanism Research Project, www.antikythera-mechanism.gr). Recently, new scanning technology has allowed researchers to find and translate script incised into some of the pieces recovered from the wreck. This text helps illuminate the thus far elusive purpose for this device. The mechanism integrated the movements of the celestial bodies with the lives of contemporary Greek peoples and their environment (see Archaeology, www.archaeology.org/news/4528-160610-antikythera-mechanism-text). Some have suggested that this mechanism may have helped with navigation, hence its presence on board a cargo ship, or that it was being delivered to its new owner. Whatever its function, perhaps its ability to determine astrological position had something to do with maritime navigation.

Land transportation

Even though maritime trade routes were preferred, eventually commodities, troops, and travelers had to venture inland to land-locked cities, customers, and military posts. To do this, rivers and tributaries were probably utilized as much as possible; however, at one point terrestrial transportation was inevitable.

An extensive network of roads extended from the Mediterranean coast to Mesopotamia and beyond. Major routes followed the coastline from Egypt to Ugarit and into Anatolia; from Aqaba at the Red Sea into Syria, Damascus, and to Mesopotamia and Turkey; and south into southern Egypt and beyond. These roads were not necessarily planned, but found as the paths of least resistance between mountain passes and freshwater sources. In essence, the terrain and topography determined early overland routes (Landels 2000:170–185; Humphrey et al. 2006: 409–442; Oleson 2008:551–605; Hodges 1992:82–89). From the Neolithic period to the Iron Age (ca. 10,000–1,000 BCE) roads that were purposefully planned and maintained occurred mostly within urban centers and villages surrounding larger city-centers. Urban streets were leveled, paved, and maintained. Paving consisted mainly of hard-packed clay soil that may or may not have been plastered or paved with pebbles, cobblestones, brick, or broken ceramic sherds. Traffic including mules, oxen, horses, and wheeled vehicles damaged earthen roads causing ruts and potholes, much like today, and required regular maintenance and an organized civil workforce. Initially, inter-city and inter-region roads were little more than forged pathways well worn by travelers and merchants moving goods from one place to another, but would be improved by the Greeks and Romans.

Walking was the most used method of terrestrial transportation. People used walking sticks for balance as well as for protection. A late period Egyptian scribe, Ankhsheshonq, said, "Do not walk the road without a stick in your hand" (Lichtheim 1980:172).

Ancient Egyptian men were often depicted carrying loads on a yoke on their back and shoulders; women carried loads on their heads or hips. Wheeled transportation may have been inspired by the field plow driven by a team of oxen.

Early examples of wheeled vehicles come from Mesopotamia, as early as 3500 BCE from reliefs and 3000 BCE from the Queen's Grave at Kjafaje where four-wheeled wagons were discovered (Forbes 1964:71). At Tepe Gawra, ca. 3000 BCE, models of carts and wagons were discovered. The Battle Standard of Ur, ca. 2500 BCE, depicts wheeled chariots. These early vehicles consisted of solid wooden wheels and a solid cart to carry its riders. The reliefs on the exterior walls of Medinet Habu, Ramessess III, ca. 1186–1155 BCE, depict the Sea Peoples arriving in what appear to be heavy, cumbersome ox-driven carts with two solid wooden wheels held in place by an axle. Two types of carts are depicted: one made of vertical sticks with horizontal cross-pieces and the other made of solid wood, with the carts balanced over the axle.

Spoked wheels replaced the solid wheel, making the vehicle lighter. Reliefs from the place at Nimroud depict carts with spoked wheels (Layard 1853, Plates 12, 13). The disadvantage to wheeled vehicles was that the terrain had to be relatively clear of debris and flat for the wheels to pass.

The best mode of transporting merchandise was by mule with human companion(s). This was the most versatile mode of transportation because mules and humans can adapt to any terrain, board a ship, and climb narrow paths; also, mules are easy to load and unload. Mules are the result of mating a female horse (mare) and a male donkey—always in this order and never vice versa. The mules' advantage is that they are amenable to carrying loads. They are less temperamental than horses, though horses are more patient, and mules are less stubborn than donkeys and easier to train. Mules are patient and hard working. Mules' skin is tougher and thicker than that of a horse, and they can stand extreme changes in weather and temperature. Mules can survive on less water for a longer period; they have tougher hooves and are sure-footed, and they travel slowly but steadily at ca. 3 mph, traveling up to 80 kilometers (50 miles) per day. Pack mules were used throughout the Graeco-Roman period and well into the modern era. The British Army used pack mules during World War I. Mules are ca. 1.32–1.52 meters tall (13 to 15 hands); their average weight is ca. 270–410 kilograms (600–900 pounds); they can carry ca. 30 percent of their own weight (90 kilograms or 200 pounds). In hilly, mountainous areas, they can carry 25 percent of their own weight (Dorsey 1991; Moorey 1999; Landels 2000:170–171). In comparison, a man could portage a limited amount of weight a limited distance: ca. 40–50 yards at a weight of 50–60 pounds (23–27 kilograms) at a distance of 300–400 yards.

The load placed onto mules had to be packed carefully and be particular in size and shape. Mules could not carry stone blocks, and whatever was placed on their backs had to be balanced and evenly distributed across the mules' back. Merchants often traveled with more than one mule and could sell the mules along with the goods. Mules could also feed along the trail on grasses or bushes. Later depictions at Roman Ostia show mules being brought up to the doors of granaries, and human workers taking sacks of grain off the mules' backs into the building.

Routes and roads

Purpose of roads

In the twenty-first century, it is difficult to imagine life without roads. From the most sophisticated city to the most rural of villages, roads are integral to travel, commerce, and communication. Roads have become so essential that literary metaphors make use of them—"the road less traveled" or "taking the high road" or "the journey of life." Roads are functional in terms of moving people, commodities, and armies, and in facilitating the movement of ideas, cultures, and politics. Thus, the practical and metaphoric functions of roads are equally important to the success of civilization.

Roads

It is thought that the first intentionally developed roads were created in Mesopotamia ca. 3500–3000 BCE (Forbes 1964:12). There were several types of roads: natural roads that developed as a result of heavy traffic from people moving from one place to another routinely; artificial roads such as work roads or ramps, such as those built at the pyramids and quarries; trade routes for caravans; urban and village streets; paved roads; and military roads. Roads developed based on the terrain; they went around or through obstacles such as mountains or buildings, or around or across bodies of water (Forbes 1964). Finally, there were intra-city or intra-village roads as well as inter-city and inter-state roads. Although most consider the fourth millennium to have been the advent of intentional road building, that assessment may need to be revised based on recent excavation of Neolithic sites such as Sha'ar HaGolan, wherein roads were intentionally built and maintained.

Most of the people travelling the roads were merchants and trade caravans; military personnel; agriculturalists bringing their produce to market; and those traveling to weddings, funerals, banquets, daily work places, to market, and for religious purposes. People travelled for political and diplomatic missions, and roads were used frequently by messengers, tax collectors, and to move commodities from one place to another, as well as for migratory purposes (Dorsey 1991).

Numerous texts reference the condition, security, construction, and use of roads for the movement of troops. In the Amarna Letters, fourteenth century BCE, a vassal prince from Jerusalem complains about the attack on a caravan he sent to Egypt containing tribute and captives for the pharaoh. It was attacked and robbed near Ayalon by the men of Milkilu, the prince of Gazru (Gezer) with the sons of Lab'ayu of Šakmu (Shekhem) (Fischer et al. 1996:9). This letter is a complaint against the Egyptian army for not providing enough protection, which was a subject of numerous other letters. In the Hebrew Bible, there are numerous references to the military and roads. Joshua 10 describes a battle along the road to Jerusalem. The Beit Horon road is where a battle between Saul and the Philistines took place (1 Samuel 13:17 ff., 14:31; 2 Samuel 5:25). Solomon is credited with having built roadside forts in strategic locations including Jerusalem, Gezr, Beit Horon, and Baalath

(1 Kings 9:17; 2 Chronicles 8:5) (Fischer et al. 1996:8). These are but two examples of multiple references to the military use of roads.

Although horses and mules were domesticated and used since 2300 BCE, horses were not commonplace until the Iron Age with the invasion of the Assyrian cavalry units during the reign of Ashurnasirpal II (883–859 BCE) and onward. Even then, horses were used mostly by military personnel. In Canaan, Mesopotamia, and Egypt, camels were not used until the Iron Age, except in the case of nomadic peoples. Nor were they native to the region prior to their domestication. The camel had been domesticated in Syria and in the North Arabian deserts. However, after the Assyrian invasions around the time of Tiglath-Pileser III (ca. 744–727 BCE), camels took on a greater role in the Near East. They were bred in large numbers and came to be associated with an increase and expansion of trade. Camels were advantageous over mules because they could go for longer periods without food and water (fourteen days without water, depending upon the season); they could carry a heavier load, almost double; required fewer drivers; did not need to be shod; and overall, camels were easier to maintain. Camels could travel at about 3 mph, loaded. Camels could carry twice as much as a cartload and could travel rougher terrain with less difficulty than mules (Moorey 1999:13). In reliefs from the palace of Sennacherib at Nimroud, camels are depicted carrying a load (Layard 1853, Plates 22, 33).

Major and minor roadways were used to control and accommodate traffic. Major roadways may include roads that extended from one city-state to another, from one country to another, and trade routes. Minor roads may include those that wound through city-states and villages and those that led from urban centers to the surrounding hinterland. Routes may also include rivers and tributaries.

The earliest roads, from the Neolithic to the Iron Age (ca. 10,000–1,000 BCE), were maintained inside cities and in villages surrounding walled cities. Urban streets were leveled, paved, and well maintained. Intra-city roads were mainly hard-packed earth "paved" with hard-packed clay/mud (Hodges 1992:166–167, 202). With carts, chariots, and increased trade, inter-city roadways and trade routes were merely beaten earth paths. Just as today, with wheeled traffic, hooved traffic, and foot traffic, roads suffered from ruts and potholes, which needed constant maintenance. Occasionally, in high trafficked areas, cobblestones, pavers, and plastered surfaces may have been installed to provide greater strength and reduce the need for such frequent maintenance. The best maintained roads were near temples, quarries, ports, and administrative buildings. Wheeled traffic was usually restricted to the public zones within cities. However, in the Hellenistic and Roman periods, roads became more substantial, ubiquitous, and better maintained. Roads were not restricted to cities or elite zones within them. Instead, they were integral to every aspect of a well-functioning empire.

Road-building materials

In Mesopotamia, the important spaces—processional roads, temple enclosures, administrative areas—were paved with stone or stone slabs. Most other roads were paved with sun-dried brick or baked brick. Mesopotamian bricks were plano-convex, formed by hand, with one flat side and one curved side, and baked in the sun or in a kiln at ca. 550–600°. There were two sizes of brick, and they were made in a mold. These date to ca. 2700–2500 BCE. The clay was prepared to produce strong bricks with few, if any, inclusions to prevent breakage. The bricks were square or rectangular in shape and measured ca. 20 × 20 × 3.5 inches. After 2700 BCE, rulers stamped bricks with their names. Bitumen was used as a mortar, as evidenced by the remnants of mortar on some plano-convex bricks. Asphaltic bitumen could be found at Hit, Ain Mamurah, and Ain el Maraj, near Kirkuk. Although asphaltic bitumen was found near the Dead Sea and in Syria, it was not likely imported from there. Bitumen mixed with sand, gravel, and clay, together with the brick, probably made for a very durable road surface (Forbes 1964).

Roadways in Mesopotamia could also be covered with cobble-pavement as found at Arpachiyah, ca. 3500 BCE. At Eridu, street surfaces were paved with com-pressed loam. Compression may have been made with limestone rollers. In cities especially, regular maintenance was necessary. With regular rains, the detritus of mudbrick structures, garbage, and wear and tear, streets were regularly covered with mud and sand. Even as city planning developed, only the most important parts of the city were paved (Forbes 1964).

As armies moved from one place to another, they also built roads to connect cities to each other. These roads were often referred to as "Road of the King" or "Royal Road." These were generally dirt roads that had been cleared of debris then leveled and hard-packed, making the surface smoother and more passable. Much later, during the Assyrian Empire (Iron Age), greater care was taken to drain and pave streets and larger roadways. Drainage was important, especially within cities, and central drains covered by limestone slabs were established, allowing excess water and sewage to drain away from the city and its streets (Forbes 1964).

Processional roadways and temple precincts were well built and maintained. For example, the processional roads to the Temple of Ishtar at Assur and to Aiburshabu in Babylon consisted of a rubble and gravel foundation, two or three courses of brick and bitumen mortar, and breccia or limestone slabs in bitumen. The main streets were ca. 12 meters wide, and secondary streets were ca. 3–4 meters wide (Forbes 1964:77–80). Some highway roads were hewn; for example, Sargon II in his eighth campaign commissioned his sappers to cut out a better road at Mt. Simirria because it was so difficult for his chariot to pass. The sappers shattered the moun-tainside and created a passable road for Sargon and his army and equipment (Dorsey 1991:28–29).

Quarry roads were built by the Egyptians to move block, particularly large blocks such as obelisks, out of the quarry, onto the chosen mode of transportation, and to its destination. Thuthotep describes building a road using skilled workers such as necropolis workers, miners and quarrymen, who hewed out a rocky trail with a rugged surface of hard stone to provide a level and smooth surface for moving a 60-ton stone block (Dorsey 1991:29).

At Ashkelon in Canaan, in the Middle Bronze Age and Iron Age, the streets were well planned but made from hard-packed earth and clay. The street that passed through the Middle Bronze Age city gate on the northern part of the tell, and the street and plaza that ran between buildings in the Iron Age marketplace were earthen, hard-packed, but well maintained and perfectly functional (Stager, Schloen and Master 2008, 2011).

At other sites in Canaan, such as at Beth-Yerah in the Early Bronze age, streets were paved with cobblestones; at Shechem in the Middle Bronze Age, streets were also cobbled; and at Joppa in the Late Bronze IIA period, a 4-meter-wide street was paved with reed and clay (Dorsey 1991:26). In Ashdod, Area K, a 3.5-meter-wide cobbled street was unearthed dating to ca. the tenth century BCE; at Gezer in the Iron II period, wedge-shaped cobblestones paved the street; and at Megiddo, at the city gate dating to ca. 1050–1000 BCE in Str. V A, the street was paved with a cement surface over a crushed stone base with a thick lime plaster. The gate passage of Str. IV was also plastered.

While urban roads were paved and well maintained, open highways were not. They were often left to develop overgrowth and potholes. Numerous texts and literary references describe the dusty nature of roads and their rough condition. In the Letter of the Satirical Scribe, the road through Megiddo is described as "filled with boulders and pebbles … and overgrown with reeds, brambles, briars(?), and 'wolf's-paw'" (Dorsey 1991:27). It was not until the Hellenistic and Roman periods that proper highways connecting cities over long distances were developed and maintained.

Roadside inns, way stations, messaging systems

One of the earliest references to a way station comes from Shulgi, King of Ur, who reigned from 2029 to 1982 BCE in Mesopotamia during the Neo-Sumerian period. He claims to have built "big houses" along the highway to serve as resting places for weary travelers. He planted gardens and settled friendly people in them (Dorsey 1991:43). The Sumerian word *éš-dam* means "house of the woman" and refers to a hostel or a tavern, which gives us a clue that these inns were most likely run by women. They provided room and board as well as recreational and social activities. There were also caravanserai, which appear to have been operated by the government and offered a safe place for travelers to stop, pass official correspondence to the next carrier, and comprise a community of travelers who were loyal to the Assyrian king (Dorsey 1991:44–45).

Herodotus (*Histories*, 5.52–53; Strassler and Purvis 2007:388–390) describes inns and way stations every ten to fifteen miles along the royal road that stretched 2600 kilometers from Susa to Ephesus. Stations were posted at regular intervals ca. 4–5 *parasangs*, a day's march (ca. 22–27 kilometers). Along with room and board, these stations also housed a permanent garrison of soldiers and grooms. A messenger could probably traverse the entire road in a matter of nine days; however, a regular army would have taken ninety days because it moved more slowly (Forbes 1964:80–81).

In addition to regularly spaced way stations, markers indicated distances along the road, and in Mesopotamia, streets were named and labeled with their names, such as the Uruk Road, meaning that this was the road that went to Uruk (Dorsey 1991:47; Forbes 1964:80–81). In Egypt and Canaan similar road names were utilized, in which the destination of the road was included. For example, the Beth-Shemesh Road (1 Samuel 6.12b) (Dorsey 1991:48–490).

Roads also functioned as information highways, delivering new ideas and knowledge of cultural traditions from one place to another. Roads also provided a network for quick long-distance communication. Persian king Cyrus the Great (ca. 550–530 BCE) created a messaging system and established posting stations approximately every 25 kilometers on the road from Susa to Sardis (Herodotus *Histories* 8.98; Strassler and Purvis 2007:642; Humphrey et al. 2006:425). The distance of a journey was calculated according to one day's ride, and horses and riders were provided for that journey. If a journey was three days, there were three riders and three horses, with each stationed a day's ride along the route. The first rider passed the message to the second, the second to the third, and the final rider delivered the message. The riders were not deterred by weather or temperature and were dedicated to completing the task. The transfer of message from one rider to another took place at posting stations staffed by attendants who provided food, water, and fresh horses to message carriers. Darius I (ca. 521–486 BCE) used this system to deliver news to Susa regarding the progress of his military campaigns. This system was much admired by the Greeks and by the Roman Emperor Augustus (ca. 63 BCE to 14 CE), who improved the system by building better roads, which allowed the transfer of written messages via a carrier and messengers. Although the system was originally meant for official messaging, private messages were also delivered (Humphrey et al. 2006:425–426).

Greek roads

The Hellenistic Greeks brought a different kind of road to the Near East. Instead of using clay, brick, and cobblestone, they used dressed stone blocks. Pausanias (ca. 110–180 CE) considered Greek roads in his Description of Greece (1.44.6; 8.54.5; 10.32.8; Humphrey et al. 2006:410):

> Originally, as they say, the road from Megara to Corinth was made from unencumbered and agile men to travel over, but the emperor Hadrian made it wider, and it was suitable for chariots to pass each other when they met. … The road to Argos from Tegea is very well suited for the carriage, and is really a superb highway. … The road across Pamassus is not entirely mountainous, but is even suited for carriages.

However, Greek roads were much maligned in antiquity because they were not as functional, well made, or well-maintained as Roman roads were. Strabo (64/63 BCE to 24 CE), in his *Geography*, noted that the Romans had especially provided for those things that the Greeks took little account of, "such as the construction of roads and aqueducts, and of sewers that could wash out the filth of the city into the Tiber" (5.3.8; Henderson and Jones 1923:404–409). The Romans established roads through the countryside by cutting into hills and embankments so that their wagons were able to transport ships' cargo (Humphrey et al. 2006:410). Perhaps the Greeks' lack of attention to road systems was because they placed greater emphasis on the people who made up the city. Nevertheless, the advancement in road technology made by the Hellenistic Greeks should not be discounted. The introduction of hewn stone blocks into road construction improved road technology mightily and provided a basis on which the Romans could develop theirs.

Introducing hewn stone block as the building material for roads was important, especially in the Near East, because it addressed the issue of erosion, a constant problem with earthen roads. The construction of Greek roads began with a leveled trench flanked on one or both sides with a channel to carry away rainwater, and the roadway had a slight camber to encourage rainwater to flow toward the channel(s). Durable stone was set where the wheels of carts, wagons, and chariots traveled. In roads used as processional ways, artificial ruts were cut into the paving stones, ca.7–10 centimeters deep on average and 30 centimeters on occasion, and 20–22 centimeters wide to provide a smooth journey for the king or for the deity's statue (Forbes 1964:101–103).

Alexander the Great adopted the Persian system of road building by using the army to build roads. Together with Thracian engineers, Alexander's army built substantial roadways and highways throughout the Near East, and he adopted the Persian's courier system (Forbes 1964:107–108).

Roman roads

The Romans improved the paving techniques of the Greeks, and devised advanced techniques for road construction. They developed a vast network of roads throughout the empire, including the Near East. There were some 120,000 miles of road, which were well maintained for more than 800 years. These roads synthesized disparate institutions, races, and cultures into Roman imperial culture. Roads were a symbol of public order, unity, strength, and infrastructure. Roads and the use of them as a unifying power was not a new idea; however, the Romans knew how to use to their advantage the qualities that roads had to offer.

Roman roads were not standardized. Their size, shape, construction method, and materials were commensurate with location and purpose. Roads were made with stone, gravel, hard-packed earth, pebble, broken tile, or a combination of these. Engineering methods adjusted to the soil, the subsoil, and available resources (Richard 2011:55–58). The few "standard" elements of Roman roads were the quality and precision with which they were built. Most roads were built so well that many of them survive today with very little, if any, deterioration. If only modern roads in the United States could be constructed with the same quality and precision!

As much as possible, Roman engineers designed direct routes, spanning marshland and valleys with bridges or embankments and tunneling through hills and mountains (Richard 2011:57). There were roadways for traveling long distances; smaller roads for the movement of troops and equipment; urban roads; country roads; and footpaths and bridleways utilized by pedestrians, pack animals, carts, carriages, chariots, and horses. One of the main functions of road building and use was to facilitate the movement of troops and equipment. These roads had to be built quickly and with strength to handle the wear and tear of troops, horses, and wagons. Within the Roman military machine, engineers oversaw construction and maintenance. Most roads were equipped with a drainage ditch at the very least or a complicated drainage and sewer system, especially in urban areas. Roman roads were engineering feats worthy of marveling. As the Roman Empire grew, this technology was incorporated into the Near East, linking the East with the West (Richard 2011:55–58).

One of the best-known Roman roads was the Via Appia, or the Appian Way. Construction began in 312 BCE by Apius Claudius Caecus, a Roman censor, for military purposes during the Samnite Wars. By 244 BCE, it extended 230 miles (196 kilometers) from Rome southeastward to Brundisium (Brindisi) in Italy. This was the Romans' first significant roadway. This route was made of a series of straight lines. The main concern seems to have been to keep the straightest line and shortest route possible, which was accomplished with the use of a groma and surveying techniques (Richard 2011:55–58).

It is considered an engineering marvel due to topography, the territory traversed, geological elevation and surveys, and enormous hydraulic projects, such as land reclamation and drainage. Hydraulics included diversion of a number of creeks/streams, land excavation for trenches, cutting bedrock, removal of excavated soil, transportation of materials for leveling and back fill, paving stones, sub-paving materials, support terracing for the road along valley and mountainsides, and bridge construction. Surveying also included back-sights taken from high points along the route to verify accuracy of the survey over long distances. Although intended to facilitate the movement of troops and equipment, the road fostered new settlements; incorporated newly conquered territories and cities; spread the Roman way of life; and facilitated trade, information, and idea sharing. Triumphal arches placed at the beginning and end of the road and at city entrances reminded inhabitants of their rulers' achievements and sovereignty (Richard 2011:57).

The Via Appia was originally constructed with a gravel surface, and gradually the entire road was paved with polygonal basalt blocks. The width of the road was consistently 4.1–4.2 meters wide, equaling 14 Roman feet. This would allow two carriages to pass in opposing directions. A camber allowed rainwater to flow to the curb drains on each side of the road. The curbs were made of upright slabs that formed a frame for sidewalks, which were ca. 1.1 to 3.0 meters wide, depending on the type of traffic that would use it. Vertical blocks were built into the curb every 3 to 5 meters to keep wheeled vehicles from riding up onto the sidewalk. Markers along the road recorded distances and named the local authorities responsible for maintaining that section of the road. Roman markers were located ca. 1000 paces, or 5000 Roman feet or ca. 1480 meters (4851 feet) apart. The counting of miles started with mile-marker 1 in Rome and continued the length of the road (Oleson 2008:555–556). Miles were measured with the hodometer (Vitruvius X.IX; Morgan 1960:301–303).

In general, Roman roads were constructed using a consistent, basic technique (www.battleoffulford.org.uk/ev_roman_rd_constrct.htm). First, a deep ditch of ca. 1 meter (3 feet) wide and nearly 0.5–1.0 meter deep was established. The bottom of the ditch was packed then leveled with packed sand or dry soil. This base layer reduced the likelihood of the road sinking or shifting over time. Next was a layer of crushed rock or large stones, and sometimes slabs called *statumen*, 20–30 centimeters thick, were laid on the base layer. The statumen created the foundation. The next layer, called the *rudus* (ca. 30–50 centimeters thick), was made of cobblestones or crushed stone mixed together with cement mortar. This also formed part of the foundation. The third layer, the *nucleus* (ca. 30–35 centimeters thick), was made of sand cement and gravel, probably to form a watertight seal. Into this third layer, the wedge-shaped stone slabs were set, the *summum dorsum* (ca. 20–30 centimeters thick), which comprised the road's surface. The road slabs were generally 30–100 centimeters square and grouted with a lime mortar, often mixed with *puzzolana*, volcanic ash. The entire road was thus 100–140 centimeters thick. The roadway was cambered so the center was ca. 30 centimeters (1 foot) higher than the edges of the road to divert rainwater. The roadway slabs were set between curbstones, which helped to keep the roadway stones in place (Forbes 1964:137–139; Fischer et al. 1996; Oleson 2008:553–558, 560–568).

Roadway systems improved in the Near East beginning with Alexander the Great and the Roman Empire. Several roads from Roman Palestine include the Jaffa-Jerusalem Road and urban roads such as those at Beth Shean and Sepphoris (Figure 15.5).

Gravel roads were not shoddy constructions either. These also began with a wide foundation trench with drainage ditches on each side. The base layer, statumen, consisted of large stones set into the hard-packed earth. The second layer, rudus, included crushed stones and pebbles. The third layer, nucleus, was made of cement or compacted sand, clay, gravel or chalk. The fourth layer, stummum dorsum, was

FIGURE 15.5   Roman roads. Left: Beth Shean. Middle and Right: Sepphoris. Note the camber of each road and the grooves in the soft stone in the road at Sepphoris

Photographs by Jill L. Baker.

comprised of stone slabs. These roads were ca. 20–30 meters wide including the drainage ditches, and the roadway proper was ca. 4–7 meters wide, with a camber that elevated the roadway some 2 meters above ground level at the top of the camber (Forbes 1964:139).

Urban road construction was a bit more complicated because the roads incorporated elaborate drainage systems. The removal of excess water from all zones of the city remained an extremely important aspect of Roman daily life, not only for the integrity of the architecture but also for the health and well-being of the inhabitants. Roadways were constructed much the same way as highways were; however, at regular intervals along the curb and in the street, drains were incorporated to divert water from the living areas of the city. These drains led to channels just below the street surface, which led to tunnels farther below.

16

TIMEKEEPING

Marking the passage of time is an innate human characteristic. It is nearly impossible to ignore the recurring cycles of the sun and moon to mark the passing of days and seasons. In some ways, time reckoning is an abstract, artificial concept that humankind has imposed on the natural world even though nature's clock is predictably precise. Nevertheless, humans devised calendars to mark the days and months, and clocks to count the minutes and hours. The more urbanized humankind became, the more precise their timekeeping.

The development of time reckoning and calendars is complex and multifaceted. Initially, timekeeping was motivated by agricultural cycles: marking the passage of seasons, identifying when to plant and when to harvest. As humankind became sedentary and urbanized, calendars also kept track of religious holy days, feast/festival days, and civil celebrations. Calendars were based on the movement of the moon, sun, and other celestial bodies. The Sumerians, Assyrians, Babylonians, Persians, Egyptians, Canaanites, Greeks, and Romans each kept their own calendars. The Hellenic Greek calendar was transported into the Near East with the conquest of Alexander and replaced by the Roman calendar later on. In the time of Julius Cesar, the Julian calendar corrected errors and became the main calendar used throughout the empire, beginning 1 January 45 BC. Eventually, the Gregorian calendar, instituted in 1582 by Pope Gregory XIII, replaced the Julian calendar.

Due to the complexity, a detailed discussion of this topic is beyond the scope of this work. Several excellent works that discuss timekeeping in detail include *Calendars and Years: Astronomy and Time in the Ancient Near East* (Steele 2007); *Lovaniensia Analecta Civil Calendar and Lunar Calendar in Ancient Egypt* (Depuydt 1997); *Calendars in Antiquity: Empires, States & Societies* (Stern 2012); *King Cult and Calendar in Ancient Israel* (Talmon 1986); *Greek and Roman Calendars: Constructions of Time in the Classical World* (Hannah 2005). This chapter will offer a general summary of select aspects of time reckoning including astronomy, astrology, the development of clocks and calendars, and the motivations for more precise timekeeping. This chapter should be considered a springboard for further study, and the resources cited within will prove valuable for continued interest in this subject.

Early timekeeping

Observing and understanding the progression of seasons was crucial to the survival of early peoples, especially to hunter-gatherers. Knowledge of changing seasons helped them know when to migrate to escape cold or inclement weather, when to harvest wild food sources and where to find them, and when to expect the migration of animals. They were also keenly aware of the biological clock of the human body, the rhythm of eating and sleeping, and the cycle of life encompassed in birth, aging, and death. As humankind became more sedentary and engaged in agriculture and animal husbandry, the need for time reckoning gained greater importance. Agriculturalists needed to know when to plant and harvest, when to breed farm animals, and when offspring would be born. Hunters needed to be familiar with the migration patterns of prey. As society became more complex, the timely performance of rituals became important, especially rituals that venerated the deities who provided food and rain. As humankind became more urbanized, there arose a need for more precise time reckoning in terms of hours, minutes, and seconds. The more precisely humankind measured time, the more distant they became from the natural clock, thus losing a connection with the natural world around them. Instead of being part of nature's rhythm, sedentary peoples became somewhat removed, creating a need to more consciously and purposefully keep track of time and record the passage of it to know what to do and when. Thus, the practice of recording the movement of celestial bodies and corresponding seasonal conditions for the purpose of growing and raising foodstuffs became crucial to urbanized society.

Archaeological evidence suggests that Upper Paleolithic and Neolithic peoples were recording the passage of time (Figure 16.1). The tusk of a wild boar, found in Smederevska Palanka, Serbia, dating to ca. 8000–6000 BCE, depicts incised markings denoting a lunar cycle of twenty-eight days and four phases of the moon. An independent researcher and research associate at Harvard University's Peabody Museum of Archaeology and Ethnology, Alexander Marshack (1918–2004), suggested that incisions on bones and stones not only marked the passage of time but were also notation systems for lunar calendars. The earliest calendars appear to have been lunar, possibly because the phases of the moon are easily observed as the moon's appearance changes, whereas the sun maintains the same appearance. Marshack realized that notches carved into bones marked the passage of time and the progression of seasons. One such calendar, the Ishango Bone, in the Museum of Natural Science in Brussels, Belgium, dates to the Upper Paleolithic period, ca. 17,000 BCE. Another early calendar, also dating to the Upper Paleolithic, is a stone depicting the phases of the moon. This stone was part of the Aurignacian Culture in Europe and dates to ca. 32,000 BCE (James and Thorpe 1995:484–486). Finally, a carved limestone slab found at Laussel shelter, Dordogne, France, dating to ca. 27,000–20,000 BCE,

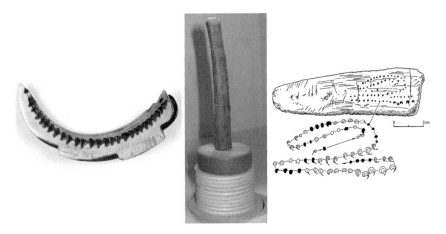

FIGURE 16.1 Early calendars. Left: Tusk from Smederevska Palanka, Serbia, ca. 8000–6000 BCE. Middle: Ishango Bone in the Museum of Natural Science, Brussels, Belgium (Ishango Bone, Royal Belgian Institute of Natural Sciences). Right: Limestone slab from the Aurignacian Culture in Europe, ca. 32,000 BCE depicts phases of the moon

Adapted from the *Daily Mail* (www.dailymail.co.uk/sciencetech/article-2511828/Could-worlds-oldest-pocket-calendar-Engraved-tusk-toldfarmers-harvest-crops-8-000-years-ago.html) (left); adapted from Wikipedia, ("Os d'Ishango IRSNB" by Ben2 – Own work. Licensed under CC BY-SA 3.0 via Commons – https://commons.wikimedia.org/wiki/File:Os_d%27 Ishango_IRSNB.JPG#/media/File:Os_d%27Ishango_IRSNB.JPG) (middle); adapted from Solar System Exploration Research (http://sservi.nasa.gov/articles/oldest-lunar-calendars/) (right).

depicts a fertility goddess/moon goddess holding a crescent-shaped horn with thirteen incised lines equaling lunar months in a year. Although Marshack's theories were at first controversial, it is now clear that very early humans measured time by observing the moon's phases.

Timekeeping was and continues to be based on the progression of the moon, sun, and other celestial bodies. Astronomers, those who regularly observed and recorded these movements, were the timekeepers of the ancient world. The Sumerians and Babylonians in Mesopotamia were among the first organized astronomers. As early as 3000–2000 BCE, they recorded constellations, stars, planets, comets, lunar eclipses, and other astronomical events. They named the constellations they identified, including Leo, Taurus, Scorpius, Auriga, Gemini, Capricorn, and Sagittarius. The Babylonians created the zodiac to mark the twelve constellations traversed by the sun, moon, and planets. The MUL.APIN is a catalog of stars and constellations and a sort of "program" for predicting the heliacal rising and setting of planets, the length of daylight as measured by a water clock, gnomon, shadows, and intercalations (the combination of lunar and solar calendars). It primarily discussed the rising and setting of constellations in relation to the calendar, and determined when to add an extra month (Britton 2002:23, 25). The earliest copy of the MUL.APIN dates to ca. 686 BCE; however, it is speculated that the original was probably completed ca. 1000 BCE (Rochberg 1999; Reiner 1999; Brack-Bernsen 1999).

The orientation and movement of the constellations, stars, sun, and planets display observable patterns which were used as an accurate method to measure time and seasons, which in turn provided a schedule for planting, harvesting, and ritual activities. Ancient astronomers recognized that astronomical phenomena are rhythmic and cyclical, and that mathematics could be applied to these to make predictions, such as the variation of the length of daylight over the course of a solar year. For example, the Enûma Anu Enlil, Tablet 63, also known as the Venus Tablet of King Ammisaduqa, discusses the appearance and disappearance of the planet Venus over a period of 21 years, ca. 1581 BCE. The Babylonians calculated the length of Venus' cycle to be 587 days. They also devised a system to mark the positions of objects in the sky. This ancient system was adopted by the Greeks, as were the constellations and their names. The system was a sexagesimal (base 60) number system to record degrees. The recently translated Plimpton 322 tablet underscores the Babylonians' use of this system (Gibbens 2017; Mansfield and Wildberger 2017). The Babylonians also calculated the "moment of a day by its distance in time to or from sunrise or sunset" (Brack-Bernsen 2002:7). The time-distance was measured in *uš*, which is the same as our time-degree measurements. The daily revolution of the earth around the sun by 360° takes twenty-four hours (Brack-Bernsen 2002:7). Further, the Chaldean astronomers adopted and supported a heliocentric model of the solar system, and in 190 BCE, Seleucus of Seleucia created a heliocentric planetary model. The Babylonians' records of astronomical events provide accurate data for establishing dates and chronology for modern archaeologists and historians.

Astronomy and calendars

Mesopotamia

Astronomical observance provided the basis for calendars that were derived from the movement of the moon and sun. The lunar calendar was the primary one. A new month began with the first sighting of the waxing crescent moon, just after sunset on the western horizon. When the chief astronomer saw this, he reported it to the king who then declared the start of the new month. The Babylonian calendar consisted of twenty-nine or thirty days, for a total of 354 days in a year. However, if the new moon was visible early, at the beginning of the thirtieth day of the month, that day was rejected, and that month had just twenty-nine days. That month was then called GUR meaning "rejected" or "hollow." If the new moon was not visible until after sunset on the third day, the month was considered GIN (confirmed), or a "full" month (Brack-Bernsen 2002:6). Since there are 365 days in a year, the Babylonian calendar began eleven days too early. As the year progressed, the lunar-based calendar no longer matched the solar calendar, which accounted for the seasons.

FIGURE 16.2 Sippar, Mesopotamia. The library in the Šamaš temple

Adapted from Al-Jadir (1998:211).

Based on records kept in the library, the astronomer could compare seasons and celestial positions for the same day in previous years and determine when to add an extra month to bring the calendar back in line with the solar calendar and thus the seasons.

One such library was discovered at Sippar in Southern Mesopotamia (Figure 16.2). Here thousands of clay tablets written in cuneiform were discovered. Sippar was occupied in the Early Dynastic period, ca. third millennium BCE, Old Babylonian period, ca. second millennium BCE, and the Neo-Babylonian period, first millennium BCE, and into the Parthian Empires.

The MUL.APIN advised how to adjust the months (Evans 1998). This correction is known as intercalation, which became standard between 383–367 BCE. However, prior to this, a thirteenth month was added every three years. Although month names varied from city to city, in general the standard Mesopotamian calendar names were the following:

Nissannu—March/April
Ajaru or Ayyaru—April/May
Simanu—May/June
Tamuau or Du-uzu—June/July
Abu—July/August
Ululu—August/September

Tashritu—September/October
Arahsamnu—October/November
Kissilimu—November/December
Tebetu—December/January
Shabatu—January/February
Addau—February/March

The extra months were called Atra sha Ululu and Atru sha Addaru, and were added to the calendar as needed. The new year began with the vernal equinox in Nisannu, March/April, or Ajaru, April/May (Rochberg 2004).

The lunar calendar was useful to the administrative branch of government for scheduling festivals and tax collection. Keeping track of the seasons had agricultural purpose. The solar year in the Mesopotamian calendar was divided into two seasons, summer and winter, a division that endured as late as 1800 BCE. However, those living in northern regions may have recognized autumn and spring. Summer was usually during the second half of the year from May to December. The winter season was from December to May.

Egypt

The Egyptian calendar began as early as the fifth millennium BCE. It is thought that the monolithic stone circle found at Nabta Playa, Aswan, was an early calendar. The southern line of stones is thought to represent Orion's belt. Modern research suggests that this formation dates to ca. 4500–3600 BCE. The Egyptian calendar consisted of 365 days, with twelve lunar months divided into three seasons of four months. This system contained errors, which were compensated for by adding five extra days, epagomenal days, at the end of the year.

At first, in the civil calendar, the New Year began with the annual flooding of the Nile River. However, the first flood day could vary by as many as eighty days, thus rendering this system inaccurate. To compensate, the Egyptians came to depend on Sirius, the Dog Star, the brightest star in the sky. Sirius disappeared for seventy days, and when it reappeared it heralded the flooding of the Nile, which became a more accurate marker for the start of the new year. This was useful for agriculturalists to know when to plant and harvest. The three seasons were known as Akhet, flood; Peret, for planting and growth; and Shomu, harvest and low water. During the Early Dynastic period, a civil calendar was established which fixed into a routine, festivals, rituals, and, most importantly, when taxes were due and when offerings had to be made. Eventually, calendars integrated solar, lunar, and astronomical cycles. They were used for religious, political, administrative, commercial, and social purposes. In 153 BCE, the Romans shifted the beginning of the year from 1 March to 1 January, and in so doing renamed the months; September, October, November, and December, based on their month number in Latin (Depuydt 1997).

From 49 to 44 BCE, during the reign of Julius Caesar, a need arose to harmonize the calendars of the conquered peoples, including the Near East, now part of the empire.

While in Egypt with Queen Cleopatra, Julius Caesar spoke with Sosigenes who suggested dropping the lunar calendar and adopting the Egyptian solar calendar and adding a day in February every fourth year to account for the slippage of days in the solar year. Thus, on 1 January 45 BCE, Julius Caesar introduced this new calendar to take effect immediately.

In 1582, a calendar was proposed by Aloysius Lilius to correct the errors in the Julian calendar. It was decreed by Pope Gregory XIII as the official calendar, thus it was termed the Gregorian calendar, and took effect on 24 February 1582. It was numbered by the perceived birth year of Jesus Christ, and it brought into alignment Christian festivals with pagan festivals, specifically Easter. This formed the basis for the modern Western calendar. It is a solar calendar, it corrects the year length, and is based on the Babylonian seven-day week. As well, day names were adopted:

English	Babylonian	Planet
Sunday	Shamash	Sun
Monday	Sin	Moon
Tuesday	Nergal	Mars
Wednesday	Nabu	Mercury
Thursday	Marduk	Jupiter
Friday	Ishtar	Venus
Saturday	Ninurta	Saturn

James and Thorpe 1995:469

Astronomy and astrology

The astronomical phenomena that the ancients observed not only carried meaning in terms of timekeeping, but communicated omens as well. Included within the Enûma Anu Enlil were seven books that discuss celestial and meteorological phenomena. These events had some predictive bearing on the king and his country, though not for individuals. The consequences could be good or poor crops (which would have an effect on taxes and tribute), success or failure in battle, and life or death of the king (Reiner 1999:22). The signs delivering these omens included thunderstorms, eclipses, earthquakes, or the helical rising of Mars (Reiner 1999:22–23). In the late second millennium BCE, much of Mesopotamian culture engaged in the reading and interpretation of celestial events and their impact on people's lives. This practice also spread to Elam and Hatti. Around 1800 BCE, the Mari Letters and Old Babylonian omen texts reveal this practice. It continued through the Middle Babylonian and Middle Assyrian periods (ca. 1200 BCE) and into the seventh century BCE in the Sargonid period when there were court astrologers. This led to nativity omens and horoscopes in the Achaemenid, Seleucid, and Arsacid periods, ca. 500–50 BCE (Rochberg 1999:39).

Eventually this led to the development of horoscopy in Babylonia around ca. 500 BCE. This form of horoscopy would spread and develop throughout the ancient Near East and Mediterranean world. To those who developed and practiced it, the arrangement of the celestial bodies at the time of one's birth was deemed important for the future of the person. Prior to this in human history, there was little regard for the individual; however, at this time there was increased focus on personal piety and happiness as well as the person's place within the divine scheme and the gods' direct influence on a person's well-being (Rochberg 1999:39). These new ideas were reflected in Babylonian wisdom literature. Focus on the individual and a personal relationship with a deity had already developed in Canaan/ancient Israel with the concept of monotheism. The wisdom literature of the Hebrew Bible reveals this well-established divine–individual relationship, as do evolving burial practices. Perhaps with the destruction of Israel in 586 BCE and the deportation of a significant portion of its population to Mesopotamia, these ideas were adopted and adapted there.

Early horoscope readings gave the positions of the planets at the time of one's birth and described the characteristics or traits that person may be likely to develop. It also described the planetary alignment necessary at the time of conception should parents wish their child to become king (Hunger and Pingree 1999:27). Planetary bodies used in early horoscopy included the moon, sun, Jupiter, Venus, Mercury, Saturn, and Mars. Elliptical constellations or stars that were "in the path of the moon" were observed in the late first millennium BCE, and zodiac names were derived from the twelve constellations that travel around the sun in one year over the course of twelve thirty-day months. They were described in degrees of longitude according to fixed stars (Rochberg 1998:29). The early zodiacal signs from the fifth century BCE included Aries, Taurus, Gemini, Cancer, Leo, Virgo, Libra, Scorpius, Sagittarius, Capricorn, Aquarius, and Pisces (Rochberg 1998:29).

The zodiac took the form of a circle with twelve divisions of thirty degrees each to represent the celestial longitude centered on the ecliptic, the sun's path across the celestial sphere during the course of the year. At the center is Helios, who drives a chariot, thus moving the sun. The twelve divisions are called signs, and act as celestial coordinates. Reference to zodiac names can be found in the Hebrew Bible in Ezekiel and Numbers and in the New Testament in Revelation. Several zodiac mosaics have been found in ancient Israel at Beth Alpha dating to the sixth century BCE; at Sepphoris dating to the fifth century BCE; and at Hammath Tiberias, also dating to the sixth century BCE. Curiously, these adorned the floors of synagogues.

Earth as a sphere

Although early Mesopotamians depicted the earth as a flat disc floating in the ocean, it did not take long for astronomers to realize the earth was a sphere, like other heavenly bodies. Some surmise this realization came by way of travelers who observed that different stars and constellations were visible at different regions. This would have been especially noticeable when traveling between the Mediterranean Sea, the Nile Delta, and Mesopotamia, due to the curvature of the Earth.

In the sixth century BCE, Pythagoras (ca. 570–495 BCE) may have been the first to introduce the idea of a spherical earth. Plato (427–347 BCE) studied Pythagorean mathematics and taught that the earth was round (*Timaeus*, Henderson and Bury 1929; Hetherington 1993:498–501; Kahn 2001). Aristotle (ca. 384–322 BCE), a student of Plato's, observed that stars seen in Egypt were not the same as those seen in Cyprus or other northern regions. He concluded this could happen only if the earth was curved (Hetherington 1993:20–25).

Aristarchus of Samos (ca. 310–230 BCE) introduced a heliocentric model of the universe, and suggested the sun was at the center and the Earth traveled around it (*Greek Mathematics II*; Henderson and Thomas 1993:2–11ff; Hetherington 1993: 17–19; Lankford 2011:32–35). Eratosthenes (ca. 276–194 BCE) was a Hellenistic astronomer who lived in Lybia. He estimated the Earth's circumference in 240 BCE. He realized that when the sun was directly overhead in Syene during the summer solstice, in Alexandria the sun cast a shadow. He used these shadows and trigonometry to calculate the estimated circumference of the earth. His answer was 20,000 stades, with 1 stade = 185 meters according to the Mathematical Association of America (www.maa.org/press/periodicals/convergence/eratosthenes-and-the-mystery-of-the-stades-how-long-is-a-stade) (Hetherington 1993:17–19).

Seleucus of Seleucia (ca. 190–150 BCE) lived in Seleucia on the west bank of the Tigris River in Mesopotamia. He wrote that Earth is a sphere, orbits around the sun, and was influenced by Aristarchus of Samos who also supported the heliocentric model (Hetherington 1993:17–19).

Strabo (64 BCE–24 CE) suggested that seafarers were likely the first to suggest the earth was spherical. He also suggested it was known as early as Homer, based on a citation in the *Odyssey* (ca. eighth or seventh century BCE).

Finally, Claudius Ptolemy (90–168 CE) of Alexandria, Egypt, wrote in support of a spherical earth in *Almagest*, a standard for astronomy, and in *Geographia* based on maritime observations (Hetherington 1993; Lankford 2011).

Time reckoning

One of the easiest ways to mark the progression of the sun throughout the day and the seasons is with a tall pole, a flat surface, and some pebbles (Figure 16.3). With the pole firmly planted vertically into the flat ground, as the sun casts a shadow against the pole and onto the ground, use the pebbles to mark the position of the tip of the pole's shadow. Begin this in the early morning at sunrise and continue until sunset in the evening. Throughout the day, more pebbles should be added to mark the interim increments. This procedure should be repeated every day until the curve formed by the marks gradually moves farther away from the stick. Eventually, the two curves will match. One curve will represent summer, and the other curve, winter (James and Thorpe 1995:487).

Some scholars suggest the earliest sundials were the Egyptian obelisks as early as 3500 BCE and shadow clocks from ca. 1500 BCE. The Hebrew Bible also mentions sundials: the "dial of Ahaz" mentioned in Isaiah 38:8 and 2 Kings, from ca. 700 BCE. The earliest sundial to have been discovered was found in Egypt in the Valley of the Kings dating to the Nineteenth Dynasty ca. 1400 BCE. It was found on the floor of

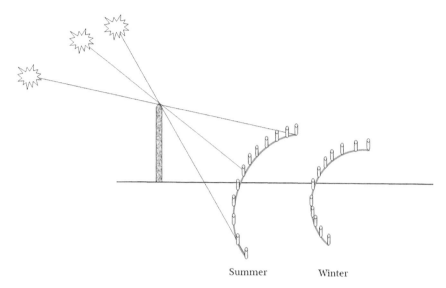

FIGURE 16.3   Calculating year length (not to scale)

Graphic by Jill L. Baker, inspired by James and Thorpe 1995:487.

a workman's house (Bryner 2013a). This is considered the oldest sundial found thus far.

Later, especially in the Roman Empire, portable sundials were utilized, which suggests the need for precise time management in a more advanced society. Numerous examples have been discovered and discussed by J. A. Talbert in his book *Roman Portable Sundials: The Empire in Your Hand* (Talbert 2017).

Parapegmata

Since using a pole and measuring its shadow required a large space, smaller time-keepers were designed for placement in a garden or a courtyard. For these, the stars visible at sunrise and sunset were important for reckoning the time. Homer and Hesiod (ca. 750–700 BCE) included such information in their works as seasonal indicators for significant agricultural or seafaring times of the year or for the migration of birds. Hesiod observed a set of five stars and recorded their data, information that was used for sowing/reaping and possibly also for the orientation of buildings for solar purposes. In the fifth century BCE, stellar events were predicted with the aid of a *parapegma*, which was invented by Meton and Euctemon of Athens (Oleson 2008:742–744).

A parapegma was a stone slab on which the days, months, moon phases, and zodiac signs were depicted. Movable pegs indicated the month, day, and celestial sign, probably oriented to the solar tropics and horizon. Roman parapegmata also depicted seven gods/planets for the seven days of the week. The zodiac represented the sun divided into twelve equal parts, each with its celestial sign, each sign divided into two parts to equal twenty-four holes in the circle. One hole is in the center of the sun. With three pegs, it was possible to show the day of the week, the month, and the day of the month.

The sundial became one of the most important timekeeping devices in the ancient world. It consisted of a gnomon and a dial. These were in use as early as 500 BCE throughout the Near East and Mediterranean. Anaximander of Miletus (610–546 BCE) is credited with introducing this Babylonian instrument to the Greeks. Herodotus (*Histories* 2.109) credits the introduction of the gnomon and the twelve-part division of the day to the Babylonians. Diogenes Laertius, *Lives of Eminent Philosophers* (2.1), credits Anaximander as being the first to use the gnomon (Humphrey et al. 2006:515–516).

The sundial confirmed fixed times of day for activities, such as feasts and daily meals. It also became easier to predict the solstices and equinoxes. Prior to this, mealtime was determined by the length of one's shadow, which varied according to the time of year. Sundials regularized the time of day throughout the year.

Eventually the shadow of the gnomon was combined with the zodiac and a system of lines for hours and seasons. Vitruvius describes Eudoxus' type of sundial as an Arachne web (*On Architecture* 9.8.1, Morgan 1960).

In addition to the flat surface gnomon and sundial, there was also the hemispheric sundial. Because Greece is located at 38° N latitude, shadows do not vary from day to day throughout the year, which is little help in distinguishing one day from another on a flat sundial. Thus, the hemispheric sundial was created. The construction and calibration of the hemispheric sundial proved to be easy, and it was more accurate, especially given the latitude in Greece. The flat sundial was more difficult to calibrate due to the curvature of the earth and the domed sky. Later, the Roman emperor Trajan in the second century CE remarked, "If you put your nose facing the sun and open your mouth wide, you'll show all the passersby the time of day" (Oleson 2008:748 quoting from *Anthologia Palatina* 111.418). Hemispheric sundials were bowl-shaped with equal divisions within the bowl marking the daylight hours. Eventually, portable sundials were also made. Evidence for miniature, personal sundials has been discovered throughout the Roman world from Spain to Greece to Africa and Germany (Talbert 2017).

Clocks

As mentioned earlier, the Mesopotamians could determine the minutes of the day by measuring the degree at which the sun had climbed or was descending. The Sumerians created the sexagesimal system we continue to use today. The Egyptians divided the day into two twelve-hour periods, and sundials kept track of the days, months, and seasons, but how did they measure time during the night hours when there is no sun? And why was it important to do so?

As society and cultures became more complex and orderly, the need arose to keep track of the smaller increments of time: hours and minutes. This was important to priests conducting nighttime rituals; to guards whose shifts changed in the middle of the night; and to astronomical record keepers. To measure minutes and hours, the Mesopotamians and Egyptians developed the water clock, or clepsydra as the Greeks called it, around 2000 BCE.

The Egyptian court official Amenemhet (ca. 1500 BCE) is credited with inventing the water clock, according to an inscription in his tomb. During the reign of Amenhotep III, ca. 1391/1388–1353/1351 BCE, water clocks were used in the Temple of Amen-Re at Karnack. The clepsydra consisted of a V-shaped bowl with marked increments on the interior and/or exterior and a small hole at the bottom of the vessel. The vessel was filled with water and the hole unplugged. The interior was divided into twelve equal parts, and as the water poured out, the "hour" was revealed. The hour marks in the pot varied according to the season. In Babylon, ca. 2000–1600 BCE, simple outflow clocks were also used. These were cylindrical in shape and aided astronomical calculations. In the Enûma Anu Enlil (ca. 1600–1200 BCE) and the MUL.APIN (ca. seventh century BCE) reference to water clocks as payment to the night and day guards was made.

Eventually there were four types of water clocks (Oleson 2008:752–754):

1) Simple outflow, which let a measured amount of water flow out.
2) Large outflow, with lines marked on the inside to indicate hours.
3) Simple inflow type, with hours marked on its interior.
4) Inflow type with a reservoir and overflow pipe that maintained constant pressure.

The fourth type of water clock, the inflow type, was instrumental in the advancement of measuring time because it resolved the problem of decreasing water pressure as the water emptied from one of the reservoirs to the other.

Water clocks came to be used in court to limit the length of time a lawyer was allowed to argue a case. However, due to the uneven flow of water, one side usually had less time as the water ran out. This is where we get the phrase "time is running out." Demosthenes in *Against Macartatus* (1.8, 8–9) discusses the lack of time for arguments (Humphrey et al. 2006:519).

Not all people were happy to have their day divided and organized by sundials and water clocks, as expressed by Plautus in his work *The Woman from Boeotia*:

> May the gods destroy that man who first discovered hours and who first set up a sundial here; who cut up my day piecemeal, wretched me. For when I was a boy, my only sundial was my stomach, by far the best and truest of all clocks. When it advised you, you ate, unless there was no food; now, even when there is food, it isn't eaten unless the sun allows it. Indeed, now, the town is so filled with sundials that the majority of its people crawl about shriveled up with hunger.

> Fragments, *Boeotia, 1, De Melo 2013:432–433;*
> *Humphrey et al. 2006:517*

Later, Ctesibius of Alexandria (ca. 270 BCE) invented an elaborate water clock that addressed the problem of diminishing water pressure by controlling the flow and pressure of water with a system of stopcocks and automata. Later these clocks came to include ringing bells, moving puppets, and singing birds (Humphrey et al. 2006:519–520).

Antikythera Mechanism

Although not a product of the Near East, the Antikythera Mechanism reflects accumulated and combined knowledge, drawing from the Near East and Hellenistic Greece, resulting in a sophisticated machine. Sponge divers discovered it in 1900 among the debris from a shipwreck on the Mediterranean Sea floor just off the coast of the island of Antikythera.

The mechanism was enclosed in a wooden box measuring 340 millimeters (13 inches) by 180 millimeters (7.1 inches) by 90 millimeters (3.5 inches), and was a complex clockwork-like machine comprised of thirty to thirty-seven interlocking gears and an inscription, which provided directions for using the machine. On the front was a ring inscribed with the 365 days of the year and twelve months according to the Egyptian solar calendar, twelve signs of the zodiac, with hands indicating the sun and moon, and moon phases. A small crank on the side of the wooden box operated the rings. On the back were two dials. The upper was inscribed with the Metonic cycle, the lunar and solar cycles over a period of nineteen years (235 lunar months). The lower dial indicated solar and lunar eclipses. These could predict when the next eclipse would occur in the Saros cycle. Meton of Athens (fifth century BCE) introduced the Metonic cycle based on his observation that nineteen years is almost equal to 235 lunar months; however, the Babylonians had incorporated this cycle into their calendars since 500 BCE (Freeth et al. 2006, 2008). This device also helped determine the cities that would host the Olympic games every four years (Freeth et al. 2008) and tracked the path of planets, such as Venus. The mechanics and data manipulation of the mechanism can inform and advance the techniques of modern watch making (see The Antikythera Mechanism Research Project, www.antikythera-mechanism.gr).

The device has been called the first known analogue computer and has been the subject of much study and debate. One of the earliest scholars to study it was De Solla Price (1974), who concluded it was made around 87 BCE based on the gears and inscription. Recent research has dated the device to the second century BCE (Freeth et al. 2006) based on epigraphy and astronomical cycles (The Antikythera Mechanism Research Project). Others date it to within one generation of the time of the shipwreck (Iversen 2017). It is surmised the ship was traveling from Rhodes or Asia Minor to Rome or Italy (The Antikythera Mechanism Research Project), based on cargo from the shipwreck, including Rhodian amphora.

17

FOOD AS TECHNOLOGY

In the twenty-first century, food and food technology is much overlooked and taken for granted, especially by those who have reliable access to foodstuffs. Nevertheless, the acquisition of food and the preparation, storage, and consumption of it played a crucial role in the rise of civilization. Food technology involves growing plant-based foodstuffs and animal husbandry, which includes growing, tending, and harvesting food sources. It is "the practical application of the principles of science and technology to the preparation, processing, storage, packaging, and transportation of food" (Oleson 1998:369). This chapter will discuss the shift humanity made from hunter-gatherer to sedentary farmer, the first flora and fauna to be domesticated, and technological achievements pertaining to food production in the ancient Near East, including processing, preservation, storage, preparation, and consumption.

Like water and shelter, food is a necessity. Recent models and studies have suggested that the adoption of sedentary farming was a blessing and a curse to humankind. While farming resulted in progress in that there was increased population growth, cultural development, a more complex society, technological invention and innovation, and a stable food supply, there were negative consequences too. It may sound strange, but the domestication of flora and fauna actually led to physical changes in the human body, poorer diets, lower nutrition, and greater vulnerability to famine and malnutrition (Garnsey 1999:2; Macintosh 2014). For example, a recent study by A. Macintosh, Cambridge University, suggests that changes in the bones of sedentary farmers can be detected. Studying the femora and tibiae of males and females from central Europe, Germany, Hungary, Austria, the Czech Republic, and Serbia from ca. 5300 BCE to ca. 850 CE, Macintosh found that the "male tibiae became less rigid, and in both males and females became less strengthened to loads in one direction more than another, such as front-to-back in walking" (Macintosh 2014). In other words, the gradual shift from hunter-gatherer to farmer affected both sexes but had a greater impact on males than females. The need for heavy, physical work and long-distance travel became less of a necessity, and the focus changed from foraging, hunting, and chasing food to farming and food production. It also resulted in specialized labor such as metalworking, ceramic production, and textile production. This relatively sedentary lifestyle required less physical activity than hunting and gathering; thus, the human body adapted. Since food was not being sought, killed, and transported at great distances from home, human anatomy no longer required bone structure and musculature necessary for long distance travel and transporting heavy loads. Thus, the male samples particularly exhibit a physical shift commensurate with sedentary farming. Although female bones also indicated some changes in terms of long distance travel, their bones also revealed performance of a wide variety of tasks, which were probably already being performed in hunting-gathering communities, hence fewer and less drastic physical changes were observed for females.

Traditional interpretations have held the opinion that reliable food supplies of good quality improved the overall health, nutrition, and longevity of a community. However, studies have shown that agriculture resulted in a limited variety of food types, limited nutrition, poor crop yields due to drought, pests, and disease, and malnutrition due to food shortages, both permanent and episodic (Garnsey 1999:2). Additionally, the accumulation of food created a more complex society by initially establishing a divide between those who were wealthy and those who were not, and later widened that gap with the advancement of technology and control over food resources. Foodstuffs came to be used as weapons as well as political and economic tools, and were given as political gifts. Diet served as an economic indicator; foodstuffs could be withheld from trade or given as tribute; and dining became a social and political tool (Garnsey 1999; Standage 2009).

Banqueting in Canaan, Mesopotamia, and Egypt, and *symposium* to the Greeks and *convivium* to the Romans, was the sharing of a meal in a social setting, which could be used as a way to solidify relationships or forge new ones, commemorate an event such as a wedding or funeral, or celebrate agreements—political or business. Sharing a meal at a banquet or symposium underscored interpersonal relationships, especially in a funerary context, emphasized social standing, and served as a mechanism whereby political, commercial, religious, or social business could be conducted (Pollock 2003; Lindsay 2001; Nielsen 2001; Jensen 2008). Regarding symposia, political, business, or social banqueting, invited guests usually possessed some social standing within the community and were in some way important to the host. Seating within the banquet hall or triclinium was equally important. There was a specific seat for the guest of honor, and those seated around him or her were seated in order of importance. Seating was usually in a reclined position on cushions around a central table tended by servants throughout the night, or days, as the banquet progressed. The foods served were equally indicative of the social setting and standing, and the type of food and drink served at the banquet was as important as those who were invited to the event. Well-established professional cooks prepared the meals using specific recipes. So, food itself, the types of foods, the recipes served, and the banquet were powerful political and economic tools which also functioned as important methods of communication within society (Garnsey 1999; Dunbabin 2003).

Whether beneficial or detrimental to humankind, the shift from hunter-gatherer may well have been necessary for the survival of humanity. Although the term hunter-gatherer elicits notions of communities constantly seeking out prey or scouring field and forest for food, these activities did not monopolize the daily schedule. While food acquisition was an important part of daily life, it was but one aspect. Studies have shown that considerable time was given to other activities such as making clothing, tools and weapons, creating artwork, and partaking in religious rituals, suggesting a certain amount of leisure time (Brewer et al. 1994:3–5). Analysis of skeletal remains indicates that the Neolithic peoples of Abu Hureyra engaged in craft specialization, making items such as cord and string, baskets, and pottery (Molleson 2014:12–15).

Refocusing on hunter-gatherers, studies have also shown that their diet was diverse, relatively consistent, and balanced, with little or no evidence of malnutrition or famine among skeletal remains of most early peoples (Eades 2009). After all, the world was their food-basket, and nature their provider. The flora and fauna they consumed consisted of a much wider variety than ours today. The foods that early peoples ate were limited by that which was seasonally available and safe for human consumption. Evidence suggests that grasses and animals such as giraffe, rhinoceros, and rodents were eaten by ancient peoples. Thus far, evidence for cooking food appears around 730,000–500,000 years ago with Peking Man (see UNESCO, www.unesco.org/ext/field/beijing/whc/pkm-site.htm). Practically any person could venture out of the village, into the wilderness, and find sustenance. Thus, hunter-gatherers had regular access to foodstuffs resulting in relatively healthy bodies and balanced nutrition. The diet of very ancient peoples was greatly varied and not limited. However, that changed once hunter-gatherers shifted to sedentary agriculturalists; there was a rise in stress rates, malnutrition, and infection (Cohen 1985). Recently, nutritionists have been suggesting that the diet of hunter-gatherers was a very healthy one that should be adopted by modern humans (Jabr 2013). Considering this one step further, beyond the limited flora and fauna that comprise our modern diet, there are numerous other wild flora and fauna that humans can safely eat. Hikers and campers are aware of edible wild plants such as elderberry, acorn, marigold, sea grape, barberry, hawthorn, and dandelion (Angier 1998).

If the hunter-gatherer diet was so successful, why did humans turn to farming and a sedentary lifestyle? Recent data and theories offer a possible explanation for the shift. The climate during the Lower, Middle, and Upper Palaeolithic periods was conducive to the growth of numerous plant and animal species. Hunter-gatherers were no doubt knowledgeable about a variety of flora and fauna and their overall nutritional and medicinal value. In general, by exploiting a wide variety of species and inadvertent (or intentional) reseeding, flora and fauna resources were not destroyed. Early Natufian sites, situated chronologically between the end of the last Ice Age and the early Younger Dryas, appear to have experienced a favorable climate, producing abundant food supplies such as wild grasses, pistachio, and almonds (Wilcox 2014:2–3). Such abundance in flora, and presumably fauna, may have encouraged the Natufian peoples to settle down, beginning the shift from a nomadic to a semi-nomadic or even sedentary way of life. Evidence from sites such as Ohalo II and Mallaha in Israel exhibit signs of permanent settlement, including storage facilities and vessels for storage of harvested foodstuffs. With this shift came liberation from daily gathering but the introduction of other chores such as food preparation, processing, and altered eating habits (Wilcox 2014:3).

The beginning Younger Dryas period, around ca. 11,000 to 10,300 BCE, brought climate change. Recent data have shown that a significant change in climate took place at about the same time humankind shifted from the hunter-gatherer lifestyle to that of sedentary farmer. Humankind had long been observing and developing knowledge of plant and animal cycles; however, increased stress on food resources likely compelled humans to control their own food sources through agriculture and animal husbandry. The shift from hunter-gatherer to sedentary farmer took place concurrently with climate change in regions where wild food sources that had once been so abundant were disappearing. It is now thought that to survive, humankind adapted to the changing climate by domesticating certain varieties of flora and fauna (Issar and Zohar 2007; Wilcox 2014:4).

At the close of the last ice age (ca. 9500–7500 BCE), the post-glacial climate changed. The ice sheets melted, sea levels rose, and previously exposed coastal plains were gradually inundated with water. The Mediterranean rose sharply and abruptly ca. 5600 BCE, spilling violently over the Bosporus, changing the smaller freshwater lake into a salt sea known today as the Black Sea (Ryan et al. 1997; Gilbert 2002:4). Habitation zones were forced further inland around the Mediterranean basin and north into areas in Europe that once were covered with ice and snow. As the climate and landscape changed, so too did the flora and fauna. Shifting habitats meant that once abundant food sources became scarce and even extinct while new species entered the scene. It was during this transition when humankind realized food sources were becoming scarce, so they adapted to this aspect of climate change by domesticating plants and animals (Brothwell and Brothwell 1998; Gilbert 2002; Ryan and Pitman 2000; Curtis 2001). The occurrence of these drastic changes would help to explain the emergence of farming over a wide area by numerous communities at about the same time.

During the Pleistocene, numerous wild species existed and were exploited: rhinoceros, camel (the camel we're familiar with as well as an extinct camel), large bovine, sheep, goat, ibex, wild cattle (aurochs), bison (wisent), horses, zebras, gazelle, oryx (now extinct), deer, jackal, fox, antelope, warthog, ostrich, and turtle; marine mammals such as seals, a sea cow or dugong, whales, dolphins; rodents, bats, birds, crocodile (Nile), bees, and locusts, to name a few (Gilbert 2002; Brewer 2002). As the climate changed, some species of flora and fauna became extinct, new ones appeared, and some migrated to temperate zones commensurate to their needs.

During this transitional period, humans learned to domesticate and cultivate certain wild species, but the question is how? What criteria did they employ in choosing which flora and fauna to domesticate? The domestication of wild species by humankind appears in the archaeological record rather abruptly; however, as previously mentioned, it is likely that knowledge of manipulating wild species developed over an extended period based on observation, experience, and trial and error. Using knowledge gleaned over the millennia, humans began selectively breeding the flora and fauna that comprised their diet. Some of the first plants to be domesticated were wheat, einkorn, emmer, hard wheat, and bread wheat; two types of barley, two- and six-row; three pulse crops, lentils, peas, chick-pea; as well as fava bean, bitter vetch, grass pea, and flax (useful for their fiber). Some of the first animals to be domesticated were sheep, goat, cattle, and pig. Evidence for the cultivation of these first appears in Mesopotamia and spread steadily to Egypt, Canaan, and Turkey, certainly by 9000 BCE, and by ca. 5000 BCE cultivation of similar crops appears in Greece and the Danube Valley. Presumably the criteria for domestication of flora included those plants which were already being eaten, were easy to domesticate, grown without too much effort, pleasing to the palate, a healthy part of their diet, and which stimulated trade. These are often referred to as "Neolithic founder crops" (Curtis 2001:66). Similarly, animals were likely chosen based on those which could be eaten and produced by-products such as milk, cheese, and wool; were healthy for the human diet; were easily domesticated, and were amenable to living among humans and accepting human instruction; could be used for transportation, and would stimulate trade (Curtis 2001:69).

Advancement in the food industry also brought about technological advancement and specialization of farming, tools, storage, and the preservation of foods. Some of these tools include plows pulled by oxen for tilling the soil, sickle blades for cutting, threshing floors, grinding stones, and milling works. Ceramic storage vessels were created for containing and transporting grains, olive oil, and wine, to name a few. Silos were built to house large quantities of grains for human consumption and as feed for livestock. Silos have been found at sites such as Mersin-Yumuktepe, as early as the Neolithic period (Curtis 2001:67; Caneva 2014).

Processing and preserving foodstuffs also advanced with the advent of bakeries, olive presses, and wineries, and spices were used for preservation, seasoning, and sweetening of culinary dishes, as well as for medicinal purposes. The basic methods of food preservation were known to the ancients, including the salting and smoking of meat and fish; using vinegar for pickling; and including honey, dried fruit, and resins in wine (Apicius, first century CE; Wilkins and Nadeau 2015; Wilkinson 1878:45; Nathan 2017; Vehling 1977). Foodstuffs were stored in cool places such as underground vaults, buildings with stone walls, and in sealed ceramic containers. Buildings, residential and administrative, had rooms dedicated to food preparation and processing (baking), and for dining. Sites such as Jerf el Ahmar, Tell 'Abr, Tell Qaramel, and Dja'de exhibit rooms used solely for the production and consumption of food (Wilcox 2014).

Kitchens were one of the busiest spaces in any home, noble or common, ancient or modern. Here food was prepared, cooked, and stored by the cook and assistants. The space that served as a kitchen could be in the courtyard around a large hearth, in a room adjacent to the courtyard, behind the house with a wood and straw covering, or in a separate building. In later periods, as the art of dining progressed, kitchens were located in a dedicated room accessed by the courtyard. Bronze Age domestic dwellings situated the hearth in the courtyard. Domestic dwellings at sites including Tell Beit Mirsim, Tell Nagilah, and Taanach had hearths in the courtyards, where meals were prepared and foodstuffs stored in small silos, clay storage jars, or perhaps skins (Beebe 1968).

It is likely that the hearth was the most common method of cooking for the majority of ancient populations. The hearth, or fire pit, could be round or rectangular with one of the short ends open and bordered by stone, brick, or clay to contain the fire. Large hearths could accommodate several cooking vessels, such as large vats, cooking pots, and even large serving bowls to keep food warm before serving. Within large hearths, the fire was confined to one side or the middle so that various temperatures and fire intensity could be achieved (Bottéro 1985). Placing a vessel directly on the fire achieved quick cooking at a high temperature, and placing a vessel next to the fire, or on hot coals, achieved slow cooking at a lower temperature. Warming could be achieved at a distance from the fire, perhaps with the aid of a few warm coals (Figure 17.1). Cooking via indirect heat was achieved by erecting a tripod with a suspended pot over hot coals or a fire, or by using an andiron or stand (Figure 17.2; Smogorzewska 2012). Cooking scenes from Egypt depict the use of tripods and stands with cooking vessels.

Evidence for cooling and refrigeration has thus far been observed as early as 1700 BCE in Mesopotamia where the ruler Zimri-lin of Mari built icehouses, *bit shuripim*, near his capital. Zimri-lin boasted at being the first to build such a thing at Turqa on the banks of the Euphrates (James and Thorpe 1995:322; Curtis 2001:253).

FIGURE 17.1 Recreation of a hearth with the main fire for cooking, and areas to the side for slow cooking or warming previously cooked foods. Does not represent an actual site. Not to scale

Graphic by Jill L. Baker.

FIGURE 17.2   Egyptian cooking scenes

Adapted from Wilkinson 1878 Figures 300 and 302 (Public Domain, PD-1923).

Apparently, ice was brought from mountainous regions and kept in the icehouse, which functioned more as a refrigeration unit than a producer of ice. Based on the texts, the ice was for cooling beverages such as wine, but perhaps it was also for keeping food cold; however, further clarification is needed. It would also seem that cooling by evaporation was understood and practiced. Based on Egyptian paintings, as early as 2500 BCE, servants fanned wine vessels in storage. This tells us they understood the process of evaporation. By wetting the amphorae and fanning them, the evaporation process was hastened, and the liquid was cooled more quickly (Curtis 2001:253–254). Athenaeus, in the second century CE in *The Learned Banqueters* (Oleson 2010), describes the way the Egyptians chilled water:

> During the day they placed the [river] water in the sun, and when the night came they strain the thick sediment and expose the water to the air in the earthen jars set on the highest part of the house, while throughout the entire night two slaves wet down the jars with water. At dawn, they take the jars downstairs. . . . They then place the jars in heaps of straw and thereafter use it without the need of snow or anything else whatever.

> *James and Thorpe 1995:323*

An important component of food technology was the slaughter of animals in preparation for sale and ultimately cooking. Specific tools for slaughter and butchering animals were crafted. Egyptian reliefs, paintings, and models depict hatchets, cleavers, knives, ropes, and hooks. Blades were made from flint or copper. Recent studies have revealed that knives of specific size and shape were used for certain animals. Most butchers processed cattle, sheep, goat, fish, pigs, and birds. Cattle, for example, were expensive and eaten mostly by the upper classes while smaller mammals were eaten by the lower classes. Butchers also preserved the meat they prepared. Texts from Egypt and Mesopotamia describe the inclusion of meat and fish in long-distance trade. Drying was the main method of preserving cattle, pig, fowl, and fish. The Egyptian tomb of Meket-re describes various cuts of meat being hung from the upper floor of a slaughterhouse where the wind and sun could dry out the meat. Once dried, the meat was placed into a storage jar for transportation to market. In the Egyptian tomb of Kha (TT8), ca. 1353 BCE, an amphora containing birds and salt suggests that salting was used as a method of preservation, which would also provide the earliest example of salting (Curtis 2001:252–253).

Cereals and breads

Early evidence for bread and beer production, both small- and large-scale, can be found in Egypt and Mesopotamia. Breads, cakes, gruel, porridge, and flatbreads were the most common staple in the ancient world. Grains such as wheat, barley, maize, and sorghum were ground into flour, which formed the main ingredient for breads. Possibly the most time consuming, labor intensive, and arduous task of the ancient world was grinding grain into flour using a quern and rubbing stone. The quern was a flat stone in an elongated, round, or basin shape upon which an oblong stone was rubbed back and forth to grind the grains. It has thus far been observed that most of the preserved breads in Egypt were made from emmer wheat (Samuel 2009:558). One of the most celebrated technological advancements in the ancient world was the grinding mill, ca. fifth to third centuries BCE, whereby mills were powered by water or by animals, thus releasing humans from this arduous task. Water wheels used for grinding cereals into flour were celebrated as a form of liberation from time-consuming work, as noted by Antipater of Thessalonica (*Greek Anthology* 9.418): "Rest your mill-turning hands, maidens who grind! Sleep on even when the cock's crow announces dawn, for Demeter has reassigned to the water nymphs the chores your hands performed" (Humphrey et al. 2006:31).

The earliest evidence for flour dates to the Upper Palaeolithic, ca. 25,000 BCE, and by 4000 BCE, flour was well established and commonly utilized. The best-preserved artifactual evidence for bread comes from Deir el-Medina, Egypt. The grain had to be pounded, sieved, and finely ground before making dough. Water was added to the flour and the dough kneaded, by hand or in a vat, to the desired consistency. Scenes from tombs such as the tomb of Ramesses III or Re'-em-Kuy,

FIGURE 17.3   Court Bakery, Ramesses III (ca. 1186–1155 BCE) Twentieth Dynasty Egypt, Valley of the Kings, Tomb KV11

Adapted from Wikimedia Commons (Public Domain, https://commons.wikimedia.org/w/index. php?curid=2113958), accessed 2 October 2017.

Antefoker, and Ken-amum depict official court bakeries (Figure 17.3). At the Giza plateau, two bakeries have been discovered. These bakeries produced bread that fed the workers and semi-cooked dough that produced beer (see AERA, www. aeraweb.org/lost-city-project/feeding-pyramid-workers/).

The dough was placed on the inside of a taboon (oven) or into molds and then into an oven. Taboons, also known as *tannur* (singular), *tananir* (plural), were utilized throughout the Near East and are commonly found in the artifactual record. Taboons are small clay cylindrical or beehive structures, ca. 125 centimeters to 1 meter high, with a diameter at the base of 40–60 centimeters. The taboon was constructed using coils of clay tempered with reeds, goat hair, pebbles, or sheep's wool, to name a few. To shape the taboon, the coils, several centimeters thick, were laid one on top of the other to form the beehive shape, and built up in narrow concentric circles to form the cone. The cone was built in stages with each stage being allowed to harden before the next was applied. A wide hole was left at the top for ventilation, and a small one at the base. The cone was then situated on a foundation of stones or mubrick, and the cone was plastered. Fuel for the fire was inserted through the top hole. Once the taboon walls were hot enough, the bread dough was placed onto the cone to bake. Tannurs were found in domestic dwellings in rural and urban houses, generally in the courtyard. Larger, industrial tannurs have also been discovered in palaces. Large-scale production of bread is also evident at Tell Beydar (Rova 2014).

To achieve various tastes and consistencies, milk, eggs, spices, honey, dates, figs, and nuts were added to the dough. To get flat bread, the dough was cooked right away; raised breads were left to rise overnight due to the natural wild yeasts present in the grain. Leavening was accomplished with yeast or lactic acid bacteria (found in milk products) or sodium bicarbonate (baking soda as we know it today) (Samuel 2009:558). Yeasts from older dough or from beer could also be added.

Beer

Production of bread and beer go hand-in-hand since it is from bread dough that beer is fermented. A recent study has indicated that some ten million years ago, our distant primate ancestors may have developed the gene that produces ADH4, an enzyme that enables humans to digest alcohol (*Archaeology*, www.archaeology.org/news/2746-141202-fermentation-digestion-alcohol). The earliest evidence for beer production and consumption may be found at Yellow River Valley, China, ca. 9000 BCE and Tepe Gawra (northeastern Iraq), ca. 4000 BCE on a stamp seal that depicts two individuals drinking beer from one ceramic vessel, each one using a straw (Curtis 2001:105–106; James and Thorpe 1995). Residue analyses of ceramic vessels from Godin Tepe (Zagros Mountains, Iran), as well as from King Midas' Tomb (Turkey), Sumerian texts, and Egyptian tomb paintings, texts, and artifacts all point to the daily consumption of beer. The earliest breweries discovered date to ca. 3500 BCE in Egypt from Hierakonpolis. Beer was a normal part of the daily diet and was consumed more commonly and frequently than wine (Renfrew 1995:197; Samuel 2009:537). Recently, in Luxor, the tomb of Khonso-Im-Heb (TT47) was discovered. He was the head of granaries and chief beer-maker for the goddess Mut during the Ramesside period, ca. 1292–1069 BCE (El-Aref 2014). This T-shaped tomb consisted of two halls and a burial chamber, and was elaborately decorated with scenes of daily life, including beer-making scenes. Middle Kingdom tomb paintings such as Amenemhat (BH2), Khnumhotep (BH3), Bakht III (BH15), and Khety (BH17) also depict baking and brewing. Texts that address bread and beer production include the Rhind Mathematical Papyrus, documents that record deliveries of goods to temple or palace kitchens, and the writings of Herodotus (ca. fifth century BCE), Pliny (first century CE), and Strabo (64 BCE–22 CE). Artifactual evidence for pharaonic beer production may be found at Abydos and Hierakonpolis, where beer production installations have been found. These include parallel rows of large vats supported by fired bricks, enveloped by a mudbrick covering (Samuel 2009:539–540). Residue analysis also confirms the presence of beer in vessels and loaves of bread. The office of chief beer-maker attests to the importance beer held in Egypt. Additionally, in Egypt, and throughout the ancient Near East, beer, like bread, was given as wages to laborers and comprised one of the most important offerings one could make to the dead (Bleiberg 1995:1379; Renfrew 1995:198; Stol 1995:497).

To make beer, the Egyptians used cereals that were especially grown and prepared for brewing: barley and emmer, yeast, and plants such as figs, coriander seeds, dates, doum fruit, and Christ's thorn. Using partially baked bread does not appear to have been practiced by the Egyptians in their brewing process (Samuel 2009:555).

In Mesopotamia, women were the primary brew masters, selling beer from their home or establishment. King Hammurabi's law code, ca. 1754 BCE, attempted to regulate these establishments regarding pricing. Women who over-charged were thrown into the river as punishment. If they served outlaws and failed to report them, the women were put to death. To aid the enjoyment of beer, there were drinking songs in honor of Ninkasi, the patron goddess of strong drink, known as "the lady who fills the mouth." A hymn from 2800 BCE to Ninkasi appears on a cylinder seal, and a Sumerian poem, dating to ca. 2800 BCE, honors Ninkasi as the patron goddess of brewing, and contains the oldest known beer recipe, which was derived from barley bread. Although brewers in Egypt were likely mostly male, an Old Kingdom statuette of a female brewer was discovered in the *mastaba* of Meresankh at Giza (JE66624) (Samuel 2009:537).

Mesopotamian beer brewing included the manufacture of *bappir*, a type of malted bread made from barley or emmer wheat that had been soaked and allowed to germinate and sprout. It was dried until it reached its most flavorsome point. Then, the malt-grain was crushed and flavored with herbs, spices, firwood chips, honey, and/or dates, and made into cakes for transport and storage. *Bappir* and hulled grains were mixed together and warmed in a slow oven until perfect, then mashed and spread onto a large cooling mat. *Oney* or dates were added to help with fermentation, and the mash was then combined with water in a large vat with a perforated base. The beer was then filtered into a vessel below the vat and was ready to drink. Beer was consumed using hollow reeds as drinking straws, probably because the beer needed filtering. Beer was high in vitamin B and a staple of one's daily diet (Renfrew 1995; Tucker 2011). A similar process was followed in Egypt (Curtis 2001:105–110) (Figure 17.4).

FIGURE 17.4   Beer drinking scenes. Left: Early Dynastic cylinder seal. Sumerian banquet including beer drinkers and musicians. "The Lady Who Fills the Mouth," hymn to Ninkasi, from 2800 BCE. Middle: Sumerians drinking beer, ca. 3500–3100 BCE. Right: Syrian mercenary drinking beer with his wife and child, ca. 1350 BCE, Egypt

Borrowed from blog http://nicolepeyrafitte.com/blog/2010/03/10/ninkasi/(left); borrowed from Epic Curiousity, http://epic-curiousity.com/2014/03/5-facts-aboutwomen-brewing-history.html (middle); borrowed from *The Guardian*, www.theguardian.com/lifeandstyle/wordofmouth/2010/oct/27/old-ale-beer-history (right).

Beer could be made any time; however, wine was made once per year when the grapes had ripened. When and where wine was initially made remains the subject of debate; however, it is speculated that wine originated in southern Europe, the Near East, and Turkmenistan and Tadzhikistan. Wine was probably consumed as early as 8000 BCE; however, artifactual evidence thus far dates it to 3500 BCE from Jericho, Arad, and Lachish, and Egypt at Abydos ca. 3100 BCE (Curtis 2001:142). The earliest wine consumed in Egypt was probably imported from the Levant; however, by 3000 BCE, the Egyptians appear to have developed a massive winemaking industry. In Mesopotamia, texts suggest that grapes were cultivated along with dates, apples, and figs, comprising the four major orchard crops, as early as 3000 BCE (Renfrew 1995:199). Wine was always an expensive commodity and a luxury item afforded only by the wealthy.

Beer has also been discovered in China, in a 9000-year-old tomb. This tomb records one of the oldest recipes for beer. Another ancient recipe comes from the tomb of King Midas, Gordion (modern Turkey), dating to ca. 740 BCE. Funerary vessels deposited with the burial consisted of one of the finest and most complete sets of drinking vessels ever discovered. In Egypt from the tomb of Pharaoh Scorpion I, ca. 3150 BCE, a recipe included thyme and coriander. A modern-day brewery, Dogfish Head, has been consulting with microarchaeologist Patrick McGovern to bring to life several brews that reflect ancient recipes, including Chateau Jiahu, based on the 9000-year-old tomb in China. This beer is made with sake rice, wildflower honey, Muscat grapes, hawthorn fruit, and chrysanthemum flowers. Theobroma is based on beer found in the chemical analyses of pottery in Honduras, which used Aztec cocoa powder, cocoa nibs, honey, chilies, and annatto. Birra Etrusca Bronze, Midas Touch, Ta Henket, and Kvasir are from a Dahish recipe (see Dogfish Head, https://dogfishalehouse.com/beers-type/ancient, accessed 2 May 2018; Dredge 2010).

Wine

One of the oldest indications for winemaking in the ancient Near East comes from Hajji Firuz Tepe, a Neolithic site located in the Zagros Mountains in Iran. Here a ceramic pot dating to ca. 5400–5000 BCE contained residue consisting of calcium salt of tartaric acid and terebinth resin, indicators for the presence of wine (Curtis 2001:73; McGovern et al. 1996). The domestication of vinifera appears to have been ca. 8000–6000 BCE in the Transcaucasia region, spreading to the Aegean, Mesopotamia, Syria, and Egypt toward the late fifth millennium BCE (Olmo 2000:36).

The winemaking process was much the same in antiquity as it is today. Grapes were picked and placed into containers. Once picked, all grapes are crushed, and the natural yeast found in grape skin begins the fermenting process. The crushed grapes, skins, and seeds form what is called must and the natural yeasts and sugar combine with the natural water, glucose fructose, acids, tannins, minerals, and amino acids. For white wine, the skins and seeds are immediately removed to reduce the tannins, which produce the color. The fermentation process requires the proper temperature and the right amount of air to encourage the yeasts to make alcohol and aroma, depending on the type of wine being made (Curtis 2001:147). Once that matures, the skins and seeds are removed, and the skins are pressed again to obtain more must. This basic process is depicted in a wall painting from the tomb of Nakht at Thebes from the Eighteenth Dynasty (Curtis 2001; McGovern 2000) (see Figure 7.15). In addition to tomb paintings, Sumerian texts, wine presses, and jars labeled "wine," "good wine," "sweet wine," "second quality," and "for merry-making" attest to a vibrant wine industry throughout ancient Egypt and the Near East (Renfrew 1995:199; Koh et al. 2014). Other fruits used for making wine included dates and pomegranates. Some of the seasonings used in winemaking include honey, storax resin, terebinth resin, juniper, mint, and myrtle (Koh et al. 2014).

In Canaan, wine and winemaking were equally important and contributed greatly to the economy. Recent excavations at Tel Kabri, located in present-day northern Israel, have yielded forty storage jars and some smaller vessels dating to the Middle Bronze Age. These jars were discovered in a palace storage room, could hold ca. 50 liters each, and, after careful analysis, the jars were determined to have contained wine. The excavators estimate this was the palace wine cellar, and altogether the jars could have held ca. 2000 liters of wine; the equivalent of 3000 modern-day bottles (Koh et al. 2014). While these jars were not meant for distribution, the wine they contained was intended for consumption by palace members and visitors.

In Canaan, wine (and/or olive) crushing installations are ubiquitous. The most simple is the rock-cut treading installations. These date to as early as the Chalcolithic period or earlier, and continue into the Iron Age and later (Frankel 1999). These vary in size, shape, and complexity; however, the basic components consist of a treading floor, collection vat, and channels. The floors and vats were rectangular, square, or round (Frankel 1999).

In the Late Bronze and Iron Ages, simple lever and weighted presses were utilized, not only in Canaan but also in Syria and Cyprus. Such levered installations have been found at Lachish from the Late Bronze Age and at Gezer, Bet Mirsham, and Tel Miqne-Ekron from the Iron Age.

Presses advanced from levers to screw presses in a variety of forms in the Hellenistic and Roman periods. In the third century BCE, Archimedes is credited with inventing (or reinventing) the screw. Used mainly to move water or grain from a lower to a higher place, the screw was also useful for crushing grapes (and olives). A screw press could exert much more force into crushing grapes than a person could do by treading or even by adding weights to a lever. Screw presses were made of wood with stone weights and a presser built into the screw. These included the direct-pressure rigid-frame press, a press with two rotating screws, a grooved-pier press, and a cross press (Frankel 1999:122–137).

Olives and olive oil

In addition to pressing grapes, olives were pressed to extract oil, as well as eaten whole. Olives and olive oil were very important staples in ancient daily diets. The oil was used in food preparation, religious rituals, medicines, as fuel for lamps, soap, lubricants, and skin care. The earliest evidence for olive pressing has been found in the Jordan Valley from about the fourth millennium BCE at Teleilat el-Ghassul, Lachish, Pella, Tell Shuna North, and Megiddo. To obtain the oil, olives had to be ground or crushed, the pit removed, the skins and meat pressed, and the water removed from the extracted liquid. This could be done by simply using stones or with an elaborate system of vats, basins, and channels. As with wine, simple rock-cut installations were used to crush the olives to obtain oil. Crushing was accomplished by treading and pressing. The earliest artifactual evidence for olive crushing has been found at a site south of Haifa, ca. 5500 BCE. Here a large quantity of olive stones was discovered around and inside a round rock-cut pit (Frankel 1999:56).

An extensive Iron Age olive oil manufacturing industry was discovered at Tel Miqne-Ekron, a Philistine site (see Figure 7.13). Some 115 oil processing installations dating to the seventh century BCE were excavated. Factory buildings included three relatively uniform rooms; one for crushing and pressing, one for separating and storage, and one for textile production. Factories were multifunctional, producing olive oil for four months of the year and textiles the rest of the year. Olive oil production included crushing the olives with a cylindrical stone in a large rectangular stone press with a weighted lever. On either side of the crushing presses were stone basins, each consisting of an upper opening and capacity of tens of liters. Fiber baskets of crushed olives were pressed with great force using a long thick wooden beam; one end was inserted into a niche in the wall, and the other hung free with large square stone weights suspended from a rope. The pressed oil flowed into the vat, and from there was transferred into jars where oil and water would separate. It has been estimated that Ekron alone produced at least 500 to 1000 tons of oil each year, making Ekron the largest oil production center thus far discovered in the ancient world (Gitin 1990; Curtis 2001:187–189; Frankel 1999). A levered press was also discovered at Maresha (Frankel 1999:76–77). Additional olive crushing devices included a round rotary crushing stone placed into a large vat. The stone was rolled over the olives to release the oil, which flowed into a collection vat. One such installation was discovered at Maresha (see Figure 7.14).

Additional olive press types included the screw and weight press, the grooved-pier press, and the cross press, all of which made use of the screw reinvented by Archimedes in the third century BCE. Variations of screw presses were described by Pliny the Elder and Hero of Alexandria in the second quarter of the first century CE (Frankel 1999:122–137).

Herbs and spices

Herbs and spices were an integral part of food preparation and consumption. Used for medicinal purposes and to enhance food's flavor, herbs and spices comprised a valuable market in the ancient world. As early as at least 3000 BCE, Egyptian,

Canaanite, Assyrian, and Babylonian gardens included items such as cumin, cinnamon, mint, basil, sesame, coriander, thyme, asafetida, bay, anise, saffron, rosemary, sage, fennel, mustard seed, capers, onions, leeks, garlic, and chives. Archaeological evidence for spices and herbs has been found in tombs, tomb paintings and reliefs, and texts. The spice trade extended from India to Greece and Rome, and formed a very important and lucrative line of commerce (Zohary 1982; Brothwell and Brothwell 1998:157–160). Recent analyses of phytoliths indicate that spices such as *Coriandrum Sativum* were used as early as 23,000 BP at the Nahal Hemar Cave in Israel, and that use of spices and herbs spread from the Mediterranean to the Atlantic coastal margins ca. 5000 cal. BP (Saul et al. 2013). Foods were sweetened with honey and dates in Egypt and the Near East (Curtis 2001:176–177, 240–242). Evidence of beekeeping has been found in Egyptian tomb paintings and texts, and an apiary was found at Tel Rehov in the Beth Shean Valley in Israel that dates to the Iron Age (Mazar 1992; Mazar and Panitz-Cohen 2007).

The earliest known cookbooks come from Mesopotamia from ca. 1750 BCE, the time of King Hammurabi. Some of the tablets from the Yale Babylonian Collection (www.library.yale.edu/neareast/exhibitions/cuisine.html) contain recipes written in elegant handwriting intended for use in the kitchens of the elite or perhaps the royal families. Recipes were mostly for meat stews, such as goat kid boiled with garlic, onion, fat, soured milk, and blood, with a side dish of braised parsnips with boiled water, fat, onion, dorsal thorn, coriander cumin and kanasu (a legume). Squeezed leek and garlic juices were spread onto a dish with onion and mint added to the braised parsnips placed on top. A recipe for wildfowl pie included fowl, water, milk, salt, fat, cinnamon, mustard greens, shallots, semolina, leeks, garlic, flour, brine, roasted dill seeds, mint, and wild tulip bulbs. The recipes generally provide a list of ingredients and describe the order in which they should be mixed or added; however, they do not provide measurements, heat temperature, or cooking time (see Yale Babylonian Collection, https://babylonian-collection.yale.edu).

Once humankind became sedentary farmers, food technology grew exponentially thus creating an interdependence between numerous task-specific industries. For example, farmers and butchers were dependent upon metalsmiths for the tools of their trades. Metalsmiths were dependent upon farmers for foodstuffs. Transportation was needed for moving raw and finished products from the farm to the market. Storage vessels and buildings were needed for the surplus of raw and finished goods. Silos were created to store large quantities of grains. Distribution centers were developed to dispense grain. Ceramic vessels were created to hold grains, olive oil, and wine, and for storage, transportation, and cooking. Although grinding stones had been in existence for some time, now milling on a larger scale could produce greater quantities of ground flour. Butcheries, bakeries, and the fermentation of grapes and production of beer became large-scale operations. Paintings from Egyptian tombs boast elaborate scenes depicting granaries, the production of cakes and breads in large-scale bakeries, beer production, wine production, and bountiful banqueting tables laden with fruits and vegetables (Curtis 2001:93–177).

In a pre-monetary society, foodstuffs functioned as currency. Remuneration for labor could be in the form of a daily food ration. For example, in Egypt, one worker could receive bread, beer, and cheese for a day's work. Taxes and tribute to pharaohs and kings, and offerings to temples and deities were also in the form of foodstuffs. Rulers owned the land and leased it to farmers, who in turn paid rent and/or taxes, which fed the royal family and staff. Temples and temple priests owned and operated their land in the same way.

Animal husbandry

Exactly when animals were domesticated remains unanswered and much debated. Archaeological clues suggest that domestication of wild animals may have begun as early as 6000–4000 BCE in Asia and Egypt. Certainly, by 3300 BCE, select wild animals had been domesticated and were being kept and bred. As with cereals, early farmers also domesticated certain animals including but not limited to sheep, goat, cattle, pig, donkey, fowl, and ostrich, though not necessarily in that order. However, it seems that domestication was most successful with these species. Criteria for choosing which wild animals to domesticate may have included those that exhibited a disposition to domestication: able to survive in captivity, accept a herder as master, possess no instinct to flee danger, and possess a disposition of calmness, placidity, and acceptance. Humans had to decide which animals would be utilized for food, work, or both. They may also have been chosen for their nutritional value and for the byproducts they could provide, such as milk, cheese, yogurt, skins, and bones. People quickly learned about selective breeding, which could provide, for example, desired types and color of wool or temperament or strength (Hesse 1982, 1989; Meadow 1989).

Animal husbandry gave rise to butcheries, cheese makers and shops, yogurt makers and shops, leather-workers and shops, specialty packaging for storage and transportation, such as ceramics, and domestic and long-distance trading. As with agriculture, animal husbandry boosted the economy and created craft specialization and niche markets.

Meats included domesticated sheep, goat, cattle, ox, and pig; poultry included chicken, duck, geese, ostrich, quail, and pigeons; fish included the Nile catfish, St. Peter's Fish, Nile perch, sea breams, groupers, gray mullets, and meagers (Nehemiah 12:39, 13:16; MacDonald 2008:37–38; Ikram 2009:656–671). Non-domesticated wild animals included deer, ibex, hippopotamus, antelopes, gazelles, hedgehog, and rabbit. Slaughtering, curing, butchering, and preserving techniques became sophisticated. Numerous tomb paintings and reliefs depict butchering techniques, curing meat, and preparation of it for consumption. Some of these include the tomb of Ty at Saqqara from the Fifth Dynasty, the tomb of Ptahhotep at Saqqara from the Fifth Dynasty, and the tombs of Ramesses III (KV 35) and Ipuy (TT217), where butchered animals are depicted hanging on a line to cure (Ikram 2009:657). Butchering techniques included severing the carotid artery of an animal that may have been rendered unconscious prior to the procedure. Inspectors scrutinized the animal, testing for purity and health by inspecting the blood and entrails. Once the arteries and veins were cut in the neck, the legs of the animal were pumped to force the blood out of the veins. Once drained, the animal was skinned and flayed, and the guts removed. Birds and fish were slaughtered and butchered in a similar manner.

Once cleaned the meat was eaten right away or hung for several hours or days depending on the temperature, time of year, and species. The hanging of carcasses is depicted in several tomb paintings such as in the tomb of Nakh (TT52) at Thebes in the Eighteenth Dynasty and the butchery scene in the tomb of Intefiqer (TT60), Thebes, from the Twelfth Dynasty. Preservation of meat included drying, salting, smoking, or a combination of these, as well as pemmicaning, which is curing meat with beer, fat, or honey (Ikram 2009:659–669).

Beekeeping and honey

The collection of combs and honey from beehives is an ancient practice. In Valencia, Spain, a cave painting dating to ca. 8000–6000 BCE depicts a person collecting honey from a hive.

It is not known when humankind attempted to domesticate wild bees; however, early artificial hives consisted of reed baskets, ceramic vessels, wooden boxes, and hollowed logs. Evidence for beekeeping in the Near East dates to ca. 3500–3100 BCE in Mesopotamia and Egypt; ca. 2500 BCE in the Indus Valley and Lower Indus regions; and ca. 2200 BCE in China (Crane 1999:162). In Mesoamerica, the Maya also kept stingless bees in hives from ca. 300 BCE to 300 CE.

In Egypt, the earliest artifactual evidence of beekeeping is from the Fifth Dynasty sun temple of Niuserra at Abu Gurob. The scene in relief depicts beehives and honey being harvested. Additional scenes have been found in the Tomb of Rekhmira (TT100), a vizier during the Eighteenth Dynasty (Figure 17.5). Tomb TT73 at Thebes (ca. 1450 BCE); and in the Tomb of Pabasa (TT279) at Thebes (ca. 660–625 BCE). These hives are depicted as horizontal cylinders or rectangular shapes and were likely made of mudbrick and/or clay.

The clay cylinders were stacked and sealed with mud and straw on one end, and a small opening was left in the other end through which bees could enter. The

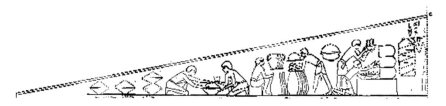

FIGURE 17.5   Beekeeping in the Tomb of Rekhmara, Vizier of Upper Egypt in the reign of Thutmose III and Amenhotep II

Adapted from Newberry 1900 Pl. 14 (Public Domain, PD-1923).

beekeeper removed the mud-straw stopper and blew smoke into the hive to ward off the bees while s/he collected the honeycombs. Once collected, the honeycomb was broken to release the honey, and the wax was used for candles, as molds, and in other daily uses. This sort of hive remains in use today in some parts of Egypt (Serpico and White 2009:410–411).

In Mesopotamia, beekeeping is attested in the eighth century BCE on a stele dated to ca. 760 BCE. Shamash-resh-usur, the governor of Suhu and the land of Mari, boasts about his attempt to introduce bees and beekeeping into Mesopotamia.

In ancient Israel, a tenth century BCE beehive was discovered at Tel Rehov. This large apiary was constructed using rows of clay cylinders, whose walls were ca. 4 centimeters thick and made from coarse unfired clay with inclusions of straw and dung. Each hive measured ca. 80 centimeters long by 40 centimeters in diameter. Each hive could hold ca. 56 liters. One end was open so the bees could enter/exit while the opposite end was sealed with a removable stopper. These clay cylinders were laid horizontally on a mud podium and were stacked two to three tiers high. In total, some 75 hives have thus far been uncovered at Rehov; however, more may exist in unexcavated areas. As in modern-day Egypt, this beekeeping technique remains in use in modern-day Israel (Mazar and Panitz-Cohen 2007).

Vegetables and fruits

Ancient food production and the economy were inextricably interwoven. After the shift from hunter-gatherer to an agrarian lifestyle, the majority of society was dependent upon food that was grown by local farmers in the rural hinterland and distributed in urban centers. Vegetables and fruits comprised an integral part of the ancient diet. Meat (sheep, goat, cattle) was expensive and therefore probably eaten mostly at feasts, rituals, and special family occasions. Vegetables and fruits, on the other hand, were more readily available, less expensive, and equally filling and nutritious. That being said, meat was favored over vegetables. Even fruit appears to be more highly regarded in Iron Age Israel than vegetables (MacDonald 2008:25–26). Nevertheless, the cultivation of fruits and vegetables was well established in Mesopotamia, Egypt, and in Canaan, and the variety can be observed in text, artwork, and the archaeological record.

Onion (*Allium Cepa Lilacaea*) first encountered in the wild in Central Asia was easily domesticated (see Chapter 13, Medicine). It is an annual or biennial herb and the bulb is edible. Onions were not only eaten but also exploited for their medicinal properties and used as a yellow or brown dye. Mesopotamian texts suggest that the onion was grown from the second millennium BCE onward (Murray 2009c: 628–630). Leeks (*A. ampeloprasum*) were also common in the Mediterranean basin. Garlic (*Allium Sativum L*) was first wild and then domesticated. It is a perennial herb and usually a winter crop. Garlic bulbs could be dried and tied in bundles, which made it easy to store and sell. Garlic was used in Egypt as early as the Naqada period. Garlic was used as a food as well as for its medicinal properties such as for respiratory problems, parasites, poor digestion, and low energy. Lettuce (*Lactuca sp. L*) has been depicted in Egyptian Old Kingdom tomb paintings. Celery was used as a food, a condiment, for medicinal purposes, and as funeral wreaths, as in the case of Tutankhamun (Murray 2009c:632). Pulses (legumes), lentils, peas, chickpeas, and fava beans were regular and important sources of protein in the ancient Near East. Like cereals, these were readily available and easy to cultivate.

Fruits that were readily available were sycamore figs (1 Kings 10:27, 1 Chronicles 27:28), melons, cucumbers, date palm, olives, and grapes; oranges, apricots, peaches, and pomegranates (Deuteronomy 8:8); pears, apples, and nuts such as pistachio (Exodus 25:33–34, 37:19–20), and almond (Genesis 43:11).

Condiments and spices were equally important in the daily diet and in commodity trading. Spices include coriander, cumin, black cumin, dill, fenugreek, sesame seeds, cinnamon, and saffron. These were used to embellish the taste of food in the ancient world just as they are used today.

Recipes

Some of the earliest known cookbooks have been found in Mesopotamia and Egypt. Cuneiform tablets housed in the Yale Babylonian Collection (www.library. yale.edu/neareast/exhibitions/cuisine.html) dating to ca. 1750 BCE, the time of King Hammurabi, discuss ingredients, procedures for preparing various foods, and recipes. Some of the recipes required meats such as sheep, goat, beef, pork, deer, and fowl; eggs from fowl; fish; turtles; grains; vegetables; fruits including figs, pomegranates, and grapes; root vegetables; truffles; mushrooms and spices such as honey, salt, and sesame. These were cooked in animal fats and oils such as olive, sesame, and linseed. Beer and wine were also used in cooking. Interestingly, recipes discuss ingredients and the order in which they should be added, but they do not discuss quantity or cooking time.

One Mesopotamian tablet (YBC 8958, Old Babylonian Period, ca. 1750 BCE), for example, discussed a recipe for wildfowl potpie, including the removal of the head and feet; cleaning of the body; retaining of the gizzard and the pluck. The gizzards were then split and cleaned. The birds were also cleaned and flattened. After a pot was prepared (presumably with fat and water), the birds, gizzards, and pluck were put into it, and the pot was placed onto the fire. After initial boiling, the pot was removed, cooled, and placed on the fire again. Another pot with fresh water mixed with beaten milk was placed onto the fire. Presumably, it was brought to a boil too. Then the pot containing the bird was drained, the inedible parts were removed, and the remaining bits were salted and added to the vessel with milk and some fat. The mixture was brought to a boil a third time, at which point rue, leeks, garlic, samidu, cinnamon, mustard greens, semolina, roasted dill leaves, wild tulip bulbs, and onion (but not too much) were added. While that was cooking, rinsed crushed grain was softened in milk and salt, samidu, leeks, and garlic to taste; then, milk and oil were combined to make a soft dough. The dough was cut into two pieces. One piece was pressed onto a large platter with the dough hanging over the edge; this was cooked on top of the oven. The same procedure was followed with the other half of the dough, but the potpie filling was spread on top of the dough and baked in the oven. Once done, the potpie was covered with the bread lid and served warm (Yale Babylonian Collection www.library.yale.edu/neareast/exhibitions/cuisine.html and Silk Road Gourmet, www.silkroadgourmet.com/mesopotamian-wildfowl-pie/, accessed 21 January 2015). Athenaeus of Naucratis, Egypt (ca. second/third century CE) was a food guide and critic. He wrote a book entitled *Deipnosophistai, The Learned Banqueters*, a 15- (or 30)-volume series regarding intelligent dinner-table conversations. Athenaeus also refers to an existing cookbook entitled *Art of Cooking: Gastronomy, Sicilian Cooking, Pickles and Vegetables*.

Although slightly later and from a different region (beyond the scope of this work), a cookbook attributed to the authorship of Marcus Gavius Apicius, a first century CE Roman food connoisseur, is worth mentioning. His cookbook, *On Cookery*, covers a range of topics. The chapters are as follows, with the English translations of the Greek titles in parentheses:

Chapter 1:   Epimeles (The Careful Cook)
Chapter 2:   Sarcoptes (The Meat Mincer)
Chapter 3:   Cepuros (The Gardener)
Chapter 4:   Pandecter (Many Ingredients)
Chapter 5:   Ospreon (Pulse)
Chapter 6:   Aeropetes (Birds)
Chapter 7:   Polyteles (The Gourmet)
Chapter 8:   Tetrapus (The Quadruped)
Chapter 9:   Thalassa (The Sea)
Chapter 10:   Halieus (The Fisherman)

Chapter 4 discussed "all kinds of dishes": nut omelets, creamed calf's brains, lettuce puree, steamed fish custard. Chapter 7 discussed recipes for tripe, port, truffles, snails, eggs, mushrooms, lungs, cakes, and sweet custards. Quadrupeds included pork, venison, mutton, veal, lamb, kid, rabbit, and hare. As a side note, Mutton was commonly eaten as early as the Early Bronze Age, as evidenced by remains of meat found in the tombs at Jericho (Tomb G 1, Kenyon 1960:443, Plate XXIII:3). Chapter 9 discussed oysters, crabs, lobsters, mussels, sardines, tuna, skate, squid, and octopus. Chapter 10 not only discussed preparation of fish but sauces for fish dishes as well.

Food management and distribution

Like any technology or commodity, relatively few people controlled food resources, the production of food, and its distribution. The actual growing and production of foodstuffs was conducted primarily in the rural hinterland near or surrounding large cities. Farmers grew crops and raised animals that were processed and turned into foodstuffs to feed the family, the village, and, ultimately, the city. With the advent and evolution of cities, non-agrarian occupations arose such as merchant, scribe, priest, administrator, and king. Those involved in non-agrarian professions had not the time or the ability to grow their own food. Thus, foodstuffs were made available via the local market, especially to those who had the ability to purchase by providing a service, bartering, or trading precious metals or stones for commodities in a pre-coinage market, or with coin after ca. sixth/fifth centuries BCE. However, for priests, kings, and their administrators, who did not accumulate wealth in a traditional way, purchasing food may have presented a challenge. To address this issue, kings imposed taxes, and temples imposed offerings and sacrifices, which could be paid in the form of processed and raw foodstuffs. This way the king and his/her administrative employees and family, and priests and his/her family and administration were provided with ample food (Ponchia 2014).

Food paid in taxes or as offerings was kept in the storehouses and managed by officials. Numerous records from the Assyrian and Neo-Assyrian empires discuss taxation, collection, and management of foodstuffs and the distribution of it. Egypt also maintained an extensive taxation system based on the annual inundation level of the Nile River. The height of the flood was measured in cubits using a nilometer (see Figure 12.1). Careful measurement of the Nile's level was kept during the course of the year. Most nilometers were situated within temple precincts where priests maintained the records. Taxation amounts were determined by the height of the inundation. A high flood level brought higher taxes; a lower flood level brought lower taxes. Additionally, some portions of the Nile River valley flooded more than others, so this was also taken into consideration when determining the tax rate. For example, 16 cubits was considered a good flood, but a flood level of 17 or 18 cubits was considered excellent (Ellenblum 2013:24–25).

Canaanite city-states would have followed a similar scenario, with the rural hinterland providing agricultural support, and farmers being taxed to support the king, the royal family, and the administration, and sacrifices and offerings to support the temple priests, their families, and their administration.

For the Mesopotamians, Egyptians, Canaanites, and Israelites, the food supply had to support not only king and temple but also the military. Each maintained extensive armies comprised of a few permanent professionals as well as a larger corpus of troops who provided annual service. These soldiers needed to be provisioned no matter where they were on duty, be it a military campaign, stationed at an outpost, or guarding the royal family (Ponchia 2014; Fales and Rigo 2014). In Assyria, for example, provisions were initially supplied from the State Archives of Assyria (Fales and Rigo 2014:420). Once these ran out, foodstuffs were obtained from the nearby provinces and territories within the empire. Texts indicate that an average daily ration for a person was ca. 2–3 liters of grain, and, for animals, 5–8 liters. Based on the numbers provided for a garrison for one month, 57,800 liters a day for men and 70,500 liters for animals per day, it can be calculated that there were 30,000 men and 8000 animals per garrison. One liter, or one *qa*, produced ca. 600–650 grams of bread. Among the soldiers were civilians performing tasks such as cupbearers, confectioners, bakers, and cooks. These individuals processed and prepared food that was distributed to the troops, not to mention the other non-military persons in the camp, such as deportee transfers (Fales and Rigo 2014).

Travelers, specifically those in caravans from Ebla, were initially provisioned by the state. Caravans were used to transport goods on an international scale. This is evidenced by texts discussing the movement of wool from Mesopotamia to Anatolia. Female woolers arranged to send their goods from Kanesh to market in Anatolia in the early second millennium BCE (Thomason 2013). Caravans were supplied with grain, vegetables, water, and even live animals such as sheep for slaughtering along the way (Milano 2014).

The ancient Canaanites and Egyptians were particularly skilled at amassing essential foodstuffs, and were known for always having ample food in times of drought, famine, and war. Silos have been used since at least the Early Bronze Age as evidenced by the remains of silos from Beth Yerah (Khirbet al-Karak), Hama, Tell Qara Quzaq, Mishrifeh (Qatna), and Tell Arqa, in Canaan and in Egypt at Tel Edfu (Tell Edfu Project, https://telledfu.uchicago.edu/about/excavation-silo-court, accessed 17 January 2018) and the Ramesseum Granaries. Long-term storage silos were constructed of a mudbrick superstructure with a thick limestone plaster on a foundation of stone or mudbrick, or slightly sunken floors lined with stone and/or lime plaster with mudbrick superstructures. The mudbrick superstructure was rounded, like a beehive with a hole at the top for ventilation. At Mishrifeh, some silos had a capacity of 30 cubic meters (Bonacossi 2014). The nine silos at Beth Yerah were ca. 10 meters wide each, and measured ca. 7 to 9 meters in diameter. Each silo was divided into four parts by a tall partition that supported the domed roof. If the average size of each silo was 8 meters in diameter and 7 meters high, each could hold ca. 200–250 cubic meters of grain making the total capacity of the silos ca. 1800–2500 cubic meters (Kempinski 1992a; Hestrin 1993).

Egyptian granaries were constructed similarly to those mentioned above; however, they also employed much larger facilities such as those depicted at Saqqara in the tomb of Ptah-het-ep and the tomb of Ti from the Fifth Dynasty, and those found at Ramasseum, Thebes, dating to Ramesses II, ca. thirteenth century BCE. These were long buildings with arched roofs, constructed of mudbrick with a very large storage capacity. They measured ca. 4 meters to 6 meters high (Curtis 2001:104). Egyptian granaries were domed and flat-roofed; however, during the New Kingdom, domed granaries appear to have been the most common (Curtis 2001:104).

Egypt was known as the "granary of the Mediterranean" (Ellenblum 2013:23) because during times of drought and famine, it supplied grain to the people of Egypt and to various other nation-states. Throughout history there have been numerous climate cycles resulting in alternating wet and dry periods. Egypt's climate cycle appears to have been different from those of Mesopotamia and Canaan since Egypt's climate is dependent more on the African cycle than the Mediterranean one. Therefore, when Canaan, Mesopotamia, and the Mediterranean basin experienced drought, Egypt did not. Thus, Egypt was able to supply foodstuffs when others could not. Granaries were maintained and managed on a daily basis. Officials such as Unas-Ankh, Overseer of the Two Granaries, managed the maintenance and distribution of foodstuffs (Curtis 2001:101). The stored food from granaries became particularly important during times of drought and famine. A well-known period of drought and famine is that of Joseph in the Hebrew Bible, who oversaw the storage of grain that fed people near and far during a drought that lasted seven years, an unusually long period. (Recurring droughts usually last one to three years.) From this story, one can learn that administrations planned for food-related crises because they understood that grain can be stored for a maximum of seven years, and foodstuffs were hoarded in very large surpluses to compensate for years of dearth (Ellenblum 2013:21).

18

WRITING, ARTS, WEIGHTS, MEASURES, AND CURRENCY

Several aspects of technology in the ancient Near East do not fit neatly within the parameters of the previous chapters, so it seemed appropriate to collect and briefly discuss them in a chapter for misfit subjects. Like many of the topics discussed, some of these subjects may not seem like technology as we consider it today; however, based on our working definition of technology, they function as such because they facilitate the achievement of goals and effect change. With that in mind, this chapter will discuss writing, art, painting, and currency.

Writing

In the beginning, oral tradition was the medium by which cultural history, mores and folkways, identity, lore, mythologies, and tradecrafts were passed from one generation to the next. These took the form of folk stories, songs, poems, and proverbs. It is through the rhythm of lyric, song, and poetry that people remember the details of an event or story. This is one reason television and radio commercials incorporate a musical jingle to sell their product: so the advertisement's message will remain in one's memory. In many early communities, the cultural history, body of laws and taboos, and traditions were entrusted to one or several individuals within the clan or tribe, who served as a sort of archivist. As the complexities of society grew, rulers used writing to promote their propaganda, communicate with distant rulers, collect knowledge in libraries, develop archives, and to facilitate business transactions.

Eventually, writing replaced memory as a more permanent and accurate way to record that which was kept in a collective memory rather than relying on one or a few people. Writing was a technology that enabled accumulated wisdom and permanent knowledge, and facilitated the intellectual process (Humphrey et al. 2006:522). Writing was a kind of early external storage device, a kind of artificial memory that could be accessed any time by any person, provided they could read (Humphrey et al. 2006:522; Oleson 2008:715–716). Eventually, members of the community who kept knowledge, wisdom, and legend in their memories were replaced by those who could write and read, and could use those skills to create permanent written records. The development of writing was complex, much more complex than this summary will make it seem, and other contemporaneous peoples also developed writing, such as the indigenous peoples of China, India, and the Americas. However, for the purposes of this work, a simplistic overview of the development of writing in the ancient Near East will suffice. A useful resource that provides a detailed account of the development of writing is A. Robinson's *The Story of Writing: Alphabets, Hieroglyphs & Pictograms* (2007).

Writing is thought by some to have begun in Mesopotamia, and from there, it spread to Egypt (Rendsburg 2003a:63a). The earliest form of writing in Mesopotamia and Egypt was glyphic or pictographic, by which a picture or pictures represented objects, concepts, events, or actions.

In Mesopotamia, glyphic representation quickly evolved into stylized symbols known as cuneiform (Figure 18.1). Multiple wedge-shaped glyphs came to represent syllables or ideograms and employed hundreds of symbols; however, vowels were not represented. Cuneiform's wedge-shaped symbols were incised onto leather-hard clay tablets by a reed stylus. Once inscribed, the clay tablet was baked, and its inscription secured forever.

The Egyptian form of writing, hieroglyphics, also progressed from pictures to signs, initially developing as a hieroglyphic system of communication. Hieroglyphics were painted on walls, incised in stone, and written on papyrus or ceramic fragments. With hieroglyphics, the symbols remained as pictures and did not become stylized in the same way cuneiform did—at least not right away; vowels were represented, and a set of twenty-four glyphs represented the consonantal sounds used in the Egyptian language (Rendsburg 2003a:63a). Hieroglyphics were considered words of the gods, and the formal writing system combined logographic and alphabetic elements. This system was used from ca. 4000–3300 BCE to ca. 391 CE when Roman Emperor Theodosius I closed all pagan temples. Hieratic developed later and was the "priestly" cursive writing system used with hieroglyphics. Hieratic was used from the Proto-Dynastic Period to the third century CE. Demotic script developed after hieroglyphics and was the "popular" or "document writing" script, derived from northern derivations of Hieratic in the Nile Delta region. It derived from northern derivations of Hieratic in the Nile Delta region. This developed during the Twenty-fifth Dynasty (ca. 650 BCE) and was used through the Roman period to approximately the fifth century CE. Finally, Coptic script developed, which was basically the Egyptian language written in an alphabetic system using script that was an adaptation of Greek. This emerged in the first century CE and remained in use in Egypt until the seventeenth century CE. The Coptic Orthodox Church continues to write and speak Coptic. Hieratic, Demotic, and Coptic were much easier to use and took up less space than hieroglyphics. Cuneiform became the lingua franca of the ancient world. It was used in Egypt, Canaan, Anatolia, and much of the ancient Near East. Specifically, it was used in business transactions,

FIGURE 18.1   Cuneiform tablet. A tablet from the Tell el-Amarna letters dating to the fourteenth century BCE

Adapted from Wikimedia.org (Public Domain, https://commons.wikimedia.org/w/index.php?curid= 629827. PD-Art).

political agreements, religious writing, to maintain royal annuls, and to record scientific observations. In comparison, Egyptian hieroglyphics and its derivatives were rarely used outside of Egypt by non-Egyptians in the same way (Rendsburg 2003a:63–64).

In Canaan in the early second millennium, an alphabet using a set of twenty-five signs, each representing a consonant, emerged. At a site known as Serabit el-Khadem in the Sinai, alphabetic inscriptions known as Proto-Sinaitic have been found which date to ca. 1500 BCE. These are considered by many to be the earliest form of alphabetic writing. This system used an alphabet of twenty-five characters and likely reflects a West Semitic language. Other, slightly later alphabetic texts have been recovered from Ugarit (Ras Shamra) and Ras ibn Hani in Syria dating to the fourteenth–thirteenth centuries BCE. The Ugaritic alphabet includes thirty characters and is a cuneiform alphabet. Ugaritic combines the Canaanite alphabet with Mesopotamian cuneiform characters and style of writing. Another script in use at this time appears to have been the Minoan Linear A. Numerous texts recovered from Crete attest to its use (Rendsburg 2003a:66–68). Later, in the Iron Age, Hebrew emerged along with the influence and use of Phoenician. During the Iron Age Hebrew evolved to include Phoenician and Aramaic forms.

It is thought by some modern scholars that the Greek alphabet was adapted from Phoenician, a form of North-Semitic writing, around the eighth century BCE in the Aegean, Euboea, and/or North Syria. However, this remains a topic of much debate. Herodotus (*Histories* 5.58–59; Strassler and Purvis 2007:391–392) states that the Phoenicians brought the alphabet to the Greeks, and that the first three letters of the Greek alphabet, alpha (aleph), beta (bet), gamma (gimel), parallel the first three letters in Phoenician (Humphrey et al. 2006:525). Pliny (*Natural History* 7.192–193; Henderson and Rackham 1952) also suggests that the alphabet was spread by Phoenician traders ca. 950–800 BCE (Humphrey et al. 2006:524–525). It is theorized that the Phoenicians' initial purpose for writing was administrative and economic. The increasingly complex administrations of Mesopotamia and Egypt required diligent and detailed recordkeeping for taxes and general bookkeeping. Temple administrations required accurate recordkeeping for similar reasons and to act as libraries or archives. For example, Uruk's temple complex provided the best place and method for collecting and preserving information on a large scale. Additionally, farmers, merchants, craftspeople, and traders needed accurate and efficient methods of recordkeeping.

This brings us to the question of who could read and write in antiquity. In Egypt, hieroglyphics were considered holy carvings, designated as such because at first only the priests and theocratic bureaucracy could read and write. Glyphics or pictorial representations were simplistic and could be universally understood, but they were cumbersome and inefficient as a writing system. Hieroglyphics and cuneiform were complicated writing systems comprised of hundreds of phonetic and symbolic signs that could be read and written only by those who had been trained to do so. However, an alphabetic system made reading and writing simpler and more accessible to everyone. The aristocratic governments of some Greek city-states actively opposed the introduction of a simple method of reading and writing because they didn't want non-aristocratic citizens to gain new power and independence. Nevertheless, it was to the advantage of Egyptian and Mesopotamian governments to have a literate citizenry because it was through the medium of pictures and writing that rulers communicated. This was made evident by the public posting of law codes, such as Hammurabi's Law Code, as well as tax codes, road and boundary markers, and the large reliefs on palace and temple walls, such as at Medinet

Habu and the Palace at Nineveh. Literature, poetry, and narratives such as the Tale of Sinhue attest to the high percentage of the population who were likely able to read and write.

Literature, poetry, and theater were very popular in the ancient world. Epic and lyric poetry such as the Epic of Gilgamesh, Epic of Atra-hasis, Enuma Eliš in Mesopotamia, and the Legend of Keret, Journey of Wen-Amun to Phoenicia, and the aforementioned Tale of Sinuhe were widespread. These works usually described heroic acts, important events, and histories that were important to the origin and development of early nations and peoples. These were likely originally handed down through oral tradition until the advent of writing, when they were permanently recorded. Based on archaeological evidence, letters, legal texts, and manuals were written and utilized as early as 2000 BCE, and the ability of common people to read and write is evidenced by personal letters to the dead (Gardiner and Sethe 1928). Historical writing was practiced from ca. 2500 BCE onward. The authors of this genre recorded military campaigns, kingship succession, royal decrees, political relationships, and other state matters. Well-known examples include 1 & 2 Kings, 1 & 2 Chronicles, and 1 & 2 Samuel of the Hebrew Bible.

As a form of technology, writing and reading performed fundamental functions in ancient society. Writing conveyed information, allowed expression of political views, recorded data, and provided a more accurate way to preserve information over and above people's memories. The ability to read was empowering because written materials conveyed knowledge, which can be considered the application of technology. To understand the laws of the land and the accomplishments of rulers, citizens had to be able to read that which was literally written on the walls of palaces, temples, and steles. If one could not read, accompanying pictorial representation of the narrative effectively translated the words to illiterate citizens or visitors from foreign lands who may not have known the local written language. Writing and reading also facilitated successful business practices and a strong economy. Merchants, tradespeople, and palace and temple administrators depended on these skills. The ability to read and write provided personal advantage and success, and continues to do so today. There was, however, a disadvantage to writing; loss of the ability to remember. Once a thought or fact was written down, it could be forgotten in memory, as long as the tablet, papyrus, or piece of paper was not lost or destroyed. Writing is an artificial form of memory, and, as such, it affects the human ability to remember. Over the course of centuries, humankind's long-term memory diminished, and the way in which information and traditions were transferred changed.

Today, in the twenty-first century, the way we remember has shifted yet again. Instead of writing, data are stored in an electronic device such as a computer, tablet, or mobile phone, and almost nothing has to be committed to human memory. M. Spitzer has described this "breakdown of cognitive abilities" as "digital dementia" (Spitzer 2012; Greenfield 2015). For example, a generation ago people memorized important addresses and telephone numbers. Today, electronic contact lists remember for us. In the elementary and secondary grades, students were required to memorize lengthy important documents such as the Gettysburg Address, the Preamble to the Constitution, and the Declaration of Independence. Students gained knowledge by memorizing it, learning it, and assimilating it, not by merely looking it up in a search engine.

Art and artistic expression

The art of the ancient Near East can be found in friezes, tomb paintings, painted ceramic vessels, figurines, and sculpture. Artistic expression can also be found in music, comedy, satire, and literature. Although it may not seem like it, art and artistic expression is a form of technology, according to our working definition, because art can function as communication. The arts are inextricably interwoven into nearly every culture and to divorce them would leave a culture and its society sterile and render it unsophisticated. Ancient peoples throughout the world were aware of the value the arts held in civilized society and cultivated their development.

The art of communication was utilized on the walls of Egyptian temples and Mesopotamian palaces. For example, the exterior walls of Egyptian temples were used to communicate the pharaoh's achievements, such as at Medinet Habu. The interior temple walls were used to communicate the basic tenets of cultic practice, mythology, and rites for the specific deity/deities being venerated. In another example, the painted walls of Egyptian tombs communicated details of the deceased's profession, family members, and perhaps achievements. Additionally, cultic mythology and ritual were included so that these could be performed for the deceased for eternity.

In Canaan, some mosaics of the fourth–sixth centuries CE express the basic tenets of Jewish and Christian beliefs. Examples can be found in the mosaics at Beth Alpha, Sepphoris, Hammoth Tiberias Ein Gedi, and the recently discovered mosaics at Huqoq (www.livescience.com/55318-bible-mosaic-found-ancient-israel-synagogue. html; www.dailymail.co.uk/sciencetech/article-3681609/Ancient-mosaics-Red-Sea-parting-Noah-s-Ark-discovered-5th-century-synagogue-Israel.html). Each mosaic contains information that would have helped the viewer understand the most basic but also presumably the most important principles of their religious system, as well as the world around them, such as the cycle of seasons. The Beth Alpha mosaic, for example, depicts a scene that brings to life the story of Abraham preparing to sacrifice Isaac to Yahweh (Genesis 22). It also depicts the symbols of Judaism: the Ark of the Covenant, the eternal light, two menorahs, a palm frond (lulav), citron (etrog), and an incense shovel (Sukenik 2007; Hachlili 1997, 2009; Magness 2005). A person, literate or illiterate, could enter the space, view the mosaic, and comprehend the most intimate tenets of Judaism. Later, churches also made use of mosaics and stained-glass windows for similar purposes. A vivid example, though not in the Near East, is the Church of Santa Maria Maggiore in Rome. These beautiful fifth century mosaics depict and express the stories of the New Testament as well as Christian doctrine and theology.

The art of communication could also be found in theater with satire, comedy, and dramatic performance. In Egypt, Mesopotamia, and Canaan, musicians, dancers, wailers, and actors were present at the king's court as entertainment during festivals, meals, and political events, as well as at funerals and important social events, and public festivals. The performing arts were executed by men and women, which offered a safe venue where both sexes, especially women, could voice their opinion in public without reprisal. Throughout the Graeco-Roman periods and the Greek and Roman empires, the performing arts became an acceptable and safe way for people to express political criticism. Even today, satire and comedy remain an acceptable non-threatening way for political criticism to be voiced. The late-night television shows *Saturday Night Live*, *The Late Show with Stephen Colbert*, and *The Tonight Show*, for example, offer a safe environment for the hosts and their guests to voice opinion about current events and politics in a humorous but piercing way. The art of humor can bring together people who might not otherwise engage in discussion and can illuminate complex and convoluted issues, which can be interpreted as a sort of information and communication technology.

Music, song, and dance can reflect current trends, historic events, rituals, politics, economic realities, and emotion. They can transport the listener/observer to another place and time and create an atmosphere of buoyant excitement, as at a rock concert, or mystery, as in a place of worship. Knowledge of ancient music, musical instruments, dance, and song comes from artwork such as reliefs and wall paintings, painted decoration on vessels, applied decoration on vessels, figurines, graffiti, textual references, and artifacts. Some of the earliest depictions of dancing and music-making come from caves, such as those found at Lascaux, France and from Near Eastern prehistoric sites such as Nevali Çori in Turkey, Choga Mami in Iran, and Tall-I Jari A in Egypt (Garfinkel 2003).

Significant evidence for the application of music, song, and dance in Mesopotamia comes from cuneiform tablets, which also mention the use of these in neighboring areas including Anatolia, Canaan, and Persia. In Sumer, music was a "fundamental element of civilization" (Yamauchi and Wilson 2016, Vol. III:421) and an integral component in the royal court, banquets, in temples, during rituals (such as weddings), funerals, military campaigns, in taverns and among the labor force. The Hebrew Bible/Old Testament references to music, song, and dance are numerous; some include Exodus 15:20; Ecclesiastes 3:4; Jeremiah 31:13 (dancing); Genesis 31:27; Exodus 32:18; 1 Chronicles 15:22 (song); 1 Chronicles 25:3; 1 Samuel 18:6; Job 21:12 (instruments) (Yamauchi and Wilson 2016, Vol. III:418–420). In the tomb of Nebamun (Dynasty XVIII), a banqueting scene depicts two dancing girls and female musicians playing wind instruments (Parkinson 2008). At Dra'Abu el-Naga, a painted scene in the tomb of Intef depicts women dressed in calf-length garments, bracelets, and anklets, dancing and striking various movements (Spencer 2003).

Artifactual examples from Mesopotamia include a decorated lyre fragment depicting an eight-stringed bovine lyre (Penn Museum, Object Number B17694A), a silver, boat-shaped harp (Penn Museum, Object Number 30-12-253), and a silver bovine-shaped lyre (British Museum, Number 121199). In addition to lyre, musical instruments included harps, mouth harps, including a recent find in the Altai

Mountains (Liesowska 2018), lutes, psalteries, clappers, scrapers, rattles, cymbals, flutes, oboes, horns, trumpets, and drums (Duchesne-Guillemin 1981; Kilmer 1998; Braun and Stott 2002). Artifactual examples from Egypt include a large flute (British Museum, Number EA6385), clarinet (British Museum, Number AF1972,24.7), an oboe (Penn Museum, Object Number AF98), and an arched harp (British Museum, Number EA38170).

An important component of successful performance is musical notation. Cuneiform tablets evidence hymns (Penn Museum, Object Number B7847), instruction for tuning instruments, such as lyres, instruction for playing and singing hymns (Penn Museum, Object Number B8037), and musical scales. The tablets indicate that in the Old Babylonian Period (ca. 1800 BCE), "there existed standardized tuning procedures that operated within a heptatonic, diatonic system consisting of seven different and interrelated scales" (Kilmer 1998:14). These scales were equivalent with Greek scales, dating ca. 1400 years later, and correspond to the major scale in use today (Kilmer 1998:14). The musical system of Mesopotamia (Sumerian and Babylonian) was known throughout the ancient Near East and Pythagoras noted that the Greeks learned musical theory and mathematics from the Mesopotamians (Kilmer 1998:14).

Painting

Painted decoration in the ancient Near East was found on ceramic vessels, papyrus (in the form of writing), wood, leather, and on walls. However, this section will focus on wall paining, specifically in Egypt. The wall surface was prepared by applying a whitewash of lime plaster for a smooth surface and a mud plaster for a rougher surface. On top of that, a smoother *gesso* layer was applied. Gesso was a white paint consisting of a binder, such as egg or animal protein, mixed with gypsum or chalk. On top of this layer, lines were added to form a straight line or grid for the artists. The gesso could then be moistened to accept the paint. This is known as *fresco a secco*, which created a more stable bond between paint and the canvas. This method of paint and wall preparation was adopted and adapted by the Greeks and Romans, especially by the Romans, as is evidenced at Pompeii and Herculaneum.

Paints in the ancient Near East were made from minerals and materials such as plants or charcoal, which helped achieve a variety of colors. These were crushed and mixed with water and some sort of binder such as egg or animal protein. Because paints were made from minerals, they were long lasting and non-fading. Color was very important because it conveyed information. For example, yellow skin indicated women or middle-aged men who worked inside; red skin denoted vigorous youth and good physical health; blue and gold were reserved for divinity because they were naturally occurring colors, as in the sky and associated with precious materials; and black was reserved for royalty and denoted fertility because it resembled the black mud of the Nile. The color black was made from carbon, from soot taken from burnt plant materials, from charcoal, or scraped from the bottom of cooking vessels. Blue hues were artificially created from a combination of silica, copper, and calcium combined with an alkali such as potash or natron, and copper ore such as malachite (Lee and Quirke 2009:108–109). Blue hues could also be produced from cobalt blue, azurite, and a mixture of calcite, carbon, and iron-titanium mixed with calcium carbonate (Lee and Quirke 2009:111).

Recent studies have shown that Egyptian blue, calcium copper silicate, is one of the oldest known artificial pigments used by humankind. One of the earliest examples of Egyptian blue has been found in a First Dynasty tomb in the region of Ka-Sen (Dhwty 2017). For the Egyptians, the color blue was very important. It was used to depict the sky, the Nile, the heavens, and the universe, and came to represent fertility, creation, life, and rebirth (Dhwty 2017; Brack 2015). The recipe for Egyptian blue included sand, copper (from azurite or malachite), and natron. Discovering and making Egyptian blue was no easy feat and underscores the knowledge and sophistication of Egyptian chemists (Brack 2015). Egyptian blue became extremely popular throughout the Near East and Mediterranean basin and was a valuable commodity. In 2009, it was discovered that Egyptian blue shows near-infrared luminescence (Brack 2015). The luminescent properties of Egyptian blue can be detected even when the color cannot be seen. This is important because works of art, such as the Elgin Marbles, can be illuminated with near-infrared radiation to detect whether Egyptian blue was applied in antiquity but lost to modernity (Brack 2015). Furthermore, the luminescent properties of Egyptian blue can have important modern applications especially when used as a biomedical pigmenting agent or in security inks.

For the color brown, iron oxide or ochre were used. Green came from malachite, though most often from a synthetic material called green frit or from copper chlorides (Lee and Quirke 2009:111–112). Red was made from iron oxides and red ochres. Yellow was made from yellow ochre including iron materials such as goethite, limonite, clay, and some silicon (Lee and Quirke 2009:115). Of course, these are just a few of the colors represented in Egyptian paintings, and the analysis and composition of paints is much more complex than recounted in this short summary. For a more thorough study, see Lee and Quirke (2009). Nevertheless, the point here is that paints were made from a variety of minerals and additives to create a stable substance that was used in artwork.

In the art of communication, color conveyed information to the viewer, such as vitality, divinity, and fertility. Dissemination of information via color remains a useful tool today. Traffic lights across the world tell a driver when to go (green), stop (red), and when to be cautious (yellow).

Weights, measures, and currency

As Mesopotamia, Egypt, and Canaan developed into nation states, their system of weights and measures became standardized. At first, each city-state maintained its own trade guilds and standards of measure. With the Akkadian Empire, Sargon of Akkad (ca. 2334–2279 BCE) established widespread standards, which Naram-Sin improved (ca. 2254–2218 BCE). These standards were generally adopted by their later empires. Egypt devised their own system of weights and measures as early as the early Dynastic Period, ca. 3100 BCE. The Palermo stone, a fragment of a stele that recorded the royal annals of the Old Kingdom from the First Dynasty (ca. 3100–2890 BCE) to the Fifth Dynasty (ca. 2392–2283 BCE), describes measurements such as a finger (ca. 0.74 inches), a palm, which equals four fingers, and a cubit, which equals seven palms. In Mesopotamia, units of length consisted of grain, finger, foot, cubit, step, reed, rod, and cord. Mass was measured as grain, shekel, pound, and load. In Canaan, weight was by talent, mina, shekel, and beqa. Length was by cubit, handbreadth, and fingerbreadth.

Items for sale were weighed and could be traded for other goods or purchased with pieces of silver or other precious metals or stones of equal weight. Balance scales were used to transact the agreement. Standardized weights were used to balance the scales. Weights have been found in Mesopotamia, Egypt, and Canaan, and can be in the shape of round stones or highly stylized and in the shape of animals. Among the most used of the precious metals were bits of silver and gold as currency (Gitin and Golani 2001). These came in the form of rings, earrings, bangles, or small ingots.

Eventually currency was invented. It is thought by most that currency originated in Anatolia during the Iron Age with a people known as the Lydians around 650 BCE. One of the first coins found thus far was made of electrum; it was bean-shaped, and stamped with the lion insignia of King Gyges on one side and marks indicating weight and purity on the other side. Herodotus (*Histories* 1.94) states that Lydia was the first Greek city-state to mint coins. The earliest coins were small blobs that resembled water-smoothed pebbles. They were made from electrum and used in the sixth century BCE by people of western Asia Minor near Sardis and in the Aegean near Athens. These coins made international trade much easier and mark an important pioneering development (Humphrey et al. 2006:486). Strabo (*Geography* 9.6.16) states that silver coins were first used on the island of Aegina by Pheidon because his palace was a center of trade due to poor agriculture (Humphrey et al. 2006:487; Hodges 1992:130–133). Coinage was a natural evolution from ingots and bullae. Coinage introduced standardized units of commerce rather than guessing at equivalent values while bartering.

Coins were manufactured of pure silver by a method known as cupellation, in which impure silver is heated in a furnace or in a crucible using materials (such as lead) to absorb the impurities and extract them from the silver. This created pure silver, from which the coins were made. The purity and weight of the coin had to be guaranteed for exchange. The ability to extract silver and gold had long existed; however, the demand for coinage provided the stimulus for gold and silver refining in unprecedented quantities and high levels of purity. The silver or gold would be fashioned into a die, which was then set onto an anvil, and each side was struck to make a specific imprint, one that was characteristic of the king and his/her kingdom. The obverse side usually contained the likeness or symbols of the king, and the reverse contained other meaningful symbols. Coins remain useful to archaeologists because they aid in dating the archaeo-historical context.

Coinage made use of well-known technology but advanced it to find new ways to purify gold and silver and mass-produce coins. It also advanced the economy by offering standardized values and quantities, which facilitated fairness in the marketplace. Fixed values and weights guaranteed that each person paid the same amount for goods in the market. Coinage also facilitated a leisure class because it enabled fixed and fair payment of services for masons, doctors, artists, actors, and architects, and it paid for a standing, professional military force. Now, instead of being paid in goods, these tradespeople could be paid in currency. Currency also contributed to greater rifts in the social structure. Now, any person could become wealthy, and those who already were wealthy could become more so (Oleson 2008:772–774). The economy shifted from being a subsistence-based market to a cash-based economy, one that we recognize today.

19

SUMMARY AND DISCUSSION

When considering technology, what comes to mind? In light of this work, and the presentation of information about the skills, practices, methods, processes, and technologies of the ancient Near East, it is hoped that the answer to that question does not include electronic or mechanical devices exclusively. According to our working definition, technology is the practical application of knowledge, scientific or otherwise, to solve a problem, achieve a goal, satisfy curiosity, make life easier, or to accomplish change. With this in mind, the peoples of the ancient Near East developed technologies that accomplished all of these without the benefit of electrical devices and systems. To construct the buildings that comprised ancient cities, pulleys, cranes, carpentry, and masonry techniques were devised. Knowledge of materials, mathematics, geometry, and physics aided in the building of those urban centers. These are the obvious technologies that helped shape the ancient world. Numerous less obvious technologies also had an impact on the advancement of humankind, including information sharing, economics, an organized labor force, writing, textiles, food systems, transportation, and items for daily use, such as soap. All of these technologies, large and small, active and passive, visible and invisible contributed to the development of the vibrant cultures and societies of the ancient Near East, and continue to do so today.

It is important to note that the machines, devices, industries, and systems discussed throughout this work were not created in a void. In many instances, the impetus for developing these technologies was due to political, cultural, economic, climatic, and/or religious reasons. The events involving and surrounding the peoples of the ancient Near East shaped them and caused them to be creative to survive. It is equally important to note that technology impacted politics, culture, economy, climate, and religion as well. The relationship between technology, people, events, and social systems is circular, interdependent, and constant.

One of the earliest examples of this relationship is humankind's shift from hunter-gatherer to sedentary agriculturalist. As noted, it is now believed that climate change was a contributing factor to this shift, and as previously available food resources moved or became scarce, humankind was forced to develop new methods of maintaining the food supply and the tools with which to do that. Several times throughout this study, reference has been made to climate change and the effect it has had on humankind, and conversely, the effect humankind has had on climate, or more accurately microclimate. Earth's climate has always experienced large and small cyclical climate changes. Evidence of past climate variations can be found in the geological record in the movement of glaciers, sediment, fossils, and trees. Changes can be detected by analyzing isotopes, pollen, and oxygen, as well as carbon and methane levels. Numerous of these changes occurred prior to human activity.

Before forging ahead, however, it is important to define climate versus weather. The term climate change refers to "any significant change in the measures of climate lasting for an extended period of time ... [which] includes major changes in temperature, precipitation, or wind patterns, among others, that occur over several decades or longer" (United States Environmental Protection Agency, www.epa.gov/climatechange/glossary.html#C, accessed March 2014). Weather is the:

> atmospheric condition at any given time or place. It [can be] measured in terms of such things as wind, temperature, humidity, atmospheric pressure, cloudiness, and precipitation. In most places, weather can change from hour to hour, day to day, and season to season. Climate in a narrow sense is usually defined as the 'average weather', or more rigorously as the statistical description in terms of the mean and variability of relevant quantities over a period of time ranging from months to thousands or millions of years.
>
> *United States Environmental Protection Agency,*
> *www.epa.gov/climatechange/glossary.html#W, accessed March 2014*

Changes to climate can be caused by variations in solar radiation, plate tectonics, volcanic eruptions, biotic processes, and anthropogenic activity. Weather and climate information has been recorded sporadically throughout human history; however, since 1860, the United States has been assiduously recording and accumulating weather-related data, and in 1870, the National Weather Service was established. These data have provided a clearer understanding of weather and climate trends and anomalies. Based on these data, some scientists and scholars have cited anthropogenic activity as the leading factor in climate change. Other scientists collecting data from ancient geological core samples of soil, ice, snow, sea, and lake floors, and archaeological excavation and texts, reveal numerous macro and microclimate changes that may not necessarily be related to anthropogenic activity. It seems that all these data should be integrated and harmonized to reveal when and what climate changes occurred and how anthropogenic activities may or may not have been a contributing factor.

When discussing climate change, it should be borne in mind that the Earth has its own cycles and experiences its own changes irrespective of anthropogenic activity.

For example, the Earth experiences regular cycles that influence warming and cooling trends. Earth's distance from the sun changes over time; every 100,000 years the Earth is farthest from the sun, resulting in a cooling phase. Earth's axial tilt has an approximate 41,000-year cycle, which results in variations in seasons and deviations to the tilt and wobble of the Earth approximately every 23,000 years (Climate, Culture and Catastrophe in the Ancient World, https://web.stanford.edu/~meehan/donnellyr/summary.html. Accessed 26 May 2018). These planetary changes result in cooling and warming trends. As the Earth orbits the sun, its axis remains the same; however, one pole is closer to the sun than the other at various positions in the orbit. Variations in the Earth's axial tilt can result in short seasonal changes or long-term climate changes.

Climate disruptions can also be caused by plate tectonics, commonly known as earthquakes, evidenced by two twenty-first century examples. In 2010, the Nazca and South American tectonic plates caused an earthquake with a magnitude of 8.8 that shook coastal, central Chile. This earthquake was so powerful that it has been determined that Santiago shifted 28 centimeters (11 inches) to the west-southwest, Concepción moved ca. 3 meters (10 feet) to the west, Buenos Aires shifted 3.0 centimeters (1.5 inches) to the west, and it is estimated that Chile's territory expanded by ca. 1.2 kilometers (.46 miles). This earthquake shifted the Earth's axis by 8 centimeters or 2.7 milliarcseconds and may have shortened the length of a day by 1.26 microseconds. In 2011, a 9.0 magnitude earthquake rocked Tóhoku, Japan, and due to the undersea thrust, caused a tsunami. According to the US Geological Survey, the main island of Honshu moved 2.4 meters (8 feet) to the east, and the northern coastline of Honshu dropped 0.6 meters (2 feet). This earthquake caused a shift of Earth's axis between 10 to 25 centimeters (4 to 10 inches). This led to an increase in the Earth's rotation thus causing the day to shorten by 1.8 microseconds due to the redistribution of the Earth's mass (Oskin 2015). Given that seasons change based on the location of the Earth and its axial tilt as it journeys around the sun, these changes to the tilt due to earthquakes would have a lasting effect on Earth's climate.

There are numerous examples in the archaeological record of climate change and the effect it has had on animals and humans, but only a few will be mentioned here: wooly mammoths and rhinos, a warming trend dated to ca. 6200–5600 BCE, Doggerland, and the Greek/Aegean crisis, ca. 2000/1177/1100 BCE.

It is generally understood that throughout Earth's long history, numerous animal species thrived then became extinct. The most obvious examples are dinosaurs (such as triceratops, tyrannosaurus, stegosaurus), very large reptiles that roamed the Earth during the Triassic period (ca. 231.4 million years ago) through the end of the Cretaceous period (ca. 80/66 million years ago). It is thought that the earth was much warmer than it is today; there were no polar ice caps, and sea level was some 100–250 meters (330–820 feet) higher than today. Many believe the extinction of these and other species of large animals was caused by a major event such as volcanic activity, asteroid collision, or gradual change due to Deccan Traps, which, at the end of the Cretaceous period, released volcanic gasses (sufur dioxide) into the atmosphere through volcanic activity, and reduced the Earth's temperature by 2° C.

Examples of climate change that occurred closer to our own time can be observed in the archaeological record. The first is that of the wooly mammoth. The Native Peoples of Siberia have been discovering mummified wooly mammoths for over a hundred years. Wooly mammoths lived during the last ice age 100,000 years ago in the Pleistocene period. Reindeer herders have found the tusks of wooly mammoths protruding from the icy surface and collected them because this ivory is valuable. In 1799, Ossip Schumachov discovered a wooly mammoth mummy and documented it. In 1901, the Berezovka Mammoth was discovered at the Berezovka River. This mammoth was a male, 35 to 40 years of age, and had fallen into a crevasse some 35,000 years ago where he died. In 1929, thirty-four mammoths were found. Other recent discoveries include the following: Dima, found in 1977 at Kilyma River dating to ca. 40,000 years ago; Mascha, found in 1988 on the Yamal Penninsula, aged 3 to 4 months old; the Jarkov Mammoth, found in 1997 in the Taymyr Penninsula, Siberia, Russia; Lyuba, discovered in 2007 in the Yuribei River, a female, 1 month old, who suffocated in the mud when the herd crossed ca. 41,800 years ago; Yuka, discovered in 2012 on the Yaymyr Penninsula, Siberia, approximately 2.5 years of age, showing signs of butchering marks, dates to ca. 30,000 years ago; and finally, Maly, found in 2013 on Lyakhovsky Island, New Siberian Islands, a female, 50 to 60 years of age at the time of her death. Additionally, a wooly rhino named Sasha was found in a frozen riverbank in Siberia. Sasha lived ca. 10,000 years ago and was 3 to 4 years of age. The sex of this wooly rhino remains unclear. S/he was covered by thick fur and had two fist-sized horns.

Thirty to fifteen thousand years ago, the climate in Siberia and Alaska was much milder than it is today. Knowing that woolly mammoths and wooly rhinos mainly ate grasses, sedges, herbaceous plants, flowering plants, and mosses, the contemporaneous terrain must not have been covered with ice and snow the way it is today. Pollen and other traces taken from the fur of these mammoths suggest a much warmer and milder climate than the one with which we are familiar in that region. The mild climate resulted in muddy terrain, rivers, and streams, and sustained flora, which in turn sustained herds of mammoths (see *Woolly Mammoth: Secrets from the Ice* (BBC; YouTube); *Raising the Mammoth* (Discovery Channel; YouTube); *Land of the Mammoth* (Discovery Channel; YouTube); Windsor Chorlton, *Woolly Mammoth: Life, Death, and Rediscovery*; www.texomashomepage.com/story/d/story/10000-year-old-remains-of-baby-woolly-rhino-found/50090/YAR03q9nVUebxKRpYcJxsw).

A second example comes from the Mediterranean basin. According to research conducted by Ryan and Pitman (2000), a warming trend caused a rapid rise in sea levels, thus displacing peoples living along the water's edge. Intrigued by the flood stories of various Near Eastern people-groups (Sumerians, Babylonians, Assyrians, Egyptians, Canaanites/Israelites, Greeks, and Romans), Ryan and Pitman wondered if there was any truth to these mythologies. Behind myth and legend, there often lies a kernel of truth. They took core samples from numerous points around the

Mediterranean basin and the Black Sea, and compared core data to archaeological data from sites such as Tell Abu Hureyra (Syrian Euphrates), Çatal Hüyük (Turkey), and Jericho (Israel). By way of review, the Younger Dryas, also known as the Big Freeze, occurred ca. 12,900 to 11,700 BP (ca. 10,800–9500 BCE), which brought cold climatic conditions and drought, after which there was a rapid return to warmer conditions in higher latitudes. Sedentary settlements of the Natufians (in Israel) occurred ca. 12,500–9500 BCE and were established during a post-glacial warming period; however, during the deterioration of the climate of the Younger Dryas, the Natufian diet changed abruptly and drastically because their food sources changed. Food resources favoring a warmer, wetter climate retreated in the drier, colder climate of the Younger Dryas. The Natufian culture collapsed, and settlements were abandoned at the height of the Younger Dryas. The level of the Dead Sea dropped by hundreds of feet. Sea level and river levels dropped. Food resources became scarce and people adapted to very difficult living conditions. The aridity of the Younger Dryas happened rapidly, probably within ten to fifty years, based on archaeological remains, soil and core samples, and water levels.

Equally rapid change from a dry, arid, cold climate to a wet and warm climate happened at the end of the Younger Dryas, which led to a rise in water levels and a restoration of flora and fauna. This was followed by a second Mini Ice Age, ca. 6200–5800 BCE, which has been confirmed by glaciologists measuring methane levels and oxygen isotopes in tiny bubbles of fossil air from the ice. This event caused the drying up of water resources (the Black Sea was some 400 feet below its "normal" level), an average temperature drop of ca. 8°, the disappearance of food resources, and massive migrations as evidenced by the abandonment of settlements. Neolithic people moved closer to water resources, such as the Black Sea, and began farming and animal husbandry to compensate for lack of wild resources. At around 5800 BCE there was a warming trend; snow and ice melted, rains returned, and water levels rose. Some waterside settlements were abandoned because of rising water levels. At approximately 5600 BCE, water levels rose substantially and rapidly, coming right up to the upper levels of the Bosporus. The sea level of the Mediterranean (Aegean) may have reached some 500 feet above the level of the Black Sea. The raging waters and pressure from the rapidly rising Mediterranean Sea caused the Bosporus to collapse, allowing very rapidly moving water to rush into the Black Sea, causing it to rise some 6 inches per day and creating a Niagara Falls-like effect over the Bosporus. Data from the core samplings provide the evidence for this scenario. Based on their research, Ryan and Pitman suggest this may provide the kernel of truth which inspired the ancient Near Eastern flood stories. Peoples living on or near the shores of the Mediterranean and the Black Sea would have had to abruptly flee their homes and relocate, and they carried with them their experience, which may have become the subject of family legends (Ryan and Pitman 2000).

Although some of Ryan and Pitman's conclusions are debated, recent evidence of submerged cities has come to light, supporting an abrupt rise in sea level in the Neolithic Period. A submerged village, Atlit Yam, has been found off the coast of Haifa, Israel. This Neolithic village dates to ca. 6900–6300 BCE, is submerged under

8–12 meters (26–39 feet) of seawater, and is estimated to have covered ca. 40,000 square meters (47,800 square yards). Underwater excavations have thus far yielded a water well and rectangular domestic dwellings. This village is thought to have been submerged by the rise in sea level at the end of the last ice age; also, the contemporaneous coastline was ca. 1 kilometer (0.6 miles) west of today's coastline (Israel Antiquities Authority, www.antiquities.org.il/article_eng.aspx?sec_id=14&subj_id=139). Evidence for Neolithic villages on the shores of the Black Sea, now submerged, has also been discovered. R. Ballard and his team discovered the remains of buildings and stone tools (Krause 2000), and further research based on Ryan and Pitman's theory has shown that a substantial and rapid rise in sea level changed the coastline and displaced numerous Neolithic peoples (Yanko-Hombach et al. 2007). Similar research has been conducted and hypotheses suggested supporting a comparable scenario for the Persian Gulf region (Rose 2010; Bryner 2010).

Another example is that of Doggerland, which resides under the North Sea. Doggerland was the landed area between the east coast of Britain, coastal Netherlands, the northern coast of Germany, northern Scotland, Denmark, and the Channel Islands. Fishermen have dredged up artifacts in their nets and on hooks for decades. These artifacts date to between 18,000 and 5500 BCE from the Mesolithic period to the Holocene period. Research conducted by Dr. Richard Bates, St. Andrews University, in collaboration with the Universities of Aberdeen, Birmingham, Dundee, and Wales Trinity St. David, and in collaboration with the oil companies who work the area, have surveyed and mapped the submerged area. This survey has enabled them to build a model of the flora and fauna and ancient people who once lived there, and establish a timeline of the dramatic events that changed the land, including sea level rise and a tsunami. The artifacts recovered from this area include flint blades and tools, standing stones, and tree stumps. Faunal remains of the animals that roamed the land include wooly mammoth, lion, hippo, hyena, forest elephant, boar, and red deer, to name a few. Sediment samplings reveal lush vegetation. It is estimated that approximately 20,000–18,000 years ago, sea level was ca. 120 meters (ca. 390 feet) below what it is today. Based on these data it can be said that Doggerland was lush and fertile, and boasted "gently sloping hills, marshland, heavily wooded valleys, and swampy lagoons" (Kessler 2012). Those who lived there were likely hunter-gatherers occupying the shores seasonally to exploit sea creatures and other flora and fauna. As the ice and snow melted due to the warming discussed earlier, the rising sea level also affected those living in the area referred to as Doggerland. Then sometime between 6500–5800 BCE, the sea rose 1 meter over the course of a decade, 100 times faster than it is rising today, and as it rose, the hills and mountains became an archipelago of low-lying islands as we know them today. Possibly initiated by a tsunami, those inhabiting Doggerland were abruptly forced to move elsewhere, leaving behind some of their belongings (Spinney 2012; Kessler 2012, *Mail Online*, www.dailymail.co.uk/sciencetech/article-2167731/Britains-Atlantis-North-sea—huge-undersea-kingdom-swamped-tsunami-5-500-years-ago.html; BBC, www.bbc.com/news/uk-scotland-edinburgh-east-fife-18687504; Flemming 2004; Gaffney et al. 2007; Video: Time

Team Special 31 (2007)—*Britain's Drowned World*, YouTube: www.youtube.com/watch?v=4P9wQj6qX2I).

The Greek/Aegean crisis of ca. 1200–1177 BCE serves as a fourth example of climate change and its impact on humankind (Cline 2014). Around 1200–1177 BCE (the exact dates remain a matter of discussion), the Mediterranean basin experienced economic decline and a massive movement of peoples resulting in what has long been referred to as the Philistine invasion into Egypt and Canaan. Until recently, the reason(s) for the collapse and relocation of peoples has been debated; however, data now suggest the upheaval may have been due to climate change resulting in possible drought, poor crop yields, and overall collapse of the economy. Core samplings and radiocarbon dating of sediment and marine fossils taken from around Larnaca Salt Lake, Cyprus (Enkomi, Hala Sultan Tekke, Kition-Bamboula) reveal that this lake, which is currently landlocked, was once a thriving sea harbor, and a dramatic shift in climate caused the waters to recede and the harbor to dry up. Lush woodlands turned into arid grasslands around ca. 3200 BCE, marking one of the driest periods of the preceding 5000 years in the Mediterranean region (Langgut et al. 2013; Kershner 2013). Data also show that between 1200–800 BCE, the area around Hala Sultan Tekke became drier, and precipitation and groundwater could not maintain agriculture. Corresponding data from across the Mediterranean show that at sites such as Ashdod, on the coast and at Soreq cave, there was an increase of $\delta^{18}O$ (Stable Oxygen isotope; used as a measure of precipitation) and decreased precipitation at Tell Breda, Ras el-Ain at the Dead Sea, reduced Nile and Tigris and Euphrates floods, and a dry event in Syria. These data confirm a major climate event for the region (Kaniewski et al. 2013; Langgut et al. 2013).

Ancient texts describe crop failures, drought, famines, and invasions, all of which correspond to ca. 1200 BCE, triggering the collapse of the Late Bronze Age civilizations. Archaeologically, many settlements saw a tremendous population loss or were abandoned altogether. It is now thought that these climatic events sparked the mass movement of Aegean peoples (and/or peoples originating from Sicily, Sardinia, Italy), including the "invasion" of the Sea Peoples comprised of tribes whose names include Sherden (Shardana), Shekelesh, Teresh, Denyen, Peleset, Tjeker, and Lukka, but who are also collectively known as the Philistines. The north exterior wall of Medinet Habu, the mortuary temple of Ramesses III, recounts from his perspective the arrival of the Sea Peoples in Egypt by sea and land. These vivid reliefs describe how the Sea Peoples were stopped, repelled, and eventually resettled in southern Canaan, where archaeological excavation has confirmed the establishment of Philistine migrants and their eventual assimilation into the culture of their new homeland. Sites such as Ashkelon, Ashdod, Tel Miqne Ekron, Gaza, and Tel es-Safi (Gath) have revealed Philistine settlement in the form of architecture, pottery, and material culture through archaeological investigation. Most consider the arrival of these peoples as a forceful invasion, interpreting the Medinet Habu reliefs in support of a hostile invasion scenario, further supported by what appears to be destruction at some sites in the archaeological record. Others have suggested that while there does appear to have been battle, some scenes depicted in the Medinet Habu reliefs can be interpreted as peaceful migration met with anger and hostility by Egypt and other city-states on the southern Levantine coast. The reliefs appear to illustrate both scenarios. The land and sea scenes depict armor, weapons, ships, and chariots; individuals in close combat; and scenes of captive Sea Peoples being led away. Concurrently, the scenes appear to depict ships' sails rolled up and oars out of the water, and in the land battle scenes, large carts with solid, heavy wheels are depicted carrying supplies, women, and children—behavior that does not seem related to war or resistance against an invading force (Singer-Avitz and Levi 1992; Dothan and Dothan 1992; Cline 2014). Whether the Sea Peoples entered Egypt and the southern Levant as invaders or migrants, the reason for their relocation may be associated with climate changes that affected their economic stability and presumably threatened their survival to such an extent that they chose to relocate to regions known to have somewhat better ecological stability.

Another driving force behind discovery, invention, and innovation is conflict. As humankind became sedentary and urbanized, competition among people became more complex, and new coping mechanisms were devised. For example, city-states developed fortification walls and gates to protect the city and its inhabitants from invading entities who sought control over local resources. These tall, thick fortification structures were made of large and dense stone and earth. To get through, over, and under them, invading armies invented strategies and devices that helped them achieve that goal. Sennacherib's siege of Lachish, as depicted in the friezes on the palace walls at Nineveh, illustrates the ingenuity of the Assyrian army. The armored vehicles allowed assailants to approach the city wall while at the same time protecting them from defenders. Battering rams on the front of the vehicle provided a way to penetrate the city gate and walls. Throughout the history of the world, the stimulus of conflict has driven humankind to invent and innovate technologies that would provide an advantage to warring factions. Even today we are witness to the integration of new technologies into conflict zones. For example, the use of drones in combat situations, though controversial, has become a useful tool.

The interplay between technological development and socio-economic evolution from the Neolithic through the Iron Age is evident. As humankind shifted from hunter-gatherer to sedentary farmer to urban dweller, needs changed. New tools, devices, and methods were needed to aid in the producing and processing of foodstuffs. With the accumulation of food and other resources such as wool, people could engage in non-agrarian professions and sedentary activities, such as weaving and marketing. The accumulation of wealth and non-agrarian tasks created a new, complex society which transformed the way people interacted with one another and lived together in communities in villages and urban centers. Leadership changed from a single clansman or chieftain making decisions to kings with administrations and a public workforce that was in charge of building and maintaining city walls, gates, streets, and public buildings such as palaces and temples. As society grew and became more complex, so did technology, which provided stronger tools, better food production, textiles, transportation, and personal daily items such as soap, perfume, and running water. Other technologies such as timekeeping, writing, and mathematics were useful for knowing when to plant/harvest, maintain business records, and for maintaining awareness of local laws. These early forms of technology helped people achieve a standard of living that honored hard work but at the same time eased the rigors and drudgery of it to a certain extent.

Another period of innovation began around 800 BCE, driven more by human ambition than by climate, starting in Greece and spreading throughout the Mediterranean basin. Early thinkers, referred to as poets and philosophers, though today we would call them engineers, scientists, physicists, and theologians, methodically asked questions about science and scientific method, logic and deductive reasoning, and theology; and through research, experimentation, and invention/innovation, they built upon and advanced knowledge which to them was already ancient. However, with these advances, attitudes toward labor, experimentation, and the trades changed. Prior to the fifth century BCE, hard work was honorable. Craftspeople, laborers, and tradespeople were held in high esteem. This attitude was evident by the laborers chosen to work at the Egyptian mines of Timna, and the status and care that was given to those who worked at the villages of Deir el-Medina, for example. The change in attitude shifted when leisure became the ultimate goal. Manual labor, manufacturing, and the skilled crafts were no longer held in high esteem. The goods they produced remained highly valued; however, those who procured the raw materials and crafted the goods were not. Greater emphasis was placed on higher learning, politics, and the military. Sharp divisions in social structure resulted even though philosophers such as Hesiod, Herodotus, and Plutarch attempted to combat these attitudes and divisions in society with logic and wisdom (Humphrey et al. 2006:579–588). Christian writers also attempted to combat this problem by extoling the virtues of good hard work (2 Thessalonians 3:6–10). While technology was beneficial to humankind in terms of making survival easier and even luxurious, it could also have detrimental effects to certain elements of society.

It is important to note that the discovery, development, and innovation of various technologies, especially those that have been discussed in this work, were not linear. In other words, technological development was not a steady forward-moving progression. Rather, it was one step forward, one or two steps backward, or even stagnation. For example, the Baghdad battery, which may have been a galvanic cell, representing knowledge of electro-chemistry, had no obvious use or none that can be detected in the archaeological record thus far. Without any real need or use for electricity, or any clear application for a battery, this technology was set aside and not rediscovered and developed until much later. Furthermore, inasmuch as historic, political, and socioeconomic events could stimulate technological development, they could also hinder it. For example, with the fall of the Western Roman Empire, the development of Eastern and Western Europe, and the Eastern Roman Empire struggling to survive, the development of technology (and science) stagnated.

Finally, we are brought to the question of why we should study the technology of the ancient world. After all, doesn't "ancient" imply obsolete? Or, is it possible to apply that which has been learned about technology and science from ancient peoples to modern civilization? When this question is posed to students in a twenty-first century classroom, it is met with audible giggles and much squirming, usually because the question seems to imply relinquishing modern conveniences. However, when reminded that numerous ancient societies lived in relative luxury, the conversation begins. Some ancient technologies could be adopted and adapted, which could maintain our current standard of living and better utilize our resources. For example, water collection systems from roofs could make use of rainwater. Water filtration systems using bio-filter systems, slow-sand filtration, and similar systems could turn filthy water into usable water, especially in rural settings. Such filtration systems already exist and have been employed in cities such as the Living Machine system (www.livingmachines.com/Home.aspx), which uses plants and beneficial bacteria to efficiently and effectively treat and reuse water. The water systems found in Jerusalem, Megiddo, and Sepphoris made use of the natural rock to purify the water. The Romans used similar systems in the aqueducts, which added collection and settlement tanks. Slow-sand filtration systems were used to purify water in the nineteenth century CE in London by John Gibb of Paisley, Scotland. This system was so effective and inexpensive to implement that, by 1852, this was the standard water purification technique, and the Metropolis Water Act required that all water taken from the River Thames within 5 miles of St. Paul's Cathedral be filtered in this manner before distributing it to the public. Another way to employ an ancient technique could be in the way homes are heated and cooled. Homes could be oriented to utilize wind in the summer months and make use of the sun's warmth in the winter months. In warmer climates, ceilings could be higher so that hot air rises and cool air falls; windows could be made bigger; the interior layout could make use of cross ventilation. In this way in temperate months, mechanical air heating/conditioning systems could be turned off, windows opened, and homes could make use of Mother Nature's natural air conditioning. From experience, this saves several hundred dollars for at least three months of the year in South Florida.

Much of what we know today is based on that which was learned millennia ago. By understanding the ancient past, we can better know ourselves and the world in which we live, and, in so doing, we will make better decisions about the future. As humankind moves forward, faced with a continuously changing natural world and developing societies and cultures, perhaps some of the technologies from the ancient past will prove useful in helping us to better utilize natural resources and become better stewards of them. Humankind was and is inventive, innovative, and relentless in its pursuit of achievement. Modern peoples can learn from the successes and failures of ancient peoples. Their achievements can serve as motivation for the future. Let us be inspired by all that they accomplished through ingenuity, perseverance, and intelligence as we pursue new ways to employ ancient ideas.

BIBLIOGRAPHY

AERA. (2016). Ancient Egypt Research Associates. www.aeraweb.org/.

Aharoni, Y. (1993). Arad. In E. Stern (ed.), *The New Encyclopedia of Archaeological Excavations in the Holy Land*. Vol. 1. Jerusalem: The Israel Exploration Society. Pp. 75–86.

Aharoni, Y. and M. Avi-Yonah. (1977). *The MacMillan Bible Atlas*. Revised edition. New York: Macmillan Publishing Co., Inc. and London: Collier MacMillan Publishers.

Ahnert, P. (2015). *Beeswax Alchemy. How to Make Your Own Candles, Soap, Balms, Salves, and Home Décor from the Hive*. Beverly, MA: Quarry Books.

Albenda, P. (1985). Mirrors in the Ancient Near East. *Notes in the History of Art*, Vol. 4, No. 2/3 (Winter/Spring), pp. 2–9.

Al-Jadir, W. (1998). XXXIVème Rencontre Assyriologique Internationale 6–10. VII. 1987 Istanbul = XXXIV. Uluslararası Assıryolojı Kongresi 6–10. VII. 1987 Istanbul = XXXIV. International Assyriology Congress 6–10. VII. 1987 Istanbul. Ankara: Türk Tarih Kurumu.

Amarna Project. (2000). The McDonald Institute for Archaeological Research. University of Cambridge. www.amarnaproject.com/index.shtml.

Ancient Arts (2012). *Prehistoric Copper Smelting in a Pit!* Ancient Arts. *Experimental Archaeology*. www.ancient-arts.org. www.youtube.com/watch?v=8uHc4Hirexc.

Ancient-Arts.org. (2013). Prehistoric Copper Smelting in a Pit! www.youtube.com/watch?v=SMeqwJFqGgU. Accessed 6 October 2017.

Ancient Discoveries. (2008a). *Ancient Mining Machines*. Season 5, Episode 5. 20 November 2008. www.youtube.com/watch?v=dsU0E48vX1s. Accessed 4 May 2018.

Ancient Discoveries. (2008b). *Ancient Special Forces*. Season 6, Episode 8.

Anderson, W. P. (1987). The Kiln and Workshops of Sarepta. *Berytus*, Vol. 35, pp. 41–66.

Angier, B. (1998). *Field Guide to Edible Wild Plants*. Mechanicsburg, PA: Stackpole Books.

Arnold, D. (1991). *Building in Egypt. Pharaonic Stone Masonry*. Oxford; New York: Oxford University Press.

Arnold, D. and J. D. Bourriau (eds.). (1993). *An Introduction to Ancient Egyptian Pottery. Fascicle 1. Techniques and Traditions of Manufacture in the Pottery of Ancient Egypt*. Mainz: Verlag Phillip von Zabern.

Aronol, D. (2014). Archaeological Institute of America. *Archaeology*. Early Human Ancestors Benefited from Fermenting Fruit. www.archaeology.org/news/2746-141202-fermentation-digestion-alcohol. Accessed 17 December 2014.

Aston, B. G., J. A. Harrell, and I. Shaw. (2000). Stone. In P. T. Nicholson and I. Shaw (eds.), *Ancient Egyptian Materials and Technology*. First edition. Cambridge, UK: Cambridge University Press. Pp. 5–77.

Aubet, M. E. (2001). *The Phoenicians and the West Politics, Colonies, and Trade*. Second edition. Cambridge, UK: Cambridge University Press.

Badler, V. R., P. E. McGovern, and R. H. Michel. (1990). Drink and Be Merry! Infrared Spectroscopy and Ancient Near Eastern Wine. In W. R. Beers and P. E. McGovern (eds.), *Organic Contents of Ancient Vessels. Materials Analysis and Archaeological Investigation. Vol. 7*. MASCA Research Papers in Science and Archaeology. Philadelphia, PA: University of Pennsylvania Press. Pp. 25–36.

Baker, J. L. (2012). *The Funeral Kit. Mortuary Practices in the Archaeological Record*. Walnut Creek, CA: Left Coast Press, Inc.

Bar-Adon, P. (1980). *The Cave of the Treasure. The Finds from the Caves in Nahal Mishmar*. Jerusalem: The Israel Exploration Society.

Barber, E. J. W. (1991). *Prehistoric Textiles*. Princeton: Princeton University Press.

Bar-Yosef, O. (1992). Building Activities in the Prehistoric Periods until the End of the Neolithic Period. In A. Kempinski and R. Reich (eds.), *The Architecture of Ancient Israel. From the Prehistoric to the Persian Periods*. Jerusalem: Israel Exploration Society. Pp. 31–39.

Bar-Yosef, O. (1998). The Natufian Culture in the Levant. Threshold to the Origins of Agriculture. *Evolutionary Anthropology*, Vol. 6, No. 5, pp. 159–177. DOI: 10.1002/(SICI)1520-6505(1998)6:5<159::AID-EVAN4>3.0.CO;2-7.

Beauchemin, M. (2016). We Tried It: Licorice "Chew Sticks" for Glowing White Teeth. *Garden Collage Magazine*. May 10, 2016. https://gardencollage.com/heal/botanical-medicine/tried-licorice-chew-sticks-glowing-white-teeth/. Accessed 18 October 2017.

Bedal, L. (2004). *The Petra Pool-Complex*. Gorgias Dissertations 7. Near Eastern Studies 5. Piscataway, NJ: Gorgias Press.

Beebe, H. K. (1968). Ancient Palestinian Dwellings. *The Biblical Archaeologist*, Vol. 31, No. 2, pp. 37–58.

Beitzel, B. J. (2005). Geography of the Levant. In S. Richard (ed.), *Near Eastern Archaeology. A Reader*. Winona Lake: Eisenbrauns. Second Printing. Pp. 3–9.

Bellwood, P. (2005). *First Farmers. The Origin of agricultural societies*. Victoria, Australia: Blackwell Publishing.

Ben-Dov, M. (1992). Middle and Late Bronze Age Dwellings. In A. Kempinski and R. Reich (eds.), *The Architecture of Ancient Israel. From the Prehistoric to the Persian Periods*. Jerusalem: Israel Exploration Society. Pp. 99–104.

Bentley, P. K. (1999). *Ancient Siege Warfare*. Bloomington, IN; Indianapolis, IN: Indiana University Press.

Ben-Tor, A. (1992). Early Bronze Age Dwellings and Installations. In A. Kempinski and R. Reich (eds.), *The Architecture of Ancient Israel. From the Prehistoric to the Persian Periods*. Jerusalem: Israel Exploration Society. Pp. 31–39.

Bhanoo, S. (2012). Remnants of an Ancient Kitchen are Found in China. *The New York Times*. 29 June 2012. www.nytimes.com/2012/07/03/science/oldest-known-pottery-found-in-china.html. Accessed 30 April 2018.

Biggs, R. D. (1995). Medicine, Surgery, and Public Health in Ancient Mesopotamia. In J. M. Sasson (ed.), *Civilizations of the Ancient Near East. Vol. III*. New York: Charles Scribner's Sons. Pp. 1911–1924.

Bilkadi, Z. (1984). Bitumen—A History. *Aramco World*. November/December, Vol. 35, No. 6, pp. 2–9. www.saudiaramcoworld.com/issue/198406/bitumen.-.a.history.htm. Accessed 7 July 2015.

Bilton, R. (2014). Apple "failing to protect Chinese factory workers". *BBC Business News*. 18 December 2014. www.bbc.com/news/business-30532463. Accessed 23 June 2015.

Binder, M., J. Eitler, J. Deutschmann, et al. (2016). Prosthetics in Antiquity—An Early Medieval Wearer of a Foot Prosthesis (6th century AD) from Hammabert/Austria. *International Journal of Paleopathology*, Vol. 12, No. 2016, pp. 29–40. DOI: 10.1016/j.ijpp.2015.11.003.

Bishop, M. C. and J. C. N. Coulston. (2016, second ed., reprinted). *Roman Military Equipment From the Punic Wars to the Fall of Rome*. Oxford: Oxbow Books.

Blackman, D. J. (1996). Further Evidence for the Use of Concrete in Ancient Harbor Construction. In A. Raban and K. G. Holum (eds.), *Caesarea Maritima A Retrospective after Two Millennia*. Leiden-New York-Köln: E. J. Brill. Pp. 41–52.

Blakely, S. W. (2015). Reinventing the Egyptian Pulley. www.egyptianpulley.com/. Accessed 7 October 2017.

Blakely, S. W. and G. Blakely. (2014). Reinventing the Egyptian Pulley. *Experimental Archaeology*. Issue 2014/3. https://exarc.net/issue-2014-3/ea/reinventing-egyptian-pulley. Accessed 7 October 2017.

Bleiberg, E. (1995). The Economy of Egypt. In J. M. Sasson (ed.), *Civilizations of the Ancient Near East. Vol. 3*. New York: Charles Scribner's Sons. Pp. 1373–1385.

Bonacossi, D. M. (2014). Early Bronze Age Storage Techniques at Mishrifeh, Central-Western Syria. In L. Milano (ed.), *Paleonutrition and Food Practices in the Ancient Near East. Towards a Multidisciplinary Approach*. History of the Ancient Near East/Monographs—XIV. S.A.R.G.O.N. Padova: S.A.R.G.O.N. Editrice e Libreria. Pp. 237–251.

Bonani, G., S. D. Ivy, I. Hajdas, et al. (1994). AMS [14]C Age Determinations of Tissue, Bone and Grass Samples from the Ötzal Ice Man. *Radiocarbon*, Vol. 36, No. 2, pp. 247–250.

BonFante, L. (1986). *Etruscan Life and Afterlife. A Handbook of Etruscan Studies*. Detroit: Wayne State University Press.

Booth, C. (2005). *The Hyksos Period in Egypt*. Buckinghamshire: Shire Publications, Ltd.

Botta, P. E. and E. Flandin. (1849). *Monument de Ninive. Tome 1 Architecture et Sculpture*. Paris: Imprimerie Nationale.

Bottéro, J. (1985). The Cuisine of Ancient Mesopotamia. *The Biblical Archaeologist*, Vol. 48, No. 1, pp. 36–47.

Boutin, A. T. and B. Porter. (2014). Commemorating Disability in Early Dilmun: Ancient and Contemporary Tales from the Peter B. Cornwall Collection. In B. W. Porter and A. T. Boutin (eds.), *Remembering the Dead in the Ancient Near East. Recent Contributions from Bioarchaeology and Mortuary Archaeology*. Boulder: University Press of Colorado. Pp. 97–132.

Brack, P. (2015). Egyptian Blue: more than just a colour. *Chemistry World*. www.chemistryworld.com/feature/egyptian-blue-more-than-just-a-colour/9001.article. Accessed 16 June 2017.

Brack-Bernsen, L. (1999). Goal-Year Tablets: Lunar Data and Predictions. In N. M. Swerdlow (ed.), *Ancient Astronomy and Celestial Divination*. Dibner Institute Studies in the History of Science and Technology. Cambridge, MA; London: The MIT Press. Pp. 149–178.

Brack-Bernsen, L. (2002). Predictions of Lunar Phenomena in Babylonian Astronomy. In J. M. Steele and A. Imhausen (eds.), *Under One Sky. Astronomy and Mathematics in the Ancient Near East*. Alter Orient und Altes Testament. Veröfentlichungen zur Kultur und Geschichte des Alten Orients und des Alten Testaments. Band 297. Munster: Ugarit-Verlag. Pp. 5–20.

Brandon, C. (1996). Cements, Concrete, and Settling Barges at Sebastos: Comparisons with Other Roman Harbor Examples and the Descriptions of Vitruvius. In A. Raban and K. G. Holum (eds.), *Caesarea Maritima A Retrospective after Two Millennia*. Leiden; New York; Köln: E. J. Brill. Pp. 25–40.

Braun, J. and D. W. Stott (translator). (2002). *Music in Ancient Israel/Palestine: Archaeological, Written and Comparative Sources.* Bible in its World. Wm. B. Eerdmans Publishing Co.

Breniquet, C. (2013). The Archaeology of Wool in Early Mesopotamia: Sources, Methods, Perspectives. In C. Breniquet and C. Michel (eds.), *Wool Economy in the Ancient Near East and the Aegean. From the Beginnings of Sheep Husbandry to Institutional Textile Industry.* Oxford: Oxbow Books. Pp. 52–78.

Breniquet, C. and C. Michel, (eds.), (2013). *Wool Economy in the Ancient Near East and the Aegean. From the Beginnings of Sheep Husbandry to Institutional Textile Industry.* Oxford; Philadelphia, PA: Oxbow Books.

Brewer, D. (2002). Hunting, Animal Husbandry and Diet in Ancient Egypt. In B. J. Collins (ed.), *A History of the Animal World in the Ancient Near East. Vol. 64.* Handbook of Oriental Studies. Section One. The Near and Middle East. Leiden; Boston; Köln: Brill. Pp. 427–456.

Brewer, D. J., D. B. Redford, and S. Redford. (1994). *Domestic Plants and Animals: The Egyptian Origins.* Warminster: Aris & Phillips, LTD.

British Museum, Mesopotamian Astronomy. www.mesopotamia.co.uk/astronomer/story/sto_set.html. Accessed on 27 May 2015.

Britton, J. P. (2002). Treatments of Annual Phenomena in Cuneiform Sources. In J. M. Steele and A. Imhausen (eds.), *Under One Sky. Astronomy and Mathematics in the Ancient Near East.* Alter Orient und Altes Testament. Veröfentlichungen zur Kultur und Geschichte des Alten Orients und des Alten Testaments. Band 297. Munster: Ugarit-Verlag. Pp. 21–78.

Brock, J. (2005). Who Were the First Surveyors? Four Surveyors of the Gods: In the XVIII Dynasty of Egypt—New Kingdom c. 1400 B.C. *Fédération Internationale des Géométres.* Article of the Month March 2005. www.fig.net/pub/monthly_articles/march_2005/brock_march_2005.pdf. Accessed 16 May 2016.

Brothwell, D. and P. Brothwell. (1998). *Food in Antiquity. A Survey of the Diet of Early Peoples. Expanded Edition.* Baltimore: Johns Hopkins University Press. Original printing 1969.

Brown, S. (1991). *Late Carthaginian Child Sacrifice and Sacrificial Monuments in their Mediterranean Context.* Sheffield: Sheffield Academic Press.

Bruce, D. (2014). *Rethinking Ancient Near East Chronology: Using A New Hebrew Kings Chronology to Re-Align the Histories of Egypt, Assyria, Babylon and Urartu (Van).* CreateSpace Independent Publishing Platform.

Bryner, J. (2010). Lost Civilization May Have Existed Beneath the Persian Gulf. *LiveScience.* December 9, 2010 05:56 a.m. ET. www.livescience.com/10340-lost-civilization-existed-beneath-persian-gulf.html. Accessed 17 June 2016.

Bryner, J. (2013a). Ancient Egyptian Sundial Discovered at Valley of the Kings. *LiveScience.* www.livescience.com/28057-ancient-egyptian-sundial-discovered.html. Accessed 1 June 2015.

Bryner, J. (2013b). Jerusalem's Ancient "City of Quarries" Reveals City-Building Rocks. *LiveScience.* www.livescience.com/29452-second-temple-quarry-uncovered.html. Accessed 23 August 2017.

Buck, B. A. (1982). Ancient Technology in Contemporary Surgery. *The Western Journal of Medicine,* Vol. 136, No. 3, pp. 99–122, 265–269.

Bullough, V. L. (2001). *Encyclopedia of Birth Control.* Santa Barbara, CA: ABC-CLIO, Inc.

Cable, K. (2017). *The Natural Soapmaking Book for Beginners. Do-It-Yourself Soaps Using All-Natural Herbs, Spices and Essential Oils.* Berkeley, CA: Althea Press.

Caneva, I. (2014). Food as Material Culture at Prehistoric Mersin. In L. Milano (ed.), *Paleonutrition and Food Practice in the Ancient Near East. Towards a Multidisciplinary Approach.* History of the Ancient Near East/Monographs IV. S.A.R.G.O.N. Editrice e Libreria. Padova. Pp. 71–84.

Cantarella, E. (2002). *Bisexuality in the Ancient World*. Second edition. New Haven; London: Yale Nota Bene, Yale University Press.

Carpino, A. (2008). Reflections from the Tomb: Mirrors as Grave Goods in Late Classical and Hellenistic Tarquinia. *Etruscan Studies. Journal of the Etruscan Foundation*, Vol. 11, No. 1, pp. 1–34.

Casey, N. (2016). Venezuelans Ransack Stores as Hunger Grips the Nation. *New York Times*. June 19, 2016. www.nytimes.com/2016/06/20/world/americas/venezuelans-ransack-stores-as-hunger-stalks-crumbling-nation.html?hp&action=click&pgtype=Homepage&clickSource=story-heading&module=second-column-region&region=top-news&WT.nav=top-news&_r=0.

Casson, L. (1995). *Ships and Seamanship in the Ancient World*. Reprinted from 1971. Princeton: Princeton University Press.

Catchpoole, D. (2014). A Tale of Ancient Toothpaste. Creation Ministries International. http://creation.com/a-tale-of-ancient-toothpaste. Accessed 25 April 2015.

Chaban, M. A. V. (2015). Cannabiso Construction: Entrepreneurs Use Hemp in House Building. *The New York Times*. www.nytimes.com/2015/07/07/nyregion/cannabis-construction-entrepreneurs-use-hemp-in-home-building.html?hp&action=click&pgtype=Homepage&module=mini-moth&region=top-stories-below&WT.nav=top-stories-below&_r=0. Accessed 6 July 2015.

Charland, C. (2013) "Visions" Photograph. *National Geographic*, September, p. 10.

Cheung, I. (2010). 10 Ancient Methods of Birth Control. *LISTVERSE*. November 14, 2010. http://listverse.com/2010/11/14/10-ancient-methods-of-birth-control/. Accessed 24 April 2015.

Choi, C. Q. (2007). World's First Prosthetic: Egyptian Mummy's Fake Toe. *LiveScience*. www.livescience.com/4555-world-prosthetic-egyptian-mummy-fake-toe.html. Accessed on 30 May 2015.

Clark, G. A. and N. R. Coinman. (2005). The Paleolithic in Syria-Palestine. In S. Richard (ed.), *Near Eastern Archaeology. A Reader*. Eisenbrauns: Winona Lake, IN. Pp. 233–243.

Clausewitz, C. Von. (1832). *On War*. Princeton, NJ: Princeton University Press.

Cline, E. H. (2014). *1177 B.C. The Year Civilization Collapsed*. Princeton, NJ; Oxford: Princeton University Press.

Cohen, M. N. (1985). Prehistoric Hunter-Gatherers: The Meaning of Social Complexity. In T. D. Price and J. A. Brown (eds.), *Prehistoric Hunter-Gatherers. The Emergence of Cultural Complexity*. Studies in Archaeology. New York: Academic Press. Pp. 99–122.

Cohen, R. (1992). Architecture in the Intermediate Early Bronze/Middle Bronze Period. In A. Kempinski and R. Reich (eds.), *The Architecture of Ancient Israel. From the Prehistoric to the Persian Periods*. Jerusalem: Israel Exploration Society. Pp. 85–90.

Cohen, S. (2002). *Canaanites, Chronologies, and Connections: The Relationship of Middle Bronze Age IIA Canaan to Middle Kingdom Egypt*. Studies in the History and Archaeology of the Levant 3. Winona Lake, IN: Eisenbrauns and Harvard Semitic Museum Publications.

Cohen, S. (2015). Interpretive Uses and Abuses of the Beni Hasan Tomb Painting. *Journal of Near Eastern Studies*, Vol. 74, No. 1. pp. 19–38. DOI: 10.1086/679590.

Cohen, S. (2016). *Peripheral Concerns. Urban Development in the Bronze Age Southern Levant*. Sheffield; Bristol, CT: Equinox Publishing Ltd.

Collon, D. (1995). Clothing and Grooming in Ancient Western Asia. In J. M. Sasson (ed.), *Civilizations of the Ancient Near East. Vol. I*. New York: Charles Scribner's Sons. Pp. 503–516.

Conan, J. (1999). Use and Trade of Bitumen in Antiquity and Prehistory: Molecular Archaeology Reveals Secrets of Past Civilizations. *The Royal Society*, Vol. 354, No. 1379, pp. 33–50.

Connolly, P. (1989). The Roman Army in the Age of Polybius. In J. Hackett (ed.), *Warfare in the Ancient World*. New York; Oxford; Sydney: Facts on File. Pp. 149–168.

Corrigan, W. J. (1932). Sanitation Under the Ancient Minoan Civilization. *The Canadian Medical Journal*, (July) Vol. 27, No. 1, pp. 77–78.

Crane, E. E. (1999). *The World History of Beekeeping and Honey Hunting*. New York and Abingdon, Oxen: Routledge.

Crubézy, E. and E. Trinkaus. (1992). Shanidar 1: A Case of Hyperostotic Disease (DISH) in the Middle Paleolithic. *American Journal of Physical Anthropology*, Vol. 89, No. 4, pp. 411–420.

Curtis, R. I. (2001). *Ancient Food Technology*. Leiden: Brill.

Czerniak, L., M. Kwiatkowska, A. Marciniak, and J. Pyzel. (2001). Çatal Höyük 2001 Archive Report. The Excavations of the TP (Team Poznan) Area in the 2001 Season. www.catalhoyuk.com/archive_reports/2001/ar01_04.html. Accessed 8 December 2014.

Dalley, S. (2013). *The Mystery of the Hanging Garden of Babylon. An Elusive World Wonder Traced*. Oxford: Oxford University Press.

Davison, C. St. C. (1961). Transporting 60 Ton Statues in Early Assyria and Egypt. *Technology and Culture*, Vol. 2/1, pp. 11–16.

De Feo, G., G. P. Antoniou, L. W. Mays, et al. (2014). Chapter 9. Historical Development of Wastewater Management. In S. Eslamian (ed.), *Handbook of Engineering Hydrology. Environmental Hydrology and Water Management*. Boca Raton; London; New York: CRC Press, Taylor & Francis Group. Pp. 163–218.

De Garis Davies, N. (1901). *The Rock Tombs of Sheikh Saïd*. Archaeological Survey of Egypt. London: Egypt Exploration Fund.

De Garis Davies, N. (1917). *The Tomb of Nakht at Thebes*. New York: The Metropolitan Museum of Art.

DeMello, M. (2014). *Inked: Tattoos and Body Art Around the World. Vol. 1: A-L*. Santa Barbara, CA: ABC-CLIO, Inc.

De Melo, W. (2013). *Plautus Stichus. Three-Dollar Day. Truculentus. The Tale of a Traveling-Bag. Fragments*. Loeb Classical Library. LCL 328. Cambridge, MA; London: Harvard University Press.

Depuydt, L. (1997). *Civil and Lunar Calendar in Ancient Egypt*. Leuven: Uitgeveru Peeters en Department of Oosterse Studies.

de Schauensee, M. (2011). Furniture Remains and Furniture Ornaments from the Period IVB Buildings at Hasanlu. In R. H. Dyson, Jr. (gen. ed.), M. de Schauensee (vol. ed.), *Peoples and Crafts in Period IVB at Hasanlu Iran*. Museum Monographs 132. Philadelphia, PA: University of Pennsylvania Museum of Archaeology and Anthropology. Pp. 1–42.

De Solla Price, D. (1974). Gears from the Greeks. The Antikythera Mechanism: A Calendar Computer from ca. 80 B.C. *Transactions of the American Philosophical Society, New Series*, Vol. 64, No. 7, pp. 1–70. DOI: 10.2307/1006146.

Desprat, S., M. Fernanda Sanchez Goni, MF. Loutre, et al. (2003). Revealing Climatic Variability of the Last Three Millennia in Northwestern Iberia Using Pollen Influx Data. *Earth and Planetary Science Letters*, Vol. 213, No. 1–2, pp. 63–78. DOI: 10.1016/S0012-821X(03)00292-9. https://ac-els-cdn-com.access.library.miami.edu/S0012821X03002929/1-s2.0-S0012821X03002929-main.pdf?_tid=2c02e547-6b36-4b31-95f9-68642aa97bbf&acdnat=1525461436_f59099d73376c7584a911d089a56c7df. Accessed 17 June 2016.

Dhwty. (2017). Egyptian Blue—The Oldest Known Artificial Pigment. *Ancient Origins*. www.ancient-origins.net/ancient-technology/egyptian-blue-oldest-artificial-pigment-ever-produced-001745. Assessed 16 June 2017.

Dimand, M. S. (1939). Rugs of the Near East in the Metropolitan Museum of Art. *The Metropolitan Museum of Art Bulletin*, Vol. 34, No. 4, pp. 90–95.

Dorsey, D. A. (1991). *The Roads and Highways of Ancient Israel*. The ASOR Library of Biblical and Near Eastern Archaeology. Baltimore, MD; London: The Johns Hopkins University Press.

Dothan, T. (1979). *Excavations at the Cemetery of Deir El-Balah*. QEDEM Monographs of the Institute of Archaeology The Hebrew University of Jerusalem 10. Jerusalem: Israel Exploration Society.

Dothan, T. and M. Dothan. (1992). *People of the Sea. The Search for the Philistines*. New York: Macmillan Publishing Company.

Draycott, J. (2016). Reconstructing the Lived Experience of Disability in Antiquity: A Case Study from Egypt. *Greece & Rome*, Vol. 62, No. 2, pp. 189–205 DOI: 10.1017/S0017383515000066.

Dredge, M. (2010). The Beer of Yesteryear. *The Guardian.com*. www.theguardian.com/lifeandstyle/wordofmouth/2010/oct/27/old-ale-beer-history. Accessed 17 December 2014.

Duchesne-Guillemin, M. (1981). Music in Ancient Mesopotamia and Egypt. *World Archaeology*, Vol. 12, No. 3, pp. 287–297.

Dunbabin, K. M. D. (2003). *The Roman Banquet. Images of Conviviality*. Cambridge, UK: Cambridge University Press.

Eades, M. R. (2009). Nutrition and health in agriculturalists and hunter-gatherers. *Protein Power*. www.proteinpower.com/drmike/low-carb-diets/nutrition-and-health-in-agriculturalists-and-hunter-gatherers/. 16 December 2014.

Eiland, M. L. and M. Eiland. (1998). *Oriental Rugs: A Complete Guide*. Revised ed. London: Laurence King.

Eitam, D. (1996). The Olive Oil Industry at Tel Miqne—Ekron During the Late Bronze Age. In D. Eitam and M. Heltzer (eds.), *Olive Oil in Antiquity. Israel and Neighbouring Countries from the Neolithic to the Early Arab Period. Vol. VII*. Series: History of the Ancient Near East/Studies. Padova: S.A.R.G.O.N. srl. Pp. 167–196.

El-Aref, N. (2014). Tomb of Chief Beer-Maker Discovered in Egypt's Luxor. *Ahramonline*. Friday, January 3, 2014. http://english.ahram.org.eg/NewsContent/9/40/90724/Heritage/Ancient-Egypt/Tomb-of-chief-beermaker-discovered-in-Egypts-Luxor.aspx. Accessed 19 December 2014.

Ellenblum, R. (2013). *The Collapse of the Eastern Mediterranean. Climate Change and the Decline of the East*. Cambridge, UK: Cambridge University Press. Pp. 950–1072.

Enoch, J. (2006). History of Mirrors Dating Back 8000 Years. *Optometry & Vision Science*, Vol. 83, No. 10, pp. 775–781.

Epstein, C. (1977). The Chalcolithic Culture of the Golan. *The Biblical Archaeologist*, Vol. 40, No. 2, pp. 56–62.

Epstein, C. (1998). The Chalcolithic Culture of the Golan. *IAA Reports, No. 4*. Jerusalem: Israel Antiquity Authority.

Evans, A. (1921). *The Palace of Minos. A Comparative Account of the Successive Stages of the Early Cretan Civilization as Illustrated by the Discoveries at Knossos. Vol. 1. The Neolithic and Early and Middle Minoan Ages*. London: Macmillan and Co., Ltd.

Evans, J. (1998). *The History and Practice of Ancient Astronomy*. New York; Oxford: Oxford University Press.

Fales, F. M. and M. Rigo. (2014). Everyday life and Food Practices in Assyrian Military Encampments. In L. Milano (ed.), *Paleonutrition and Food Practice in the Ancient Near East. Towards a Multidisciplinary Approach. History of the Ancient Near East/Monographs IV*. Padova: S.A.R.G.O.N. Editrice e Libreria. Pp. 413–429.

Fant, J. C. (2008). Quarrying and Stoneworking. In J. P. Oleson (ed.), *The Oxford Handbook of Engineering and Technology in the Classical World*. Chapter 5. Oxford: Oxford University Press. Pp. 121–135.

Fessenden, M. (2015). As Glaciers Retreat, They Give up the Bodies and Artifacts They Swallowed. *Smithsonian.com*. www.smithsonianmag.com/smart-news/glaciers-retreat-they-give-mummies-and-artifacts-they-swallowed-180955399/?no-ist. Accessed 18 June 2016.

Finch, J. (2012). Egyptian Toes Likely to be the World's Oldest Prosthetics. University of Manchester. www.manchester.ac.uk/discover/news/article/?id=8774. Accessed 30 May 2015.

Firth, R. (2013). Considering the Finishing of Textiles Based on Neo-Sumerian Inscriptions from Girsu. In M.-L. Nosch, H. Koefoed, E. A. Strand (eds.). *Textile Production and Consumption in the Ancient Near East. Archaeology, Epigraphy, Iconography*. Oxford: Oxbow Books. Pp. 140–160.

Fischer, M., B. Isaac, and I. Roll. (1996). *Roman Roads in Judea II. The Jaffa-Jerusalem Roads*. BAR International Series 628. Oxford: Tempus Reparatum.

Flemming, N. (2004). *Submarine Prehistoric Archaeology of the North Sea (CBA Research Project)*. Council for British Archaeology.

Fletcher, J. (2009). Hair. In P. T. Nicholson and I. Shaw (eds.), *Ancient Egyptian Materials and Technology*. Cambridge, UK: Cambridge University Press. Pp. 495–501.

Flintknapping—Beginners Part 1. (2009). Flintknapping—Beginners Part 1. YouTube www.youtube.com/watch?v=wyzNIa-U5Nc. Accessed 21 June 2016.

Forbes, R. J. (1964). *Notes on the History of Ancient Roads and their Construction*. Amsterdam: Adolf M. Hakkert Leiden: E. J. Brill.

Forshaw, R. J. (2009). The Practice of Dentistry in Ancient Egypt. *British Dental Journal*, Vol. 206, No. 9, pp. 51–58. www.nature.com/bdj/journal/v206/n9/pdf/sj.bdj.2009.355. pdf. Accessed 31 May 2015.

Fournet, T. (2012). The Ancient Baths of Southern Syria in their Near Eastern Context. Introduction to the Balnéorient Project. In R. Kreiner and W. Letzner (eds.), *Spa Sanitas Per Aquam. Tagungsband des Internationalen Frontinus-Symposiums zur Technik- und Kulturgeschichte der antiken Thermen*. Aachen, 18–22. März 2009. Leuvan: Peeters. Pp. 327–336.

Frankel, R. (1999). *Wine and Oil Production in Antiquity in Israel and Other Mediterranean Countries*. JSOT/ASOR Monograph Series 10 Sheffield: Sheffield Academic Press.

Frayer, D. W., R. Macchiarelli, and M. Mussi. (1988). A Case of Chondrodystrophic Dwarfism in the Italian Late Upper Paleolithic. *American Journal of Physical Anthropology*, Vol. 75, No. 4, pp. 549–565.

Freeth, T., Y. Bitsakis, X. Moussas, et al. (2006). Decoding the Antikythera Mechanism: Investigation of an Ancient Astronomical Calendar. *Nature*, Vol. 444, No. 7119, pp. 587–591. DOI: 10.1038/nature05357. www.nature.com/articles/nature05357. Accessed 20 October 2017.

Freeth, T., A. Jones, J. M. Steele, and Y. Bitsakis. (2008). Calendars with Olympiad Display and Eclipse Prediction on the Antikythera Mechanism. *Nature*, Vol. 464, No. 7204, pp. 614–617. DOI: 10.1038/nature07130. www.nature.com/articles/nature07130. Accessed 20 October 2017.

Friend, G. (1998). *Tell Taannek 1963–1968 III: The Artifacts, 2: The Loom Weights*. Publications of the Palestinian Institute of Archaeology Excavations and Surveys. Published with the sponsorship of the American Schools of Oriental Research. Palestine: Birzeit University.

Gabriel, R. A. (2003). *The Military History of Ancient Israel*. Westport, CT; London: Praeger.

Gaffney, V., K. Thomson, and S. Fitch (eds.) (2007). *Mapping Doggerland. The Mesolithic Landscapes of the Southern North Sea*. Oxford: Archaeopress.

Gale, R., P. Gasson, N. Hepper, and G. Killen. (2009). Wood. In P. T. Nicholson and I. Shaw (eds.), *Ancient Egyptian Materials and Technology*. Cambridge, UK: Cambridge University Press. Pp. 334–371.

Galor, K. (2002). Qumran's Plastered Installations: Cisterns or Immersion Pools? In C. Ohlig, Y. Peleg, and T. Tsuk (eds.), *Cura Aquarum in Israel. In Memoriam Dr. Ya'akov Eren. Proceedings of the 11th International Conference on the History of Water Management and Hydraulic Engineering in the Mediterranean Region*. Israel 7–12 May 2001. Schriften der Deutschen

Wasserhistorischen Gesellschaft. Band 1. Siegburg: DWhG c/o Wahnbachtalsperenverb. Pp. 33–46.

Gannon, M. (2014). Workers at Biblical Copper Mines Ate Quite Well. *LiveScience*. November 25, 2014. www.livescience.com/48908-metalworkers-diet-biblical-mines.html. Accessed 30 August 2017.

Garcia, M. J. G., M. B. R. Zapata, J. I. Santisteban, R. Mediavilla, E. López-Pamo, and C. J. Dabrio (2007). Late Holocene Environments in Las Tablas de Daimiel (South Central Iberian Peninsula, Spain). *Vegetation History and Archaeobotany*, Vol. 16, No. 4, pp. 241–250. DOI 10.1007/s00334-006-0047-9. https://link.springer.com/article/10.1007/s00334-006-0047-9. Accessed 17 June 2016.

Gardiner, A. H. and K. Sethe. (1928). *Egyptian Letters to the Dead. Mainly from the Old and Middle Kingdoms*. London: The Egypt Exploration Society.

Garfinkel, Y. (2003). The Earliest Dancing Scenes of the Nar East. *Near Eastern Archaeology*, Vol. 66, No. 3, pp. 84–95.

Garfinkel, Y. and D. Ben-Shlomo. (2009). *Sha'ar Hagolan. Vol. 2.* The Rise of Urban Concepts in the Ancient Near East. *Qedem Reports 9*. Jerusalem: Israel Exploration Society (Book 9).

Garfinkel, Y. and S. Cohen. (2007). *The Middle Bronze Age IIA Cemetery at Gesher: Final Report. Vol. 2.* The Annual of The American Schools of Oriental Research. Boston, MA: American Schools of Oriental Research.

Garfinkel, Y., A. Vered, and O. Bar-Yosef. (2006). The Domestication of Water: The Neolithic Well at Sha'ar Hagolan, Jordan Valley, Israel. *Antiquity*, Vol. 80/309, pp. 686–696.

Garnsey, P. (1999). *Food and Society in Classical Antiquity. Key Themes in Ancient History*. Cambridge, UK: Cambridge University Press.

Gheorghiu, D. (ed.). (2009). *Early Farmers, Late Foragers, and Ceramic Traditions: On the Beginning of Pottery in the Near East and Europe*. Newcastle upon Tyne: Cambridge Scholars Publishing.

Ghose, T. (2012). Human Greenhouse Gas Emissions Traced to Roman Times. *LiveScience*. October 3, 2012. www.livescience.com/23678-methane-emissions-roman-times.html. Accessed 22 June 2016.

Gibbens, S. (2017). Ancient Tablet May Show Earliest use of This Advanced Math. *National Geographic*. August 24, 2017. http://news.nationalgeographic.com/2017/08/ancient-babylonian-trigonometry-tablet-plimpton-322-video-spd/. Accessed 18 September 2017.

Gilbert, A. S. (2002). The Native Fauna of the Ancient Near East. In B. J. Collins (ed.), *A History of the Animal World in the Ancient Near East. Vol. 64.* Series, Handbook of Oriental Studies. Section One. The Near and Middle East. Leiden; Boston; Köln: Brill. Pp. 3–78.

Gitin, S. (1990). Ekron of the Philistines, Part II: Olive-Oil Suppliers to the World. *Biblical Archaeology Review*, Vol. 16, No. 2, pp. 32–42, 59.

Gitin, S. and A. Golani (2001). The Tel Miqne-Ekron Silver Hoards: The Assyrian and Phoenician Connections. In M. S. Balmuth (ed.), *Hacksilver to Coinage: New Insights into the Monetary History of the Near East and Greece*. Numismaatic Studies No. 24, New York: The American Numismatic Society. Pp. 27–48.

Gonen, R. (1992). The Late Bronze Age. In A. Ben-Tor (ed.), *The Archaeology of Ancient Israel*. New Haven, CT; London: Yale University Press. Pp. 211–257.

Gordetsky, J., J. O'Brien. (2008). Mysticism and Urology in Ancient Egypt. *The Journal of Urology*, Vol. 179, No. 4, p. 309. www.urologichistory.museum/content/exhibits/historyforum/mysturo.pdf. Accessed 31 May 2013. DOI: 10.1016/S0022-5347(08)606904-0/.

Greenfield, S. (2015). Digital Dimentia. *Psychology Today*. Posted 1 July 2015. www.psychologytoday.com/blog/mind-change/201507/digital-dementia. Accessed 15 June 2016.

Greenwich Point Conservancy. The Feake-Ferris House Circa 1645–1689. www. greenwichpoint.org/the-ferris-homestead/#current-condition. Accessed 6 October 2017.

Griffiths, S. (2016). Sorry Tefal, Romans Used Non-stick Cookware 2, 000 Years Ago. *Daily Mail.com*. 30 March 2016. www.dailymail.co.uk/sciencetech/article-3515952/Sorry-Tefal-Romans-used-non-stick-cookware-2-000-years-ago-Cumanae-testae-slippery-coating-stop-stews-sticking.html. Accessed 8 May 2018.

Gruber, M. I. (1995). Private Life in Ancient Israel. In J. M. Sasson (ed.), *Civilizations of the Ancient Near East. Vol. I*. New York, NY: Charles Scribner's Sons. Pp. 633–648.

Hachlili, R. (1997). *Ancient Jewish Art and Archaeology in the Land of Israel*. Leiden: Brill.

Hachlili, R. (2009). *Ancient Mosaic Pavements. Themes, Issues and Trends. Selected Studies*. Leiden and Boston: Brill.

Hackett, J. (ed.). (1989). *Warfare in the Ancient World*. New York; Oxford; Sydney: Facts on File.

Hackett, J. W. (1990). *Warfare in the Ancient World*. New York: Checkmark Books.

Haggerty, S. E. (2015). Discovery of a Kimberlite Pipe and Recognition of a Diagnostic Botanical Indicator in NW Liberia. *Economic Geology*, Vol. 110, No. 4, pp. 851–856. DOI: 10.2113/econgeo.110.4.851. Accessed 6 October 2017.

Halioua, B. and B. Ziskind. (2005). *Medicine in the Days of the Pharaohs*. Cambridge, MA: Harvard University Press.

Hamblin, W. J. (2006). *Warfare in the Ancient Near East to 1600 BC. Holy Warriors at the Dawn of History*. London; New York: Routledge.

Hamilton, R. W. and B. L. Milgram. (2007). *Material Choices: Refashioning Bast and Leaf Fibers in Asia and the Pacific*. Los Angeles: Fowler Museum at the University of California Los Angeles.

Hand, E. (2015). Rare African Plant Signals Diamonds Beneath the Soil. *Science*. www. sciencemag.org/news/2015/05/rare-african-plant-signals-diamonds-beneath-soil. Accessed 8 May 2018.

Handwerk, B. (2002). Pyramid Builders' Village Found in Egypt. *News.nationalgeographic.com*. http://news.nationalgeographic.com/news/2002/08/0805_020805_giza_2.html. Accessed 16 May 2016.

Hannah, R. (2005). *Greek and Roman Calendars. Constructions of Time in the Classical World*. London and New York: Bloomsbury Academic and Gerald Duckworth & Co. Ltd.

Harrell, J. A. and V. M. Brown. (1992). The World's Oldest Surviving Geological Map: The 1150 B.C. Turin Papyrus from Egypt. *The Journal of Geology*, Vol. 100, No. 1, pp. 3–18.

Hassan, S. (1943). *Excavations at Giza. Vol. 4, 1932–1933. With Collaboration of Banoub Habashi*. Cairo: General organization for Government Printing Offices.

Hauptmann, A., R. Maddin, and M. Prange. (2002). On the Structure and Composition of Copper and Tin Ingots Excavated from the Shipwreck of Uluburun. *Bulletin of the American Schools of Oriental Research*, Vol. 328, pp. 1–30.

Henderson, J. (2013). *Ancient Glass. An Interdisciplinary Exploration*. Cambridge, UK: Cambridge University Press.

Henderson, J. (ed.). C. L. Brownson (transl.). (2001, reprinted). *Xenophon III*. Loeb Classical Library. LCL 90. Cambridge, MA: Harvard University Press.

Henderson, J. (ed.) and R. G. Bury (transl.). (1929). *Plato Timaeus, Critias, Cleitophon, Menexenus Epistles*. Loeb Classical Library. LCL 234. Cambridge, MA; London: Harvard University Press.

Henderson, J. (ed.) and W. D. Hooper (transl.). (1935). *Marcus Porcius Cato On Agriculture. Marcus Terentius Varro on Agriculture*. Loeb Classical Library. LCL 283. Cambridge, MA; London: Harvard University Press.

Henderson, J. (ed.) and A. Hort (transl.). (1916). *Theophrastus Enquiry into Plants Books I-V*. Loeb Classical Library. LCL 70. Cambridge, MA; London: Harvard University Press.

Henderson, J. (ed.) and A. Hort (transl.). (1926). *Theophrastus Enquiry into Plants and Minor Works on Odours and Weather Signs II*. Loeb Classical Library. LCL 79. Cambridge, MA; London: Harvard University Press.

Henderson, J. (ed.) and H. L. Jones (transl.). (1923). *Strabo Geography Books 3–5*. Loeb Classical Library. LCL 50. Cambridge, MA; London: Harvard University Press.

Henderson, J. (ed.) and H. L. Jones (transl.). (1935). *Strabo VII. Strabo Geography Books 15–16*. Loeb Classical Library. LCL 241. Cambridge, MA; London: Harvard University Press.

Henderson, J. (ed.) and W. H. S. Jones. (1963). *Pliny Natural History Books 28–32*. Loeb Classical Library. LCL 418. Cambridge, MA; London: Harvard University Press.

Henderson, J. (ed.) and W. Miller (transl.). (1914). *Xenophon Cyropaedia Books V-VIII*. Loeb Classical Library. LCL 52. Cambridge, MA; London: Harvard University Press.

Henderson, J. (ed.) and C. H. Oldfather (transl.). (1933). *Diodorus of Sicily. The Library of History Books I-II.34*. Loeb Classical Library. LCL 279. Cambridge, MA; London: Harvard University Press.

Henderson, J. (ed.) and C. H. Oldfather (transl.). (1935). *Diodorus of Sicily The Library of History Books II.35-IV.58*. Loeb Classical Library. LCL 303. Cambridge, MA; London: Harvard University press.

Henderson, J. (ed.) and C. H. Oldfather (transl.). (1954). *Diodorus of Sicily Books XIV-XV.19*. Loeb Classical Lobrary, LCL 399. Cambridge, MA; London: Harvard University Press.

Henderson, J. (ed.) and A. L. Peck. (1970). *Aristotle History of Animals IV-VI*. Loeb Classical Library. LCL 438. Cambridge, MA; London: Harvard University Press.

Henderson, J. (ed.) and B. Perrin (transl.). (1917). *Plutarch. Lives. Agesilaus and Pompey Pelopidas and Marcellus*. Loeb Classical Library. LCL 87. Cambridge, MA; London: Harvard University Press.

Henderson, J. (ed.) and H. Rackham (transl.). (1952). *Pliny Natural History. Volume IX: Books 33–35*. Loeb Classical Library. LCL 394. Cambridge, MA; London: Harvard University Press.

Henderson, J. (ed.) and H. Rackham. (1968, reprinted from 1945). *Pliny Natural History, Volume IV: Books 12–16*. Loeb Classical Library, LCL 370. Cambridge, MA; London: Harvard University Press.

Henderson, J. (ed.) and J. C. Rolfe (transl.). (1946). *Aulus Gellius The Attic Nights Books I-V*. Loeb Classical Library. LCL 195. Cambridge, MA; London: Harvard University Press.

Henderson, J. (ed.), W. H. D. Rouse (transl.), and J. F. Smith (revised). (1992). *Lucretius De Rerum Natura*. Loeb Classical Library. LCL 181. Cambridge, MA; London: Harvard University Press.

Henderson, J. (ed.), I. Thomas (transl.). (1993, revised). *Selections Illustrating the History of Greek Mathematics*. Loeb Classical Library. LCL 362. Cambridge, MA; London: Harvard University Press.

Hendon, J. A. (2003). Feasting at Home. Community and House Solidarity among the Maya of Southeastern Mesoamerica. In T. L. Bray (ed.), *The Archaeology and Politics of Food and Feasting in Early States and Empires*. New York, NY: Kluwer Academic/Plenum Publishers. Pp. 203–234.

Herzog, Z. (1992). Settlement and Fortification Planning in the Iron Age. In A. Kempinski and R. Reich (eds.), *The Architecture of Ancient Israel. From the Prehistoric to the Persian Periods*. Jerusalem: Israel Exploration Society. Pp. 231–274.

Hesse, B. (1982). Animal Domestication and Oscillating Climates. *Journal of Ethnobiology*, Vol. 2, No. 1, pp. 1–15.

Hesse, B. (1989). Paleolithic Faunal Remains from Ghar-i-Khar, Western Iran. In P. J. Crabtree, D. Campana, and K. Ryan (eds.) *Early Animal Domestication and Its Cultural Context*. MASCA Research Papers in Science and Archaeology. The University Museum of Archaeology and Anthropology. Philadelphia: University of Pennsylvania. Pp. 37–45.

Hestrin, R. (1993). Beth Yerah. In E. Stern (ed.), *The New Encyclopedia of Archaeological Excavations in the Holy Land. Vol. 1.* Jerusalem: The Israel Exploration Society. Pp. 255–259.

Hetherington, N. S. (1993). *Encyclopedia of Cosmology: Historical Philosophical, and Scientific Foundations of Modern Cosmology.* New York: Garland.

Hodge, A. T. (2000a). Wells. In Ö. Wikander (ed.), *Handbook of Ancient Water Technology.* Leiden/Boston/Köln: Brill. Pp. 29–33.

Hodge, A. T. (2000b). Aqueducts. In Ö. Wikander (ed.), *Handbook of Ancient Water Technology.* Leiden/Boston/Köln: Brill. Pp. 29–33.

Hodges, H. (1992). *Technology in the Ancient World.* New York: Barnes & Noble Books. (1970; reprinted 1992).

Höflmayer, F. (2014). Egypt and the Southern Levant in the Late Early Bronze Age. In F. Höflmayer and R. Eichmann (eds.), *Egypt and the Southern Levant in the Early Bronze Age.* Orient-Archäologie Band 31. Raden: Verlag Marie Leidorf. Pp. 134–148.

Hohfelder, R. L., C. Brandon, and J. P. Oleson. (2007). Constructing the Harbour of Caesarea Palaestina, Israel: New Evidence From the ROMACONS Field Campaign of October 2005. *The International Journal of Nautical Archaeology,* Vol. 36, No. 2, pp. 409–415. DOI: 10.1111/j.1095-9270.2007.00156.x.

Howard, D. (2011). *Bronze Age Military Equipment.* Barnsley, South Yorkshire: Pen & Sword Military.

Howley, A. (2010). 70th Anniversary of the Discovery of Lascaux. *National Geographic Society.* Posted on September 17, 2010. http://voices.nationalgeographic.com/2010/09/17/70th_anniversary_lascaux/. Accessed on 7 July 2015.

Huehnergard, J. and H. Liebowitz. (2013). The Biblical Prohibition Against Tattooing. *Vetus Testamentum,* Vol. 63, No. 1, pp. 59–77.

Humphrey, J. W., J. P. Oleson, and A. N. Sherwood. (2006). *Greek and Roman Technology: A Sourcebook. Annotated Translations of Greek and Latin Texts and Documents.* London; New York: Routledge. Digital Printing.

Hunger, H. and D. Pingree. (1999). *Astral Sciences in Mesopotamia.* Leiden: Koninklijke Brill.

Ikram, S. (2009). Meat Processing. In P. T. Nicholson and I. Shaw (eds.), *Ancient Egyptian Materials and Technology.* Cambridge, UK: Cambridge University Press. Pp. 656–672.

Institute of Nautical Archaeology. http://nauticalarch.org/projects/all/southern_europe_mediterranean_aegean/uluburun_turkey/introduction/. Accessed 4 June 2015.

Irving, J. (2013). Trephination. Definition. *Ancient History Encyclopedia.* Last modified May 01, 2013. www.ancient.eu/Trephination/. Accessed 10 June 2016. https://nauticalarch.org/projects/cape-gelidonya-late-bronze-age-shipwreck-excavation/. Accessed 30 September 2017.

Issar, A. S. and Zohar M. (2007). *Climate Change—Environment and History of the Near East.* Second edition. Berlin Heidelberg: Springer.

Isserlin, B. S. J. (2001). *The Israelites.* Reprinted. Minneapolis, MN: Fortress Press.

Iversen, P. (2017). The Calendar on the Antikythera Mechanism and the Corinthian Family of Calendars. *Hesperia,* Vol. 86, pp. 129–203.

Jabr, F. (2013). How to Really Eat Like a Hunter-Gatherer: Why the Paleo Diet is Half-Baked [Interactive & Infographic]. *Scientific American.* www.scientificamerican.com/article/why-paleo-diet-half-baked-how-hunter-gatherer-really-eat/. Accessed 16 December 2014.

Jackson, C. M., P. T. Nicholson, and W. Gneisinger. (1998). Glassmaking at Tell el-Amarna: An Integrated Approach. *Journal of Glass Studies,* Vol. 40, pp. 11–23.

James, P. and N. Thorpe. (1995). *Ancient Inventions.* Wonders of the Past! (First trade paperback edition). New York: Ballantine Books.

Janssen, R. M. H. (1995). Costume in New Kingdom Egypt. In J. M. Sasson (ed.), *Civilizations of the Ancient Near East. Vol. I.* New York: Charles Scribner's Sons. Pp. 383–394.

Jarus, O. (2005). Lost and Found: Ancient Shoes Turn Up in Egypt Temple. *Livescience*. February 26, 2013.

Jarus, O. (2014). Ancient Egyptian Woman with 70 Hair Extensions Discovered. *Livescience*. September 17, 2014. www.livescience.com/47875-ancient-egyptian-woman-with-hair-extensions.html. Accessed 18 April 2015.

Jensen, R. M. (2008). Dining with the Dead: From the Mensa to the Altar in Christian Late Antiquity. In L. Brink and D. Green (eds.), *Commemorating the Dead: Texts and Artifacts n Context. Studies of Roman, Jewish, and Christian Burials*. Berlin; New York: Walter de Gruyter. Pp. 107–144.

Johnston, I. and G. H. R. Horsley (eds.), (2011). *Galen Method of Medicine Books 5–9*. Cambridge, MA; London: Harvard University Press.

Kahn, C. J. (2001). *Pythagoras and the Pythagoreans. A Brief History*. Indianapolis, IN; Cambridge: Hackett Publishing Company, Inc.

Kaniewski, D., E. Van Campo, J. Guiot, et al. (2013). Environmental Roots of the Late Bronze Age Crisis. *PLoS ONE*, Vol. 8, No. 8, pp. e71004. DOI: 10.1371/journal.pone.0071004. http://journals.plos.org/plosone/article?id=10.1371/journal.pone.0071004. Accessed 17 June 2016.

Kemp, B. (2009). Soil (Including Mud-Brick Architecture). In P. T. Nicholson and I. Shaw (eds.), *Ancient Egyptian Materials and Technology*. Cambridge, UK: Cambridge University Press. Pp. 78–103.

Kempinski, A. (1992a). Fortifications, Public Buildings, and Town Planning in the Early Bronze Age. In A. Kempinski and R. Reich (eds.), *The Architecture of Ancient Israel From the Prehistoric to the Persian Periods*. Jerusalem: Israel Exploration Society. Pp. 68–80.

Kempinski, A. (1992b). Middle and Late Bronze Age Fortifications. In A. Kempinski and R. Reich (eds.), *The Architecture of Ancient Israel. From the Prehistoric to the Persian Periods*. Jerusalem: Israel Exploration Society. Pp. 127–142.

Kempinski, A. (1992c). The Middle Bronze Age. In A. Ben-Tor (ed.) and R. Greenberg (translator), *The Archaeology of Ancient Israel*. New Haven and London: Yale University Press. Ch. 6. Pp. 159–210.

Kempinski, A. (1992d). Chalcolithic and Early Bronze Age Temples. In A. Kempinski and R. Reich (eds.), *The Architecture of Ancient Israel From the Prehistoric to the Persian Periods*. Jerusalem: Israel Exploration Society. Pp. 53–59.

Kennedy, M. (2014). Babylonian tablet shows how Noah's ark could have been constructed. *The Guardian*, Friday 24 January. www.theguardian.com/culture/2014/jan/24/babylonian-tablet-noah-ark-constructed-british-museum. Accessed 3 June 2015.

Kenyon, K. M. (1960). *Excavations at Jericho. Volume One. The Tombs Excavated in 1952–1954*. London: British School of Archaeology in Jerusalem.

Kenyon, K. M. (1965). *Excavations at Jericho. Volume Two. The Tombs Excavated in 1955–58*. London: British School of Archaeology in Jerusalem.

Kenyon, K. M. (1981). *Excavations at Jericho. Volume Three. The Architecture and Stratigraphy of the Tell, Text and Plates*. The British School of Archaeology in Jerusalem. Oxford: Oxford University Press.

Kershner, I. (2013). Pollen Study Points to Drought as Culprit in Bronze Age Mystery. *New York Times*. October 22, 2013. www.nytimes.com/2013/10/23/world/middleeast/pollen-study-points-to-culprit-in-bronze-era-mystery.html?_r=0.

Kessler, B. (2012). Doggerland—The Europe that was. The British Isles were once neither British nor Isles. *National Geographic Society*. http://nationalgeographic.org/maps/doggerland/. Accessed 17 June 2016.

Keyes, K., M. D. Lee, and J. J. Maurer. (2003). Antibiotics: Mode of Action, Mechanisms of Resistance, and Transfer. In M. E. Torrence and R. E. Isaacson (eds.), *Microbial Food Safety in Animal Agriculture Current Topics*. Ames, IA: Iowa State Press. Ch. 6. Pp. 45–71.

Keyser, P.T. (1993). The Purpose of the Parthian Galvanic Cells: A First-Century A.D. Electric Battery Used for Analgesia. *Journal of Near Eastern Studies*, Vol. 52, No. 2, pp. 81–98.

Khalifeh, I. A. (1988). *Sarepta II. The Late Bronze and Iron Age Periods of Area II, X.* Beyrouth: Publications de l'Université Libanaise. Philadelphia, PA: University of Pennsylvania University Museum.

Killebrew, A. E. (1997). Baths. In E. M. Meyers (ed.), *The Oxford Encyclopedia of Archaeology in the Near East. Vol. I.* New York: Oxford University Press. Pp. 283–285.

Kilmer, A. D. (1998). The Musical Instruments from Ur and Ancient Mesopotamia. *Expedition*, Vol. 40, No. 2, pp. 12–18.

Klein, R. G. (2009). *The Human Career. Human Biological and Cultural Origins.* Third edition. Chicago: University of Chicago Press.

Klingman, W. K. and N. P. Klingman. (2013). *The Year Without Summer. 1816 and the Volcano That Darkened the World and Changed History.* New York: St. Martin's Press.

Köcher, F. (1963). Die *Babylonisch-Assyrische Medizin in Texten und Untersuchungen. Band 1.* Leinen: Walter de Gruyter Verlag.

Koh, A. J., A. Yasur-Landau, and E. H. Cline. (2014). Characterizing a Middle Bronze Palatial Wine Cellar from Tel Kabri, Israel. *PLoS ONE*, Vol. 9, No. 8, pp. e106406. DOI: 10.1371/journal.pone.0106406.

Koren, Z. C. (2005). The First Optimal All-Murex All-Natural Purple Dyeing in the Eastern Mediterranean in a Millennium and a Half. *Dyes in History and Archaeology*, Vol. 20, pp. 136–149, Color Plates 15.1-15.5 (Archetype Publications, London).

Krause, L. (2000). Ballard Finds Traces of Ancient Habitation Beneath Black Sea. *National Geographic News.* 13 September 2000. http://news.nationalgeographic.com/news/2000/12/122800blacksea.html. Accessed 17 June 2016.

Krebs, R. E. and C. A. Krebs. (2003). *Groundbreaking Scientific Experiments, Inventions and Discoveries of the Ancient World.* Westport, CT: Greenwood Publishing Group.

Kreston, R. (2012). Ophthalmology of the Pharaohs: Antimicrobial Kohl Eyeliner in Ancient Egypt. *Discover Magazine*, 20 April 2012. http://blogs.discovermagazine.com/bodyhorrors/2012/04/20/ophthalmology-of-the-pharaohs/#.VTUf1JMe2sM. Accessed 20 April 2015.

Kuniholm, P. I., M. Newton, H. Sherbiny, and H. Bassir. (2014). Dendrochronological Dating in Egypt: Work Accomplished and Future Prospects. *Tree-Ring Research*, Vol. 70, No. 3, pp. S93–S102. DOI: 10.3959/1536-1098-70.3.93.

Kvavadze, E., S. E. Connor. (2005). Zelkova Carpinifolia (Pallas) K. Koch in Holocene Sediments of Georgia—an Indicator of Climatic Optima. *Review of Palaeobotany & Palynology*, Vol. 133, No. 1, pp. 69–89. DOI: 10.1016/j.revpalbo.2004.09.002. https://ac-els-cdn-com.access.library.miami.edu/S0012821X03002929/1-s2.0-S0012821X03002929-main.pdf?_tid=81654e5a-01d6-4617-b639-68f8ce2cf177&acdnat=1525464155_81163f465764361a5b61527c9655267b. Accessed 17 June 2016.

Landels, J. G. (2000). *Engineering in the Ancient World.* Berkeley, CA; Los Angeles, CA: University of California Press.

Langgut, D., I. Finkelstein, T. Litt. (2013). Climate and the Late Bronze Collapse: New Evidence from the Southern Levant. *Tel Aviv*, Vol. 40, No. 2, pp. 149–175.

Lankford, J. (ed.). (2011). *History of Astronomy. An Encyclopedia.* New York; London: Routledge.

Lassen, A. W. (2013). Technology and Palace Economy in Middle Bronze Age Anatolia: the Case of the Crescent Shaped Loom Weight. In M.-L. Nosch, H. Koefoed, and E. Andersson Strand (eds.), *Textile Production and Consumption in the Ancient Nar East. Archaeology, Epigraphy, Iconography.* Oxford; Oakville: Oxbow Books. Pp. 78–92.

Layard, A. H. (1849). *The Monuments of Nineveh: From Drawings Made on the Spot.* London: John Murray.

Layard, A. H. (1853). *A Second Series of the Monuments of Nineveh Including Bas-Reliefs from the Palace of Sennacherib and Bronzes from the Ruins of Nimrud. From Drawings Made On The Spot, During a Second Expedition to Assyria.* London: Murray.

Lazenby, J. (1989). Hoplite Warfare. In. J. Hackett (ed.), *Warfare in the Ancient World.* New York; Oxford; Sydney: Facts on File. Pp. 54–81.

Lee, L. and S. Quirke. (2009). Painting Materials. In P. T. Nicholson and I. Shaw (eds.), *Ancient Egyptian Materials and Technology.* Cambridge: Cambridge University Press. Pp. 104–120.

Lehner, M. (1992). *This Old Pyramid.* Nova. Season 19, Episode 15. WGBH Boston for PBS.

Lehner, M. (1997). *The Complete Pyramids. Solving the Ancient Mysteries.* New York: Thames and Hudson.

Levey, M. (1956). Babylonian Chemistry: A Study of Arabic and Second Millennium B.C. Perfumery. *Osiris,* Vol. 12, pp. 376–389. www.jstor.org/stable/301716. Accessed 13 June 2016 14:16 UTC.

Levey, M. (1958). Gypsum, Salt and Soda in Ancient Mesopotamian Chemical Technology. *Isis,* Vol. 49, No. 3, pp. 336–342.

Levey, M. (1960). A Group of Akkadian Texts on Perfumery. *Chymia,* Vol. 6, pp. 11–19. www.jstor.org/stable/27757190. Accessed 13 June 2016 14:23 UTC.

Levy, T. E. (ed.). (1995). *The Archaeology of Society in the Holy Land.* New York: Facts on File.

Li, X., M. Wagner, X. Wu, et al. (2013). Archaeological and Palaeopathological Study on the Third/Second Century BC Grave from Turfan, China: Individual Health History and Regional Implications. *Quaternary International,* Vol. 290–291, No. 2013, pp. 335–343. DOI: 10.1016/j.quaint.2012.05.010.

Lichtheim, M. (1975). *Ancient Egyptian Literature. Volume I: The Old and Middle Kingdoms.* Berkeley, CA; Los Angeles, CA; London: University of California Press.

Lichtheim, M. (1980). *Ancient Egyptian Literature. Volume III: The Late Period.* Berkeley, Los Angeles, CA; London: University of California Press.

Liesowska, A. (2018). Ancient Jew's Harps Found in Altai Mountains as Musical Instruments Reappear after 1,700 Years. *The Siberian Times.* January 9, 2018. http://siberiantimes.com/science/casestudy/news/ancient-jews-harps-found-in-altai-mountains-as-musical-instruments-reappear-after-1700-years/. Accessed 19 January 2018.

Lindsay, H. (2001). Eating with the Dead: The Roman Funerary Banquet. In I. Nielsen and H. S. Nielsen (eds.), *Meals in a Social Context.* Aarhus, Denmark: Aarhus University Press. Pp. 67–80.

Lineberry, C. (2007). Tattoos. The Ancient and Mysterious History. *Smithsonian.com.* www.smithsonianmag.com/history/tattoos-144038580/?all. Accessed 22 April 2015.

Livet, J. (2001). Djeserkareseneb. *OsirisNet.net.* www.osirisnet.net/tombes/nobles/djeserkareseneb38/e_djeserkareseneb_03.htm. Accessed 18 September 2017.

Loades, M. (2010). *Swords and Swordsmen.* Barnsley, South Yorkshire: Pen & Sword Military.

Lobell, J. A. and E. A. Powell. (2013). Ancient Tattoos. *Archaeology,* Wednesday, 9 October 2013. http://archaeology.org/issues/109-1311/features/1360-cucuteni-jomon-lapita-thracian-moche-mississippian-ibaloi. Accessed 22 April 2015.

Long, D. J., P. Milburn, M. J. Bunting, R. Tipping, and T. G. Holden. (1999). Black Henbane (*Hyoscyamus niger L.*) in the Scottish Neolithif: A Re-Evaluation of Palynological Findings from Grooved Ware Pottery at Balfarg Riding School and Henge, Fife. *Journal of Archaeological Science,* Vol. 26, pp. 45–52. Article No. jasc.1998.0308, www.idealibrary.com. Accessed 13 October 2017.

Lorenzi, R. (2012). Ancient Egyptian Fake Toes Earliest Prosthetics. *Discovery News.* http://news.discovery.com/history/ancient-egypt/ancient-egypt-wooden-toes-prosthetics-121002.htm. Accessed 30 May 2015.

Lucas, A. (1930). Cosmetics, Perfumes and Incense in Ancient Egypt. *The Journal of Egyptian Archaeology*, Vol. 16, No. 1/2, (May), pp. 41–53.

Lucas, A. and J. Harris. (2011). *Ancient Egyptian Materials and Industries*. Fourth edition. Mineola, NY: Dover Publications.

Lyons, H. (1927). Ancient Surveying Instruments. *The Geographical Journal*. The Royal Geographical Society (with the Institute of British Geographers) Vol. 69, No. 2, pp. 132–139. JSTOR www.jstor.org/stable/1782725. Accessed 13 August 2013.

McClellan, J. E. and H. Dorn. (2006). *Science and Technology in World History. An Introduction*. Second edition. Baltimore: The Johns Hopkins University Press.

MacDonald, N. (2008). *What Did the Ancient Israelites Eat? Diet in Biblical Times*. Grand Rapids: William B. Eerdmans Publishing Company.

McDonald Institute for Archaeological Research. (2000). Amarna Project. University of Cambridge. www.amarnaproject.com/pages/recent_projects_old/.

McGovern, P. E. (2000). The Funerary Banquet of "King Midas." *Expedition*, Vol. 42, pp. 21–29.

McGovern, P. E., S. J. Fleming, and S. H. Katz. (2000). *The Origins and Ancient History of Wine*. Australia/Canada/France: Gordon and Breach Publishers/Taylor & Francis e-Library, 2005. Third Printing.

McGovern, P. E., D. L. Glusker, L. J. Exner, and M. M. Voigt. (1996). Neolithic Resinated Wine. *Nature*, Vol. 381, pp. 480–481.

McGovern, P. E., D. L. Glusker, R. A. Moreau, et al. (1999). A Funerary Feast Fit for King Midas. *Nature*, Vol. 402 (December 23), pp. 863–864.

McGovern P. E. and R. H. Michel. (1990). Royal Purple Dye: The Chemical Reconstruction of the Ancient Mediterranean Industry. *Accounts of Chemical Research*, Vol. 23, pp. 152–158. www.penn.museum/sites/biomoleculararchaeology/wp-content/uploads/2010/03/AccountsPurple.pdf

Macintosh, A. (2014). From Athletes to Couch Potatoes: Humans through 6,000 Years of Farming. www.cam.ac.uk/research/news/from-athletes-to-couch-potatoes-humans-through-6000-years-of-farming.

McLaughlin, R. (2016). *The Roman Empire and the Silk Routes. The Ancient World Economy and the Empires of Parthia, Central Asia and Han China*. Barnsley: Pen & Sword History.

Magness, J. (2005). Heaven on Earth: Helios and the Zodiac Cycle in Ancient Palestinian Synagogues. *Dunbarton Oaks Papers*, Vol. 59, pp. 1–52.

Manderscheid, H. (2000). The Water Management of Greek and Roman Baths. In Ö. Wikander (ed.), *Handbook of Ancient Water Technology. Vol. 2. Technology and Change in History*. Leiden: Brill. Pp. 467–538.

Maniatis, Y. (2009). The Emergence of Ceramic Technology and its Evolution as Revealed with the use of Scientific Techniques. In A. J. Shortland, I. C. Freestone, and T. Rehren (eds.), *From Mine to Microscope: Advances in the Study of Ancient Technology*. Oxford: Oxbow Books. Pp. 11–28.

Mansfield, D. F. and J. J. Wildberger. (2017). Plimpton 322 is Babylonian Exact Sexagesimal Trigonometry. *Science Direct*, Vol. 44, No. 4 (November), pp. 395–419. DOI: 10.1016/j.hm.2017.08.001.

Martinez-Cortizas, A., X. Pontevedra-Pombal, E. García-Rodeja, J. C. Nóvoa-Muñoz, and W. Shotyk (1999). Mercury in a Spanish Peat Bog: Archive of Climate Change and Atmospheric Metal Deposition. *Science*, Vol. 284, No. 5416, pp. 939–942. DOI: 10.1126/science.284.5416.939.

Mazar, A. (1990). *Archaeology of the Land of the Bible. 10,000–586 B.C.E.* The Anchor Bible Reference Library. New York; London: Doubleday.

Mazar, A. (1992). Temples of the Middle and Late Bronze Ages and the Iron Age. In. A. Kempinski and R. Reich (eds.), *The Architecture of Ancient Israel. From the Prehistoric to the Persian Periods*. Jerusalem: Israel Exploration Society. Pp. 161–190.

Mazar, A. and N. Panitz-Cohen. (2007). It Is The Land of Honey: Beekeeping at Tel Rehov. *Near Eastern Archaeology*, Vol. 70, No. 4, pp. 202–219.

Mazow, L. (2013). Throwing the Baby Out with the Bathwater: Innovations in Mediterranean Textile Production at the End of the 2nd/Beginning of the 1st Millennium BCE. In M. L. Nosch, H. Koefoed, and E. B. Andersson Strand (eds.), *Textile Production and Consumption in the Ancient Near East: Archaeology, Epigraphy, Iconography*. Oxford: Oxbow Books.

Mazza, P. P. A., F. Martini, B. Sala, et al. (2006). A New Palaeolothic Discovery: Tar-hafted Stone Tools in a European Mid-Pleistocene Bone-Bearing Bed. *Journal of Archaeological Science*, Vol. 33, No. 9, pp. 1310–1318. www-sciencedirect-com.access.library.miami.edu/science/article/pii/S0305440306000197?via%3Dihub. DOI: 10.1016/j.jas.2006.01.006.

Meadow, R. H. (1989). Prehistoric Wild Sheep and Sheep Domestication on the Eastern Margin of the Middle East. In P. J. Crabtree, D. Campana, and K. Ryan (eds.) *Early Animal Domestication and Its Cultural Context*. MASCA Research Papers in Science and Archaeology. The University Museum of Archaeology and Anthropology. Philadelphia: University of Pennsylvania. Pp. 25–36.

Meek, T. J. (1992, fifth printing). The Code of Hammurabi. In J. B. Pritchard (ed.), *Ancient Near Eastern Texts Relating to the Old Testament. Third Edition with Supplement*. Fifth printing. Princeton: Princeton University Press. Pp. 163–179.

Meiggs, R. (1982). *Trees and Timber in the Ancient Mediterranean World*. Oxford: Oxford University Press.

Merchant, J. (2011). Ancient Egyptians used "Hair Gel." *Nature*. Published online 19 August 2011. DOI: 10.1038/news.2011.487. www.nature.com/news/2011/110819/full/news.2011.487.html. Accessed 18 April 2015.

Merrillees, R. S. (1962). Opium Trade in the Bronze Age Levant. *Antiquity*, Vol. 36, No. 144, pp. 287–292.

Metropolitan Museum of Art. (2000–2015). Heilbrunn Timeline of Art History. Lascaus (ca. 15000 B.C.). www.metmuseum.org/toah/hd/lasc/hd_lasc.htm. Accessed 11 December 2015.

Mielach, D. (2012). Is It Ethical to Own an iPhone? *Business News Daily*. February 2, 2012. www.businessnewsdaily.com/1979-owning-iphone-ethical.html. Accessed 23 June 2015.

Milano, L. (2014). Eating on the Road. Travel Provisions in the Ebla Archives. In L. Milano (ed.), *Paleonutrition and Food Practice in the Ancient Near East. Towards a Multidisciplinary Approach*. History of the Ancient Near East/Monographs IV. Padova: S.A.R.G.O.N. Editrice e Libreria. Pp. 281–296.

Miller, J. A. (1993). Women in Chemistry. In G. Kass-Simon and P. Farnes (eds.), *Women of Science: Righting the Record*. Midland Book Edition. Pp. 300–335.

Mithen, S. (2010). The Domestication of Water: Water Management in the Ancient World and its Prehistoric Origins in the Jordan Valley. Philosophical *Transactions of the Royal Society A*, Vol. 368, pp. 5249–5274. DOI: 10.1098/rsta.2010.0191.

Moghadasi, A. N. (2014). Artificial Eye in Burnt City and Theoretical Understanding of How Vision Works. *Iranian Journal Public Health*, Vol. 43, No. 11, pp. 1595–1596. http://ijph.tums.ac.ir.

Molleson, T. (2014). Craftsmen for Food Production: The Human Bone Evidence for Methods of Food Processing at Abu Hureyra. In L. Milano (ed.), *Paleonutrition and Food Practice in the Ancient Near East. Towards a Multidisciplinary Approach*. History of the Ancient Near East/Monographs IV. Padova: S.A.R.G.O.N. Editrice e Libreria. Pp. 1–24.

Moorey, P. R. S. (1999). *Ancient Mesopotamian Materials and Industries*. Winona Lake: Eisenbrauns.

Morgan, M. H. (1960). *Vitruvius. The Ten Books on Architecture*. M. H. Morgan, (translator). New York: Dover Publications, Inc.

Moussaieff, A., N. Rimmerman, T. Bregman, A. Straiker, C. C. Felder, S. Shoham, Y. Kashman, S. M. Huang, H. Lee, E. Shohami, K. Mackie, M. J. Caterina, J. M. Walker, E. Fride, and R. Mechoulam. (2008). Incensole Acetae, An Incense Component, Elicits Psychoactivity by Activating TRPV3 Channels in the Brain. *He FASEB Journal*, Vol. 22, No. 8, pp. 3024–3034. www.fasebj.org/content/22/8/3024.full.pdf+html. Accessed 31 May 2015.

Muhly, J. D. (2003). Metalworking/Mining in the Levant. In S. Richard (ed.), *Near Eastern Archaeology. A Reader*. Winona Lake: Eisenbrauns. Pp. 174–183.

Murray, M. A. (2009a). *Egyptian Temples*. London; New York: Routledge.

Murray, M. A. (2009b). Viticulture and Wine Production. In P. T. Nicholson and I. Shaw (eds.), *Ancient Egyptian Materials and Technology*. Digitally Printed Version. Cambridge, UK: Cambridge University Press. Pp. 577–608.

Murray, M. A. (2009c) Fruits, Vegetables, Pulses and Condiments. In P. T. Nicholson and I. Shaw (eds.) *Ancient Egyptian Materials and Technology*. Cambridge, UK: Cambridge University Press. Pp. 609–655.

Nathan, J. (2017). A Dig in Israel Unearths Clues About Ancient Food and Drink. *The New York Times*. October 20. www.nytimes.com/2017/10/20/dining/israel-ancient-wine-canaanite.html?emc=edit_tnt_20171021&nlid=19839618&tntemail0=y&login=email. Accessed 21 October 2017.

Naville, E. (1908). *The Temple of Deir El Bahari. Part VI. Plates CLL-CLXXIV. The Lower Terrace, Additions and Plans*. London: The Egypt Exploration Fund.

Naville, E. (1898). *The Temple of Deir El Bahari. Part III. Plates LVL-LXXXVI. End of the Northern Half and Southern Half of the Middle Platform*. London: The Egypt Exploration Fund.

Nemet-Nejat, K. R. (1998). *Daily Life in Ancient Mesopotamia*. Westport, CT: Greenwood Publishing Group.

Nerlich, A. G., A. Zink, et al. (2000). An Egyptian Prosthesis of the Big Toe. *The Lancet*, Vol. 356, December 23/30 2000, pp. 2176–2179.

Netzer, E. (1992). Massive Structures: Process in Construction and Deterioration. In. A. Kempinski and R. Reich (eds.), *The Architecture of Ancient Israel. From the Prehistoric to the Persian Periods*. Jerusalem: Israel Exploration Society. Pp. 17–30.

Neuburger, A. (1930, transl. by J. L. Brose). *The Technical Arts and Sciences of the Ancients*. London: Methuen & Co. Ltd.

Newberry, P. E. (1893a). *Beni Hasan Part I. Archaeological Survey of Egypt*. London: Egypt Exploration Society.

Newberry, P. E. (1893b). *Beni Hasan Part II. Archaeological Survey of Egypt*. London: Egypt Exploration Society.

Newberry, P. E. (1895). *El Bersheh Part 1. The Tomb of Tehuti-Hetep*. London: Egypt Exploration Society.

Newberry, P. E. (1900). *The Life of Rekhmara Vezîr of Upper Egypt Under Thothmes III and Amenhetep II (circa B.C. 1471–1448) With Twenty-Two Plates*. Westminster: Archibald Constable and Co. Ltd.

Newman, R. and M. Serpico. (2009). Adhesives and Binders. In P. T. Nicholson and I. Shaw (eds.), *Ancient Egyptian Materials and Technology*. Cambridge, UK: Cambridge University Press. Pp. 475–494.

Newton, A., R. Thunell, and L. Stott. (2006). Climate and Hydrographic Variability in the Indo-Pacific Warm Pool during the last Millennium. *Geophysical Research Letters*, Vol. 33, No. 1, pp. 19710. DOI: 10.1029/2006GL027234, 2006. https://agupubs.onlinelibrary.wiley.com/doi/epdf/10.1029/2006GL027234. Accessed 17 June 2016.

Nicholson, P. T. (2000). Glass. In P. T. Nicholson and I. Shaw (eds.), *Ancient Egyptian Materials and Technology*. Cambridge, UK: Cambridge University Press. Pp. 195–226.

Nicholson, P. T. and J. Henderson (2000). Glass. In P. T. Nicholson and I. Shaw (eds.) *Ancient Egyptian Materials and Technology*. Cambridge, UK: Cambridge University Press. Pp. 195–224.

Nicholson, P. T. and I. Shaw (eds.). (2000). *Ancient Egyptian Materials and Technology*. First edition. Cambridge; New York. Cambridge University Press.

Nicholson, P. T. and I. Shaw. (2009). *Ancient Egyptian Materials and Technology*. Cambridge; New York: Cambridge University Press. Digitally Printed Version.

Nielsen, I. (2001). Royal Banquets: The Development of Royal Banquets and Banqueting Halls from Alexander to the Tetrarchs. In I. Nielsen and H. S. Nielsen (eds.), *Meals in a Social Context*. Aarhus, Denmark: Aarhus University Press. Pp. 102–133.

Nosch, M.-L., H. Koefoed, and E. A. Strand (eds.). (2013). *Textile Production and Consumption in the Ancient Near East. Archaeology, Epigraphy, Iconography*. Oxford: Oxbow Books.

Nunn, J. F. (2002, reprinted). *Ancient Egyptian Medicine*. Red River Books. Norman: University of Oklahoma Press.

Nutton, V. (2013). *Ancient Medicine*. Sciences of Antiquity Series. Second edition. London; New York: Routledge.

Ogden, J. (2009). Metals. In P. T. Nicholson and I. Shaw (eds.), *Ancient Egyptian Materials and Technology*. Cambridge, UK: Cambridge University Press. Pp. 148–176.

Ohlig, C., Y. Peleg, and T. Tsuk (eds.). (2004). *Cura Aquarum in Israel*. In Memoriam Dr. Ya'akov Eren. Proceedings of the 11th International Conference on the History of Water Management and Hydraulic Engineering in the Mediterranean Region, Israel, 7–12 May 2001. Siegburg.

O'Kelley, M. (1975). And Into the Dye Pot. In *Bittersweet. Vol. II. No. 4*. Summer. https://thelibrary.org/lochist/periodicals/bittersweet/su75h.htm.

Oleson, D. S. (ed. & transl.) (2010) *Athenaeus The Learned Banqueters Books 12-13.594b*. Loeb Classical Library. LCL 237. Cambridge, MA; London, England: Harvard University Press.

Oleson, J. P. (1998). *The Oxford Handbook of Engineering and Technology in the Classical World*. Oxford; New York: Oxford University Press.

Oleson, J. P. (2000a). Irrigation. In Ö. Wikander (ed.), *Handbook of Ancient Water Technology*. Technology and Change in History, Vol. 2. Leiden: Brill. Pp. 183–216.

Oleson, J. P. (2000b). Water-Lifting. In Ö. Wikander (ed.), *Handbook of Ancient Water Technology*. Technology and Change in History, Vol. 2. Leiden: Brill. Pp. 183–216.

Oleson, J. P. (2008). Introduction. The Greek and Roman View of Technology. In J. P. Oleson (ed.), *The Oxford Handbook of Engineering and Technology in the Classical World*. Oxford: Oxford University Press. Pp. 3–14.

Olmo, H. P. (2000). Origin and Domestication of the Vinifera Grape. In P. E. McGovern and S. J. Fleming, and S. H. Katz (eds.), *The Origins and Ancient History of Wine*. Australia/Canada/France: Gordon and Breach Publishers/Taylor & Francis e-Library, 2005.

Oppenheim, A. L., R. H. Brill, A. Von Saldern. (1988). *Glass and Glassmaking in Ancient Mesopotamia. An Edition of the Cuneiform Texts which Contain Instruction for Glassmakers with a Catalogue of Surviving Objects*. Corning: The Corning Museum of Glass Press.

Oren, E. D. (1987). The "Ways of Horus" in North Sinai. In A. Rainey (ed.), Egypt, Israel, Sinai: Archaeological and Historical Relationships in the Biblical Period. Tel Aviv: Tel Aviv University. Pp. 69–120.

Oren, E. D. (1992). Palaces and Patrician Houses in the Middle and Late Bronze Ages. In A. Kempinski and R. Reich (eds.), *The Architecture of Ancient Israel. From the Prehistoric to the Persian Periods*. Jerusalem: Israel Exploration Society. Pp. 105–120.

Ortloff, C. R. (2005). The Water Supply and Distribution System of the Nabataean City of Petra (Jordan), 300 BC—AD 300. *Cambridge Archaeological Journal*, Vol. 15, No. 1, pp. 93–100. DOI: 10. 1017/S0959774305000053.

Ortloff, C. R. (2009) *Water Engineering in the Ancient World. Archaeological and Climate Perspectives on Societies of Ancient South America, the Middle East, and South-East Asia.* Oxford: Oxford University Press.

Oskin, B. (2015). Japan Earthquake & Tsunami of 2011: Facts and Information. *LiveScience.* 7 May 2015. www.livescience.com/39110-japan-2011-earthquake-tsunami-facts.html. Accessed 15 June 2016.

Oxenham, M. F., L. Tilley, H. Matsumura, et al. (2009). Paralysis and Severe Disability Requiring Intensive Care in Neolithic Asia. *Anthropological Science*, Vol. 117, No. 2, pp. 107–112. Published online 10 April 2009 in J-STAGE (www.jstage.jst.go.jp). DOI: 10.1537/ase.081114. Accessed June 2016.

Paleomanjim. (2009). Flintknapping—Beginners Part 1. *YouTube.* 27 November 2009. www.youtube.com/watch?v=wyzNIa-U5Nc. Accessed 17 August 2017.

Parkinson, R. B. (2008). *The Painted Tomb Chapel of Nebamun.* British Museum Press.

Paszthory, E. (1989). Electricity Generation or Magic? The Analysis of an Unusual Group of Finds from Mesopotamia. *MASCA Research Papers in Science and Archaeology*, Vol. 6, pp. 31–38.

Patel, S. S. (2012). The First Pots. *Archaeology.* 6 December 2012. www.archaeology.org/issues/61-1301/features/271-top-10-2012-neolithic-china-pottery. Accessed 30 April 2018.

Paton, W. R. (1917). *The Greek Anthology Book 9.* Loeb Classical Library. Vol. III. Cambridge, MA: Harvard University Press.

Peck, W. H. (2013). *The Material World of Ancient Egypt.* Cambridge, UK: Cambridge University Press.

Perath, I. (1984). *Stone Building and Building Stone in Israel. A Historical Review.* State of Israel. The Ministry of Energy and Infrastructure. The Geological Survey of Israel. Environmental Geology Division. Report EG/38/84. Defus Hai, Jerusalem.

Perry, W. (2011). Bones of Roman-Era Babies Killed at Birth Reveal a Mystery. *Livescience.* 12 September 2011. www.livescience.com/15961-baby-graves-infanticide.html. Accessed 25 April 2015.

Petrie, W. M. F. (1886). *Naucratis I: 1884-5.* London: Egypt Exploration Fund.

Petrie, W. M. F. (1888). *Tanis II.* London: Egypt Exploration Fund.

Petrie, W. M. F. (1898). *Deshasheh 1987.* Fifteenth Memoir of The Egypt Exploration Fund. St. John's House, Clerkenwell: Gilbert and Rivington, Ltd.

Petrie, W. M. F. and F. L. Griffith. (1898). *Hieratic Papyri from Kahun and Gurob (Principally of the Middle Kingdom).* The Petrie Papyri. Bernard Quaritch.

Philip, G. (2003). Weapons and Warfare in Ancient Syria-Palestine. In S. Richard (ed.), *Near Eastern Archaeology. A Reader.* Winona Lake, IN: Eisenbrauns. Pp. 184–192.

Pinhasi, R., Gasparian, B., Areshian, G., Zardaryan, D., Smith, A., et al. (2010). First Direct Evidence of Chalcolithic Footwear from the Near Eastern Highlands. *PLoS ONE*, Vol. 5, No. 6, pp. e10984. DOI: 10.1371/journal.pone.0010984.

Place, V. (1867) *Ninive et L'Assyrie. Tome Troisiéme.* Ministère de la Maison de L'empereur et des Beaux-Arts. Imprimerie Impériale, Paris.

Pollock, S. (2003). Feasts, Funerals, and Fast Food in Early Mesopotamian States. In T. L. Bray (ed.), *The Archaeology and Politics of Food and Feasting in Early States and Empires.* New York: Kluwer Academic/Plenum Press. Pp. 17–38.

Ponchia, S. (2014). Management of Food Resources in the Neo-Assyrian Empire. In L. Milano (ed.), *Paleonutrition and Food Practice in the Ancient Near East. Towards a Multidisciplinary Approach.* History of the Ancient Near East/Monographs IV. S.A.R.G.O.N. Editrice e Libreria. Padova. Pp. 385–412.

Porath, Y. (1992). Domestic Architecture of the Chalcolithic Period. In A. Kempinski and R. Reich (eds.), *The Architecture of Ancient Israel. From the Prehistoric to the Persian Periods.* Jerusalem: Israel Exploration Society. Pp. 40–50.

Porter, B. W. and A. T. Boutin. (2014). *Remembering the Dead in the Ancient Near East. Recent Contributions from Bioarchaeology and Mortuary Archaeology.* Boulder: University of Colorado Press.

Potts, D. T. (ed.). (2012). *A Companion to the Archaeology of the Ancient Near East. Vol. I.* Chichester: Blackwell Publishing, Ltd.

Pritchard, J. (1975). *Sarepta: A Preliminary Report on the Iron Age.* University Museum Monograph, No. 35. Philadelphia, PA: The University Museum, University of Pennsylvania.

Pritchard, J. (1980). *The Cemetery at Tell es-Sa'idiyeh, Jordan.* University Museum Monograph, No. 41. Philadelphia, PA: The University Museum, University of Pennsylvania.

Quinn, P. S. (2013). *Ceramic Petrography. The Interpretation of Archaeological Pottery & Related Artefacts in Thin Section.* Oxford: Archaeopress.

Rawlinson, G. (1875). *History of Herodotus. In Four Volumes. Vol. II.* London: John Murray, Albemarle Street.

Rehren, T. (2000). New Aspects of Ancient Egyptian Glassmaking. *Journal of Glass Studies,* Vol. 42, pp. 13–24.

Rehren, T. and E. B. Pusch. (2005). Late Bronze Age Glass Production at Qantir-Piramesses, Egypt. *Science,* New Series, Vol. 308, No. 5729, pp. 1756–1758.

Reich, R. (1992). Building Materials and Architectural Elements in Ancient Israel. In A. Kempinski and R. Reich (eds.), *The Architecture of Ancient Israel. From the Prehistoric to the Persian Periods.* Jerusalem: Israel Exploration Society. Pp. 1–16.

Reiner, E. (1999). Babylonian Celestial Divination. In N. M. Swerdlow (ed.), *Ancient Astronomy and Celestial Divination.* Dibner Institute Studies in the History of Science and Technology. Cambridge, MA; London: The MIT Press. Pp. 21–38.

Rendsburg, G. A. (2003a). Writing and Scripts (with Special Reference to the Levant). In S. Richard (ed.), *Near Eastern Archaeology. A Reader.* Winona Lake: Eisenbrauns. Pp. 63–70.

Rendsburg, G. A. (2003b). Semitic Languages (with Special Reference to the Levant). In S. Richard (ed.), *Near Eastern Archaeology. A Reader.* Winona Lake: Eisenbrauns. Pp. 71–73.

Renfrew, J. (1995). Vegetables in the Ancient Near Eastern Diet. In J. M. Sasson (ed.), *Civilizations of the Ancient Near East. Vol. 1.* New York: Charles Scribner's Sons. Pp. 191–202.

Richard, C. J. (2011). *Why We're All Romans. The Roman Contribution to the Western World.* New York: Rowman and Littlefield Publishers, Inc.

Riddle, J. M. (1992). *Contraception and Abortion from the Ancient World to the Renaissance.* Cambridge, MA; London: Harvard University Press.

Roach, J. (2007). Oldest Perfumes Found on "Aphrodite's Island". *National Geographic News.* Thursday, 28 October 2010. http://news.nationalgeographic.com/news/2007/03/070329-oldest-perfumes.html. Accessed 18 April 2015.

Robinson, A. (2007). *The Story of Writing. Alphabets, Hieroglyphs & Pictograms.* Second edition. London: Thames and Hudson.

Robinson, H. R. (2002). *Oriental Armour.* New York: Dover Publications, Inc.

Rochberg, F. (1998). *Babylonian Horoscopes.* Transactions of the American Philosophical Society. Held at Philadelphia For Promoting Useful Knowledge. Vol. 88, Pt. 1. Philadelphia, PA: American Philosophical Society.

Rochberg, F. (1999). Babylonian Horoscopy: The Texts and Their Relations. In. N. M. Swerdlow (ed.) *Ancient Astronomy and Celestial Divination.* Dibner Institute Studies in the History of Science and Technology. Cambridge, MA; London: The MIT Press. Pp. 39–60.

Rochberg, F. (2004). *The Heavenly Writing Divination, Horoscopy, and Astronomy in Mesopotamian Culture.* Cambridge, UK: Cambridge University Press.

Rollefson, G. O. (2005a). The Neolithic Period. In. S. Richard (ed.), *Near Eastern Archaeology. A Reader.* Second printing. Winona Lake: Eisenbrauns. Pp. 244–253.

Rollefson, G. O. (2005b). Prehistoric Chipped-Stone Technology. In: S. Richard (ed.), *Near Eastern Archaeology. A Reader*. Second printing. Winona Lake: Eisenbrauns. Pp. 254–262.

Rose, J. I. (2010). New Light on Human Prehistory in the Arabo-Persian Gulf Oasis. *Current Anthropology*, Vol. 51, No. 6, pp. 849–883.

Rose, M. (1997). Ashkelon's Dead Babies. *Archaeology Archive*, Vol. 50, No. 2, pp. 12–13. March/April. http://archive.archaeology.org/9703/newsbriefs/ashkelon.html. Accessed 25 April 2015.

Rova, E. (2014). Tannurs, Tanur Concentrations and Centralized Bread Production at Tell Beydar and Elsewhere: An Overview. In L. Milano (ed.) *Paleonutrition and Food Practice in the Ancient Near East. Towards a Multidisciplinary Approach*. History of the Ancient Near East/Monographs IV. S.A.R.G.O.N. Padova: Editrice e Libreria. Pp. 121–169.

Ryan, W. and W. Pitman. (2000). *Noah's Flood. The New Scientific Discoveries about the Event that Changed History*. New York: Touchstone—Simon & Schuster.

Ryan, W., W. Pitman, C. O. Major, et al. (1997). Abrupt Drowning of the Black Sea Shelf. *Marine Geology*, Vol. 138, Nos 1–2, pp. 119–126.

Rye, O. S. (1981). *Pottery Technology: Principles and Reconstruction*. Washington, DC: Taraxacum.

Sachers, J. H. (2009). Mesolithic Bows from Denmark and Northern Europe. In N. Lee (ed.), *Study of Structures, Materials & Manufacturing Process of World Traditional Bows & Arrows, Cheonan*. www.academia.edu/11765815/Mesolithic_Bows_from_Denmark_and_Northern_Europe. Accessed 9 October 2017.

Salmon, I. (2003). *Surveying in Ancient Egypt*. Sydney, Australia: School of Surveying and Spatial Information Systems, The University of New South Wales. www.sage.unsw.edu.au/currentstudents/ug/projects/salmon/salmon.htm. Accessed 16 May 2016.

Samuel, D. (2009). Brewing and Baking. In P. T. Nicholson and I. Shaw (eds.), *Ancient Egyptian Materials and Technology*. Cambridge, UK: Cambridge University. Pp. 537–576.

Sanford, M. T. and A. Dietz. (1976). The Fine Structure of the Wax Gland of the Honey Bee (*APIS MELLIFERA L.*). *Apidologie*, Vol. 7, No. 3, pp. 197–207. DOI: 10.1051/apido: 19760301.

Sapart, C. J., G. Monteil, M. Prokopiou, et al. (2012). Natural and Anthropogenic Variations in Methane Sources During the Past Two Millennia. *Nature*, Vol. 490, pp. 85–88. DOI: 10.1038/nature11461.

Sapir-Hen, L. and E. Ben-Yosef. (2014). The Socioeconomic Status of Iron Age Metalworkers: Animal Economy in the "Slaves' Hill", Timna, Israel. *Antiquity*, Vol. 88, No. 341, pp. 775–790. DOI: 10.1017/S0003598X00050687. Published online: 2 January 2015.

Saul, H., M. Madella, A. Fischer, A. Glykou, S. Hartz, O. E. Craig. (2013). Phytoliths in Pottery Reveal the Use of Spice in European Prehistoric Cuisine. *PLoS One*, August, Vol. 8, No. 8, pp. E70583.

Schultz, R. (1998). *Egypt. The World of the Pharoahs. Knemann*. Cologne: Konemann.

Scott, J. (2014). My No-Soap, No-Shampoo, Bacteria-Rich Hygiene Experiment. *New York Times Magazine*. http://nyti.ms/TunQ8w. Accessed 25 May 2014.

Scurlock, J. (2014). *Sourcebook for Ancient Mesopotamian Medicine*. Atlanta, GA: SBL Press.

Scurlock, J. and B. R. Anderson. (2005). *Diagnoses in Assyrian and Babylonian Medicine*. Champaign, IL: University of Illinois Press.

Sear, F. (1982). *Roman Architecture*. Ithaca, NY: Cornell University Press.

Sekunda, N. (1989). Hellenistic Warfare. In J. Hackett (ed.), *Warfare in the Ancient World*. New York/Oxford/Sydney: Facts on File.

Serpico, M. (2009). Resins, Amber and Bitumen. In P. T. Nicholson and I. Shaw (eds.) *Ancient Egyptian Materials and Technology*. Cambridge, UK: Cambridge University Press. Pp. 430–474.

Serpico, M. and R. White. (2009). Oil, Fat, and Wax. In P. T. Nicholson and I. Shaw (eds.), *Ancient Egyptian Materials and Technology*. Cambridge, UK: Cambridge University Press. Pp. 390–429.

Sesen, S. Em Hotep. (2010). *Egypt for the Curious Layperson and the Budding Scholar. Building the Great Pyramid Year 1: Six Letters from Hemienu.* http://emhotep.net/2010/08/04/locations/lower-egypt/giza-plateau-lower-egypt/building-the-great-pyramid-year-1-six-letters-from-hemienu/. Accessed 28 August 2016.

Shafer, B. E. (ed.) (2005) *Temples of Ancient Egypt.* London; New York: I. B. Tauris.

Shea, J. J. (2013). *Stone Tools in the Paleolithic and Neolithic Near East A Guide.* Cambridge, UK: Cambridge University Press.

Shokeir, A. A. and M. I. Hussein. (1999). The Urology of Pharaonic Egypt. *BJU International*, Vol. 84, No. 7, pp. 755–760. https://onlinelibrary.wiley.com/doi/epdf/10.1046/j.1464-410x.1999.00313.x. Accessed 10 June 2016.

Shortland, A., P. Nicholson, and C. Jackson. (2001). Glass and Faience at Amarna: Different Methods of both Supply for Production, and Subsequent Distribution. In A. J. Shortland (ed.), *The Social Context of Technological Change. Egypt and the Near East, 1650-1550 BC. Proceedings of a Conference Held at St. Edmund Hall, Oxford, 12–14 September 2000.* Oxford: Oxbow Books. Pp. 147–160.

Shortland, A. J., S. Kirk, K. Eremin, P. Degryse, and M. Walton. (2017). The Analysis of Late Bronze Age Glass from Nuzi and the Questin of the Oritin of Glass-Making. *Archaeometry*. DOI: 10.1111/arcm.12332. https://onlinelibrary-wiley-com.access.library.miami.edu/doi/full/10.1111/arcm.12332. Accessed 25 October 2017.

Singer-Avitz, L., and Levi, Y. (1992). MB IIA Kiln at the Nahal Soreq Site. *Atiqot*, Vol. XXI, No. 9*–14*, pp. 143–147.

Sloley, R. W. (1926). An Ancient Surveying Instrument. *Ancient Egypt.* September Part III. Pp. 65–67.

Smith, M. E., Wharton, J. B., and Olson, J. M. (2003). Aztec Feasts, Rituals, and Markets: Political Uses of Ceramic Vessels in a Commercial Economy. In T. L. Bray (ed.) *The Archaeology and Politics of Food and Feasting in Early States and Empires.* New York/Boston/Dordrecht/London/Moscow: Kluwer Academic/Plenum Publishers. Pp. 235–270.

Smogorzewska, A. (2012). Fire Installations in Household Activities. Archaeological Study from Tell Arbid (North-East Syria). *Paléorient*, Vol. 38, No. 1/2, Préhistoire des Textiles au Proche-Orient/Prehistory of Textiles in the Near East. Pp. 227–247.

Sonnedecker, G. (translator). (1976). *Kremers and Urdang's History of Pharmacy.* American Institute of the History of Pharmacy, Fourth edition. South Tyrol Museum of Archaeology, Südtiroler Archäologiemuseum. www.iceman.it/en/the-iceman/.

Speiser, E. A. (1969). The Epic of Gilgamesh. In J. B. Pritchard (ed.), *Ancient Near Eastern Texts Relating to the Old Testament.* Third edition with supplement. Princeton, NJ: Princeton University Press. Pp. 72–99.

Spencer, P. (2003). Dance in Ancient Egypt. *Near Eastern Archaeology*, Vol. 66, No. 3, pp. 111–121.

Spinney, L. (2008). Archaeology: The Lost World. *Nature*, Vol. 454, pp. 151–153. DOI: 10.1038/454151a. Published online 9 July 2008. www.nature.com/news/2008/080709/full/454151a.html. Accessed 4 May 2018.

Spinney, L. (2012). A World Beneath the Sea. *National Geographic*, Vol. 222, No. 6, pp. 132–143.

Spitzer, M. (2012). *Digitale dimenz: Wie wir uns und unsere Kinder um den Verstand bringen.* München: Droemer, 7.

Stager, L. E. and S. R. Wolff. (1984). Child Sacrifice at Carthage: Religious Rite or Population Control? *Biblical Archaeology Review*, Vol. 10, No. 1, pp. 30–51.

Stager, L. E., J. D. Schloen, and D. M. Master. (2008). *Ashkelon I. Introduction and Overview (1985-2006) The Leon Levy Expedition to Ashkelon.* Final Reports of the Leon Levy Expedition to Ashkelon. Harvard Semitic Museum Publications. Winona Lakes: Eisenbrauns.

Stager, L. E., D. M. Master, and J. D. Schloen. (2011). *Ashkelon 3. The Seventh Century B.C. The Leon Lev Expedition to Ashkelon.* Final Reports of the Leon Levy Expedition to Ashkelon. Harvard Semitic Museum Publications. Winona Lakes: Eisenbrauns.

Standage, T. (2009). *An Edible History of Humanity*. New York: Walker & Company.

Stanley, A. (1995). *Mothers and Daughters of Invention: Notes for a Revised History of Technology*. New Brunswick, NJ: Rutgers University Press.

Steele, J. M. (ed.). (2007). *Calendars and Years. Astronomy and Time in the Ancient Near East*. Oxford: Oxbow Books.

Stern, S. (2012). *Calendars in Antiquity. Empires, States, & Societies*. Oxford: Oxford University Press.

Stol, M. (1995). Private Life in Ancient Mesopotamia. In J. M. Sasson (ed.) *Civilizations of the Ancient Near East. Vol. 1*. New York: Charles Scribner's Sons. Pp. 485–501.

Strassler, R. B. and A. L. Purvis. (2007). *The Landmark Herodotus. The Histories*. New York: Pantheon Books.

Streily, A. H. (2000). Early Pottery Kilns in the Middle East. In *Paléorient*, 2000, Vol. 26, No. 2. *La pyrotechnologie à ses débuts. Evolution des premières industries faisant usage du feu*. Pp. 69–81; DOI: 10.3406/paleo.2000.4711. www.persee.fr/doc/paleo_0153-9345_2000_num_26_2_4711.

Stromberg, J. (2013). Air Pollution has been a Problem Since the Days of Ancient Rome. *Smithsonian.com*. www.smithsonianmag.com/history/air-pollution-has-been-a-problem-since-the-days-of-ancient-rome-3950678/?no-ist. Accessed 22 June 2016.

Sukenik, E. L. (2007). *The Ancient Synagogue of Beth Alpha*. New Jersey: Geogias Press.

Talbert, R. J. A. (2017). *Roman Portable Sundials. The Empire in Your Hand*. Oxford: Oxford University Press.

Talmon, S. (1986). *King, Cult and Calendar in Ancient Israel*. Jerusalem: Magnes Press.

Tassie, G. J. (2003). Identifying the Practice of Tattooing in Ancient Egypt and Nubia. *Papers from the Institute of Archaeology*, Vol. 14, pp. 85–101.

The Antikythera mechanism Research Project. (n.d.). www.antikythera-mechanism.gr/project/overview. Accessed 20 October 2017.

The Central Timna Valley Project (n.d.). Tel Aviv University. The Sonia and Marco Nadler Institute of Archaeology. http://archaeology.tau.ac.il/ben-yosef/CTV/. Accessed 30 August 2017.

The Metropolitan Museum of Art. (2000–2015). The Nahal Mishmar Treasure. www.metmuseum.org/toah/hd/nahl/hd_nahl.htm. Accessed 4 June 2015.

The Siberian Times reporter. (2012). Siberian Princess Reveals Her 2,500 Year Old Tattoos. *The Siberian Times*. 14 August 2012. http://siberiantimes.com/culture/others/features/siberian-princess-reveals-her-2500-year-old-tattoos/. Accessed 1 May 2018.

Thomason, A. K. (2013). Her Share of the Profits: Women, Agency, and Textile Production at Kültepe/Kanesh in the Early Second Millennium BC. In M. L. Nosch, H. Koefoed, and E. Andersson Strand (eds.), *Textile Production and Consumption in the Ancient Nar East. Archaeology, Epigraphy, Iconography*. Oxford; Oakville, CA: Oxbow Books. Pp. 93–112.

Tsoucalas, G., M. Karamanou, M. Lymperi, V. Gennimata, and G. Androutsos. (2014). The "Torpedo" Effect in Medicine. *International Maritime Health*, Vol. 65, No. 2, pp. 65–67. DOI: 10.5603/IMH.2014.0015. www.intmarhealth.pl. Accessed 24 January 2018.

Tucker, A. (2011). The Beer Archaeologist. *Smithsonian Magazine*. August 2011. www.smithsonianmag.com/history/the-beer-archaeologist-17016372/. Accessed 22 June 2016.

Tylor, J. J. and F. Ll. Griffith. (1894). *Monuments of El Kab. The Tomb of Paheri*. London. Egypt Exploration Fund.

University College, London. (2003). The Geology of Egypt. Digitalegypt.ucl.ac.uk. www.digitalegypt.ucl.ac.uk/geo/geology.html. Accessed 9 June 2014.

University of Colorado, Boulder. (2009). 13,000-year-old-Stone Tool Cache in Colorado Shows Evidence of Camel, Horse, Butchering. www.colorado.edu/news/releases/2009/02/25/13000-year-old-stone-tool-cache-colorado-shows-evidence-camel-horse. Accessed 12 December 2015.

University of Colorado, Boulder. (2015). 13,000-year-old Stone Tool Cache Set for Exhibit at CU-Boulder. www.colorado.edu/news/releases/2015/10/07/13000-year-old-stone-tool-cache-set-exhibit-cu-boulder. Accessed 12 December 2015.

University of Oregon. (2000). The World's Oldest Shoes. http://pages.uoregon.edu/connolly/FRsandals.htm. Accessed 12 December 2015.

Vandenbeusch, M. (2014). Tattoos in Ancient Egypt and Sudan. *The British Museum.* June 26, 2014. http://blog.britishmuseum.org/2014/06/26/tattoos-in-ancient-egypt-and-sudan/. Accessed 22 April 2015.

van den Brink, E. C. M. and T. E. Levy. (2002). *Egypt and the Levant Interrelations from the 4ᵗʰ through the Early 3ʳᵈ Millennium BCE.* London; New York: Leicester University Press.

Van Driel-Murray, C. (2000). Leatherwork and Skin Product. In P. T. Nicholson and I. Shaw (eds.) *Ancient Egyptian Materials and Technology.* Cambridge, UK: Cambridge University Press. Pp. 299–319.

Van Driel-Murry, C. (2009). Leatherwork and Skin Products. In P. T. Nicholson and I. Shaw (eds.), *Ancient Egyptian Materials and Technology.* Cambridge, UK: Cambridge University Press. Pp. 299–319.

Vehling, J. D. (1977, reprinted). *Apicius Cookery and Dining in Imperial Rome. A Bibliography, Critical Review and Translation of the Ancient Book Known as Apicius de re Coquinaria.* New York: Dover Publications, Inc.

Veldmeijer, A. J. (2009). *Studies of Ancient Egyptian Footwear. Technological Aspects. Part XII.* Fibre Shoes. British Museum Studies in Ancient Egypt and Sudan, 14, Pp. 97–129.

Veldmeijer, A. J. (2011). *Tutankhamun's Footwear. Studies of Ancient Egyptian Footwear.* Leiden: Sidestone Press.

Vogelsang-Eastwood, G. (2000). Textiles. In P. T. Nicholson and I. Shaw (eds.), *Ancient Egyptian Materials and Technology.* Cambridge, UK: Cambridge University Press. Pp. 268–298.

Wachsmann, S. (1998). *Seagoing Ships and Seamanship in the Bronze Age Levant.* College Station: Texas A&M University Press.

Wachsmann, S. (2009). *Seagoing Ships and Seamanship in the Bronze Age Levant.* Second printing. College Station: Texas A&M University Press.

Wadley, L. (2010). Compound-Adhesive Manufacture as a Behavioral Proxy for Complex Cognition in the Middle Stone Age. *Current Anthropology,* Vol. 51, pp. S111–119, Supplement 1. DOI: 10.1086/649836.

Watkins, T. (1989). The Beginnings of Warfare. In J. Hackett (ed.), *Warfare in the Ancient World.* New York; Oxford; Sydney: Facts on File. Pp. 15–35.

Watson, T. (2014). Ancient Hunting Camp Found Beneath Lake Huron. USA Today. www.usatoday.com/story/tech/2014/04/28/hunting-camp-lake-huron/8113975/. Accessed 17 June 2016.

Webb, M. A. and R. Craze. (2004). *The Herb & Spice Companion.* New York: Metro Books.

Weeks, K. (1995). Medicine, Surgery, and Public Health in Ancient Egypt. In J. M. Sasson (ed. in chief), *Civilizations of the Ancient Near East Vol. III.* New York: Charels Scribner's Sons. Pp. 1787–1798.

Wendrich, W. Z. (2009). Basketry. In P. T. Nicholson and I. Shaw (eds.), *Ancient Egyptian Materials and Technology.* Cambridge, UK: Cambridge University Press. Pp. 254–267.

Wendrich, W. and P. Ryan. (2012). Phytoliths and Basketry Materials at Çatalhöyük (Turkey): Timelines of Growth, Harvest and Objects Life Histories. *Paléorient,* Vol. 38, No. 1/2, Préhistoire des textiles au Proche-Orient/ Prehistory of Textiles in the Near East. Pp. 55–63.

White, K. D. (1984). *Greek and Roman Technology.* Ithica, NY: Cornell University Press.

Wikander, O. (2000). The Neolithic and Bronze Ages. In Ö. Wikander (ed.), *Handbook of Ancient Water Technology.* Leiden: Brill. Pp. 607–616.

Wilcox, G. (2014). Food in the Early Neolithic of the Near East. In L. Milano (ed.), *Paleonutrition and Food Practice in the Ancient Near East. Towards a Multidisciplinary Approach.* History of the Ancient Near East / Monographs IV. S.A.R.G.O.N. Padova: Editrice e Libreria. Pp. 1–10.

Wilkins, J. and R. Nadeau (eds.). (2015). *A Companion to Food in the Ancient World.* Chichester: Wiley Blackwell.

Wilkinson, J. G. (1837a). *Manners and Customs of the Ancient Egyptians. Volume 1.* London: John Murray.

Wilkinson, J. G. (1837b). *The Manners and Customs of the Ancient Egyptians. Volume 3.* London: John Murray.

Wilkinson, J. G. (1878). *The Manners and Customs of the Ancient Egyptians. Volume 2.* London: John Murray.

Williams, A. R. (2016). Ancient Royal Boat Tomb Uncovered in Egypt. *National Geographic.* 7 November 2016. http://news.nationalgeographic.com/2016/11/royal-burial-boat-ancient-egypt-found/#/03-ancient-egypt-boats.jpg. Accessed 17 June 2017.

Wilson, A. (2000a). Industrial uses of Water. In Ö. Wikander (ed.), *Handbook of Ancient Water Technology. Vol. 2. Technology and Change in History.* Leiden: Brill. Pp. 127–150.

Wilson, A. (2000b). Drainage and Sanitation. In Ö. Wikander (ed.), *Handbook of Ancient Water Technology. Vol. 2. Technology and Change in History.* Leiden: Brill. Pp. 151–179.

Wilson, J. A. (1992a, fifth printing). The Journey of Wen-Amon to Phoenicia. In J. B. Pritchard (ed.), *Ancient Near Eastern Texts Relating to the Old Testament. Third Edition with Supplement.* Princeton, NJ: Princeton University Press. Pp. 25–29.

Wilson, J. A. (1992b, fifth printing). The Instruction of Amen-em-opet. In J. B. Pritchard (ed.), *Ancient Near Eastern Texts Relating to the Old Testament. Third Edition with Supplement.* Princeton, NJ: Princeton University Press. Pp. 421–425.

Wiseman, D. J. (1989). The Assyrians. In J. Hackett (ed.), *Warfare in the Ancient World.* New York; Oxford; Sydney: Facts on File. Pp. 36–53.

Wolff, S. R. (1996). Oleoculture and Olive Oil Presses in Phoenician North Africa. In D. Eitam and M. Heltzer (eds.), *Olive Oil in Antiquity. Israel and Neighbouring Countries from the Neolithic to the Early Arab Period. Vol. VII.* Series: History of the Ancient Near East/Studies—Padova: S.A.R.G.O.N. srl. Pp. 129–136.

World Museum of Man. www.worldmuseumofman.org.

Wright, G. R. H. (2005). *Ancient Building Technology. Volume 2. Materials. Parts 1 and 2.* In series, Technology and Change in History. Volume 7/1. Brill: Leiden/Boston.

Wu, X., C. Zhang, P. Goldberg, D. Cohen, Y. Pan, T. Arpin, and O. Bar-Yosef (2012). Early Pottery at 20,000 Years Ago in Xianrendong Cave, China. *Science,* Vol. 336, No. 6089, pp. 1696–1700. DOI: 10.1126/science.1218643.

Yadin, Y. (1963). *The Art of Warfare in Biblical Lands in the Light of Archaeological Discovery.* London: Weidenfeld and Nicolson.

Yale Babylonian Collection. (2017). http://babylonian-collection.yale.edu/. Accessed 14 October 2017.

Yamauchi, E. M. and M. R. Wilson. (2016). *Dictionary of Daily Life in Biblical & Post-Biblical Antiquity. Volumes I-IV.* Peabody, MA: Hendrickson Publishers.

Yanko-Hombach, V., A. S. Gilbert, N. Panin, and P. M. Dolukhanov, (eds.). (2007). *The Black Sea Flood Question: Changes in Coastline, Climate, and Human Settlement.* Dordrechet, The Netherlands: Springer.

Yeakel, J. D., M. M. Pires, L. Rudolf, et al. (2014). Collapse of an Ecological Network in Ancient Egypt. *Proceedings of the National Academy of Sciences of the United States of America,* Vol. 111, No. 40, pp. 14472–14477. DOI: 10.1073/pnas.1408471111. www.ncbi.nlm.nih. gov/pmc/articles/PMC4210013/. Accessed 9 May 2018.

Zaki, M. E., A. M. Sarry El-Din, M. Al-Tohamy Soliman, et al. (2010). Limb Amputation in Ancient Egypt from Old Kingdom. *Journal of Applied Sciences Research*, Vol. 6, No. 8, pp. 913–917.

Zias, J. (1982) Three Trephinated Skulls from Jericho. *Bulletin of the American Schools of Oriental Research*, Vol. 246, No. Spring, pp. 55–58.

Zias, J. (1991). Health and Healing in the Land of Israel—A Paleopathological Perspective. In O. Rimon, (ed.), *Illness and Healing in Ancient Times*. Reuben and Edith Hecht Museum Catalogue 13. Haifa: University of Haifa. Pp. 13–19.

Zias, J. and K. Mumcuoglu. (1996). "Pre-Pottery Neolithic B Head Lice from Nahal Hemar Cave." *'Atiqot*, Vol. 20, pp. 167–168.

Zoech, I. (2003). The Ancient Egyptian Recipe for Toothpaste. *The Telegraph*. 19 January 2003. www.telegraph.co.uk/news/worldnews/europe/austria/1419375/The-ancient-Egyptian-recipe-for-toothpaste.html. Accessed 25 April 2015.

Zohary, M. (1982). *Plants of the Bible*. Cambridge, UK: Cambridge University Press.

INDEX